JUSTINIAN'S DIGEST: CHARACTER AND COMPILATION

Justinian's Digest: Character and Compilation

TONY HONORÉ

OXFORD
UNIVERSITY PRESS

OXFORD
UNIVERSITY PRESS

Great Clarendon Street, Oxford OX2 6DP

Oxford University Press is a department of the University of Oxford.
It furthers the University's objective of excellence in research, scholarship,
and education by publishing worldwide in

Oxford New York

Auckland Cape Town Dar es Salaam Hong Kong Karachi
Kuala Lumpur Madrid Melbourne Mexico City Nairobi
New Delhi Shanghai Taipei Toronto
With offices in
Argentina Austria Brazil Chile Czech Republic France Greece
Guatemala Hungary Italy Japan South Korea Poland Portugal
Singapore Switzerland Thailand Turkey Ukraine Vietnam

Oxford is a registered trade mark of Oxford University Press
in the UK and in certain other countries

Published in the United States
by Oxford University Press Inc., New York

Reprinted 2012

ISBN 978-0-19-959330-9

Printed in the United Kingdom by
Lightning Source UK Ltd., Milton Keynes

To All Souls College, Oxford

Acknowledgements

I am grateful to Boudewijn Sirks, Alan Rodger and Detlef Liebs for their help with this work and especially to Liebs for his careful reading of the manuscript.

Chapter 3

This chapter was first published in *Roman Legal Tradition* 3:1 (2006) 1–47. ISSN 1551–1375. The author thanks Detlef Liebs and Ernest Mezger for their helpful suggestions.

Contents

1

Introduction

This work aims to assess the character of Justinian's Digest and to provide up-to-date information about its compilation. Given its importance in western and, by derivation, worldwide history it is remarkable how rare have been the attempts to provide a coherent picture of these matters. Leaving aside the text, the book embodies my latest (and probably final) thoughts on the character and compilation of the work. On what lines was the *magnum opus* conceived? How was it compiled and what serves to explain its impact? My views, though the fruit of long reflection and analysis, are inevitably to some extent speculative.

The problem of compilation has a lively attraction given the difficulty of the compilers' task, the speed with which its was accomplished (if the account given by Justinian and Tribonian is to be believed), and its lasting influence on law in the western tradition. The emperor and his minister claim that the Digest was compiled in the three years 530–533 AD by a commission that read and edited some 2,000 *libri* (chapters) composed by legal authors many years previously. If that claim is correct the Digest's 9,132 texts were excerpted from ancient works and edited by Justinian's compilers in three years—a mere fraction of what it would now take with the added complexities of computers and email. Understandably the claim has been doubted, but no convincing evidence has come to light of a pre-existing collection of material that could have served as a preliminary draft of the Digest. There is, however, an alternative explanation of its character, set out below, that sees it as an updated version of earlier writing.

To deal first with the work's compilation, Bluhme proposed that the difficulty about the alleged time scale of the compilation was less serious than at first appeared.[1] The reading and excerpting of the texts was not done by all 17 commissioners but was divided between three

[1] 'Die Ordnung der Fragmente in den Pandektentiteln' in *ZGR* 4 (1820) 257 f.

committees. From the leading works that they were thought to have perused and sifted these are called the Sabinian, edictal and Papinian committees. Bluhme listed the order in which, in his view, the three committees had been told to read and/or had in fact read and excerpted the works assigned to them. This order, which governs about five-sixths of the Digest texts, was refined by Krüger and has come to be known as the Bluhme-Krüger order (BK Ordo). Bluhme also proposed that many of the principal ancient works, such as the commentaries on the praetor's edict and Sabinus, were grouped together so that works by different authors on the same subject would be read in conjunction. This would help to explain the relatively short time that the compilation took and the existence in the completed work of sequences of texts from two or more authors relating to the same subject-matter.

In 1970, with the help of Alan Rodger, I wrote an article that was designed to take Bluhme's ingenious suggestions further.[2] Our idea was to count the lines excerpted from each ancient work, as recorded by the inscriptions that precede the published texts, so as to determine the rate of excerpting from different works and at different stages of the process of excerpting. We went on to argue that each committee was comprised of two of the six senior commissioners on the Digest commission. These two divided the excerpting between them, if necessary with the help of advocates attached to the commission. This would have further reduced the time taken to complete the work. So far as works not read together were concerned, these were divided into groups. In each group an equal number of books was assigned to each of the two commissioners on the committee. The reading and excerpting was done at a prescribed rate, in order that it should be completed in time for the texts excerpted to be put together by the end of 533 in the 50 books and 432 titles of which the published work consists. The article suggested a grouping of the works not read together and a subdivision of each group into an equal number of books. A timetable for the process of reading and exerpting was proposed.

This theory attracted both support and criticism. A critic complained that we had grouped the works not read together in an arbitrary way. Many different groupings were possible and the ones proposed rested on no coherent principle.[3] Another objection was that we had treated the Appendix works as if they constituted a mass like the three main

[2] *SZ* 87 (1970) 246–314.

[3] D. Osler, 'The Compilation of Justinian's Digest', *SZ* 102 (1985) 129–84.

masses, and supposed that they were read and excerpted contemporaneously with them and as part of the Papinian mass. Mantovani's careful analysis[4] showed rather that they were read after the three main masses. Excerpts from them were incorporated in the draft Digest as the work of editing the various books and titles progressed.

In my eighties (*extremus labor*)[5] I have come to a revised view which retains the essence of the previous analysis but seeks to meet the main criticisms. This view was published in outline in 2004,[6] and forms chapter 2 of the present work. The revised theory retains the idea that the works not read together were grouped according to settled criteria. These groupings are not, however, now taken to be directed principally towards securing an equal numerical division of books between two commissioners. A study of the way in which the authors and works were allocated to the three main commissions, previously a neglected topic, led to the conclusion that the allocation was based on one of four factors: authorship (each author being assigned to a basic mass or, in the case of Paul, to two masses), subject-matter, literary genre and the desire to secure an equal or nearly equal division of books between the two senior commissioners assigned to the committee in question.[7] Short monographs (*libri singulares*) were also grouped in one of these ways. They were allocated to the committee in charge of the author's basic mass (or, in Paul's case, masses) unless they formed part of a group concerned with a particular subject, such as adultery. The principle of grouping the works assigned to the three committees is therefore retained but the principles on which works are allocated to groups are refined and elucidated. This study forms chapter 3 of the present work.

In 1973 I published an article 'Editing the Digest' which dealt with the displacement of texts by the compilers from the order and position in which they had been excerpted by the original three committees.[8] This position (the 'BK Ordo') was established in its original form by Bluhme and Krüger and a revised version that takes account of modern scholarship forms Addendum A. The 1973 article distinguished types of displacement, such as texts displaced to form the introduction to or

[4] D. Mantovani, *Digesto e masse Bluhiame* (1987).

[5] Virgil, *Eclogues* 10.1: Extremum hunc, Arethusa, mihi concede laborem.

[6] T. Honoré, 'How Tribonian organised the Compilation of Justinian's Digest', *SZ* 121 (2004) 1–43.

[7] T. Honoré, 'Justinian's Digest: The Distribution of Authors and Works to the Committees' in M. Hoeflich & E. Mezger (eds), *Roman Legal Tradition* 3:1 (2006) 1–47.

[8] T. Honoré, 'The Editing of the Digest Titles' *SZ* 90 (1973) 262–304.

coda of a title or mass, and texts displaced within a mass. A revised version of this forms chapter 4 of the present work. The new version lists 17 rather than the previous 16 per cent of the texts as displaced from the BK Ordo.[9] This is largely because more texts introducing titles are now taken to be displaced. In Addenum B each of the 50 books of the Digest is analysed to show which texts have been displaced and how they have been displaced. This analysis is developed from Krüger's valuable footnotes in the stereotype edition of the Digest but quite often departs from them either on the ground that his view was mistaken or in the light of more recent scholarship.

The new version also lists the sequences of linked texts created by the compilers. Most of the links occur in reverse chronological order; hence the original texts were not linked. It also deals with the compilers' use of linking expressions in order to make the result read smoothly. Finally the new article lists short but authentic phrases taken from classical authors and inserted in the Digest, a practice that shows how reluctant Justinian and Tribonian were to allow the commissioners to insert even a few words on their own initiative, except when that was necessary to link classical texts that had not originally been connected.

The character of the Appendix is dealt with in an article[10] reprinted in an expanded form in chapter 5. The new theory owes much to Mantovani's treatise but differs in the conclusion it draws about the nature of that group of works. In my view the Appendix consisted of late arrivals, not available when the allocation of texts to the three committees was originally made. In this respect I agree with what has long been thought to be the case. As these later works became available they were allocated to the appropriate committee, generally to the committee to which the author's basic mass was assigned. But this extended the list of works to be read and excerpted by the three committees before the editing of the excerpts into books and titles could begin. In consequence it upset the time schedule for the completion of the work. At a certain stage of the project it was therefore decided to call a halt to the reading by the three committees and to begin collecting and editing the texts excerpted into books and titles, so that publication would be possible on the planned date. The late arrivals not yet read and excerpted by the three committees were assembled in a group of their own, the Appendix.

[9] 1532 instead of 1416.

[10] T. Honoré, 'Late Arrivals: The Appendix in Justinian's Digest Reconsidered' in A. Burrows and Lord Rodger of Earlsferry (eds), *Mapping the Law: Essays in Memory of Peter Birks* (2006) 497–512.

These works then ceased to be allocated to one of the three committees. As a result of this decision there were a few late arrivals (e.g. Scaevola's *digesta* and Labeo's *posteriora*) the first books of which had been read and excerpted by one of the original three committees, but the remainder of which became part of the Appendix. The Appendix works were read by commissioners chosen for the purpose (they can be thought of as the 'Appendix committee') and the excerpts were allocated progressively to the books and titles being edited by other commissioners.

A short chapter completes this work. It deals with an aspect of the compilers' linking of texts. The linking often took the form of a comment on or modification of an Ulpian text by a text from another author, such as Paul. Although each text was meant to be preceded by an inscription that listed its author and work, the compilers or later copyists sometimes forgot to insert an inscription when they returned to the original text after the comment or modification. In this way, for example, some texts of Ulpian came to be attributed to Paul. A chapter on this misattribution forms chapter 6.[11]

This last essay leads into a wider theme. The Digest, as explained in chapter 4, was intended to present the law set out by juristic opinion in a coherent and updated form. But a neglected aspect of the Digest concerns its literary genre. On what model was the work based? Justinian's Codex is expressly designed to incorporate in a revised and shortened version the three previous codices (Gregorian, Hermogenian and Theodosian) with more recent constitutions including Justinian's own enactments.[12] His Institutes are, again, principally taken from Gaius' Institutes and *Res Cottidianae* and from other institutional works. They constitute a modified and updated version of those works, as explained in the constitution Imperatoriam maiestatem which singles out 'Gaius noster' as a source.[13] This does not imply that Justinian and Tribonian always prefer the text of Gaius to that of other institutional writers or that Justinian's version is free from reference to his own later innovations. It does imply that Gaius' introductory works are the main source of Justinian's text.

In my view Justinian's Digest relates in a similar way to the works of Ulpian. Over 40 per cent of the Digest texts are expressly attributed by

[11] Earlier version in 'Some Texts of Ulpian Attributed to Paul' in *Fides, humanitas, ius. Studii in onore di Luigi Labruna* (2007–8) 2529–42.

[12] C. Summa 1.

[13] C. Imperatoriam 6: praecipue ex commentariis Gaii nostri tam institutionum quam rerum cottidianarum.

inscription to Ulpian. Nearly 60 per cent of the texts introducing titles are similarly attributed. A reader of the Digest is primarily reading a selected and revised version of Ulpian's writings, incorporating alternative versions of the law when appropriate. His views are not always preferred to the views of other jurists, but other views are mostly treated as provisos to or modifications of his exposition of the law. His clarity, scholarly citation of authority and ingenuity in finding the route to a just solution holds the wide-ranging work together. But his importance, unlike that of Gaius, is not expressly acknowledged. He is not *Ulpianus noster*.[14] Given his listing of constitutions hostile to Christianity as a guide to provincial governors,[15] it would not have been politically correct to single him out in this way. But his prominence throughout the work cannot be an accident. Tribonian must have told the commissioners to treat him as the lead author.

If that is right, all three volumes of the Corpus Iuris should be regarded as updated versions of earlier writings. They express both the emperor's respect for certain past models and his determination to present them with modifications of which he approves and, in that way, to make them his own.

Ulpian's work is central to the Digest. Hence it is important in assessing its long-term influence through generations of lawyers and administrators to understand the theoretical point of view from which Ulpian writes, which he calls the true philosophy. I have called him a pioneer of human rights.[16] Though this description can be criticized on the ground that there is no rubric *de iure hominis* in his work or in the Digest, he, his pupils and coevals of the cosmopolitan Severan age adopt certain values incorporated in the Stoic law of nature. This equates nature with reason and treats human beings as born free and equal. That equation is open to objection because an 'is' (nature) cannot logically imply an 'ought' (what reason recommends or requires). But no great leap is demanded in this instance. Human beings possess the capacity to recognize alternatives and to decide between them, settling on what to think or do for a reason or reasons. They can do this and can communicate with one another by language to a greater extent than other animals. Why should we not exercise the capacities to reason and communicate that we possess? To

[14] There is an appreciative essay by D. Liebs, 'Mein Ulpian' in M. Schauer and G. Thome (eds), *Altera Ratio. Klassische Philologie zwischen Subjectivität und Wissenschaft. Festschrift für Werner Suerbaum zum 70. Geburtstag* (2003) 74–81.

[15] Lactantius, *Divinae Institutiones* 5.11.19.

[16] *Ulpian. Pioneer of Human Rights* (2002) especially 76–93.

Ulpian and those lawyers who think like him this carries with it the mandate to interpret authority and to fill gaps in the law in the light of reason and to express their conclusions clearly and intelligibly. The extension of this idea to the determination of where authority resides is an added contribution of modern human rights thinking.

Whatever may be thought of this train of ideas it is, via Ulpian and other writers of the cosmopolitan age, embodied in the Digest. It has in the long run served to produce a balance between freedom and obligation in societies exposed to this way of thinking about law.

2

How Tribonian Organized the Compilation of Justinian's Digest[1]

I. Introduction

In 1970 Alan Rodger[2] and I published an article on how Justinian's commissioners read books and excerpted texts for the Digest.[3] It attracted controversy. We dealt with the reading and excerpting of the classical literature rather than the later phase of the Digest project in which the texts were edited and put together in titles and books. We were concerned with how Tribonian organized the project rather than with identifying his interventions in the Digest texts.[4] Our thesis was that the key

[1] The original version of this chapter was published in *SZ* 121 (2004) 1–43. I thank Dario Mantovani and Detlef Liebs for their comments on an earlier draft. Neither is committed to my conclusions.

[2] His help was invaluable but he was not responsible for the article's shortcomings. This revised version is wholly my responsibility.

[3] 'How the Digest Commissioners worked' *SZ* 87 (1970) 246–314 (henceforth *Commissioners*), filled out in Honoré, 'Justinian's Digest: Work in Progress' (1971) *Law Quarterly Review* 88 (1972) 30–56; idem, 'Justinian's Digest: Following the Trail', ibid. 530–42 (henceforth *Trail* 1972); 'The Distribution of the Digest texts into Titles' SZ 89 (1972) 351–62; 'The Editing of the Digest Texts' SZ 90 (1973) 262–304; 'The Background to Justinian's Codification' *Tulane LR* 48 (1974) 859–93; 'Labeo's Posteriora and the Digest Commission', in A. Watson (ed.), *Daube Noster* (1974) 161–81. Much was incorporated in Honoré, *Tribonian* (1978) 139–86 (henceforth *Tribonian*).

[4] For which see *Tribonian* (n. 3), chs 3, 6. This research, despite criticism by certain writers (A. Watson, LQR 94 (1978) 459; TR 50 (1982) 409; Averil Cameron, JRS 69 (1979) 200–1; H. L. W. Nelson, *Uberlieferung, Aufbau und Stil von Gai Institutiones* (1981) 182 n. 1, 187 n. 8; T. Wallinga, *Tanta Δεδωκεν* (1989) 564 contra R. Syme, *SZ* 97 (1980) 78, 94f.; Alan Rodger (below n. 5) 385; F. Millar, 'A New Approach to the Roman Jurists' JRS 76 (1986) 272–80 has been endorsed in three detailed studies, one dealing with Tribonian as the composer of many of Justinian's Novels (G. Lanata, *Legislazione e Natura nelle Novelle Giustineanee* (1984): x, 12–13, 45–7, 54, 67–8, 86, 91–8, 154, 166–8, 201–3, 238–9); a second with his interventions in Justinian's Institutes (G. Falcone, 'Il metodo di compilazione delle Institutiones di Giustiniano' *Annali Palermo* 45 (1998), 223–426 at 228f. and M. Varvaro, 'Lo stile di Triboniano e la

to the completion of the Digest in three years was that the task of reading and excerpting classical texts was delegated according to a timetable to six senior commissioners organized in the three committees conventionally called the Sabinian, edictal and Papinian committees.

How does this theory now stand? A number of authors have since put forward theories about the compilation of the Digest.[5] Some have treated our hypothesis as discredited.[6] But Wieacker in a 1993 article paid tribute to it as the most coherent reconstruction of recent years.[7] So it may be of interest to review the theory in the light of recent scholarship. Though some elements of the 1970 article are untenable, it remains, in my view, the best explanation of the speed with which the task of reading and excerpting was completed. That part of the work was delegated by Tribonian in accordance with a timetable to each of the six senior commissioners organized in three committees.

It is true that no clear line can be drawn between excerpting and editing. The commissioners appear to have selected only about 5 per cent of the original works and to have jettisoned the rest. That was not a mechanical operation. It required judgment, for the reader had to pick out the best and most useful texts.[8] He must decide where the excerpt should begin

compilazione delle Institutiones di Giustiniano' SDHI 68, 2002, 319–98 at pp. 321–31) and the third with his drafting of the Fifty Decisions (M. Varvaro, 'Contributo allo studio delle Quinquaginta Decisiones' Annali Palermo 46, 2000, 361–539 at 518 and passim). In view of these studies I assume without further argument, contrary to the view of Wallinga, above, that Tribonian was the author of the introductory constitutions C. Deo auctore, C. Tanta and C. Omnem.

[5] Especially F. Wieacker, 'Zur Technik der Kompilatoren' *SZ* 89 (1972) 293–323 modified in 'Zur Herstellung der Digesten', in *Ars boni et aequi. Festschrift W. Waldstein* (1993) 417–42; O. Verrey, *Leges geminatae à deux auteurs et la compilation du Digeste* (1973); W. Waldstein, 'Tribonianus' *SZ* 97 (1980) 232–55; A. Rodger, 'Behind the Scenes of Roman Law' *Oxford Journal of Legal Studies* 3 (1983) 382–404; L. Solidoro, 'Triboniano e la legislazione Giustinanea', *Labeo* 28 (1982) 74–81; D. Pugsley, 'Some reflections on the compilation of Justinian's Digest' *Irish Jurist* 19 (1984) 350–9; D. Osler, 'The Compilation of Justinian's Digest' *SZ* 102 (1985) 129–84 (henceforth Osler 1985); idem, 'Following Bluhme: a note on Dario Mantovani, "Digesto e masse Bluhmiane"' *IVRA* 39 (1988) 137–58; D. Mantovani, *Digesto e masse Bluhmiane* (1987—henceforth Mantovani); W. Kaiser, 'Digestenentstehung and Digestenüberlieferung' *SZ* 108 (1991) 330–50; P. Furlong, *Justinian and Mathematics: An Analysis of the Digest's Compilation Plan* (2003) based on a 1996 honours thesis for the University of Melbourne, Department of Classics and Archaeology; revised version available at http://users.ox.ac.uk/~alls0079 (henceforth Furlong).

[6] Osler 1985 (n. 5) 184: 'the numerical foundation of the theory is invalidated'; Mantovani (n. 5) 52, 133; 'di questa originale teoria, ... non resta piu nulla'.

[7] Wieacker (n. 5, 1993) 439: 'und der strenge Anspruch auf nahtlose Kohärenz beschränkt den Fachgenossen auf—vielleicht dürftige—Randbemerkungen'.

[8] C. Tanta 1: *quae necesse esset omnia* [nearly 2000 *libri*] *et legere et perscrutari et ex his si quid optimum fuit eligere... in quinquaginta libros omne quod utilissimum erat collectum est.*

and end and put it in a grammatically correct form. There was nevertheless a distinction between the excerpting and the editorial phase of the project. The distinction holds even if the reading and excerpting of the works known as the Appendix went on in parallel with the task of assembling the excerpts already made into titles and books.[9] In that case the two operations were for a time in the hands of different commissioners.

II. How Demanding was the Digest Project?

In the article we steered a middle course between two views: that the Digest could not have been compiled from scratch in three years,[10] and that to do this was not difficult.[11] We rejected the idea that the work proceeded quickly because the commissioners used an existing collection of material, either a single predigest[12] or a number of separate collections put together for teaching purposes.[13] Nor did we think, as Pescani was to argue, that the compilers sometimes read not the whole original work but only a few pages.[14] Assuming that they read through and made

[9] Mantovani (n. 5) 121–3.

[10] F. Hofmann, 'Die Compilation der Digesten Justinians' *Kritische Studien von Dr. Franz Hofmann* (1900): P. Pescani, 'II piano del digesto e Ia sua attuazione' *BIDR* 77 (1974) 237–405.

[11] T. Mommsen, 'Hofmann versus Bluhme' *SZ* 22 (1901) at p. 6.

[12] The leading proponents were R. Ehrenzweig, 'Die Compilation der Digesten Justinians' *ZS für priv. u. offentl. Recht* 28 (1901) 320f.; H. Peters, *Die oströmischen Digestenkommentare und die Entstehung der Digesten* (1913); reprinted in *Labeo* 16 (1970) 214, 335; H. Kruger, 'Römische Juristen und ihre Werke' *Studi Bonfante* 2 (1930) 302–37; P. Collinet, *La génèse du Digeste, du Code et des Institutes de Justinien* (1952) contra O. Lenel, 'Zur Entstehung der Digesten' *SZ* 34 (1913) 381f.; L. Mitteis, ibid. 408f.; F. Wieacker, *Textstufen klassischer Juristen* (1960) 129f.; Mantovani (n. 5) 22–33, 66–73, esp. 68 n. 135.

[13] V. Arangio Ruiz, 'Precedenti scolastici del Digesto' *Conferenze per il XIV centenario delle Pandette*, 15 dicembre 1930 (1931) 287f.; 'Di alcuni fonti postclassiche del Digesto' *Atti della Accademia di Scienze morali e politiche di Napoli* 54 (1931) 1Of. *Rariora* (1946) 171f.; E. Albertario, *Introduzione storica allo studio del diritto romano giustinaneo* I (1935) l6f.; A. Guarino, 'La méthode de la compilation', *RIDA* 4 (1957) 269–88; 'La compilazione delle Digesta Iustiniani' *Atti Acc. Napoli sc. e pol.* 79 (1968) 527–62; *Studi Scherillo* 2.717f.; C. Tomulescu, 'On the Activity of Justinian's Compilers' *Index* 2 (1971) 139–44; L. Solidoro, Triboniano (n. 5) 74–81; G. L. Falchi, 'Sul possibile coordinamento tra le masse bluhmiane e le partes del Digesto' *SDHI* 49 (1983) 51–90; idem, 'Gli spostamenti fuori massa dei frammenti del Digesto' *Sodalitas, Scritti in onore Guarino* 6 (1984) 2691–715; idem, 'Osservazioni sulle "L Decisiones" di Giustiniano' *Studi Biscardi* 5 (1984) 121–50; idem, 'Digesto e masse Bluhmiane', *Labeo* 35 (1989) 98–103; contra Mantovani (n. 5) 22–33; W. Kaiser (n. 5) 332–3.

[14] P. Pescani, 'Il piano del digesto e la sua attuazione', *BIDR* 77 (1974) 237–405.

excerpts from the original texts,[15] we tried to explain how, even so, they could have compiled the Digest in the three years between December 530 and December 533.[16] About half of this period would be devoted to reading and making excerpts, the other half to editing and assembling the texts, securing the emperor's approval, drafting Justinian's Institutes and having enough copies of the Digest made before it was promulgated. On the other hand we did not think that Justinian's commissioners had an easy task. Diósdi, following Mommsen,[17] was to argue that three years was plenty of time for the commissioners to read, excerpt and edit the 50 books of the Digest.[18] There was no great hurry and no need to ask how exactly they did it.

Was Diósdi right? Assume a book to be on average a *liber* of 1,500 lines,[19] each line (*versus*) to average 39 letters or 15–16 syllables,[20] and the books to be read to number somewhere between the 'nearly 2,000' mentioned in C. Tanta[21] and the 1,510 of which we found evidence.[22] Allowing for books found to be neither useful nor new,[23] and omitted from the Digest, perhaps there were 1,600 books to read in all. These would contain about 2,400,000 lines. To cover this volume of material in, say, 18 months requires an average of about 4,400 lines or 75 pages to be read and excerpted every day.[24] The commission could not do this in joint session, even supposing that its 17 members were regularly available, which in the case of the 11 advocates is unlikely.

[15] As does Mantovani (n. 5) 33, 37, 64 following Mommsen (n. 11) 7f.; P. Krüger, *SZ* 22 (1901) 42f.; Jörs, *RE* 5.511f.; P. de Francisci, 'Alcune osservazioni sul metodo dei compilatori delle Pandette' *Rend. Ist. Lomb. sc. e lett.* 2.44 (1911) 185f.

[16] For the exact period F. Pringsheim, 'Die Entstehungszeit des Digestenplanes und die Rechtschulen' *Atti del congresso intemazionale di diritto romano* I (1934) 449f.

[17] Mommsen, 'Hofmann versus Bluhme' *SZ* 22 (1901) 1.

[18] Diósdi, 'Das Gespenst der Pre-digesten' *Labeo* 17 (1971) 187–92. Contra Cenderelli, *Digesto e Predigesti, Reflessioni ed ipotesi di ricerca* (1983) 14f.

[19] Diósdi (n. 18 above at 189) gives a figure of 1,488 lines per book for the Codex Veronensis.

[20] Derived by Diósdi (above at 190) from the Veronese manuscript of Gaius.

[21] C. Tanta 1: duo paene milia librorum esse conscripta.

[22] The figure in *Commissioners* p. 314 was 1,528, from which should be subtracted 19 books: in the Appendix Valens 7 *actionum*, Proculus 3 *ex posterioribus Labeonis*, Paul 2 instead of 6 *imperialium sententiarum;* in the Sabinian mass Gaius 3 instead of 7 *aureorum;* in the Papinian mass Pauli 1 *de articulis liberalis causae*—a duplicate of Paul 1 *de liberali causa* in the Sabinian mass.

[23] C. Tanta 17: *sed huius operis conditores non solum ea volumina perlegerunt, ex quibus leges positae sunt, sed etiam alia multa quae, nihil vel utile vel novum in eis invenientes, quod exceptum nostris digestis applicarent, optimo animo respuerunt.*

[24] 2,400,000 divided by 4,400 gives 545 days, which is close to 18 months.

The task must have been divided up. Bluhme's hypothesis[25] that the commission was divided into three committees, corresponding to the three masses (Sabinian, edictal and Papinian) was not prompted by the idea that this would have saved time, but the time factor strengthened his thesis. If the work was divided between three committees each had to read on average a little under 1,500 lines or 25 pages a day. The lines may have been slightly shorter than a line in a modern column,[26] but this still seems too much. The committees had both to read the material and to select the texts to be included in the Digest. The selection could not be entrusted to the advocates attached to the commission, though the advocates could usefully read out texts, once or repeatedly, so that an informed choice could be made. The choice must have been that of one or more senior commissioners, consulting Tribonian when necessary. That was possible, since the commissioners were brought into the palace (though they cannot have been permanently confined to it) and worked subject to Tribonian's orders.[27] The chosen excerpts had also to be allocated to a suitable title, as required by C. Deo auctore, if possible immediately.[28]

So it seems that, despite Diósdi, we need to investigate the detailed organization of the work. The claim that the enterprise when first broached was thought likely to take 10 years[29] smacks of propaganda, but to complete it within a reasonable time presented a challenge. Six aims had to be reconciled. One was to work quickly, since the commissioners could not be kept from their normal duties indefinitely.[30] A second was to ensure that only the best and most useful texts were excerpted.[31]

[25] F. Bluhme, 'Die Ordnung der Fragmenta in den Pandektentiteln' *ZGR* 4 (1820) 257–452, reprinted in *Labeo* 6 (1960) 50–96, 235–77, 368–404. Osler (n. 5, 1988) 138–9 points to a hint of Bluhme's discovery in Antoninus Augustinus, *Emendationes et Opiniones* (Venice 1543) 1.1. at p. X line 29.

[26] A line in a column of Lenel's *Palingenesia* averages about 43 or 44 letters, which is 10 per cent longer than Diósdi's figure of 39.

[27] C. Deo auctore 3: *his* [the commissioner's] *itaque collectis et in nostrum palatium introductis nobisque tuo testimonio placitis totam rem faciendam permisimus, ita tamen, ut tui vigilantissimi animi gubernatione res omnis celebretur.*

[28] Deo auctore 5; Honoré, *Tribonian* (n. 3) 149.

[29] C. Tanta 12: *Omni igitur Romani iuris dispositione... perfecta et in tribus annis consummata, quae ut primum sperari coepit, neque in totum decennium compleri sperabatur.*

[30] C. Deo auctore 14: *Haec igitur omnia deo placido facere tua prudentia una cum aliis facundissimus viris studeat et tam suptili quam celerrimo fini tradere.*

[31] C. Tanta 1: *plus quam trecenties decem milia versuum a veteribus effusa, quae necesse esset et legere et perscrutari et ex his si quid optimum fuisset eligere.*

A third was to reduce the classical works to 50 books.[32] A fourth was to avoid inconsistency and repetition,[33] a fifth to ensure that the product should be sophisticated[34] and a sixth to make the texts attractive to read and listen to.[35]

In reconstructing how the works were read and excerpted our database was made up of a line count, derived from Lenel's *Palingenesia*, of the excerpts from each work cited in the Digest. Not all the excerpts made can have been included in the final text, because some texts excerpted as part of one mass will have duplicated texts in another. If 'about 2,000' books were to be reduced to 50 books there must have been an instruction about the permissible volume of excerpts. But we assumed that it was meaningful to calculate on the basis of the excerpts included in the final text the rate, in terms of lines per book, at which the different works were excerpted.

Our data made it possible to calculate the approximate number of lines that the three committees excerpted from each classical work. It also made possible an overview, from which it emerged that the Sabinian and edictal committees excerpted a nearly equal number of books (apart from the Appendix),[36] the Papinian committee about five-sevenths (or, if the Appendix is subtracted, one-half) of that number.[37] All three excerpted more from works read earlier than those read towards the end.[38] The Sabinian committee took excerpts at a rate just over one-third greater than the other two committees.[39] The data collected are central to any serious attempt to reconstruct the process by which the Digest was compiled.

[32] C. Deo auctore 14: *ut codex consummatus et in quinquaginta libros digestus nobis offeratur.*

[33] C. Deo auctore 4: *Iubemus igitur vobis libros ad ius Romanum pertinentes et legere et elimare, ut ex his omnis materia colligatur nulla (secundum quod possibile est) neque similitudine neque discordia derelicta.*

[34] *subtilis*: C. Deo auctore 14 (above n. 30).

[35] C. Deo auctore 4: *Sed et hoc studiosum vobis esse volumus, ut... omne opus moderatum et quam pulcherrimum ostendatis.*

[36] In the event there were minor adjustments between them: *Commissioners* 252–3.

[37] *Commissioners* 252–3, 295, 306, 314; Honoré, *Tribonian* (n. 3) 169.

[38] Sabinian committee: first 168 books, 171 lines per book; last 152 books, 41 lines. Edictal committee: first 152 books, 160 lines per book; last 171, 20 lines. Papinian committee: first 174 books, 87 lines per book; last 152, 44 lines. The figures are derived from *Commissioners* 295, 306, 314.

[39] Sabinian mass 90.41 lines per book; edictal 65.93 lines; Papinian (omitting Appendix) 73.54. The reason for this was no doubt that Ulpian was to be treated as the lead author, who accounted for over 40 per cent of the Digest in volume and 60 per cent of the introductory texts in the Digest titles. 62 per cent of his books were allocated to the Sabinian committee which therefore had to be given a greater allowance of material (below n. 161).

III. The Bluhme/Krüger Ordo

We assumed that the reconstruction of the order of excerpting and editing in Bluhme/Krüger's *Ordo librorum iuris veteris in compilandis digestis observatus*[40] (BK Ordo) was broadly accurate,[41] including its allocation of works to the Sabinian, edictal and Papinian masses and the Appendix.[42] This assumption has been confirmed by older[43] and more recent[44] studies so far as the major works in the three main masses are concerned. It is less reliable as regards the allocation of minor works, the precise location of which is often uncertain, especially for works placed by Bluhme near the end of the Sabinian and Papinian masses and given an ordinal numeral by Paul Krüger.[45] Bluhme himself stressed that when there were few fragments of a work its position within a mass was often dubious. There were even some cases in which the mass to which a work should be assigned was doubtful, but in general the correct mass was clear.[46] Occasionally a work was included by Bluhme in the BK Ordo only because of a wrong inscription.[47] Of these, three survived Paul Krüger's scrutiny: Proculus 3 *ex posterioribus Labeonis*, a work listed in the Appendix at BK Ordo 266 on the basis of a single text,[48] Valens 7 *actionum* listed at BK Ordo 272 also on the basis of a single text[49] and Modestinus 4 *de praescriptionibus* at BK Ordo 145 on the same basis.[50] But the elimination of these works makes little difference except to the composition of the Appendix,[51] which is in any

[40] *Corpus Juris Civilis* (ed. Krïuger/Mommsen) I.874–8 Additamentum 1. The numbering of the items in the BK Ordo goes back to the stereotype edition of the Digest of 1905.

[41] Honoré, *Tribonian* 151; Wieacker (1972, n. 5) 297; Mantovani 134–5. We noted minor amendments in *Commissioners* 251–2; Waldstein (n. 5) 248. As Bluhme pointed out (n. 25 above at 439, cf. Mantovani 78) the accuracy of his allocations depended on the number of fragments incorporated in the Digest from each classical work.

[42] On the status and composition of the Appendix (the designation dates from 1837 and is due to G. Hugo, 'Der von Bluhme entdeckten Reihe sind Vier' *Civilistisches Magazin* 6.4); see Mantovani 1–3, 16–19, 109–24.

[43] G. Rotondi, 'L'indice Fiorentino delle Pandette e l'ipotesi del Bluhme' *Scr. Giur.* 1 (1922) 298–339.

[44] Mantovani 124–30.

[45] Mommsen, *Digesta Iustiniani Aug.* II.50*–58*; *Corpus Iuris Civilis* 927–31, with slight modifications in the stereotype edition.

[46] Bluhme (n. 25) 368.

[47] Nine instances are cited by Mantovani 82.

[48] D. 33.6.16: idem [i.e. Proculus] by mistake for Iavolenus.

[49] D. 36.4.15: Valens 7 act. for Venuleius.

[50] Lenel, *Palingenesia* 1, 723[1]; *Commissioners* 252. A mistake for his *liber singularis* on the subject.

[51] The third was omitted in our article: *Commissioners* 302.

case uncertain, since Paul's *Imperiales sententiae* (BK Ordo 263) may belong to the beginning of the Appendix or the end of the Papinian mass or may possibly have been read as a separate part of the editorial process.[52]

A good start on the work of revising the BK Ordo in order to distinguish the items whose position is settled exactly or within narrow limits, from those where the range of possibilities is wide, was made by Hugo Krüger[53] and taken further in Mantovani's detailed study of the Bluhmian masses,[54] of which considerable use has been made in the present study.[55] Mantovani confirms that even the minor works were for the most part read in a fixed order.[56] About six texts out of seven in the Digest appear in the standard order; but one in seven has been displaced by the editors for reasons of substance or elegance of exposition.[57] Despite the difficulties, one should not exaggerate the uncertainty that surrounds Bluhme's theory, as does Osler,[58] who even doubts whether the three committees existed and worked simultaneously.[59]

We assumed that the committees did exist and that the three masses were assigned to them, the Appendix going to the Papinian committee. This last assumption Mantovani rejects. He proposes, partly on the basis of a study by the present author,[60] to treat the Appendix as a continuation of the Sabinian mass rather than as a group of works allocated to the

52 Mantovani 109–10; but Kaiser (n. 5) 339–40; Osler 1988 (n. 5) 146–7. In my view this work, in a two-book epitome of the original six-book work, belongs to the Appendix; cf. Liebs, 'Jurisprudenz', *Hist. Lat. Lit.* 4 (1997) § 423 no. 79.

53 H. Krüger, 'Römische Juristen und ihre Werke' *Studi Bonfante* 2 (1930) 302–37, especially 317.

54 Mantovani, especially 79–81 and Table 91–103.

55 I do not assume that Mantovani, any more than Bluhme/Krüger, is right in every detail, only that a plausible theory of the composition of the Digest must be consistent with cogent recent research.

56 Mantovani 126–7.

57 Honoré 1973 (n. 3) 262–304; Mantovani 11–22.

58 Osler 1988 (n. 5) 140, 158.

59 Osler ibid. 158.

60 Honoré, 'Labeo's *Posteriora*' (1974, n. 3) 160–81; Mantovani 117–21; Kaiser (n. 5) 338–9. This study showed that Iavolenus' edition of Labeo's *posteriora,* excerpts from which are inscribed sometimes in the name of Iavolenus and sometimes in that of Labeo, were part of the Sabinian mass up to the middle of book 2 and of the Appendix thereafter, though in the BK Ordo the Iavolenus series is put at the end of the Sabinian mass and the Labeo series is part of the Appendix. Osler (n. 5, 1988, 153) confirms that no fragment after book 2 falls unambiguously in the Sabinian mass, though he points out that within book 2 the allocation to the Sabinian mass and the Appendix does not obviously correspond to the earlier and later parts of that book. The conclusion Mantovani draws is that this and the rest of the Appendix works were assigned to the Sabinian committee but read at a later stage, after the part of the Sabinian and other masses already read had begun to be edited into titles and books.

Papinian committee.[61] In his view it was decided at a certain juncture that the editorial process of assembling texts into titles and books should begin, although the Sabinian committee had not finished reading all the works assigned to it—in particular those now labelled the Appendix.[62] On this view either the commission was working to a timetable which included these books, but the Sabinian committee failed to keep to it; or, after the timetable had been settled, that committee was saddled with an extra list of books which had become available after the initial timetable had been fixed but which there had not yet been time to read.[63] In either case the commissioners who had been reading and excerpting the other masses could not be left to cool their heels while the Sabinian commissioners, according to Mantovani, finished reading the Appendix books. So the commissioners assigned to the other committees began the task of assembling the excerpts already made into titles and books.

The new excerpts from the Appendix works were, on his view, inserted into the Digest titles in positions that varied with the point reached in the editorial process.[64] At least up to D. 22.3 the process of editing was complete when the reading of the Appendix works was finished. This process included choosing initial and codal texts to begin and end the titles, so that the Appendix texts had to be put after the codal texts. From about book 33.1 onwards the Appendix precedes the codal texts. The explanation given for this is that, between about books 22 and 33, the editors had arranged the three masses in order, but had not completed editing the titles, for example by choosing introductory and codal texts. The Appendix texts were therefore inserted after the last of the three masses, which was generally the Papinian mass. This created the impression that the Appendix was part of the Papinian mass. In the last stages,

[61] Mantovani 114–15, 121; Kaiser 339–41, 348 mentions some difficulties with this thesis; Osler (n. 5, 1988) 146f. is sceptical.

[62] Above n. 42.

[63] It is possible that the Appendix works, or most of them, came to light during the period when excerpting was taking place, for instance because they had to be sent from provincial libraries to Constantinople. If so, they may either have been allocated to one of the existing committees as they arrived, or left over to be allocated later. Certainly Pomponius' *Epistulae* and *Senatusconsulta*, had they been available from the beginning, would have been allocated to the edictal committee, as the 'residuary heir' of Pomponius' works (below nn. 106, 123). Hence it is possible that the committees, including the Sabinian committee, were up to date or nearly up to date with the excerpting of the works originally assigned to them when the decision was made to begin editing. My considered view of the Appendix is set out in chapter 5.

[64] The accuracy of this theory depends on determining the positioning of the Appendix group of works in the various Digest titles, which is at times controversial: Mantovani (n. 5) 109–10; Kaiser (n. 5) 339–40; Osler (n. 5, 1988) 144–6.

from book 40 onwards, the editors had not yet arranged the three masses in order when the Appendix excerpts were ready to be added. Hence the Appendix need not now come after the three main masses but could be put in whatever position the editors thought best.[65]

If Mantovani's theory that the Appendix was excerpted after and separately from the three main masses is correct,[66] it lends support to the existence of a timetable, since it implies that the Sabinian committee's work of reading and excerpting was broken off in order that editorial work could begin on the excerpts so far gathered by all three committees. Osler argues that there was a second instance of a work being assigned partly to one of the three main masses and partly to the Appendix. In his view Scaevola's *Digesta*, most of the excerpts from which belong to the Appendix[67] was allotted to the Papinian committee. Only the first two books, however, fall in the main Papinian mass while the remainder form part of the Appendix.[68] Just as the Sabinian committee excerpted only the first one-and-a-half books of Labeo's *Posteriora*, so the Papinian committee excerpted only the first two books of Scaevola's *Digesta* before the excerpting of the main masses was broken off.[69] This argument, if correct, reinforces the case for supposing that the committees were working to a timetable.

It does not follow that Mantovani is right in allocating the Appendix works to the Sabinian committee.[70] These works could have been read by any of the existing committees or by a committee specially chosen for the purpose. If the excerpting by the Sabinian and Papinian committees was broken off at a certain moment[71] so that the editing could begin, we cannot be sure who read the Appendix works.

[65] Mantovani 114–15.

[66] Some objections to Mantovani's correlation of the reading and excerpting of the Appendix works with the process of editing the Digest are raised by Kaiser (n. 5) 340–1. But there is much to be said in favour of Mantovani's conclusion that the Appendix was excerpted after and separately from the three main masses, though in my view most of the Appendix works were not allocated to one of the three committees from the outset. For example, if Scaevola's *Digesta* had been part of any committee's task from the beginning, it should have been allocated to the Papinian committee (below n. 119) and excerpted earlier, before the short works at BK Ordo 225–62 with which the main mass ends.

[67] BK Ordo 267.

[68] Osler (n. 5, 1988) 154–8. Osler's theory, if correct, would help to answer Kaiser's objection.

[69] Osler does not attempt to explain the phenomenon: the explanation given above is mine.

[70] Osler 1988 (n. 5) 146.

[71] At what moment? Assuming a long-term rate of reading and excerpting of a book a day for the Sabinian and edictal committees and a book every two days for the Papinian

IV. The Timetable

In our article we put forward the hypothesis[72] that the commissioners were told to work to a timetable, beginning from 15 December 530. By reading and excerpting at a steady rate of so many books per week the excerpts they collected would be ready to be edited in titles and books after about 19 months, say from July 532.[73] Various factors such as absence, illness or political crisis might cause delays, but these could be made up, for the task, if delegated to the six senior commissioners with assistance from the advocates, would not be unduly heavy. Each of the three committees was headed, we argued, by two senior commissioners, to whom we gave the initials A and B for the Sabinian committee, C and D for the edictal and E and F for the Papinian committee. Since there were only five senior commissioners apart from Tribonian, this implied that Tribonian himself, besides supervising the whole operation, took part in the detailed work of reading and making excerpts.[74] It pointed to exceptional dynamism on his part. An attempt was made to identify membership of the three committees on the basis that the three most senior commissioners each headed a committee.[75] On that basis Tribonian headed the senior committee (the Sabinian)[76] and Constantinus,[77] holding an office that required him to deal with petitions and judicial proceedings before the emperor, headed the Papinian committee, which had fewer books to read. Theophilus, the senior professor, headed the edictal committee. Each committee was allotted the works of a major lawyer. Those of Ulpian, Paul and Gaius could not

committee, the three committees finished reading their main mass and the editing began about 7 June, 12 July or 25 July 532.

[72] 'Arbeitshypothese' (Wieacker, 11. 3, 1993, 440). In *Tribonian* (n. 3) xvii I described this as a 'discovery'.

[73] Honoré (n. 3, 1972) 538–41; *Tribonian* (n. 3) 171 contra Furlong (n. 5) 18–21, who would extend the excerpting phase to October 532.

[74] C. Deo auctore 3: *et iussimus quos probaveris... ad* ***sociandam*** *laborem eligere; 4: Iubemus igitur* ***vobis*** *antiquorum prudentiam... et legere et elimare* [my emphasis]; *Tribonian* 164–5; Rodger (n. 5) 394.

[75] Honoré (1971) 24–33; *Tribonian* 164–70. Furlong (n. 5) 22–3 suggests a different distribution of commissioners to committees.

[76] Senior in respect of the amount excerpted per book (90 lines as against 60 to 70), and the assignment to it of the most distinguished lawyer (Julian), the commentaries on the most ancient type of law, the *ius civile,* and the majority of books by the lawyer (Ulpian) from whom the greatest volume of work was chosen and whose texts introduced 60 per cent of the Digest titles.

[77] C. Tanta 9: *magister scrinii libellorum sacrarumque cognitionum.*

be allotted exclusively to any one committee, given the range of their works and that all three wrote edictal commentaries which, in view of their bulk, had to be split between the Sabinian and edictal committees.[78] The Sabinian committee was charged with reading the works of the greatest lawyer, Julian;[79] the Papinian committee with those of the second, Papinian;[80] and the edictal committee received the works of Modestinus,[81] the remaining member of the five listed in Valentinian's Law of Citations. The remaining professors, Dorotheus, Anatolius and Cratinus should be allocated to the Sabinian, Papinian and edictal committees also, perhaps in order of seniority.[82]

Responsibility for reading and excerpting the classical works assigned to each committee was divided, we argued, between two senior commissioners. The commissioners either worked on their own, when works were read separately,[83] or with the advocates on the commission when works were read jointly.[84] In the case of joint reading the advocates would presumably read out the text, once or several times, to the responsible commissioner, as they would in court, and the commissioner would decide if the passage read should be excerpted.[85] In deciding which works were read separately and which jointly we followed the

[78] In the case of Gaius, the Papinian committee which acted as his 'residuary heir': below n. 122.

[79] *Index auctorum* (so-called Index Florentinus) I; C. Tanta 18: *ipse Iulianus legum et edicti perpetui suptilissimus conditor.* All 101 of his books were allotted to the Sabinian committee. On the importance of Rangwert see Kaiser (n. 5) 338.

[80] *Index auctorum* II; C. Omnem 4: *ad sublimissimum Papinianum... acutissimi Papiniani; ipse pulcherrimus Papinianus... maximi Papiniani... viri sublimissimi praefectorii Papiniani...* Fifty-eight out of 62 of his books were allotted to this committee. Three, on adultery, go with the Sabinian group of works on that subject. The location of his Αστυνομικος is uncertain (BK Ordo 111; Mantovani 94).

[81] All Modestinus' books, numbering 67, were allotted to the edictal committee, though Mantovani expresses a doubt about the mass into which two *libri singulares (de inofficioso testamento, de differentia dotis)* fall. His 4 books *De praescriptionibus* (BK Ordo 145) should be eliminated and have not been included in the count (Lenel, *Palingenesia* 1,723[1]; Mantovani 96) but two *libri singulares* from the *Index auctorum*, *de testamentis* and *de legatis,* should be added and, like the others, assigned to the edictal mass, making 69 books in all: *Commissioners* 252.

[82] Honoré (n. 3, 1971) and *Tribonian* 169–70 gave reasons for assigning Anatolius to the edictal and Cratinus to the Papinian committee, but it may be that considerations of seniority should prevail.

[83] *Commissioners* 250–1.

[84] *Commissioners* 248–50. On the possible ambiguity as to whether works were read together or separately, caused by Krüger's editing of the BK Ordo, see Mantovani (n. 5) 107 n. 20; Kaiser (n. 5) 330–1.

[85] C. Tanta 14: sometimes repetition was inevitable *ne tam sensus quam aures legentium ex hoc perturbentur.* This reminds us of the importance of reading aloud.

analysis of Bluhme.[86] When he thought that two or more works were read jointly he divided the joint work into sections read successively. When works were read separately Bluhme listed them in the sequence in which they were incorporated in the Digest titles. Although the work was divided between the commissioners the output must have remained a committee responsibility, since, to account for the BK Ordo, the committee must have been obliged to present the excerpts in a fixed order, either in the order of the list of works assigned to it or in the order in which they had in fact been read.[87]

We suggested that the two senior commissioners between them, with or without help from the advocates, read and excerpted seven books a week in the case of the Sabinian and edictal committees and five in the case of the Papinian committee. If the Appendix works were not part of any of the main masses but were read later the first two committees must have read at about twice the rate of the Papinian committee, which in that case averaged only seven books a fortnight. The mean length of a book being a little over 1,500 lines[88] this was strenuous but not unmanageable.

The commissioners on the three committees could consult one another or Tribonian about the excerpts they proposed to make. But the key to rapid progress was, in our view, sub-delegation. Works excerpted separately were divided into groups and in each group the two senior commissioners heading a committee were assigned an equal or nearly equal number of books to read and excerpt. It may have been left to the commissioners to decide how exactly the works in a group should be divided up between them. For works read jointly equal division was not appropriate,[89] but in the interests of speed alternating sections of the joint works were divided between the two senior commissioners.

There must have been a timetable, since otherwise there was no way of ensuring that the three committees proceeded in tandem and finished at the same time. The timetable was largely respected in practice, since when the texts were edited in titles and books they mostly drew on all three masses. In principle the editing should have begun only when the

[86] Bluhme (n. 25) 282f., 445f.; Mantovani 39–53.

[87] This may seem counter to Bluhme's view (n. 25, p. 296) that it was a matter of indifference to the compilers whether the order in which the texts appeared in the Digest titles was the same as the order of excerpting. Rather, the order of reading and excerpting was a matter of indifference provided that the excerpts were presented to the commission group by group in a fixed order. As to the order within each group the committee could exercise a discretion.

[88] C. Tanta I says that the commission read nearly 2,000 books and more than 3,000,000 lines, cf. n. 21 above.

[89] Furlong (n. 5) 17.

excerpting was finished. Mantovani's hypothesis[90] that it began before the Appendix works had been read suggests that this aim was modified in the interests of speed. It confirms by implication the existence of a timetable, not only for the excerpting, but also for the completion of the whole project. If, as he thinks, the reading of the Appendix works was undertaken concurrently with editing the titles and books, this was in order that the Digest project as a whole could finish on time.

In order, then, to ensure that the committees finished reading and excerpting at the same time, Tribonian had to prescribe the rate at which the work should proceed. That he did so is indicated both by Mantovani's analysis of the Appendix and by the fact that the ratio of number of books excerpted by the three committees up to the editorial stage is close to 2:2:1 or 7:7:5 depending on whether the Appendix is counted among the books excerpted before that stage began.[91] This in turn implies that Tribonian settled the identity and number of books to be excerpted by each committee on the basis of the works available when the operation of reading and excerpting began. He and Justinian planned to finish the Digest in far less than 10 years. The Codex project, which had taken only 14 months, was an encouraging precedent. They may have aimed from the outset to complete the Digest in three years, though to say so in advance would have been to give hostages to fortune.

But the specific division into groups that we put forward represents, as Osler pointed out,[92] only one possible way in which the works may have been divided up.[93] This conclusion is reinforced by Mantovani's study which shows that the position of many minor works from which few fragments survive is in doubt. Moreover the timetable implied by the group-by-group sequence set out in our article could not have been insisted on from day to day. The committees could not in practice have worked at a 'stated and invariable rate'.[94] Relatively more time had to be

[90] Mantovani 114–15, 121.

[91] In principle 559 to the first two (Commissioners 251–3) and 291 (52 per cent of 559) to the third, though in the upshot the Sabinian committee excerpted 546 books and the edictal committee 573 (*Commissioners* 251–3; *Tribonian* 168–9; Furlong, above n. 5, 3). These figures are subject to some adjustment to the extent that the BK Ordo has assigned books to the wrong mass. Mantovani's reconstruction suggests that the doubts, which mainly concern some *libri singulares* of Paul will, however resolved, not greatly alter the picture. It remains possible that, as was earlier believed, the Appendix works, or most of them, came to light only during the course of the commission's work, in which case the initial assignments to the Sabinian and edictal committees may have been equal or nearly equal, as we thought.

[92] Osler 1985, 155–62.

[93] We did not argue that it was the only way, though we should have made this clearer.

[94] Honoré, *Trail* (1972) 535 contra Furlong (n. 5) 3, 5.

spent on the most important books, which came early in each committee's task. If, however, a committee fell behind hand when reading the leading works it was, in my view, expected to catch up later, so that the three committees finished excerpting at much the same time. It is a feature of those who undertake a stint of so much per day, week or month that they check their progress against the timetable from time to time and, though they may fall quite a long way behind, make up the deficit in the end.[95]

If Mantovani is right, the other committees finished their initial task before the Sabinian committee. If Osler is also right[96] the edictal committee finished first, which one would expect if it was composed of two professors.[97] The plan then had to be changed and the Appendix works excerpted while the editorial process was going on. But if most of the Appendix works had come to light only recently, as is not implausible, the Sabinian committee, like the others, need not have been far behind with its original stint. Whichever hypothesis is correct, to give the committees a timetable was an essential feature of the planning of the Digest project.

According to the 1970 article the works to be read by the three committees were divided into groups, which we numbered from I to XLIII. These groups, listed in chronological order for each mass, were based on the reconstruction of the masses by Bluhme and Krüger.

The BK Ordo distinguishes between works excerpted jointly and those excerpted separately. The works excerpted jointly bring together the authors of commentaries on Sabinus, on the praetor's edict, on appeals, on adultery and so on. The basis for joint excerpting is that two or more authors have written on the same topic and that what they have to say is likely to overlap. Joint excerpting then helps to avoid duplicating texts and makes it easier to select the best statement of the law on a given point. The works excerpted separately are also grouped together. Sometimes they come between two jointly excerpted groups. Once they come at the beginning of the works assigned to a committee.

V. The Allocation of Works to Committees

The method by which works were allocated to committees is, at least in outline, clear. The method combined considerations of prestige and seniority with the grouping together of subjects and genres and an

[95] Honoré, *Ulpian, Pioneer of Human Rights* (2002) 169, 187.
[96] Osler (1988) 154–8 and above n. 68. [97] Above nn. 76–82.

attempt to achieve equity between the committees, in the light when necessary of numerical equality. The works of each author, apart from Paul, were in principle allocated to a committee, subject to exceptions in the interest of drawing together works of the same genre or on the same subject. The system resembles that of instituting an heir subject to legacies. Not only is each committee allotted the whole or nearly the whole work of a major legal author (Julian, Papinian and Modestinus)[98] but it also acquires lesser authors. Sometimes, if only one work by the author was in the hands of the commissioners, it was inevitable that it should be allotted just one committee, but sometimes there was a choice. Marcianus,[99] Neratius,[100] Alfenus Varus,[101] Florentinus,[102] Africanus,[103] Rutilius Maximus[104] and perhaps Labeo[105] went to the Sabinian committee; Pomponius,[106] Celsus,[107] Marcellus,[108] Iavolenus,[109] Callistratus,[110] Papirius Iustus,[111] Terentius Clemens,[112] Licinnius Rufinus,[113] Proculus,[114] Tertullian,[115] Mauricianus,[116]

[98] Above nn. 79–81.

[99] Thirty-three books out of 34 (BK Ordo 22, 40, 42, 44, 55, 57, 63, 66). The other book, *ad senatus consultum Turpillianum* (BK Ordo 229) yields one fragment (D. 48, 16, 1), which begins a title, and is unplaceable as regards mass, see Mantovani 100. It should however probably be allotted to the Sabinian committee along with his other books.

[100] Twenty-two books out of 25 (BK Ordo 36, 60), with his three books of *Responsa* being allocated to the Papinian committee to accompany Paul's four books *Ad Neratium* (BK Ordo 217–18); Mantovani 98.

[101] All 15 books, seven from his *Digesta* and eight from Paul's *epitome* of his work (BK Ordo 15, 16); *Commissioners* 251–2.

[102] His 12 books of *Institutiones.*

[103] His nine books of *Quaestiones.*

[104] His book *Ad legem Falcidiam* (BK Ordo 68).

[105] Assuming that Mantovani is right in attributing Iavolenus' *Posteriora Labeonis* to the Sabinian committee and that this work is to be treated as essentially a work of Labeo.

[106] Below n. 123.

[107] His 39 books of *Digesta.*

[108] Thirty-seven books out of 38 (BK Ordo 135), the exception being his one book of Responsa, allotted to the Sabinian committee (BK Ordo 59) for a reason that escapes me (see however Chapter 3 nn. 227–30).

[109] Thirty-four books (BK Ordo 125, 127, 130, 152, 153), i.e. all apart from 10 *ex posterioribus Labeonis,* which should probably be treated as Labeo's or at any rate grouped with Labeo's 10 books of *Posteriora a Iavoleno epitomatorum* (BK Ordo 94, 265).

[110] Sixteen books out of 21 (BK Ordo 100, 158, 160, 176), three going to the institutional group in the Sabinian mass (BK Ordo 26) and two with the *quaestiones* of Paul.

[111] His 20 books of *Constitutiones:* BK Ordo 177.

[112] His 20 books *ad legem Juliam et Papiam:* BK Ordo 164.

[113] His 12 or 13 books of *Regulae:* BK Ordo 175.

[114] His 11 books of *Epistulae* (BK Ordo 155, 157).

[115] All nine books (BK Ordo 161, 173).

[116] His six books *ad legem Juliam et Papiam* (BK Ordo 166).

Menander[117] and Taruttienus Paternus[118] to the edictal committee; Scaevola,[119] Tryphoninus,[120] and Hermogenianus[121] to the Papinian committee. The Papinian committee also inherited Gaius, subject to his edictal commentary, institutional works and commentary on the lex Julia et Papia being grouped with similar works in the Sabinian and edictal masses.[122] Pomponius went to the edictal committee, subject to similar legacies.[123] For lesser authors the allocation is sometimes debatable,[124] or the fragments are too few to be sure.[125] But all the leading authors, apart from Paul, whose works were too lengthy and

[117] His four books *De re militari* (BK Ordo 171).

[118] His four books *De re militari* (BK Ordo I72); Liebs, 'Jurisprudenz', *Hist. Lat. Lit.* 4 (1997) § 419.6.

[119] Twenty-seven books out of 31 (BK Ordo 184, 187, 189, 191, 193), the exceptions being his four books of *regulae* which go to the Sabinian committee with the bulk of *regulae* (BK Ordo 38). Scaevola's *Digesta* and the spurious *liber singularis quaestionum publice tractatatum* belong to the Appendix (BK Ordo 267, 271). They would have been given to the Papinian committee had they been available in time and, if Osler is right (above nn. 67–8), perhaps the *Digesta* were so given.

[120] The 21 books of *Disputationes:* BK Ordo 219, 221.

[121] All six books of *Iuris epitomae:* BK Ordo 206, 208, 210, 212, 214.

[122] All 22 books (BK Ordo 197, 215, 223–4, 245–7) apart from 15 *ad edictum,* 11 (or 7) of institutional works, 1 *de formula hypothecaria* which went with the only other work on the subject, by Marcianus (BK Ordo 57–8) in the Sabinian mass and *27 ad edictum* and 15 *ad legem Iuliam et Papiam* in the edictal mass. There is one text inscribed *ad legem Glitiam* (D. 5.2.4; BK Ordo 169), inserted between excerpts from Mar*cellus' Digesta.* Lenel treats the work as spurious and to H. Kruger and Mantovani the text is unplaceable. If there was such a (spurious) work it should go in the Papinian mass. The example of Gaius shows how Tribonian's principles of allocation could in practice lead to a distribution of works by which each committee had a substantial number of an author's books.

[123] Fifty-four books (BK Ordo 154, 156), which is all apart from the 36 *Ad Sabinum* and one of *Regulae* that go to the Sabinian committee with other similar works (BK Ordo 2, 45), the three *Enchiridii* (BK Ordo 248) that go to the Papinian committee to accompany Gaius' *Ad legem XII tabularum* and the seven *ad Plautium* (BK Ordo 126, 128; 131) which belong to *ad Plautium* group in the edictal mass. His 25 books of *epistulae* and *senatusconsulta* in the Appendix (BK Ordo 269, 270) cannot have formed part of the original allocation to either the Papinian or the Sabinian committees.

[124] Eight books of Macer belong to the Sabinian committee (BK Ordo 52, 61, 65, 86) and it is not clear why the two *ad legem vicesimae hereditatium* were allotted to the edictal committee (BK Ordo 168), unless it was to go with the Augustan legislation *ad legem Iuliam et Papiam* at BK Ordo 162–7. Venuleius Saturninus (including in the compilers' estimation Claudius Saturninus) seems to belong to the Sabinian committee (eight books in BK Ordo 53, 91, 92), of which BK Ordo 53 belongs to a group on *publica iudicia,* but his 19 books of *Stipulationes* go to the Papinian committee (BK Ordo 216).

[125] Arcadius Charisius perhaps belongs to the Sabinian committee (BK Ordo 62; Mantovani 92). Two texts of uncertain placement were allotted to the Papinian committee by BK Ordo 261, 262: Mantovani 100. The one text of Aelius Gallus (BK Ordo 178) is also unplaceable: Mantovani 96. The two texts of Iulius Aquila's book of *Responsa* do not allow his mass to be determined (BK Ordo 179): Mantovani 96. Quintus Mucius and Furius Anthianus appear only in the Appendix.

varied to confine to one committee, were assigned to a committee that was, as it were, either the sole heir to their works, or the residuary heir to those not bequeathed elsewhere.[126]

Ulpian's basic committee is the Sabinian committee. This allocation, in my view, is connected with the fact that Ulpian is treated as the lead author for the Digest, in which 60 per cent of the titles begin with an Ulpian text.[127] It goes hand in hand with the fact that the Sabinian committee excerpted at a markedly greater rate per book than the other committees.[128] The works of Paul were distributed rather evenly between the three committees, irrespective of subject-matter. Unlike the other Digest jurists he possesses two basic committees, the Sabinian and the Papinian. A striking feature is that the BK Ordo allots 24 *libri singulares* of Paul to each of the Sabinian and Papinian committees. Only one, of uncertain mass,[129] is allotted to the edictal committee, and it should be transferred to one of the other committees. Chapter 3 deals with the allocations outlined above in greater detail, author by author, and in particular with the allocations to Ulpian and Paul.

Some think that Bluhme relied too heavily on affinities of authorship and subject-matter in compiling the BK Ordo,[130] but the examples given show that Tribonian followed an orderly principle in distributing the work between the committees, though there had to be compromises between the claims of authorship and subject-matter. But the crucial question in the present inquiry is whether numerical considerations also played a part in the make-up of the groups.[131] Osler did not show that the groups, however constituted—and some of our suggestions took too little account of subject-matter—were not subdivided into equal lots to be read by individual commissioners. As Furlong puts it, 'Osler's main findings can be shown to actually support Honoré's division of texts among the six subcommittees, but only when understood in terms of Justinian's "5 per cent compilation limit" plan.'[132]

Osler, however, rightly rejected the theory that the commissioners regularly adhered to a timetable for reading and excerpting each group

[126] Maecianus cannot be assigned to a committee, because his 14 books on *iudicia publica* go with a group on this topic in the Sabinian mass and his 16 books on *fideicommissa* with that topic in the Papinian mass. His *liber singularis ex lege Rhodia* provides only one Digest fragment (D. 14.2.9) which comes between the Sabinian mass and the appendix: BK Ordo 93; Mantovani 92.

[127] Honoré, *Ulpian. Pioneer of Human Rights* (2002) 229.

[128] Above n. 39.

[129] *Ad legem Cinciam:* BK Ordo 170; Mantovani 97.

[130] Mantovani 78–9.

[131] *Commissioners* 262; Furlong 15.

[132] Furlong (n. 5) 11; below nn. 143–63.

of works. Our findings about the rate at which books were excerpted within each group were inconsistent with the assumption that the two commissioners always worked together on the same group to the same deadline. If they had, and if the amount excerpted depended on how industrious they were, the output would have consistently reflected their relative zeal. But according to our data their relative rate of excerpting varied considerably.[133] Moreover our scheme, if strictly adhered to, would have resulted in some senior commissioners 'being inactive for a substantial amount of time'[134] because they finished their group work earlier than their colleague. In some groups one of the commissioners excerpted at a much greater rate than the other. For example in group XL commissioner E on our analysis excerpted at three times the rate of F,[135] but in group XXXV F excerpted at nearly four times the rate of E.[136] The reasons we gave (pressure of public business, non-availability of certain books) could not convincingly explain the unevenness. There were groups in all three masses that showed very different rates of excerpting between the assumed senior commissioners, for example groups III, IV and XI in the Sabinian mass,[137] and groups XXV to XXVIII in the edictal mass.[138]

So either the commissioners did not always excerpt the same groups of works at the same time or they did not consistently maintain a rate of excerpting that reflected how assiduous they were. If they were to excerpt only the best and most useful texts the rate of excerpting must have depended on the quality of the texts read and the total amount of text that could be included in the Digest. The uneven rate of excerpting would be easier to explain if the work was divided between commissioners who were free, within the constraint of an overall limit on the amount to be excerpted, to move on to the next works to be read, though in a different group, when they had finished their present task, or to fall behindhand for a time provided that they caught up later. Then we would expect that sometimes one commissioner and sometimes his colleague would excerpt more. We may need to distinguish between the order in which individual commissioners read and excerpted the books assigned to them and the order in which the excerpts were presented to Tribonian and Justinian for incorporation

133 *Commissioners* 295, 306, 314.

134 Osler (1985) 183.

135 129 lines per book against 39.

136 53 lines per book against 14; *Commissioners* 314.

137 121, 61 and 71 lines per book for A; 50, 16 and 121 for B.

138 28, 20, 14 and 20 lines per book for C; 46, 31, 4 and 4 for D.

in the Digest. The scheme of division into groups seems to have been preserved when the excerpts were handed over. But within each group of works excerpted separately the excerpts were presented, it appears, either in the order in which the work had been assigned to the committee or in that in which they were actually read.[139] So far as works read jointly were concerned, the excerpts were presented in the order of the successive sections—a feature that attracted Bluhme's attention.

The grouping of the works excerpted in our original article in groups from I to XLIII has been retained in this revised chapter. An updated grouping from a reduced number of groups, labelled (i) to (xxxv), interspersed with works left unattached (largely *libri singulares* not grouped with others) is presented in chapter 3 and Addendum A. For reasons explained above and in chapter 5 the updated grouping does not attempt to group the Appendix works .

Another objection to our theory was that the decline in the rate of excerpting with the passage of time, common to all three committees,[140] could not be reconciled with a timetable based on an invariable rate of work. The decline was to be expected, since the committees read the most important works first. Relatively more time must have been spent on these works.[141] The decline could be better explained if all three committees had to work to a deadline, such as July 532, but were allowed, while respecting that deadline, which was based on a prescribed rate of work of seven books per week or per fortnight, to fall behind temporarily while they were reading the more important works. They might 'borrow' time during the early stage of excerpting knowing that they would have to repay it later on.[142] Not merely might a commissioner fall behind his colleague for a time, but the committee as a whole might temporarily fall behind. In that case he or they would have to hurry to catch up towards the end, and this would help to explain the decline in excerpting common to all three committees.

[139] This second possibility would account for the phenomenon of 'split works' (the *Regulae* of Marcianus, the *Epistulae* of Proculus, Tryphoninus' *Disputationes*): BK Ordo 40, 42, 44; 155, 157; 219, 221; Osler (1985) 163–9; Furlong (n. 5) 14 and of 'sandwich groups': BK Ordo 48–56; 88–94; 124–33; 141–9; 150–4; 220–3; 263–6; Osler 1985, 177–84; Furlong 17. Mantovani 105–6 throws doubt on whether the *Disputationes* of Tryphoninus were read in two separate sections. The work of Tryphoninus may have been read jointly with Paul's *Manualia* and *Decreta.* It may be noted that on Mantovani's reconstruction (n. 5, 106–7) the first section in this group amounts to 14 books out of 27.

[140] Above n. 38. [141] Mantovani 177. [142] Furlong (n. 5) 9.

VI. Reduction to 5 per cent?

Furlong, in an article that concentrates on the statistical aspect of the problem,[143] argues for Justinian's '5 per cent compilation limit plan'.[144] In his view the unevenness in excerpting within particular groups points to a defect in our theory. That theory concentrated on speed of excerpting[145] at the expense of an equally important feature of the project, that of reducing the classical works to 50 books.[146] It was pointless to excerpt quickly unless the volume of excerpts fitted this aim.[147] While the length of individual books could vary, the Digest as a whole could not be of indefinite bulk if it was to be used in practice and teaching. What instructions, then, were given to the commissioners about the volume of text to be excerpted? According to Furlong, a controlling factor was that each of the six commissioners was allotted a fixed and precise overall excerpting rate within which to accomplish the task, based on the aim of reducing the classical material to 5 per cent of the original.[148] The commissioners might 'borrow' lines when excerpting the more important works but these would have to be 'repaid' later.

C. Deo Auctore and C. Tanta contain clues as to what this overall excerpting rate may have been. They instruct Tribonian to collect the classical works and to extract their core (*enucleare*)[149] and polish (*elimare*)[150] them according to a certain scheme of control (*certum moderamen*).[151] According to C. Tanta over 3 million lines were in the upshot reduced to nearly 150,000.[152] So it is plausible to think that the scheme of control involved reducing the classical works to about 5 per cent of the originals.[153] It is true that the average Digest book, according to C. Tanta, is about twice the length of the original books,

143 Furlong (n. 5).

144 Furlong (n. 5) 5–10.

145 Furlong (n. 5) 26. Nevertheless speed was an essential factor.

146 C. Deo Auctore 5.

147 Furlong (n. 5)11; Pugsley (n. 5) 354.

148 Furlong (n. 5) 5–10. He attributes this directive to Justinian rather than Tribonian. I am not convinced that the assessment in *Tribonian* 252–4 of their respective roles, political for Justinian and executive for Tribonian, is wrong.

149 C. Deo auctore 11.

150 C. Deo auctore 4.

151 C. Tanta 1: *ipsa vetustatis studiossissima opera iam paene confusa et disssoluta eidem viro excelso* [Tribonian] *permisimus tam colligere quam certo moderamini tradere* cf. *C. Tanta pr.: in novam pulchritudinem et moderatum pervenire compendium.*

152 C. Tanta 1: *a praefato viro excelso suggestum est... plus quam trecenties decem milia versuum a veteribus effusa, quae necesse esset omnia legere et perscrutari... et quod undique fuit collectum, hoc in sinus suos receperunt, in certum quinquaginta paene milia versuum totum opus consummantes.*

153 Wieacker (n. 5) 441 'pauschale Ratio 1:20'.

3,000 lines instead of average of 1,500.[154] That may have been acceptable, but the length could not be extended to 4,000 or 5,000 lines per book.

Five per cent was roughly the fraction to which the original works were in fact reduced. Tribonian's figures can be compared with those for the number of books and lines excerpted that we published as part of our article.[155] The number of books recorded was on our count 1,528 rather than nearly 2,000.[156] The lower number may partly reflect the fact that according to C. Tanta many of the books read contained nothing useful or original that called for inclusion in the Digest.[157] But there can hardly have been over 400 books of this worthless sort, especially as C. Deo auctore ruled out from the start books lacking imperial authority and not cited by later authors.[158] There was an element of exaggeration in 'nearly 2,000'. The number of lines should therefore have been proportionately less than the figure given in C. Tanta—not 'nearly 150,000' but about 120,000. The total number of lines that we counted was close to this figure: 113,301.[159] It is true that our count was of single column lines as printed in a modern book, Lenel's *Palingenesia*.[160] If we take Diósdi's figure of 39 letters per line instead of Lenel's 43 or 44, the Digest figure was really about 10 per cent more than our 113,301, say 125,000. Even so the amount excerpted and included in the Digest comes to no more than 5.2 per cent of the originals. It may be argued that, while in the upshot just over 5 per cent was excerpted, this is merely because the good and useful texts happened to come to that amount, not because the commissioners were instructed to aim at that figure. There might have been twice as many good and useful texts. But this would not explain the consistent ratio of excerpting as between committees or, on our analysis, by individual commissioners within each committee.

While the overall level of excerpting fits C. Tanta well, the three committees did not all excerpt at the same rate. Five per cent of 1,500

[154] 150,000 divided by 50. In reality 2,500 lines is closer to the mark.

[155] *Commissioners* 285–314.

[156] *Commissioners* 314.

[157] C. Tanta 17: *sed huius operis conditores non solum ea volumina perlegerunt, ex quibus leges positae sunt, sed etiam alia multa quae, nihil vel utile vel novum in eis invenientes, quod exceptum nostris digestis applicarent, optimo animo respuerunt.*

[158] C. Deo auctore 4: *quia autem at alii libros ad ius pertinentes scripserunt, quorum scripturae a nullis auctoribus receptae sunt, neque nos eorum volumina nostram inquietare dignamur sanctionem.*

[159] *Commissioners* 314.

[160] They average 43 or 44 letters. If we take the Corpus Iuris Civilis stereotype edition of the Digest there are about 71 lines per column of about 40 letters each, which for 897 pages of two columns each comes to 127,374 lines.

lines is 75 lines, and 113,301 lines divided by 1,600 books comes to 71 Lenel lines per book. This is reasonably close to 5 per cent even if, taking the lines of an ancient text to be a tenth shorter, we increase the number of lines excerpted to 125,000 and so to 78 lines per book. If the overall figures are broken down, they yield an average of 90.41 Lenel lines per book for the Sabinian mass as a whole without the Appendix, 65.93 for the edictal mass as a whole and 73.54 for the Papinian mass less the Appendix.[161] The level of excerpting for the edictal and Papinian masses is therefore around three-quarters that for the Sabinian mass: 73 per cent of the Sabinian for the edictal mass and 81 or 71 per cent for the Papinian mass, depending on whether the Appendix is included. These proportions are independent of the length of the lines. Furlong, who treats the Appendix as part of the Papinian mass, suggests that the scheme was for the edictal and Papinian committees to excerpt at three-quarters of the rate allotted to the Sabinian committee. This would ensure that the classical material was reduced to 5 per cent of the original.[162] Consistent with the overall excerpting rate, the main Sabinian mass was given a higher rate of excerpting and the other two committees a lower one. Though the figures for the edictal and Papinian committees are a little below or above three-quarters of the Sabinian rate, depending on whether the Appendix is assigned to the Papinian committee, Furlong's hypothesis may be on the right lines. This would be likely if, as argued in *Tribonian,*[163] Tribonian himself headed the Sabinian committee, and so could insist on a higher overall rate of excerpting for that committee.

VII. Sub-delegation?

None of this shows that within each committee the work was divided between two senior commissioners. But Furlong's argument is strengthened when the rate of excerpting per book is calculated separately, on our hypothesis, for the individual Sabinian and edictal commissioners. For the main Sabinian mass commissioner A excerpts overall at a rate of

[161] *Commissioners* 295, 306, 314. Including the Appendix the Papinian mass averages 63.96 lines per book, which is 71 per cent of the Sabinian mass. Including the Appendix the Sabinian mass averages 81.51 lines per book.

[162] Furlong (n. 5) 6f.

[163] *Tribonian* 164–70; Rodger (n. 5) 394–5; above n. 76; contra Solidoro (n. 13) 77; Pugsley (n. 5) 354; Furlong (n. 5) 21–3.

91.10 per book, B at a rate of 92.60.[164] For the edictal mass C excerpts at a rate of 66.82 and D. at a rate of 67.68.[165] If our assignments to individual commissioners had been arbitrary, because there was in fact no sub-delegation, the probability of these figures coming so close by chance is, he calculates, no more than 6.78 and 3.59 per cent respectively, which gives a combined probability for these two masses of 0.24 per cent, or less than 1 in 400.[166] This argument in favour of sub-delegation supports the conclusion that our division of the text between the two Sabinian and two edictal commissioners was more or less accurate.

It suggests that the senior commissioners in those committees were excerpting separately but adhered closely to a prescribed norm. The same is not true of the Papinian mass, at least if taken to include the Appendix. There the excerpting rate of the two postulated commissioners diverged. So far as the main mass was concerned E excerpted at a rate of 77.78 lines per book, F at 69.41. For the Appendix the figures we arrived at were that one commissioner excerpted at 18.81 lines per book, the other at 61.83.[167] But these Appendix figures are not reliable, since doubt attaches both as to the exact composition of the Appendix, and as to how the works which genuinely belonged to it should be grouped.[168] On the other hand the figure for F in the main Papinian mass is very close to that for the edictal commissioners C and D, which may suggest that F was adhering to the same norm for volume of excerpt.[169]

Another argument for sub-delegation is that this was a sensible way of speeding the work of the commission, which could not have been finished so quickly without it. Once the idea of delegation had been adopted in order to speed the work of excerpting it was logical, given the presence of six senior commissioners, to extend it further.

A third argument is numerical. This depends on an analysis of certain sequences of works in the BK Ordo. In some of these there occurs a sudden reduction in the rate of excerpting that we termed 'collapse'. It is best explained, we argued, by supposing that the sequences of works excerpted separately were divided into two equal lots, each allocated to one of the commissioners on the committee.[170] The argument is best set out in visual as well as numerical terms.

164 *Commissioners* 295, 314.
165 *Commissioners* 306, 314.
166 Furlong (n. 5) 10, 23–5.
167 *Commissioners* 314.
168 Mantovani 109–12 (casting doubt on fourteen books assigned to the Appendix).
169 Furlong (n. 5) 14.
170 *Commissioners* 262, 265; Furlong 15–16.

Take for example our groups III to V.[171] They form part of the Sabinian mass and come between two sets of works (II, edictal commentary and VI, institutional works) excerpted jointly. The order of their arrangement points to planning.[172] In the Bluhme/Krüger Ordo they run, using Krüger's enumeration, as follows:

III.	10.	Ulpianus 10 disputationum	10 books	
	11.	Ulpianus 10 de omnibus tribunalibus	10 books	
IV.	12.	Ulpianus 6 opinionum	6 books	
	13.	Ulpianus 6 de censibus	6 books	
V.	14	(i). Iulianus digestorum 1–62	62 books	
	14	(ii). Iulianus digestorum 63–90	28 books)	
	15.	Alfeni Vari 7 digestorum epitomae	7 books)	
	16.	Paulus 8 epitomarum Alfeni digestorum	8 books)	
	17.	Iulianus 1 de ambiguitatibus	1 book)	= 63 books
	18.	Iulianus 4 ad Urseium Ferocem	4 books)	
	19.	Iulianus 6 ad Minicium	6 books)	
	20.	Africanus 9 quaestionum	9 books)	

The position of item 13, Ulpianus *De censibus* is uncertain. H. Krüger marked its position as hypothetical and Mantovani would place the work near the end of the Sabinian mass.[173] There are seven fragments, four (unsurprisingly) in Digest title 50.15, *De censibus*. These merely show that Ulpian's *De censibus* belongs to the Sabinian mass. In support of his view Mantovani points to D. 47.15.7, a generalizing text that ends the title *De praevaricatione*,[174] and D. 44.7.26, another generalizing text that, in the long title *De obligationibus et actionibus*, ends the 26 texts of the Sabinian mass.[175] Neither of these texts serves to fix the position of *De censibus* in the BK Ordo. They illustrate rather the liking of the compilers for codal texts that end a title or mass with a generalization.[176] Well-known examples are the last texts of the titles *De furtis*[177] and *De iniuriis*.[178] The remaining text from *De censibus* is 41.1.34, where the text comes between two excerpts from Ulpian's

[171] *Commissioners* 287–8. [172] *Commissioners* 263–4, 287–8; *Tribonian* 162–3.

[173] Mantovani 90.

[174] *In omnibus causis, praeterquam in sanguine, qui delatorem corrupit, ex senatus consulto pro victo habetur.*

[175] *Omnes poenales actiones post litem inchoatam et ad heredes transeunt.*

[176] Mantovani 15–16.

[177] D. 47.2.93 (Ulp. 38 ed: *Meminisse oportebit nunc jura plerumque criminaliter agi et eum qui agit in crimen subscribere...*).

[178] D. 47.10.45 (Herm. 5 epit: *De iniuria nunc extra ordinem ex causa et persona statui solet*).

Disputationes. It could therefore belong where Bluhme placed it, but this is not demonstrable.

Whether or not it did so, our idea was that the next seven items fall into two equal or very nearly equal lots by virtue of a break between books 62 and 63 of Julian's *Digesta*. Item 14(i) amounts to 62 books, and items 14(ii) to 20 to 63 books.[179] But why should we suppose that a break occurs between books 62 and 63 of Julian's *Digesta*? One reason is that this corresponds to a striking collapse in the rate of excerpting.

Here are the figures for excerpts from Julian's *Digesta* book 50 onwards:

Books 50–62: 9, 49, 146, 45, 103, 38, 66, 49, 15, 28, 79, 97, 97

Books 63–90: 3, 45, 22, 0, 0, 0, 21, 27, 0, 0, 7, 0, 0, 0, 4, 45, 0, 8, 5, 14, 5, 16, 2, 67, 3, 5, 3, 11

The first 62 books of that work average 49 lines per book (those from 50 to 62 average 63 lines), but the last 28 only 11. The explanation we gave of the collapse was twofold. A different commissioner (B) was required to read from book 63 of Julian's *Digesta* onwards in order that B's lot should be equal or nearly equal to A's. But B, in contrast to commissioner A, who had read the first 62 books, chose very few texts from the later books. Items 10, 12 and 14 (i) were allocated to commissioner A, and items 11, 13 and 14 (ii) to 20 to his colleague B. It was not that B was averse to making excerpts on a substantial scale. Though he took very little material from the last 28 books of Julian's *Digesta* he excerpted at a good rate from items 15 to 20.[180] Commissioners could presumably choose the order in which to read the books allotted to them, and B may have read the works that came later in the BK Ordo first and felt pressed either for time or for volume of material when he came to his part of Julian's *Digesta*. In any event, the collapse pointed to a change at that point in the commissioner responsible for reading and excerpting Julian's *Digesta* from book 63 onwards.

Osler proposed a different explanation.[181] He pointed out that in works such as *Digesta, Quaestiones* and *Responsa* the author, after dealing with the topics treated in the praetor's edict, tacks on the discussion of statutes at the end. The commissioners in general excerpt at a lower rate in the statutory than in the edictal part.[182] There are several instances of this phenomenon.[183] But it does not account for the location of the

[179] The discrepancy of one book is not serious, especially as the location of some one book monographs is uncertain.

[180] 59 lines per book.

[181] Osler (1985) 172–7.

[182] Osler (1985) 176.

[183] Papinian's *Responsa,* Paul's *Quaestiones,* Paul's *Responsa,* Scaevola's *Quaestiones,* Modestinus' *Responsa,* Marcellus' *Digesta* and Celsus' *Digesta:* Osler (1985) 173–7.

collapse in Julian's *Digesta*. In that work the statutory part begins at book 59 (*ad legem Cinciam*), and the first four books of the statutory part (59 to 62) average an excerpting rate of 75 lines per book, which is higher than the average for the first 62 books and much higher than that for the last 28.

On Osler's view the collapse should coincide with the beginning of the statutory material. If that were the case the change would be noticeable from book 59 onwards. But the phenomenon of collapse does not in this instance coincide with the beginning of the statutory material, but comes within that material. Osler's explanation is therefore inadequate. No collapse occurred at the beginning of the statutory material in Julian's *Digesta*. Some other factor accounted for the collapse that began at book 63. One suggestion, put informally by Mantovani, is that in the sixth century the statutory material from book 63 onwards (the *leges Aelia Sentia, Julia de maritandis ordinibus, Papia, Aquilia, Rhodia de iactu, Julia de adulteriis, Appuleia, Publilia de sponsu* (?) and the *senatus consultum Libonianum*) was less important than the material in books 59 to 62 (the *leges XII tabularum, Cincia de donationibus, Falcidia, Cornelia de captivis* and the *senatus consulta Tertullianum* and *Iuventianum*). The difference is not obvious and is not reflected in any of the seven instances in which the collapse does coincide with the beginning of the statutory material.[184] The numerical explanation therefore seems the more promising. It is reinforced if my hypothesis about the membership of the three committees is correct.[185] The professors did not teach the statutory material and are likely to have been less interested in it than in the edictal material which they did teach. In uncodified systems of law such as the Roman and English professors teach and students learn from juristic writings or decided cases. They are reluctant to teach or study statutes. Indeed, even after Justinian's reforms, the Codex Justinianus was studied only in the fifth year, as had been the case in the fifth century.[186] The point of view of judges, ministers and government officials is of course different. If the change over at book 63 of Julian's *Digesta* was from a minister, Tribonian, to a professsor, Dorotheus, the collapse would not be surprising.

Papinian's *Quaestiones*, excerpted by the Papinian committee, provides another example.[187] Papinian's main works come together at the

[184] Below nn. 209–18. [185] Above nn. 76–82.

[186] C. Omnem 5 and for the previous system of education P. Collinet, *Histoire de l'école de droit de Beyrouth* (1925) 234–40.

[187] *Commissioners* 262–5. Contra Osler (1985) 171–2.

beginning of the Papinian mass.[188] They precede a jointly excerpted set of works, the *Quaestiones* of Paul and Scaevola. On our analysis Papinian's works, consisting of 58 books divided into two lots of 29, constitute group XXXI and were divided as follows:

180 (i). Papinianus quaestionum 1–29	29 books	
180 (ii). Papinianus quaestionum 30–37	8 books)	
181. Papinianus responsorum 1–19	19 books)	= 29 books
182. Papinianus definitionum 1–2	2 books)	

The position of these works at the beginning of the BK Ordo is not in doubt,[189] though Hugo Krüger thought the position of the *Definitiones* no more than probable.[190] Item 180 (i) consists of 29 books and items 180 (ii) to 182 also of 29. The figures for the excerpting of Papinian's *Quaestiones* from book 20 onwards are as follows:

Books 20–9: 227, 44, 37, 107, 6, 15, 273, 237, 162

Books 30–7: 14, 23, 25, 8, 2, 22, 70, 38

The first 29 books of Papinian's *Quaestiones* average 90 lines per book, and within this figure books 20 to 29 a little more, 110 lines per book. But the last eight books, 30 to 37, average only 20 lines per book. The collapse begins at book 30. Yet the statutory section of this work begins at book 29 (*ad legem duodecim tabularum, ad legem Falcidiam, ad legem Cinciam, ad legem Corneliam de captivis*). On Osler's theory the collapse should begin there, yet book 29 yields 162 lines.[191] The explanation is perhaps to be like that for Julian's *Digesta*. Papinian's works formed a group of 58 books divided into two equal lots. As with Julian, it was convenient to make the division somewhere near the transition from edictal to statutory topics, so that there was something like a change of subject-matter as well as a numerical division of the books to be read. But subject-matter was subordinated to the division into an equal number of books. There was also, if the membership of the committees has been correctly identified, a changeover from an official, Constantinus,

[188] On Papinian's *Quaestiones* and *Responsa* (to which one could add *Definitiones*) being edited and hence perhaps excerpted as a separate group within the Papinian mass see Kaiser (n. 5) 322.

[189] *Commissioners* 262; *Tribonian* 161; Osler (1985) 172–4.

[190] Mantovani 98.

[191] 'Wahrscheinlich richtig.' The caution is unfounded, since there are 12 sequences in which Papinian's *Definitiones* are sandwiched between his *Responsa* or *Quaestiones* and the *Quaestiones* of Paul, Scaevola or Callistratus, which follow immediately in the BK Ordo: D. 12.6.58–60; 23.2.62–64; 23.4.26–28; 26.7.41–43; 26.9.5–7; 27.3.20–22; 28.6.41–3; 31.79–81; 35.1.78–80; 46.2.27–29; 46.3.96–98; 50.17.82–84.

to a professor, Anatolius or Cratinus, who was less likely to attach weight to the statutory material.

These examples tend to show that, for works excerpted separately, Tribonian's[192] scheme involved the division of books into lots consisting of an equal or nearly equal number of books. As Furlong puts it 'that the collapse [in these instances] should have occurred by chance alone and yet somehow have managed to make up lots containing an equal number of books seems improbable'.[193] He concludes after a statistical analysis of the phenomenon of collapse that in the three examples highlighted here (Julian's *Digesta*, Papinian's *Responsa* and—to be discussed shortly—Scaevola's *Digesta*), in comparison with the other seven works in which collapse is observed,[194] the extent of the collapse in the three is due roughly half to the transition from edictal to statutory material and half to the numerical division that we claim to detect.[195]

In the other seven works the collapse coincides exactly or very closely with the transition from edictal to statutory material. In Celsus' *Digesta* the statutory part begins at book 28 (*ad legem duodecim tabularum*) and there is a collapse from 32.8 to 14.2 lines per book. In Marcellus' *Digesta* it starts from book 22, which has a text *ad legem Falcidiam* or, preferably, the latter part of book 21 (*ad legem Aquiliam*),[196] and there is a collapse from 43.2 to 20.9 lines per book. In Modestinus' *Responsa* the transition to statutes and the accompanying collapse from 60.2 to 9.3 lines per book occur on Lenel's view from book 14.[197] Book 15 has a text *ad legem Cinciam* and book 16 one *ad legem Falcidiam*. In Paul's *Quaestiones* the statutes start at book 17 (*ad legem duodecim tabularum*) with an accompanying collapse from 125.0 to 26.6 lines per book). In Paul's *Responsa* the transition begins at book 19 (*ad legem Iuliam et Papiam*)[198] and the collapse is from 74.2 to 7.8 lines per book.[199]

In Scaevola's *Quaestiones*[200] it may begin at book 14, from which no fragment survives; in any case book 15 has a text *ad legem Falcidiam*[201]

[192] It could be argued that the commissioners in each committee chose to adopt the system of equal division. But it appears to be common to all three committees, so that it is more probably to be attributed to Tribonian's *gubernatio*.

[193] Furlong (n. 5) 15.

[194] Below nn. 209–18.

[195] Furlong (n. 5) 16–17.

[196] Lenel, *Palinenesia* vol. 1. p. 627 n. 2.

[197] Lenel, *Palingenesia* vol. 1 p. 198 n. 1.

[198] Not book 16 as stated by Osler (n. 5) 176.

[199] Not from 83.8 to 14.8 lines per book, as he supposes.

[200] Collapse from 36.8 to 7.4.

[201] D. 35.2.23.

and one *ad legem Corneliam de captivis.*[202] Taking book 14 as the start of the statutory material the collapse is from 36.8 to 7.4 lines. For these six instances Osler gives detailed figures book by book.[203] In Papinian's *Responsa*, which he does not list, the statutory part begins in the middle of book 12 (*ad legem XII tabularum*[204] and *ad legem Cinciam*)[205] and the collapse is from 236.6 to 55.9 lines per book. In these seven works the earlier and later parts of the statutory material are treated on a level. Why, then, contrary to the general picture, do the two not coincide in the case of Julian's *Digesta* and Papinian's *Quaestiones*? Is the explanation that there was a numerical division of books to be read by the two senior commissioners, who differed as to the relative importance of the statutory material?

If the system of numerical division was adopted in these two cases there is reason to suppose that it was adopted throughout, though we cannot know exactly how the groups and lots were constituted. In our 1970 article we put forward one possible division.[206] There are, however, in many parts of the BK Ordo a number of different ways of grouping books and ensuring an equal division of lots within them. Why is the division specially visible in Julian's *Digesta* and Papinian's *Quaestiones*? The clue may lie in the length of these works, 90 and 37 books respectively, along with their difficulty and legal importance. Julian's *Digesta* was far the longest work to be excerpted separately, and he[207] and Papinian[208] were regarded as the leading classical lawyers. These works were so copious and demanding that to allot them to a single commissioner would be to overburden him. The same is not true of the other seven works in which less is excerpted from the statutory than the edictal material.[209] All are shorter and none equally prestigious. Several were excerpted jointly and divided into sections, where the problem did not arise, since alternate sections were, we argued, excerpted by different commissioners. This is true of Paul's and Scaevola's *Quaestiones*, running to 26 and

202 D. 28.6.29.

203 Osler (1985) 175–6. Furlong's figures (n. 5) at 16, 25–6 include Papinian's *Responsa* with a breakdown for each book but are slightly different because not in every case based on all the books preceding the collapse.

204 D. 38.16.16.

205 D. 3.5.29.

206 *Commissioners* 285–314.

207 *Index auctorum* I; C. Tanta 18: *ipse Iulianus legum et edicti perpetui suptilissimus conditor:* Tribonian is making a point on scholarly grounds of revising the ranking in the Valentinian Law of Citations.

208 *Index auctorum* II; C. Omnem 4: *acutissimi Papiniani... ipse pulcherrimus Papinianus... maximi Papiniani... viri sublimmisimi praefectorii Papiniani...*

209 Below nn. 210–18.

20 books respectively,[210] and of Celsus' and Marcellus' *Digesta* in 39 and 31 books respectively.[211] Papinian's[212] and Modestinus'[213] *Responsa*, both in 19 books, were excerpted separately—a heavy but not overwhelming task for a single commissioner. Paul's *Responsa*, in 23 books, was also, it seems, excerpted separately but broken into four lots, interspersed with the *Responsa* of Scaevola, so that the lots would be excerpted by alternate commissioners,[214] neither of whom was overburdened.

Two other works, which in view of their length might have been divided between two commissioners, were excerpted separately. One of them is Scaevola's *Digesta*, generally regarded as part of the Appendix,[215] though on Osler's view the first two books were excerpted as part of the main Papinian mass. At whatever juncture this work came into the hands of the commissioners, in principle it was correctly assigned to that mass, to which the *Quaestiones* and *Responsa* of Scaevola already belonged. But it was probably not so assigned from the outset, since in that case one would have expected it to be excerpted earlier in the Papinian mass, along with the more bulky works. In any event it features first a notable increase and then a spectacular collapse in the rate of excerpting. It was in our view divided between commissioners in two places, between books 13 and 14 and between books 29 and 30.[216] The reason for not discussing it along with Julian's *Digesta* and Papinian's *Quaestiones* is that the second point of division may coincide—the evidence is not clear—with the beginning of the statutory material. If it does, this work does not serve to decide between Osler's theory and mine. If, however, the idea of dividing works excerpted separately into groups and lots is accepted as a guiding principle, it offers an instructive example of how this was done.

According to our article group XLII consisted of Scaevola's *Digesta* and Labeo's *Pithana* epitomized by Paul.[217] The group comprised 48 books in all:

267 (i). Scaevola digestorum 1–13	13 books
267 (ii). Scaevola digestorum 14–29	16 books
267 (iii). Scaevola digestorum 30–40	11 books
268. Labeo pithanon a Paulo epitomatorum 1–8:	8 books

210 BK Ordo 183–4.
211 BK Ordo 134–5.
212 BK Ordo 181.
213 BK Ordo 146.
214 BK Ordo 186–93. This may have been a case of joint excerpting.
215 On Osler's view divided between the Papinian mass and the Appendix.
216 *Commissioners* 312–13.
217 *Commissioners* 265, 312–13; *Tribonian* 163–4.

The position of these two works in the BK Ordo is treated by Hugo Krüger as probably correct and is not doubted by Mantovani. Items 267 (i) and 267 (iii) come to 24 books, as do items 267 (ii) and 268. We argued that they were read and excerpted by commissioners E and F respectively.[218] The reason for considering Scaevola's work and Labeo's to form a group is the two abrupt changes in the rate of excerpting that take place within Scaevola's *Digesta.* These would be unlikely if the same commissioner excerpted the whole 40 books. The figures are striking:

267 (i). Scaevola books 1–13: 69, 49, 10, 48, 142, 43, 118, 9, 32, 30, 51, 0, 6.

267 (ii). Scaevola books 14–29: 74, 176, 260, 260, 197, 260, 118, 227, 276, 359, 59, 111, 70, 47, 86, 121, 58.

267 (iii). Scaevola books 30–40: 4(?), 26, 11, 33, 9, 0, 0, 0, 0, 0, 0.

268. Labeo books 1–8: 101, 48, 7, 35, 20, 64, 15, 9.

Books 1–13 average 46 lines per book, the last six of these books only 21 lines per book. The next 16 books however average 156 lines, over three and a half times as much as the first 13. There is then a dramatic collapse in the last 11 books of Scaevola, where the average is only seven lines—less than a twentieth of the preceding 16. If the first break was determined by considerations of substance, it should come at book 13 (*de testamentis*), which begins a long series of books on wills and succession. In fact it comes at book 14 (*de legatis et fideicommissis*). From book 13 only six lines are excerpted. The change occurs about but not exactly at the point of the change of subject-matter. As regards the second change, it is unclear what book 30 is about. The four lines attributed to it seem to have been misplaced.[219] But certainly book 31 is on statutory material (*ad legem Cinciam*). So the collapse occurs at or close to the beginning of the statutory material and is to that extent consistent with Osler's thesis that the reason for the collapse was that the statutory material began at that point. But that the same commissioner excerpted the whole of Scaevola's *Digesta* is unlikely given the two striking changes in the rate of excerpting noted above. The figures suggest that two commissioners were responsible for this group of works and that the first had less time to devote to it than the second.

It is not surprising that the reading and excerpting of the Appendix works should have been somewhat rushed. The pressure on time could

[218] Since we do not know by whom the Appendix works were read, this cannot any longer be assumed.

[219] Lenel *Palinenesia* 2, 270 n. 1.

have been connected with the aftermath of the Nika riots or with the process of editing the Digest.[220]

The other long work that might well have been subdivided is Pomponius' 39 books *ad Quintum Mucium*.[221] Why was it not divided between two commissioners, like Julian's *Digesta*, Papinian's *Quaestiones* and (in my view) Scaevola's *Digesta*? Perhaps because, though long, it was not thought to be of great importance. Only 1,001 lines were excerpted from it, an average of 25 lines per book, which is below the average excerpting rate for the other very long works: Julian's *Digesta* (53 per book), Papinian's *Quaestiones* (90 per book) and Scaevola's *Digesta* (80 per book), despite the 'collapse' that occurs in those three. But it may be noted that Mantovani regards two of the works following Pomponius' *ad Quintum Mucium* (Callistratus 4 *de iure fisci*[222] and Paul 2 *de censibus*[223]) as of uncertain mass. If these two works really belong elsewhere, then Pomponius' long treatise of 39 books is followed by 40 books of lesser works, consisting of Pomponius 15 *variarum lectionum*, Proculus 11 *epistularum*, Callistratus 6 *cognitionum*, and Tertullianus 8 *quaestionum*.[224] These fill the space between works by Iavolenus[225] and a group of treatises *ad legem Iuliam et Papiam* and the arrangement would then conform to the pattern of the other long works.

In the upshot three really long works excerpted separately, Julian's *Digesta*, Papinian's *Responsa* and Scaevola's *Digesta*, give signs of a division between two commissioners reading an equal or nearly equal number of books. In each case the sequence begins with the long work. This is possibly also true of the fourth, Pomponius *ad Quintum Mucium*. And if this is true of these works the same is likely also to be true of shorter works whose position in the BK Ordo is doubtful or from which fewer fragments survive. In particular Mantovani's suggestion[226] that at certain points, for example in excerpting material on criminal law, the commissioners charged with the task chose the books with which to supplement the main sources, is not acceptable if it means that Tribonian did not specify which works were to be read by which committee and did not insist that the reading and excerpting of works read separately be divided equally or nearly equally between the senior commissioners.

[220] Honoré (1972) 30-I.

[221] BK Ordo 154. The explanation that follows differs from that suggested in *Commissioners* 302–3 and *Tribonian* 159.

[222] BK Ordo 158.

[223] BK Ordo 159.

[224] BK Ordo 155, 156, 157, 160, 161.

[225] BK Ordo 152, 153.

[226] Mantovani 149f.

The example Mantovani gives is, however, consistent with these principles. It concerns the excerpting by the Sabinian committee of penal works. The author suggests that that committee's reading of a group of these works influenced the order of exposition in books 47 and 48 of the Digest (the *libri terribiles*). Departing from the order in Justinian's Codex the Digest editors adopted an original arrangement. Civil delicts were followed by extraordinary crimes and then by public offences.[227] If this is correct, it confirms the hypothesis that Tribonian was an active member of the Sabinian committee. For he alone could have introduced the revised order in the editing of the 'penal mass', which is rooted in works read by the Sabinian committee, in particular Ulpian *De officio proconsulis*. Around this work and Marcianus' *Institutiones* book 14 this 'mass within a mass' was grouped,[228] and influenced the innovative arrangement of the titles.[229]

It may be of interest to mention another sequence in the BK Ordo where a concentration of subject-matter corresponds with a possible division into groups and lots that points to numerical ordering. A sequence in the edictal mass (group XX in our article) comes between a section of edictal commentary and the *Digesta* of Celsus and Marcellus, both of which were excerpted jointly. These intermediate works form a group of which the main organizing principle is to bring together commentaries on Plautius. It runs as follows:

124.	Paulus ad Plautium books 1–14		
125.	Iavolenus ad Plautium book 1		
126.	Pomponius ad Plautium book 1		18 books
127.	Iavolenus ad Plautium book 2		
128.	Pomponius ad Plautium books 2–3 (?2)		
129.	Paulus ad Plautium books 15–18	)	
130.	Iavolenus ad Plautium books 3–5	)	
131.	Pomponius ad Plautium books 4(?3)–7	)	18 books
132.	Paulus ad Vitellium 4 books	)	
133.	Paulus de iure fisci 2 books	)	

I do not defend our analysis of this sequence in the 1970 article.[230] The position of these works in the BK Ordo is, however, in no real doubt. Item 132 is accepted by Hugo Krüger and not doubted by Mantovani, while item 133 is also accepted by Hugo Krüger and placed by Mantovani between 95 and 135. Since the items from 95 to 123 all

[227] Mantovani 175.
[228] Mantovani 157–61.
[229] Mantovani 157–8, 161–75.
[230] *Commissioners* 300; *Tribonian* 157–8.

consist of edictal commentary, while the *Digesta* of Celsus in 39 books occupies 134, Paul *De iure fisci* should be somewhere in group XX in the BK Ordo, though only one fragment survives.[231] We have therefore a group of 36 books. The question arises why, after all 30 books of commentary on Plautius had been included in items 124 to 131, another six books of Paul on other topics were added at 132–133. A possible answer is that the earlier parts of the commentary on Plautius were read at items 124 to 128 by one commissioner, the later parts at items 129 to 131 by another. But that left a disparity between the number of books allotted to each, which was made up by the six extra books of Paul. This suggestion depends on assuming that the Bluhme/Krüger Ordo errs in allotting Pomponius' third book *Ad Plautium* to item 128 rather than 13l. A passage from book 17 of Paul *Ad Plautium*[232] immediately follows a text in Pomponius book 3 *Ad Plautium*,[233] both apparently dealing with *mora*.[234] So it seems right to make this slight correction to the BK Ordo. What reason, other than a numerical one, could there have been for the additional six books, unrelated in point of substance to the commentaries *Ad Plautium*?

It seems that it is a feature of the principal works excerpted separately that, though groups consist largely of works related to one another in substance or authorship, we also find numerical patterns that point to the sub-division of the work of excerpting into equal or nearly equal lots. The sequences tend to begin with a long or medium-sized work, which is balanced by another or other works that are jointly of similar length, or is divided in such a way as to permit such a balance. Though many details escape us, these examples point to a method of organization adopted by Tribonian that consisted in insisting on the division of works excerpted separately into equal or nearly equal lots to be read by different commissioners.

VIII. Works Excerpted Jointly[235]

According to the Bluhme/Krüger Ordo all three committees excerpted some works jointly. This was often the case when two or more authors had written about the same subject-matter, notably in the Sabinian

231 D. 34.9.5. 232 D. 45.1.91.4–5 (Paul 17 Plaut.).
233 D. 45.1.90 (Pomp. 3 Plaut.). 234 Lenel *Palinenesia* 2, 80 n. 3.
235 *Commissioners* 248–50; Osler (1985) 136–53; Furlong (n. 5) 11–13.

and edictal commentaries. The Sabinian committee did this in five groups (I, II, VI, VII and XIV), the edictal committee in four (XVIII, XIX, XXI and XXVI) and the Papinian committee in two (XXXII and XXXIV). Bluhme divided the jointly excerpted works into sections of text from both or all the authors. The sections were, he considered, inserted into the Digest titles successively. For example a long mass of commentary *ad Sabinum* by Ulpian, Pomponius and Paul was in this way divided into nine successive sections of text—(i), (ii), (iii) etc.—each comprising a section of commentary on Sabinus by all three authors. When edited the Digest texts from section (ii) came after those from section (i), texts from section (iii) after those from section (ii), and so on. We argued that the two senior commissioners in each committee were in charge of excerpting alternative sections of text. One would excerpt the odd-numbered sections, the other the even-numbered sections. In this way the text could be read and excerpted more quickly and the work of the commission speeded up. There is some evidence that this system of alternating sections was adopted. In the section of edictal commentary excerpted by the Sabinian committee (group II in our article) Gaius *ad ed. prov.* and Paul *brevia* both appear in three sections. Gaius comes before Paul in the odd-numbered sections (i) and (iii) but after Paul in the even-numbered section (iv).[236] This is consistent with different commissioners being responsible for excerpting the odd- and even-numbered sections.

But if Bluhme identified the sections correctly, the two commissioners when excerpting jointly did not read and excerpt an equal number of books. Considerations of speed prevailed. 'It made absolutely no difference which of the two committee members excerpted which book or how may books, provided that the committee maintained its overall reading timetable.'[237] The commissioner excerpting the odd-numbered sections (i, iii, v etc.) generally excerpted more. This was true in all the groups in the Sabinian and edictal committees except group IV, where each commissioner read four books. In the Sabinian committee A was responsible for 147 of the books excerpted jointly, B for only 78.[238] In the edictal committee C covered 163 3/4 books, D 124 1/4.[239] In the Papinian committee on the other hand in one jointly excerpted

[236] *Commissioners* 253, 286–7. [237] Furlong (n. 5) 12.

[238] Group I: A 68 1/2, B 33 1/2; group II: A 36 1/2, B 28 1/2; group VI: A 30, B 9; group VII: A 8, B 3; group XIV: A 4, B 4.

[239] Group XVIII: C 38 2/3, D. 25 1/12; group XIX: C 50 1/12; D. 34 1/6; group XXI C 36; D. 34; group XXVI C 39, D. 31.

group (XXXII) E excerpted 21 books and F 25, though E excerpted more lines than F, while in the other (XXXIV) they either did an equal number or E did one more book than F.[240]

We assumed that in case of joint excerpting only the length of the first section was fixed initially and assigned to one commissioner. His colleague started from the point beyond this section. When the first commissioner had finished his allotted section he proceeded to a point beyond that reached by his colleague, and so on by a system of leap-frogging until the end. The two commissioners did not therefore necessarily handle the same number of books or the same number of sections.[241] As one would expect, the commissioner who did the first section generally excerpted more books. This, as Osler pointed out,[242] was not compatible with commissioners engaged in excerpting works jointly observing a rigid timetable. But, as Furlong stresses, Osler fails to explain the statistically improbable event that in groups excerpted jointly the odd-numbered sections in seven groups out of eight in the Sabinian and edictal committees contain more books than the even-numbered sections.[243] Moreover the method suggested is compatible with the existence of a flexible timetable for the committee as a whole, a timetable that would account for the leapfrogging method we suggested. Respecting the timetable would depend on the availability of advocates who, we argued, were essential in cases of joint excerpting when two or more manuscripts had to be read in parallel. Presumably they had to adapt their practice before the praetorian prefect, so far as possible, in order to enable them to fulfil their duties to Justinian's commission.

Osler also made the point that there was considerable variation in the excerpting rates for the odd- and even-numbered sections. In the Sabinian mass B excerpts at a higher rate than A in groups I, II and VI, though in all three groups A excerpts more lines overall. A however excerpts at a higher rate than B in group XIV. In the edictal mass D excerpts at a higher rate in groups XVIII, XIX, XXI and XXVI but again C excerpts more lines overall in groups XVIII and XIX though not in the other two. In the Papinian mass E excerpts at a higher rate than F in group XXXII but F at a higher rate in group XXXIV. In both these groups E excerpts more lines overall. These figures are consistent with the leap-frogging method that we proposed, though they do not prove

240 *Commissioners* 308–9.
241 *Commissioners* 249. The number of sections was odd in groups I and XXI.
242 Osler 139.
243 Furlong (n. 5) 12.

that it was adopted. To Osler this variation in the rate of excerpting was not compatible with the hypothesis of a single commissioner being responsible for the odd- and even-numbered sections respectively. But once we substitute a flexible committee timetable for one addressed to each individual commissioner, this objection falls away so far as works excerpted jointly are concerned.

What about the comparative rate of excerpting per book? To take the figures for all the groups whether excerpted separately or jointly, in the Sabinian mass A excerpts more lines than B in 10 groups out of 17 and averages more per book in 7 out of 17. In the edictal mass C excerpts more lines than D in 9 groups out of 13 but averages more per book in 7 out of 17. In the Papinian mass E excerpts more lines than F in 7 groups out of 10 and also averages more per book in 7 groups. If the commissioners were held to a settled overall rate of excerpting, but not to a fixed rate for each group, the variation in the rate of excerpting in both the groups read jointly and those read separately becomes explicable, and is indeed what one would expect.[244]

In sum, there are serious arguments both for the view that the Digest commissioners worked to a timetable and that the work was speeded up, within the committee structure, by delegating the task of reading and excerpting to individual senior commissioners. Moreover these arguments cohere with other elements of the theory, such as the identification of the senior members of the three committees and the distribution of authors and works to the three committees. Though hypothetical, the theory here reformulated can claim to be the most plausible.

[244] Furlong (n. 5) 12–13.

3

The Distribution of Authors and Works to the Committees

I. Introduction

This chapter addresses a set of related problems about the compilation of Justinian's Digest. Suppose that, as scholars have long believed, Bluhme was right in detecting the existence of three separate masses of works to be read and excerpted by the Digest commissioners and of three separate committees (the Sabinian, the Papinian and the edictal) to read them.[1] How, then, was it decided which works to allot to each mass, and which works should be read together?[2] The allocation was crucial, because Tribonian could not personally supervise the selection of texts made by the committees, at any rate those on which he did not himself serve. How did he ensure that the best texts would be chosen?

Much inevitably turns on the reconstruction by Bluhme and Krüger of the order in which the works were read by the committees (the BK Ordo).[3] Their list allots works to masses on the basis of the sequences of inscriptions found in the Digest titles and seeks to fix the order in which they were read and excerpted within each mass. Krüger numbered the works in the presumed order in which they were read, listing first the Sabinian mass, then the edictal and Papinian masses. Despite some mistakes and uncertainties his numbering is for convenience retained in this chapter. The mistakes and uncertainties should not be exaggerated. The

[1] F. Bluhme, 'Die Ordnung der Fragmenten in den Pandektentiteln' *ZGR* 4 (1820) 257–420 = *Labeo* 6 (1960) 50–96, 235–77, 368–404.

[2] T. Honoré, 'How Tribonian Organised the Compilation of Justinian's Digest' in *SZ* 121 (2004) at 18–25 touches on this topic. See above chapter 2 nn. 98–142.

[3] 'Ordo librorum iuris veteris' in *Corpus Iuris Civilis* 16th stereotype ed. 1 (T. Mommsen & P. Krüger (eds), *Iustiniani Digesta* (Berlin 1954) 927–31. A revised and updated version of the Bluhme-Krüger Ordo is printed in Addendum A below.

reworking of the BK Ordo by Mantovani[4] shows that, on the evidence available from the inscriptions, at most 48 of the 1,522 books read by the Digest commissioners, 3 per cent of the total, were put by Bluhme and Krüger in a particular mass although the mass to which they were really assigned cannot be determined.[5]

The true figure is in my view lower, since about half the books that Mantovani lists as indeterminate were either placed by Bluhme in the correct mass,[6] or their correct mass can be fixed on the basis, set out in this article, of the way in which authors were allotted to masses.[7] It is true that greater uncertainty attaches to the order in which works were read within each mass, a matter that is touched on only marginally in this chapter.

The BK Ordo allocation of works to masses is broadly reliable. For ease of reference an updated version of it is printed in Addendum A. But the principles governing the allocation have hardly been studied. Clearly the task of allotting authors and works to masses fell to Tribonian as part of his *rei omnis gubernatio*.[8] This chapter deals with how authors and

[4] D. Mantovani, *Digesto e masse Bluhmiane* (1987) 90–103.

[5] All the works that Mantovani marks in his Retractatio (above n. 4, pp.90–103) with ID ('impossibile determinazione'), less the non-existent Proculus 3 *ex posterioribus Labeonis* (BK Ordo 266) and Valens 7 *actionum* (BK Ordo 272). The remaining ID works are: Paulus 6 *imperialium sententiarum*, 2 *de censibus*, 1 *de iure patronatus*, 1 *ad SC Silanianum*, 1 *de senatusconsultis*, 1 *ad SC Velleianum*, 1 *de intercessionibus feminarum*, 1 *ad orationem divi Severi*, 1 *ad legem Cinciam*, 1 *de poenis omnium legum*, 1 *ad regulam Catonianam*, 1 *de inofficioso testamento*, 1 *de tacitis fideicommissis*, 1 *de instrumenti significatione*, 1 *de gradibus et adfinibus*, 1 *de officio praefecti urbi*; Venuleius 6 *de interdictis*; Callistratus 4 *de iure fisci*; Ulpian 1 *de officio praefecti vigilum*; 1 *de officio praefecti urbi*; 1 *de officio quaestoris*; Arcadius Charisius 1 *de muneribus civilibus*; 1 *de officio praefecti praetorio*; Modestinus 1 *de differentia dotis*, 1 *de inofficioso testamento*; Gaius 1 *ad legem Glitiam*, 1 *regularum*; Aquila 1 *responsorum*; Anthianus 1 *ad edictum*; Gallus 1 *de verborum significatione*; Maecianus 1 *ex lege Rhodia*; Marcianus 1 *ad SC Turpillianum*; Papinianus 1 *αστυνομικος*; Quintus Mucius 1 ορων.

[6] All 14 books listed in the Appendix but doubted by Mantovani (Paul 6—in reality 2—*imperialium sententiarum*, Quintus Mucius 1 *ορων*, Venuleius 6 *de interdictis*, Anthianus 1 *ad edictum*) on which see Chapter 5 nn. 20–55. Two *libri singulares* of Modestinus (BK Ordo 141, 151) can safely be located in the edictal mass, since the other works of Modestinus nearly all belong to this mass: below notes 170–84. Seven *libri singulares* of Paul (*de iure patronatus*, *ad SC Silanianum*, *ad SC Velleianum*, *de intercessionibus feminarum*, *ad orationem divi Severi* in the Sabinian mass; *de tacitis fideicommissis* and *de instrumenti significatione* in the Papinian) are in my view located in the correct mass in the BK Ordo (see below nn. 268–87). This would account for 23 of the 48 books doubted.

[7] A *liber singularis* of Gaius (*ad legem Glitiam*?) should go in the Papinian mass and his *liber singularis regularum* should remain there; one of Papinian (*αστυνομικος*) goes in the Papinian mass or the Appendix: see below nn. 119–24, 138–61. This covers another three doubtful cases.

[8] C. Deo auctore 3.

works were allotted to the three masses before the reading and excerpting began. It does not, except incidentally, discuss either the sections of edictal commentary that were later transferred from the Sabinian to the edictal committee[9] or the allocation of works that, according to a long-standing opinion that I share, arrived after the three committees had begun to read the list of works assigned to them. These late arrivals form the subject of a separate chapter on the Appendix and its sources.[10] In a major project such as the Digest there were inevitably some changes of plan as the work progressed.

II. The Principles of Allocation

A number of factors guided the way in which authors and works were allotted to the three masses and were grouped together within each mass. I first set out the principles that seem to have guided the allocation and then examine the evidence for how they were applied to different authors and masses:

(i) Each author was allocated to a mass. Thus, Julian went to the Sabinian mass, Modestinus to the edictal mass and Papinian to the Papinian mass. The only exception is Paul who, in view of the number of his works, especially *libri singulares*, was allocated half to the Sabinian and half to the Papinian mass.[11] The mass to which an author is allocated I shall call his 'basic mass'. When an author's works are read in succession, like the works of Modestinus in the edictal mass, they make up what I shall call an 'author-group'.[12]

(ii) The author's basic mass received all his works with three exceptions:

(a) A work of his was transferred to another mass when this was necessary to make up a group of works dealing with the same subject-matter. Thus, although Papinian's basic mass is the Papinian mass, his *libri 2 de adulteriis* and *liber singularis de adulteriis* are put in the Sabinian mass, along with works of Ulpian and Paul *de adulteriis*, to

[9] BK Ordo 108–123; Bluhme (n. 1), 283–87 = *Labeo* 6 (1960) 61–63; F. Wieacker, *Vom Römischen Recht* (2nd edn, Stuttgart 1961) 280–1; A. M. (T.) Honoré and A. Rodger, 'How the Digest Commissioners worked' *ZSS rom. abt.* 87 (1970) 276–9.

[10] Chapter 5 below. [11] Below nn. 249–98.

[12] Within this author-group (BK Ordo 137–151) a *liber singularis* of Modestinus (BK Ordo 142) together with two of Ulpian (BK Ordo 143–144) make up a subject-group of works on excuses from tutelage. On subject-groups see below, ii (a).

complete a group dealing with adultery.[13] Such a group I call a 'subject-group'. Works in subject-groups are read jointly or in succession in order to make it easier to choose the best texts on the subject.[14] Ancient authors copied one another a good deal, so that it saved time to read treatises on the same subject together. A reader had, however, to be alert to the possibility that the later author might add to, modify or disagree with the earlier. With few exceptions, works relating to the same subject were read together in a group. Some 40 per cent of the books read by the Digest commission were read in subject-groups.

(b) A work of the author in a given genre could be transferred from his basic mass to another mass to compose a group of works in the same genre. I shall term such a group a 'genre-group'. Thus, the group of 41 books of *regulae* in the Sabinian mass[15] include Pomponius' *liber singularis regularum*[16] and Scaevola's *libri 4 regularum*[17] although Pomponius' basic mass is the edictal[18] and Scaevola's the Papinian.[19] But, in contrast with subject-groups, transfer to a genre-group was optional. For example, though six or seven authors of *regulae* come in the *regulae* group in the Sabinian mass (Neratius, Ulpian, Scaevola, Paul, Marcianus, Pomponius and perhaps Gaius), two do not. Modestinus' 10 books of *regulae*[20] remain with his other works in the edictal mass and Licinius Rufinus' 12 or 13 books[21] are also in the edictal mass. Transfer on the basis of genre is optional because works in the same genre, unlike works on the same subject, do not necessarily deal with the same points of law. *Regulae*, for example, might be on almost any topic. But it was often convenient to read works of the same genre together or in close succession, since a later author might copy, develop or dissent from an earlier writer in that genre.

[13] BK Ordo 28–31.

[14] C. Deo auctore 5: *omnibus auctoribus iuris aequa dignitate pollentibus et nemini quadam praerogativa servanda, quia non omnes in omnia, sed certi per certa vel meliores vel deteriores inveniuntur:* confirmed by C. Tanta 1: *plus quam trecenties decem milia versuum a veteribus effusa quae necesse esset omnia et legere et perscrutari et ex his si quid optimum fuisset eligere.*

[15] BK Ordo 36–40, 42–46 and possibly 224. Two unrelated books of Ulpian's *responsa* are inserted in this group at BK Ordo 41. This is done in my view for numerical reasons, explained in (c) below, so that the total number of books in the group would be 44, which is conveniently divisible into two sub-groups of 22 books each, the first being constituted by Neratius 15 reg. and Ulpian 7 reg. (BK Ordo 36–37). See below nn. 227–230.

[16] BK Ordo 45. [17] BK Ordo 38. [18] Below nn. 202–14.

[19] Below nn. 125–31. [20] BK Ordo 139. [21] BK Ordo 175.

(c) Although the matter is controversial, there is in my view a third ground on which a work was sometimes transferred from an author's basic mass to another mass. This could be done to make a group numerically balanced. Thus, though the edictal mass is not Paul's basic mass, two of his works (libri 4 *ad Vitellium*, 2 *de iure fisci*)[22] are appended, I argue, to the subject-group *ad Plautium*[23] in the edictal mass in order to create a group conveniently divisible into two sub-groups, each with an equal number of books.[24] These transfers are however on a small scale and are relatively rare. Apart from the six books of Paul just mentioned there appear to be two other cases of transfer for numerical reasons, that of Ulpian's three books *de officio consulis*[25] and Marcellus' *liber singularis responsorum*.[26]

(iii) Of the works that are not transferred to another mass some form part of a subject- or genre-group, but others do not. Those that do not I shall call 'unattached'. Many *libri singulares* are unattached, because they are on specialized topics and so do not need to be read with other works. The composition of *libri singulares* did not count as a special genre of legal writing. Unattached works are important in fixing the author's basic mass because, if they do not form part of a subject- or genre-group, there was, apart from the occasional transfer on numerical grounds under (c) above, no reason to transfer them from the author's basic mass. This is important, for example, for Gaius, most of whose works form part of subject- or genre-groups in the Sabinian and edictal masses but whose unattached works are concentrated in the Papinian mass, which is therefore his basic mass.[27]

(iv) There can be composite groups. Thus the Julian group in the Sabinian mass[28] is mainly an author-group but partly also a subject- and genre-group.[29] Various combinations of the three basic elements are possible.

The system described is sophisticated and may at first be difficult to grasp. This is unsurprising. Tribonian admired sophistication, *subtilitas*.[30]

22 BK Ordo 132, 133.
23 BK Ordo 124–31.
24 Honoré (2004, above n. 2) 39–40.
25 Below nn. 180–4.
26 Below nn. 227–30.
27 Below nn. 138–61.
28 BK Ordo 14–20.
29 Below nn. 53–7.
30 C. Deo auctore (*nam qui non suptiliter factum emendat laudabilior est eo qui primum invenit*), 14 (*tuaprudentia una cum aliis facundissimis viris studeat.....tam suptili quam celerrimo fini tradere*); C. Tanta 18 (*ipse Iulianus legum et edicti perpetui suptlissimus conditor*). In section 6 (*nam qui non suptiliter factum emendat laudabilior est eo qui primum invenit*) the text does not make sense as it stands and should perhaps read *non insuptiliter*.

In the allocation of authors to masses prestige was important. The so-called Valentinian Law of Citations gave priority to the works of Papinian, Paul, Gaius, Ulpian, and Modestinus.[31] Tribonian modifies this, as we see from the so-called Florentine *Index Auctorum*, which records the books read by the Digest commission.[32] Composed by someone close to the commission in a mixture of Greek and Grecized Latin,[33] it lists Julian first,[34] Papinian second.[35] After Papinian the *Index* abandons precedence and lists the authors in presumed chronological order. Hence the third author is the Republican Quintus Mucius Scaevola, of whom the commission read just one book.[36] Julian's leading status in the age of Justinian is confirmed in C. Tanta.[37]

The ranking throws light on the relative standing of the three masses and the committees reading them. All 101 books of Julian went to the Sabinian mass.[38] Of the 62 books attributed to Papinian 58 went to the mass named after him.[39] The Sabinian mass is, it seems, the most honoured; next to it the Papinian. The edictal mass is not overlooked, for it is allotted all 69 books of Modestinus,[40] though on any view Modestinus comes below the other two. So, judging from the prestige of the authors allotted to it, the edictal mass ranks third. The allocation of Ulpian, Paul and Gaius confirms this ranking. Ulpian's basic mass, we shall see, is the Sabinian,[41] Gaius' the Papinian.[42] Paul is shared by those two masses.[43] So, of the six leading jurists (Julian plus the five listed in the Law of Citations) the Sabinian and Papinian masses have two and a half each, the edictal mass one. But the Sabinian mass trumps the Papinian not only in the volume of works read and excerpts made but by acquiring

[31] CTh. 1.4.3 (7 Nov. 426).

[32] See *Iustiniani Digesta*, in the stereotype edition (above, n. 3) 25–8. Though the *Index auctorum* is incomplete and contains mistakes it is a contemporary list.

[33] The title is Greek: ΕΞ ΟΖΩΝ ΑΡΧΑΙΩΝ ΚΑΙ ΤΩΝ ΥΡ'ΑΥΤΩΝ ΓΕΝΟΜΕΝΩΝ ΒΙΒΛΙΩΝ ΣΥΝΚΕΙΤΑΙ ΤΟ ΠΑΡΟΝ ΤΩΝ DIGESTON ΗΤΟΙ ΤΟΥ ΡΑΝΔΕΚΤΟΥ ΣΥΝΤΑΓΜΑ.

[34] *Index auctorum* I Ιουλιανου.

[35] *Index auctorum* II Papinianu.

[36] *Index auctorum* III Quintu Muciu Scaevola 1 ορων βιβλιον εν.

[37] C. Tanta 18 (quoted above, n. 30).

[38] *Digesta* 90, *de ambiguitatibus* 1, *ad Urseium Ferocem* 4, *ex Minicio* 6 (BK Ordo14, 17, 18, 19).

[39] *Quaestiones* 37, *responsa* 19, *definitiones* 2 (BK Ordo 180, 181, 182).

[40] Differentiae 9, de manumissionibus 1, regulae 10, de ritu nuptiarum 1, de differentia dotis, 1, excusationes 6, responsa 19, de enucleatis casibus, 1, de praescriptionibus 1, pandectae 12, de heurmaticis 1, de inofficioso testamento 1 (BK Ordo 137, 138, 140, 141, 142, 145, 146, 147, 148, 149, 150, 151). One may add two libri singulares listed in the *Index auctorum* of which no excerpts appear in the Digest: de legatis et fideicommissis and de testamentis. His de poenis (BK Ordo 174) was also allotted to the edictal mass.

[41] Below nn. 58–84.

[42] Below nn. 138–61.

[43] Below nn. 249–98.

Julian, the greatest jurist, rather than Papinian, the second greatest, and by acquiring Ulpian, whereas Paul is shared by the Sabinian and Papinian masses. In the context of the Digest Ulpian is preferred to Paul, since the commissioners took more than twice as much from Ulpian as from Paul.[44]

I now go through the 37 Digest authors in order to fix their basic mass.[45] There were in fact more, since the inscriptions did not distinguish, as does modern scholarship, between various Pauls,[46] Scaevolas and Ulpians,[47] some of whom may genuinely have borne those names. Thus, one suspects that the similarity of their names has fused Cervidius Scaevola, the well-known author of *Quaestiones, Responsa* and *Digesta*,[48] with another Scaevola, author of *Quaestionum publice tractatarum liber singularis.*[49]

Only in five cases is the allocation to a basic mass uncertain. Normally the basic mass is that in which the bulk of the author's work was read, but we have always to ask what works, if any, were transferred to another mass to form a subject- or genre-group or to achieve numerical balance.

III. The Authors' Basic Masses

(1) Authors whose Basic Mass is the Sabinian

As stated, the works of the most prestigious author, **Julian**, are in the Sabinian mass. They fall in a group[50] that lies between certain works of Ulpian[51] and a group belonging to the elementary genre of *institutiones* and *res cottidianae.*[52] The Julian group is mainly an author-group, composed of Julian's *digesta, de ambigitatibus, ad Urseium Ferocem* and *ex Minicio*, 101 books in all,[53] but sandwiched within it are excerpts

[44] 41 per cent against 17 per cent.

[45] Above nn. 11–12. Since the allocation of each author to a basic mass was a crucial feature of the project the name of the jurist so allocated is given in boldface.

[46] D. Liebs, *Handbuch der lateinischen Literatur der Antike*, 5 (Munich 1989) § 507.1 (Pseudo-Paulus I); 507.2 (Pseudo-Paulus II); 508.3 (Pseudo-Paulus III); 509.1 (Pseudo-Paulus IV).

[47] D. Liebs, *Handbuch der lateinischen Literatur der antike*, 4 (Munich 1997); Liebs (note 46) § 428.5 (Pseudo-Ulpianus II); 428.6 (Ulpianus II); *HLL* 5 (1989) §§ 507.3 (Ulpianus III); 507.4 (Pseudo-Ulpianus II).

[48] BK Ordo 184, 187, 189, 191, 193, 267.

[49] BK Ordo 271; Liebs (note 47) § 415.7 (Scaevola IV).

[50] BK Ordo 14–20.

[51] BK Ordo 10–12 or 13.

[52] BK Ordo 21–27.

[53] BK Ordo 14, 17, 18, 19.

from the *digesta* of Alfenus Varus,[54] an author who worked in the same genre. After Julian's last work come the *quaestiones* of Africanus,[55] a pupil of Julian whose work is mainly a comment on Julian's. Africanus' work had to be read with Julian's because of its close relation to Julian's work. But the Alfenus excerpts need not have been sandwiched between Julian's works. There the link is the genre, *digesta*. But not all *digesta* were read in the same mass, since the *digesta* of Celsus and Marcellus are read together in the edictal mass.[56] The explanation for the decision to read the *digesta* of Julian and Alfenus together is in my view partly numerical—the desire to balance a reading by one commissioner of 62 books of Julian's *digesta* with an equal stint made up of other related works.[57] This is not the place to pursue that theme, but clearly for **Julian**, **Africanus** and **Alfenus** the Sabinian is their basic mass. No works of theirs appear elsewhere.

A number of other authors belong to the Sabinian mass. Apart from Julian the most important is **Ulpian**. Most of his work, in 152 or 153 books, comes in the Sabinian mass, about 78 books in the edictal mass and six to nine books in the Papinian mass. To begin with the Papinian mass, it has his six books on *fideicommissa*,[58] which fall in a subject-group with works by Valens, Ulpian, Maecianus, Gaius, Paul and Pomponius.[59] The BK Ordo also assigns to a place near the end of the Papinian mass three *libri singulares* of Ulpian on the *officia* of the *praefectus vigilum*,[60] the *praefectus urbi*[61] and the *quaestor*.[62] According to Mantovani, however, all three are of indeterminate mass,[63] as is Paul's *liber singularis* on the urban prefect,[64] with which Ulpian's must have been grouped on the basis of subject-matter. Since Paul's monograph on the *praefectus vigilum* belongs in the Papinian mass,[65] Ulpian's *liber singularis* on the same subject should belong with it in a small subject-group. We do not know where the other two *libri singulares* belong. Hence, though the allocation of an author's unattached *libri singulares* to a mass usually points to his basic mass, these three *libri* of Ulpian do not show that the Papinian was his basic mass.

That leaves the Sabinian and edictal masses. Ulpian's 51 books *ad Sabinum* head the group of commentaries by him, Paul and Pomponius

[54] BK Ordo 15, 16. [55] BK Ordo 20. [56] BK Ordo 134–135.
[57] Honoré (2004, above n. 2) 29–31. [58] BK Ordo 195, 203.
[59] BK Ordo 194–204; Mantovani (above n. 4) 107–8. [60] BK Ordo 257.
[61] BK Ordo 258. [62] BK Ordo 262. [63] Mantovani (above n. 4) 101.
[64] BK Ordo 259. [65] BK Ordo 256.

in the Sabinian mass.[66] His 83 books *ad edictum praetoris* and *ad edictum aedilium curulium*, grouped with those of Paul and Gaius are divided, roughly in the proportion of 1 to 2, between the Sabinian and edictal masses. The edictal commentaries were too bulky to be assigned to a single committee. Ulpian's seven books of *regulae*,[67] four *de appellationibus*,[68] and four *ad legem Aeliam Sentiam*[69] fall in groups of like works in the Sabinian mass,[70] while his 20 books *ad legem Iuliam et Papiam*[71] go in the edictal mass with other commentaries on that law or laws.[72] All these fall in subject-groups and so do not settle Ulpian's basic mass, though they fall mostly in the Sabinian mass. That leaves a number of unattached works. His 10 books of *disputationes* and ten *de omnibus tribunalibus*, along with six of *opiniones* and six *de censibus* are in the Sabinian mass.[73] His *liber singularis de sponsalibus*[74] is regarded as of uncertain mass.[75] But his *libri singulares pandectarum*,[76] *de officio curatoris reipublicae*,[77] and *de officio consularium*[78] are confirmed as Sabinian.[79] These 35 unattached books point to the Sabinian as Ulpian's basic mass. So does the fact that he has about twice as many books in that mass as in the edictal mass. One work of his does not fit this scheme. His three books *de officio consulis*[80] go in the edictal mass and are not related by subject or genre to either the preceding *digesta* of Celsus and Marcellus[81] or the succeeding works by Modestinus. This exception is in my view to be explained on numerical grounds, for reasons explained in connection with the discussion of Modestinus' place in the edictal mass.[82]

There was good reason for Tribonian to assign Ulpian to the Sabinian mass. He provides more lines of text than any other author (40 or 41 per cent of the Digest) and, though not the greatest or second greatest lawyer, is treated as the leading author from the point of view of expounding the law. Indeed an Ulpian text comes first in three-fifths of the Digest titles.[83] Consistently with the decision to treat Ulpian as the lead author, the Sabinian committee excerpted at a higher rate per book than the other committees: some 90 lines per book against between 65 and 75.[84]

[66] BK Ordo 1–3. [67] BK Ordo 37. [68] BK Ordo 64.
[69] BK Ordo 71. [70] BK Ordo 36–40, 42–45, 64–67, 70–71.
[71] BK Ordo 162. [72] BK Ordo 162–167.
[73] BK Ordo 10–13; Mantovani (above n. 4) 90. [74] BK Ordo 32.
[75] Mantovani (above n. 4) 91. [76] BK Ordo 85. [77] BK Ordo 88.
[78] BK Ordo 89. [79] Mantovani (above n. 4) 93. [80] BK Ordo 136.
[81] BK Ordo 134–135. [82] Below nn. 180–4.
[83] Honoré, *Ulpian. Pioneer of Human Rights* (2nd edn, 2002) 229 (260 titles out of 432).
[84] Sabinian 90.41; Papinian 73.54; edictal 65.93: Honoré and Rodger (above n. 9) 295, 306, 314.

Three authors apart from Julian, Alfenus and Africanus have their only work in the Sabinian mass. One is **Florentinus** whose surviving work, 12 books of *institutiones*,[85] heads a group of institutional works by him, Marcianus, Ulpian, Gaius, Callistratus and Paul.[86] **Rutilius** Maximus[87] and **Claudius** Saturninus,[88] each with one *liber singularis*, are other Sabinian authors. The *Index auctorum* treats Venuleius Saturninus and Claudius Saturninus as the same,[89] though the inscriptions to their works distinguish them, since D. 48.19.16 is inscribed Claudius Saturninus *libro singulari de poenis paganorum*, whereas 48.19.15 has Venuleius Saturninus *de officio proconsulis*. The commissioners, though not the compiler of the *Index auctorum*, therefore knew that these two authors were distinct.

Other Sabinian authors have at least one book transferred to another mass. **Marcianus**' 16 books of *institutiones*,[90] two *de appellationibus*,[91] two *de publicis iudiciis*,[92] five *regularum*[93] and one *ad formulam hypothecariam*[94] all fall into genre- or subject-groups in the Sabinian mass.[95] Apart from these 26 books, his *liber singularis de delatoribus*[96] is an unattached work in that mass, which serves to confirm that it is his basic mass. One *liber singularis* is however in the Papinian mass,[97] where it forms a small subject-group with a *liber singularis* of Paul,[98] both *ad SC Turpillianum*.[99] **Neratius** also belongs to the Sabinian mass, which acquires not only his 15 books of *regulae*,[100] heading a *regulae* group,[101] but seven unattached books of *membrana*.[102] So the Sabinian mass has 22 books of his total of 25. Three books of *responsa*, however, go in the Papinian mass where, given their subject-matter, they form a small subject-group with Paul's four books *ad Neratium*,[103] based on Neratius' *responsa*.[104] **Macer** probably also belongs to the Sabinian mass, which has eight of his 10 books. They include his two books each of *publica*

[85] BK Ordo 21. [86] BK Ordo 21–27.
[87] BK Ordo 68: Mantovani (above n. 4) 92.
[88] BK Ordo 92: Mantovani (above n. 4) 93.
[89] *Index auctorum* XXI Βενουλειου 4 de poenis paganorum βιβλιον εν.
[90] BK Ordo 22. [91] BK Ordo 66. [92] BK Ordo 55.
[93] BK Ordo 40, 42, 44. [94] BK Ordo 57.
[95] BK Ordo 21–27, 36–46, 52–56, 57–58, 64–66. [96] BK Ordo 63.
[97] BK Ordo 229. [98] BK Ordo 228; Mantovani (above n. 4) 99.
[99] Mantovani (above n. 4) 99. [100] BK Ordo 36. [101] BK Ordo 36–46.
[102] BK Ordo 60. [103] BK Ordo 217–218.
[104] C. Ferrini, 'I libri di Paolo ad Neratium' [1894], in *Opere*, 2 (Milan 1929) 229–34; R. Greiner, *Opera Neratiii. Drei Textgeschichten* (Karlsruhe 1973) 139–50; T. Honoré, 'A Study of Neratius and a Reflection on Method' *TR* 43 (1975) 238–9; Liebs above (n. 47) § 423–4.

iudicia,[105] *de officio praesidis*,[106] *de appellationibus*,[107] and *de re militari*.[108] Of these *iudicia publica* and appeals are grouped with others on the same subject,[109] but those on the office of governor and military law are unattached. This points to the Sabinian as his basic mass, but his two books on the Julian inheritance tax (*ad legem vicesimam hereditatum*)[110] come in the edictal mass immediately or shortly after the group of works *ad legem Iuliam and Papiam*.[111] It is not clear why they are in the edictal mass. Hence, though likely, it is not certain that Macer's basic mass is the Sabinian. **Arcadius Charisius** perhaps also belongs to the Sabinian mass, to which his unattached monograph *de testibus* is allotted.[112] The text from *de muneribus civilibus*,[113] a single long text at the end of a title, could end the Papinian mass—but then why is this important text put at the end of the title? It could alternatively be part of the Appendix. His *de officio praefecti praetorio*, in a title with only a single text,[114] is unplaceable. Finally **Labeo** should be accounted Sabinian, since all the texts from the first book of his *posteriora* epitomized by Iavolenus and some from the second book belong to that mass.[115] The attribution of this work by the BK Ordo[116] to Iavolenus was a mistake. The unattached works of Iavolenus come in the edictal mass,[117] to which Labeo's *posteriora* would also have been allotted if it had been regarded as a work of Iavolenus. The only other work of Labeo that became available to the compilers, his *pithana* epitomized by Paul,[118] belongs to the Appendix and so does not count in assessing his basic mass.

In the outcome the Sabinian is the basic mass of 10 writers (Alfenus, Africanus, Claudius Saturninus, Florentinus, Julian, Labeo, Marcianus, Neratius, Rutilius and Ulpian) and probably of two more (Arcadius and Macer).

(2) Authors whose Basic Mass is the Papinian

The **Papinian** group[119] is a self-contained author-group of 58 books but does not include quite all Papinian's works. As mentioned, his three

[105] BK Ordo 52. [106] BK Ordo 61. [107] BK Ordo 65.
[108] BK Ordo 86. [109] BK Ordo 52–56, 64–66. [110] BK Ordo 168.
[111] BK Ordo 169; Mantovani (above n. 4) 97.
[112] BK Ordo 62; Mantovani (above n. 4) 92. [113] BK Ordo 260; D. 50.4.18.
[114] BK Ordo 261; D. 1.11.1; Mantovani (above n. 4) 101.
[115] T. Honoré, 'Labeo's *posteriora* and the Digest Commission' in A. Watson (ed.), *Daube Noster* (Edinburgh 1974) 161–81; Mantovani (above n. 4) 117 n. 48; Osler, 'Following Bluhme: a note on Dario Mantovani, "Digesto e masse Bluhmiane"' *IVRA* 39 (1988) 150–3. [116] BK Ordo 94.
[117] BK Ordo 152 and 153. [118] BK Ordo 268. [119] BK Ordo 180–182.

books on adultery are assigned to the Sabinian committee to form part of a group of works by Ulpian, Papinian and Paul on that topic.[120] There is also his one-book αστυνομικος, with only one Digest text, which forms the whole title *de vi publica et si quod in ea factum esse dicatur.*[121] BK Ordo puts this in the edictal mass after the commentaries on the edict of the aediles[122] and before the transferred group of edictal commentaries.[123] Mantovani treats it as of uncertain mass.[124] There is no good reason to put it in the edictal mass. It belongs either in the Papinian mass as his basic mass or in the Appendix.

Another author whose basic mass is the Papinian is Cervidius **Scaevola**, whose 20 books of *quaestiones* and six of *responsa* come near its beginning.[125] In both cases they are read jointly with Paul's work in the same genre,[126] Paul having been a pupil of Scaevola,[127] so that there was good reason to read these works together. Scaevola's books of *regulae*[128] go in the *regulae* group headed by Neratius in the Sabinian mass.[129] Osler has shown, convincingly, that the first two books of Scaevola's *digesta* were read as part of the Papinian mass.[130] So his 40 books of *digesta* must have been assigned to that mass. But they cannot have been assigned to it from the outset, since otherwise they would have been read with his *quaestiones* and *responsa*, with which they overlap. Indeed they would in any case have been read early in the Papinian mass, since it was the practice in this mass to read the most substantial works near the beginning. The remaining 38 books of *digesta* form part, indeed the most substantial part, of the Appendix.[131] There are three authors whose only surviving work comes in the Papinian mass. Aburnius **Valens** seven books of *fideicommissa*[132] heads the *fideicommissa* subject-group in that mass.[133] **Hermogenianus**' six books of *iuris epitomae*[134] are in a genre-group along with Paul's *sententiae*,[135] a work of similar length and of the same type and period,[136] though the compilers could hardly have known this. **Tryphoninus**' 21 books of *disputationes* also come in the Papinian mass.[137]

[120] BK Ordo 28–31.
[121] BK Ordo 111; D. 43.10.
[122] BK Ordo 108–110.
[123] BK Ordo 112–123.
[124] Mantovani (above n. 4) 94.
[125] BK Ordo 184, 187, 198, 191, 193.
[126] BK Ordo 183, 186, 188, 190, 192.
[127] D. 23.3.56.3; Liebs (above n. 47) §423.
[128] BK Ordo 38.
[129] BK Ordo 36–46.
[130] Osler (above n. 115) 154–7.
[131] BK Ordo 267; chapter 5 below nn. 96–112.
[132] BK Ordo 194, 201.
[133] BK Ordo 194–204.
[134] BK Ordo 206, 208, 210, 212, 214.
[135] BK Ordo 205, 207, 209, 211, 213.
[136] Liebs (n. 46) §507.1; *Römische Jurisprudenz in Africa mit Studien zu den pseudopaulinischen Sentenzen* (2nd edn, Berlin 2005) 41–128.
[137] BK Ordo 219, 221.

The most surprising author whose basic mass is Papinian is **Gaius.** His 42 books on the urban and provincial edicts and that of the curule aediles[138] are grouped with the corresponding works of Ulpian and Paul in the Sabinian[139] and edictal masses.[140] His 15 books *ad legem Iuliam et Papiam*[141] go in the edictal subject-group devoted to those laws.[142] The *institutiones* and *res cottidianae*[143] are part of a Sabinian genre-group of elementary works.[144] His *liber singularis ad formulam hypothecariam*[145] goes with a similar work of Marcianus in the Sabinian mass to form a small subject-group.[146] Two books on *fideicommissa*[147] fall in that subject-group in the Papinian mass.[148] All these works are in subject- or genre-groups, spread over all three masses, and so they do not serve to identify Gaius' basic mass. But his unattached works, comprising 19 books, (*regulae* 3,[149] *de manumissionibus* 3,[150] *de verborum obligationibus* 3,[151] *ad legem XII tabularum* 6,[152] *de casibus* 1,[153] *de tacitis fideicommissis* 1,[154] *ad SC Tertullianum* 1,[155] *ad SC Orfitianum* 1)[156] all fall in the Papinian mass. This must therefore be Gaius' basic mass. The *Index auctorum* lists a *liber singularis 'dotalicion'*,[157] and the BK Ordo assigns the mysterious *lex Glitia*, with a single text, to the edictal mass.[158] To Mantovani, however, this latter work is of uncertain mass.[159] The BK Ordo puts Gaius' *liber singularis regularum* in the Papinian mass,[160] though Mantovani treats its mass as uncertain.[161] Two or three of these *libri singulares* should go in the Papinian mass with Gaius' other 19 unattached books, making 21 or 22 in all, but the *liber singularis regularum* perhaps belongs in the Sabinian mass with other works of *regulae*. In the end, counting the works that belong to subject- and genre-groups, 23 or 24 books of Gaius' fall in the Papinian mass against 40 in the edictal mass and 25 or 26 in the Sabinian, though the Papinian is his basic mass. This paradoxical distribution, in which the basic mass has fewer books than the other two, serves to honour the Papinian mass, which secures in Papinian and Gaius two leading authors to compare with the Sabinian mass's Julian and Ulpian. The

[138] BK Ordo 7–9, 98–99, 104–107, 110, 114–115, 118–119, 122–123.
[139] BK Ordo 4–9.
[140] BK Ordo 95–99, 101–110, 112–123.
[141] BK Ordo 165.
[142] BK Ordo 162–167.
[143] BK Ordo 24–25.
[144] BK Ordo 21–27.
[145] BK Ordo 58.
[146] BK Ordo 57.
[147] BK Ordo 197.
[148] BK Ordo 194–204.
[149] BK Ordo 223.
[150] BK Ordo 245.
[151] BK Ordo 246.
[152] BK Ordo 247.
[153] BK Ordo 215.
[154] BK Ordo 242.
[155] BK Ordo 243.
[156] BK Ordo 244.
[157] *Index auctorum* XX.12.
[158] D. 5.2.4; BK Ordo 169.
[159] Mantovani (above n. 4) 97.
[160] BK Ordo 224.
[161] Mantovani (above n. 4) 99.

edictal mass secures more of Gaius' books than any other, but is not his basic mass.

Venuleius Saturninus' basic mass is also the Papinian. His 19 books of *stipulationes* is an unattached work in that mass, though it could have been grouped with Gaius 3 *de verborum obligationibus*.[162] Four books *de officio proconsulis* go in the Sabinian mass[163] with two of Paul on that subject[164] to form a small subject-group. Three books on *iudicia publica*[165] also belong to a Sabinian subject-group.[166] The rest of his works go in the Appendix[167] but will originally have been assigned to the Papinian mass as his basic mass.[168] **Claudius** Saturninus, on the other hand, belongs to the Sabinian mass.[169]

There are in all seven authors (Gaius, Hermogenianus, Papinian, Scaevola, Tryphoninus, Valens, and Venuleius) whose basic mass is the Papinian.

(3) Authors whose Basic Mass is the Edictal

The basic mass of the remaining authors is the edictal. The first is **Modestinus.** The Modestinus group is an author-group amounting to 59 books[170] but it sandwiches[171] two *libri singulares* of Ulpian, *excusationes*[172] and *de officio praetoris tutelaris*,[173] which were read with Modestinus' six books of *excusationes* because they dealt with the same subject.[174] Mantovani regards two of Modestinus' *libri singulares* in this sequence as of uncertain mass.[175] But, given that no work of Modestinus is shown to belong to another mass, they are surely edictal and should come between BK Ordo 137 and 151.[176] Somewhere in this same sequence two *libri singulares* of Modestinus mentioned in the *Index auctorum* (*de testamentis* and *de legatis et fideicommissis*) should be added.[177] The only Modestinus work outside this sequence is his four

[162] BK Ordo 216. [163] BK Ordo 91. [164] BK Ordo 90.

[165] BK Ordo 53. [166] BK Ordo 52–56.

[167] *Actionum* 10 and *interdictorum* 6 (BK Ordo 273, 274).

[168] Chapter 5 below nn. 116–17. [169] Above nn. 88–9.

[170] BK Ordo 137–42, 146–151. Modestinus' supposed 4 books *de praescriptionibus* (D. 45.1.101; BK Ordo 145) should, with Lenel *Pal.* I.732 and the *Index auctorum* be eliminated, though the commission did have his *liber singularis de praescriptionibus* (BK Ordo 148; *Index auctorum* XXXI.7).

[171] BK Ordo 143, 144.

[172] BK Ordo 143. [173] BK Ordo 144. [174] BK Ordo 142–144.

[175] *De differentia dotis*; *de inofficioso testamento*: BK Ordo 141, 151.

[176] The only Modestinus work outside this sequence is his 4 books *de poenis* at BK Ordo 174, towards the end of the mass.

[177] *Index auctorum* XXXI 10, 11.

books *de poenis* towards the end of the edictal mass.[178] One may suspect that this was a late arrival, and so was put in Modestinus' basic mass, but, along with other unattached works, towards the end.[179]

The Modestinus sequence, including the two *libri singulares* of Ulpian, comes to 67 books.[180] Ulpian's 3 books *de officio consulis* come just after the *digesta* of Celsus and Marcellus and before the sequence of Modestinus' works.[181] This work would normally be expected to go in the Sabinian mass as Ulpian's basic mass.[182] Its place at the beginning of the Modestinus sequence has no merit from the point of view of authorship, subject-matter or genre. In my view it can be explained as bringing the total of books in the sequence to 70, which can be conveniently divided into two lots of 35 each.[183] There are many ways of doing this, but one is to run one lot from BK Ordo 146 to 151,[184] the other from BK Ordo 136 to 144 with the addition of the two from the *Index auctorum*.

Apart from Modestinus[185] the edictal mass acquires Iuventius **Celsus**' only surviving work, his *digesta*.[186] It has the only works of eight other writers: **Proculus**,[187] **Terentius Clemens**,[188] **Mauricianus**,[189] **Arrius Menander**,[190] **Tarrutienus Paternus**,[191] **Tertullianus**,[192] **Licinius Rufinus**[193] and **Papirius Iustus**.[194] Several of these come towards the end of the mass and constitute a sort of mass coda to which otherwise unassigned authors were allotted. This coda is analogous to the *libri singulares* of Paul and others which form codas in the Sabinian and Papinian masses.[195]

Iavolenus' 15 books *ex Cassio*[196] and 14 *epistularum*[197] form a short author-group in the edictal mass, which also has his five books *ad Plautium*,[198] the latter grouped with other commentaries *ad Plautium*.[199] His basic mass is therefore the edictal. The BK Ordo

[178] BK Ordo 174.

[179] The unattached works begin after a small subject-group on military law at BK Ordo 171–2.

[180] BK Ordo 137 to 144 = 30 books; 146 to 151 = 35 books; *Index auctorum* XXXI 10, 11 provides two more *libri singulares* of Modestinus.

[181] BK Ordo 137–151; Mantovani (above n. 4) 95–6.

[182] Above, nn. 58–84.

[183] If Bluhme has correctly analysed the successive sections of Celsus and Marcellus *digesta*, the odd- and even- numbered sections also come to 35 books each.

[184] *Responsorum* 19, *pandectarum* 12 and 3 *libri singulares*.

[185] Above nn. 170–84.

[186] BK Ordo 134.

[187] BK Ordo 155, 157.

[188] BK Ordo 164.

[189] BK Ordo 166.

[190] BK Ordo 171.

[191] BK Ordo 172.

[192] BK Ordo 161, 173.

[193] BK Ordo 175.

[194] BK Ordo 177.

[195] BK Ordo 72–93, 225–259.

[196] BK Ordo 152.

[197] BK Ordo 153.

[198] BK Ordo 127, 130.

[199] BK Ordo 124–131.

allotted his 10-book selection from Labeo's *posteriora* to the Sabinian mass.[200] Since the initial allocation of this work was to the Sabinian mass, the compilers must have regarded it as a work of Labeo rather than Iavolenus, as does the *Index auctorum*.[201] Otherwise it would have gone to the edictal mass, as Iavolenus' basic mass. **Pomponius**' basic mass is also the edictal. His *ad Sabinum*[202] goes in the Sabinian mass in a subject-group with the Sabinian commentaries of Ulpian and Paul.[203] His *liber singularis regularum*[204] falls in the *regulae* group in that mass.[205] Five books on *fideicommissa*[206] are in the Papinian mass group on that topic.[207] His historical works (*libri enchiridii*)[208] are probably attracted by Gaius on the Twelve Tables, the only other historical work read by the commission, to a small historical genre-group.[209] His seven books *ad Plautium*[210] are in the edictal mass with other commentaries *ad Plautium*.[211] All these are in subject- or genre-groups. But Pomponius' unattached works, 39 books *ad Quintum Mucium*[212] and 15 *variarum lectionum*[213] go in the edictal mass, which must therefore be his basic mass. It is to the edictal mass that two works of his that appear in the Appendix[214] will have been initially assigned. **Callistratus** also belongs to the edictal mass, with six books *de cognitionibus*,[215] four *edicti monitorium*,[216] and four *de iure fisci*.[217] Of these the first two books *edicti monitorium* are mistakenly grouped in the edictal mass with the edictal commentaries of Ulpian, Paul and Gaius.[218] His two books of *quaestiones*[219] accompany a *quaestiones* group in the Papinian mass,[220] and his three of *institutiones*[221] belong to the institutional group in the Sabinian mass.[222] Most of his books (14 out of 19), including all 14 unattached books, point to the edictal as his basic mass.

200 BK Ordo 94.

201 *Index auctorum* VII Λαβεωνος 2 posteriorum βιβλια δεκα.

202 BK Ordo 2.

203 BK Ordo 1–3.

204 BK Ordo 45.

205 BK Ordo 56–46.

206 BK Ordo 199, 202.

207 BK Ordo 194–204.

208 BK Ordo 248, 249.

209 BK Ordo 93.

210 BK Ordo 126, 128, 131.

211 BK Ordo 124–133.

212 BK Ordo 154.

213 BK Ordo 156.

214 *epistularum* 20, *de senatusconsultis* 5: BK Ordo 269, 270.

215 BK Ordo 160.

216 BK Ordo 100, 176. They come towards the end of the edictal mass: Mantovani (above n. 4) 94, 97.

217 BK Ordo 158. Mantovani (above n. 4) 96 thinks that this work might belong to the Appendix. If so, D. 49.14 would be the only title in the Digest that begins with Appendix texts (49.14.1–3).

218 BK Ordo 95–100 but see Mantovani (above n. 4) 94.

219 BK Ordo 185.

220 BK Ordo 183–184.

221 BK Ordo 26.

222 BK Ordo 21–27.

Marcellus presents a difficulty. His 31 books of *digesta*,[223] grouped with those of Celsus in a genre-group,[224] and his six *ad legem Iuliam et Papiam*,[225] in a subject-group of commentaries,[226] come in the edictal mass, which is prima facie his basic mass. But his *liber singularis responsorum*, an unattached work, goes in the Sabinian mass.[227] Mantovani, reviewing its position in that mass, would move it from BK Ordo 59 to the end of the *regulae* group running from BK Ordo 37 to BK Ordo 46. It would then be 46 bis in the BK Ordo. Mantovani's argument is that 10 of the 14 texts from Marcellus' *responsa* come immediately after the *regulae* group, which already contains another extraneous work, Ulpian's two books of *responsa*.[228] If Mantovani is right, the *regulae* in the group preceding Marcellus' *responsa* come to 41 books (Neratius 15, Ulpian 1 + 7, Scaevola 4, Paul 8, Marcianus 5, Pomponius 1). The extraneous works (two of Ulpian's *responsa* and one of Marcellus' *responsa*) could have been added to yield 44 books, an even number easily divided into two sub-groups of 22 books each. For example the 44 books could have been split into the 22 made up by the first two items in the sequence (Neratius 15 reg. and Ulpian 7 reg.)[229] and the 22 made up by the rest.[230] That is speculative, but Mantovani's proposal makes this explanation possible.

The edictal mass emerges as the basic mass of 12 and perhaps 13 or even 15 authors: certainly Callistratus, Celsus, Clemens, Iavolenus, Licinius Rufinus, Mauricianus, Menander, Modestinus, Papirius, Pomponius, Proculus, Tarrutienus Paternus and probably Marcellus. To judge from the coda of this mass, it is the residuary mass for authors not otherwise assigned, such as Menander, Tarrutienus, Licinnius, and Papirius,[231] to whom, it will be seen, we may plausibly add Aelius Gallus and Iulius Aquila.

(4) Authors of Uncertain Mass

There remain five authors of uncertain mass: Aelius Gallus, Aquila, Furius, Quintus Mucius Scaevola and Maecianus. The single text of **Gallus**[232] comes at the end of the edictal mass in the generally regular title *de verborum significatione*. Though Mantovani treats it as of

[223] BK Ordo 135. [224] BK Ordo 134–135. [225] BK Ordo 167.
[226] BK Ordo 162–167. [227] BK Ordo 59. [228] BK Ordo 41.
[229] BK Ordo 36–37. [230] BK Ordo 38–46 bis.
[231] BK Ordo 171, 172, 175, 177. [232] D. 50.16.157.

uncertain mass,[233] it may really belong to the end of the edictal mass, since, as we saw, a collection of one-work authors forms a major element of its coda.[234] The same is true of Iulius **Aquila**, from whose book of *responsa* we have two texts, one at the end of the edictal mass[235] and the other at the end of a title. The latter may be a codal text.[236] Furius **Anthianus**' five books *ad edictum*,[237] of which only one book or collection of texts was available to the compilers, belongs to the Appendix.[238] So does **Quintus Mucius** Scaevola's ορων.[239] Their original mass cannot be determined because there are no works by these authors outside the Appendix. The basic mass of Volusius **Maecianus** is uncertain. His *iudicia publica* in 14 books[240] are in the Sabinian mass in a group with works by Macer, Venuleius, Paul and Marcianus on that subject.[241] His 16 books on *fideicommissa*[242] go in the Papinian mass with the similar works of Valens, Ulpian, Gaius, Paul and Pomponius.[243] This leaves the *liber singularis ex lege Rhodia*, with a single text[244] that follows the Sabinian mass[245] and precedes an Appendix text.[246] The BK Ordo puts it in the Sabinian mass.[247] To Mantovani it is of uncertain mass.[248] It cannot be placed, and might even belong to the Appendix. So it is impossible to determine Maecianus' basic mass.

(5) Paul

Paul is unique. He has no single basic mass. This is because his 310 books[249] outstrip those of any other author, even Ulpian's 239, and include 59 *libri singulares*. The *Index auctorum* makes a distinction between longer works and *libri singulares*, for which it uses the term μονοβιβλα. It lists these for Ulpian, Paul, Marcianus and Modestinus but not for Gaius or Papinian. The separate listing suggests that the commission dealt with them in a different way from the longer works.

233 Mantovani (above n. 4) 97. 234 Above nn. 187–95.
235 D. 26.7.34. 236 D. 26.10.12. 237 *Index auctorum* XXXVI.
238 BK Ordo 275; chapter 5 nn. 47–55.
239 BK Ordo 264; chapter 5 nn. 30–8. 240 BK Ordo 56.
241 BK Ordo 52–56. 242 BK Ordo 196, 200. 243 BK Ordo 194–204.
244 D. 14.2.9. 245 D. 14.2.6–8. 246 D. 14.2.10 (Lab. 1 pith.).
247 BK Ordo 93. 248 Mantovani (above n. 4) 93.
249 This figure includes his 23 books of *brevia* listed by the *Index auctorum* XXV.4, of which 1–5 and 16–23 seem to belong to the edictal committee, 6–8 to the Sabinian. The intervening seven books have been divided so that about two-thirds go to the Sabinian committee, to which I have chosen to assign books 9–13, with 14–15 going to the edictal committee.

For Paul the *Index* records 49[250] *libri singulares* out of 59.[251] The other 10 are not listed in the *Index auctorum* but excerpts from them appear in the Digest.[252] On the other hand there are 11 books mentioned in the Index of which no fragments are inserted in the Digest.[253] The BK Ordo attributed 24 of Paul's *libri* to the Sabinian mass, 24 to the Papinian mass, and one to the edictal mass. Mantovani treats this allocation as uncertain in 15 cases,[254] seven of which were placed by BK Ordo in the Sabinian mass,[255] seven in the Papinian mass,[256] and one in the edictal mass.[257] The allocations that he finds to be secure are always in the Sabinian (17 *libri singulares*)[258] or the Papinian masses (also 17).[259] BK Ordo puts only one *liber singularis* of Paul, with a single text, in the edictal mass, and this allocation is insecure.[260] So it seems likely that no *libri singulares* of Paul were allotted to the edictal mass. The possible exception is his *de excusatione tutelarum*, allotted by BK Ordo to the Sabinian

[250] Treating *ad senatusconsultum Libonianum* (BK Ordo 230) and *ad senatusconsultum Claudianum* (BK Ordo 231) as separate.

[251] At times it is questionable whether two titles evidenced in the sources refer to the same or different works e.g. *de liberali causa* and *de articulis liberalis causae*, and whether some of the work listed in the *Index auctorum* really existed (*de actionibus*, *ad municipalem*, *de instrumento et instructo*): Liebs (above n. 47), 155–74; Liebs (above n. 46) 67–71 but, whatever the truth, the overall picture is not seriously affected.

[252] F. Schulz, *History of Roman Legal Science* (Oxford 1946) 146.

[253] Below n. 267.

[254] *De iure patronatus*; *ad senatusconsultum Silanianum*; *de sentusconsultis*, *ad senatusconsultum Velleianum*; *de intercessionibus feminarum*; *de excusatione tutelarum*; *ad orationem divi Severi*; *ad legem Cinciam*; *de poenis omnium legum*; *ad regulam Catonianam*; *de inofficioso testamento*; *de tacitis fideicommissis*; *de instrumenti significatione*; *de gradibus et adfinibus*; *de officio praefecti urbi*; see Mantovani (above n. 4) 90–103.

[255] BK Ordo 35, 48, 78, 79, 80, 82, 83.

[256] BK Ordo 232, 234, 236, 237, 238, 254, 259.

[257] BK Ordo 170.

[258] *De dotis repetitione*; *de adsignatione libertorum*; *regularum*; *de portionibus quae liberis damnatorum conceduntur*; *de conceptione formularum*; *de iudiciis publicis*; *de appellationibus*; *ad legem Fufiam Caniniam*; *de libertatibus dandis*; *de liberali causa*; *de secundis tabulis*; *de iure codicillorum*; *de centumviralibus (septemviralibus) iudiciis*; *de adulteriis*; *ad orationem divi Marci Antonini et Commodi*; *de variis lectionibus*; *de poenis militum* (BK Ordo 33, 34, 39, 49, 51, 54, 67, 69, 72, 73, 74, 75, 76, 77, 81, 84, 87). Four of these belong to subject-groups: *regularum*, *de publicis iudiciis*, *de appellationibus* and *de adulteriis*. The rest are unattached.

[259] *De cognitionibus*; *de concurrentibus actionibus*; *de usuris*; *ad SC Turpillianum*; *ad SC Libonianum (et edictum Claudianum)*; *ad senatusconsultum Claudianum*; *de poenis paganorum*; *de forma testamenti (= de testamentis?)*; *ad sc. Tertullianum*; *ad sc. Orfitianum*; *ad legem Falcidiam*; *de iure libellorum*; *de articulis liberalis causae* (?); *de iuris et facti ignorantia*; *de iure singulari*; *de officio adsessorum*; *de officio praefecti vigilum* (BK Ordo 225, 226, 227, 228, 230, 231, 233, 235, 239, 240, 241, 250, 251, 252, 253, 255, 256). All these appear to be unattached.

[260] D. 1.3.29 (*ad legem Cinciam*: BK Ordo 170); Mantovani (above n. 4) 97.

mass.[261] This should have been read in the edictal mass as part of a subject-group along with works of Modestinus and Ulpian.[262] But two of the three surviving texts from this work of Paul fall in the Sabinian mass,[263] while the third is in the edictal mass.[264] One must agree with Mantovani that the correct mass remains uncertain.[265]

The edictal mass therefore contains at most one *liber singularis* of Paul, and moreover one allocated to it, if at all, as part of a subject-group. This suggests that the other 14 *libri singulares* whose mass is uncertain belong in the Sabinian or Papinian masses, which each have at least 17 of these monographs securely allotted to them.[266] Presumably the 11 monographs listed in the *Index auctorum* from which no Digest texts have been excerpted also belong to the Sabinian or Papinian masses.[267]

A few of the *libri* that Mantovani regards as of indeterminate mass have in my view been placed by BK Ordo in the correct mass.[268] Five seem to belong to the Sabinian mass. One is *de iure patronatus*,[269] with three texts. D. 38.1.28 seems to be correctly placed in the Sabinian mass, with D. 38.1.17 moved to an earlier place in the same title and mass to qualify what Paul says in 38.1.16. The third text from this work is codal[270] and might come from this work or from a *liber singularis de iure patronatus quod ex Iulia et Papia venit*, a work attributed to Paul in the *Index auctorum*.[271] *Ad SC Silanianum*[272] is similar. All three texts come in the Sabinian mass. D. 29.5.10 and 12, with a qualifying fragment from Tryphoninus at 29.5.11, come before the Sabinian subject-group on *publica iudicia*,[273] while 29.5.7 is moved to an earlier position where it qualifies a text of Paul. *Ad SC Velleianum*[274] and *de intercessionibus feminarum*[275] each provide a single text (D. 16.1.23 and 24) at the end of the Sabinian mass in the title *Ad SC Velleianum*. There is no reason to suppose that they have been shifted from another mass. *Ad orationem divi Severi*[276] yields three texts. Two of these qualify texts of Ulpian in the Sabinian mass,[277] while the third[278] ends the Sabinian mass and does not belong to the Papinian mass, since the last text in the

[261] BK Ordo 82.
[262] BK Ordo 142–144.
[263] D. 27.1.26; 26.3.4.
[264] D. 27.1.11.
[265] Mantovani (above n. 4) 83.
[266] Above nn. 258–9.
[267] *De actionibus*; *de donationibus inter virum et uxorem*; *de extraordinariis criminibus*; *υποθηκαρια*; *de instructo et instrumento* (= *de instrumenti significatione*?; Liebs (1997), 166 no. 55); *de iure patronatus ex lege Iulia et Papia*; *ad legem Velleam*; *de legibus*; *de legitimis hereditatibus*; *ad municipalem*; *de officio praetoris tutelaris*.
[268] Above n. 6.
[269] BK Ordo 35.
[270] D. 25.3.9.
[271] *Index auctorum* XXV 63.
[272] BK Ordo 48.
[273] BK Ordo 52–56.
[274] BK Ordo 79.
[275] BK Ordo 80.
[276] BK Ordo 83.
[277] D. 27.9.2, 4.
[278] D. 27.9.13.

title, D. 27.9.14, which belongs to the Papinian mass,[279] has a mistaken repetition of Paulus in the inscription. There is, again, no reason to suppose that 27.9.13 has been transferred from another mass. Two more *libri singulares* of Paul that have been doubted belong in my view in the Papinian mass. In *de tacitis fideicommissis* one text[280] is inserted between two texts from Paul's *decreta* in the Papinian mass while the other[281] comes between a text from Paul *de cognitionibus*,[282] which belongs to the Papinian mass, and two texts *ad SC Orfitianum* and *Tertullianum*,[283] both in the same mass.[284] The order of texts in this title 50.16 is generally reliable. In *de instrumenti significatione*[285] one text appears at the end of the Papinian mass and before the Appendix.[286] The other qualifies a text of Paul *ad Sabinum* on *suppellex*.[287] No other *liber singularis* of Paul is assigned to the Appendix, and so the Papinian mass is to be preferred.

The figures suggest that the number of Paul's *libri singulares* allocated to these two masses was about equal. The two masses were joint heirs, as it were, to these works.

There are on my count 99 books of Paul in the Sabinian mass,[288] 88 in the Papinian mass,[289] and 105 in the edictal mass.[290] Eighteen are indeterminate, including those *libri singulares* that may be either Sabinian or Papinian.[291] The works in the edictal mass are nearly all grouped according to subject-matter: *ad edictum praetoris* 53, *brevia* (about) 15;[292] *ad edictum aedilium* 2; *ad Plautium* 18; *ad legem Iuliam et Papiam* 10.[293] The apparent exceptions are four books *ad Vitellium* and two *de iure*

[279] Paulus 9 resp.; BK Ordo 188. [280] D. 49.14.49. [281] D. 50.16 229.

[282] D. 50.16.228: BK Ordo 225. [283] D. 50.16.230, 231.

[284] BK Ordo 240 and 239, respectively. [285] BK Ordo 238.

[286] D. 32.99. [287] D. 33.10.4, between two texts of Paul *ad Sab.*

[288] *Ad Sabinum* 16; *ad edictum* 24 (including ed. 48 fin.–51 transferred from edictal mass: above note 9); *brevia* 10?; *epitomarum Alfeni digestorum* 8; *institutionum* 2; *de adulteriis* 3; *regularum* 7; *ad leg. Iuniam* 2; *de off. proconsulis* 2; *ad leg. Aeliam Sentiam* 3 and 22 *libri singulares* (above nn. 258, 269–79).

[289] *Quaestionum* 26; *responsorum* 23; *de fideicommissis* 3; *sententiarum* 5; *ad Neratium* 4; *manualium* 3; *decretorum* 3; *imperialium sententiarum* 2 (of six: transferred to Appendix) and 19 *libri singulares* (above nn. 259, 280–7).

[290] *Ad edictum* 54 (not counting 48 fin.–51 transferred to the Sabinian mass: above n. 9); *brevia* 1–5, 16–23 (?); *ad ed. aedilium curulium* 2; *ad Plautium* 18; *ad Vitellium* 4; *de iure fisci* 2; *de censibus* 2; *ad leg. Iuliam et Papiam* 10.

[291] Above nn. 253–7. One of these may belong to the edictal mass: above n. 261. These figures include as determinate the *libri singulares* that Mantovani treats as indeterminate but that I think can be allocated to the Sabinian or Papinian masses respectively (above nn. 268–87).

[292] The 23 books of Paul's *brevia* seem to have been available to the commissioners, but their distribution between the Sabinian and edictal masses is uncertain, apart from the few from which excerpts survive. [293] BK Ordo 96, 102, 103, 109, 124, 163.

fisci.[294] But are these works really unattached, or do they form part of the *ad Plautium* group? Though they are not related by subject-matter to the group *ad Plautium* that they follow, they may have been put in to make up a numerical balance.[295] Of the other unattached works, Paul's two books *ad legem Iuniam*[296] go in the Sabinian mass, while three books *manualium*[297] and three *decretorum*[298] are in the Papinian mass. So it is probably right to think of Paul as having two basic masses, the Sabinian and the Papinian, to which his residuary works are more or less evenly assigned.

IV. Identity and Character of the Groups

The allocation of authors and works to masses depends, as has been seen, on the existence within each mass of groups of works. The grouping was essential in order that the works dealing with the same subject should be read together or in close succession. In that way the best texts on the subject could be chosen and excerpted for inclusion in the Digest. This accounts for the existence of subject-groups. But there were also two other classes of group, author-groups and genre-groups.[299] In these cases it was convenient, but not essential, to read works by the same author or belonging to the same genre together or in close succession. The members of a committee would by this means become familiar with a particular author's style and mode of thought, or with the characteristics of a certain genre of legal writing. This would make for greater speed and economy than if the reader were to be continually switching from one author or genre to another.

A group that belonged predominantly to one of these three main classes could be mixed in that it could incorporate an element of another class. For example the Julian group in the Sabinian mass is an author-group that incorporates a genre element and a subject element.[300] Not all the works assigned to the three committees were assigned in groups, pure or mixed, of these three types. *Libri singulares*, unless forming part of a subject-group, tended not to be attached to any subject- or genre-group. Some four-fifths of the books read by the commission were, however, read in groups of one of these standard types.[301]

294 BK Ordo 132, 133.
295 Honoré (2004, above n. 2) 39–40; above nn. 22–4.
296 BK Ordo 50.
297 BK Ordo 220.
298 BK Ordo 222.
299 Above nn. 13–21.
300 Above nn. 50–7.
301 On my calculation 81 per cent: below nn. 332–4.

It can be assumed that the division into groups was part of Tribonian's design for the execution of the Digest project, his *gubernatio*. The allocation of an author's work to a mass other than his basic mass depended on the existence in the other mass of a group to which his work was to be transferred. Beginning from a list of authors and their works of the sort enshrined in the *Index auctorum*, and a decision as to their basic mass, the identity of these groups had to be worked out in advance. This in turn affected the balance between the three masses, which had to be settled from the outset, so that the commissioners assigned to each committee knew the extent of their overall responsibilities for reading and excerpting the classical authors.

To identify a group demands care and their precise boundaries are sometime in doubt. The groups that Rodger and I proposed in 1970[302] paid too little attention to subject-matter and too much to numerical balance. We assumed that all the works read were divided into groups, including the unattached works. That is uncertain. But the grouping remains a major feature of the enterprise and to settle the composition of the groups that can be detected is important. The works that comprise a group should be consistent with the Digest inscriptions, and should be based on a particular author, subject or genre, though there can be combinations of these elements and, in my view, sometimes additions to secure numerical balance.

A serious effort was made to draw together all the works dealing with the same subject-matter. But there are a few cases in which works on the same topic were not read together. Rutilius Maximus on the *lex Falcidia* comes in the Sabinian mass (BK Ordo 68) and Paul on the same statute in the Papinian mass (BK Ordo 241). Paul's *liber singularis de adulteriis* (BK Ordo 77) was not read with the rest of the adultery group, which included his three-book work on adultery (BK Ordo 31), though it was in the same mass. His *liber singularis* on excuses from guardianship may or may not have been read with the works of Modestinus and Ulpian on this subject in the edictal mass.[303] Paul and Venuleius *de officio proconsulis* (BK Ordo 90–91) were not read with Ulpian *de officio proconsulis* (BK Ordo 47) and may not have been read together.[304] Modestinus *de inofficioso testamento* does not seem to have been read with the monograph by Paul on the subject in the Papinian mass.[305]

In general, however, when it was desirable to read two or more works together, either jointly or in succession, and the evidence of inscriptions leaves open whether they were in fact grouped, I have assumed

302 Honoré and Rodger (above n. 9), 285–314. 303 Above nn. 261–5.
304 Mantovani (above n. 4) 93. 305 BK Ordo 151, 236.

that they were. An example is that of commentaries on the same office, *lex* or *senatusconsultum* or the same specialized branch of the law. Thus the BK Ordo puts in succession in the Sabinian mass Paul's three and Ulpian's four books *ad legem Aeliam Sentiam.*[306] In the edictal mass we have Menander' and Paternus' four books *de re militari.*[307] The Papinian mass has Paul's and Gaius' monographs on the *sc. Tertullianum* and *sc. Orfitianum*, each pair of which should have been read together,[308] as in the case of the same authors' works on secret trusts (tacit *fideicommissa*),[309] and Paul and Marcianus on the *sc. Turpillianum.*[310]

Works of the same genre are not grouped together to the same extent as those belonging to subject-groups. It was not essential, for example, to gather together all *regulae* or *quaestiones*. Though these genres had enough in common to be worth reading alongside one another their subject-matter was variable and could range across large areas of the law. I have treated Gaius on the Twelve Tables[311] and Pomponius' *enchiridia*,[312] works concerned with legal history, as a group of this sort.

Groups normally begin with the most important or longest work. Thirty-five groups appear to satisfy the criteria set out. The Labeo *posteriora* group (BK Ordo 94, 265) is not included, since it probably consists wholly or in part of works that arrived late and were put at the end of the Sabinian mass, to which they were assigned. The military law group (BK Ordo 171–172) in the edictal mass is included, although it is possible that it also consists of late arrivals.

(1) Groups in the Sabinian Mass

In this mass eleven groups can be detected:

(i) *ad Sabinum* group (BK Ordo 1–3) 103 books (Ulpian 51, Pomponius 36, Paul 16);
(ii) middle edictal commentaries group[313] (BK Ordo 4–9, 112–123) 80 books (Ulpian 30, Paul ed. 25, Paul brev. 8, Gaius ed. prov. 12, Gaius ed. urb. 5);
(iii) Ulpian '10-book group' (BK Ordo 10–11) 20 books (Ulpian 10, Ulpian 10);
(iv) Julian group (BK Ordo 14–20) 125 books (Julian 90 + 1 + 4 + 6, Alfenus 7, Paul 8, Africanus 9);

[306] BK Ordo 70–71. [307] BK Ordo 171–172.
[308] BK Ordo 239, 240, 243, 244. [309] BK Ordo 237, 242.
[310] BK Ordo 228–229. [311] BK Ordo 247. [312] BK Ordo 248, 249.
[313] Before the transfer of BK Ordo 112–123 from the Sabinian to the edictal mass: above n. 9.

(v) institutional group (BK Ordo 21–27) 42 books (Florentinus 12, Marcianus 16, Ulpian 2, Gaius 7, Callistratus 3, Paul 2);
(vi) adultery group BK Ordo 28–31) 11 books (Ulpian 5, Papinian 2 + 1, Paul 3);
(vii) *regulae* group (BK Ordo 36–46, 59?) 44 books (Neratius 15, Ulpian 7 + 1 + 2, Scaevola 4, Paul 7 +1, Marcianus 5, Pomponius 1, Marcellus 1?);
(viii) *iudicia publica* group (BK Ordo 52–56) 22 books (Macer 2, Venuleius 3, Paul 1, Marcianus 2, Maecianus 14);
(ix) *formula hypothecaria* group (BK Ordo 57–58) two books (Marcianus 1, Gaius 1);
(x) appeals group (BK Ordo 64–66) nine books (Ulpian 4, Macer 2, Marcianus 2, Paul 1);
(xi) *lex Aelia Sentia* group (BK Ordo 70–71) seven books (Paul 3, Ulpian 4).

I have omitted Ulpian's six books of *opiniones* and *de censibus* (BK Ordo 12–13), which might, like (iii) above, be considered a group based on authorship and numerical equality. Mantovani would however place *de censibus* between the *iudicia publica* group and the end of the Sabinian mass.[314] The possible 'office of proconsul' group at BK Ordo 90–91 is also omitted, since the precise location of these works of Paul and Venuleius in the Sabinian mass is uncertain,[315] and they are not grouped with Ulpian's major work on that topic.[316] In all 465 books are included in these 11 Sabinian groups, of which 234 (all except iii, iv, v and vii) are grouped by subject-matter, 145 mainly by authorship (iii and iv) and 86 (v, vii) by genre. The larger groups come at the beginning of the mass, the smaller ones later, and the mass, as originally conceived, ends mostly with short works, especially *libri singulares*. The total number of books initially allocated to the Sabinian mass can be estimated in the following way. From the total of 546 embodied in our earlier study[317] subtract the last four books of Gaius' *res cottidianae*,[318] of which Tribonian had available only an epitome of three books,[319] Iavolenus' 10 *ex posterioribus Labeonis*, which was probably a late arrival,[320] and four of the *libri singulares* (Paul 2, Ulpian 1, Maecianus 1) that Mantovani regards as of uncertain mass.[321]

314 Mantovani (above n. 4), 90.
315 Mantovani (above n. 4), 93.
316 BK Ordo 47 (Ulp. 10 *off. proc.*).
317 Honoré and Rodger (above n. 9) 295.
318 BK Ordo 24.
319 Schulz (above n. 252), 167–8.
320 Chapter 5 nn. 72–83.
321 Mantovani (above n. 4) 91–3 lists Paul 1 *de iur. patron.*, 1 *ad SC Silian.*, 1 *de SCC.*, 1 *ad SC Velleian.*, 1 *de intercess. fem.*, and *1 ad orationem divi Severi*); Ulp. *1 de sponsalibus*;

To the remaining 528 books add 13 *libri singulares* of Paul to make up his notional total of 30 such books in this mass, and restore Ulpian's *de sponsalibus*,[322] since the Sabinian is his basic mass.[323] This yields an initial allocation of 542 books, of which 465 (86 per cent) are in groups—a high proportion. Of these 234 (43 per cent) are in subject-groups, 145 (27 per cent) in author-groups, 86 (16 per cent) in genre-groups.

(2) Groups in the Papinian Mass

In this mass 14 groups can be detected:

- (xii) Papinian group (BK Ordo 180–182) 58 books (quaestiones 37, responsa 19, definitiones 2);
- (xiii) *quaestiones* group (BK Ordo 183–184) 48 books (Paul 26, Scaevola 20, Callistratus 2);
- (xiv) *responsa* group (BK Ordo 186–193) 29 books (Paul 23, Scaevola 6);
- (xv) *fideicommissa* group (BK Ordo 194–204) 39 books (Valens 7, Ulpian 6, Maecianus 16, Gaius 2, Paul 3, Pomponius 5);
- (xvi) *sententiae-iuris epitomae* group (BK Ordo 205–214) 11 books (Paul 5, Hermogenianus 6);
- (xvii) Neratius *responsa* group (BK Ordo 217–218) seven books (Neratius 3, Paul 4);
- (xviii) Tryphoninus group (BK Ordo 219–222) 27 books (Tryphoninus 21, Paul 6);
- (xix) SC Turpillianum group (BK Ordo 228, 229) two books (Paul 1, Marcianus 1);
- (xx) *tacita fideicommissa* group (BK Ordo 237, 242) two books (Paul 1, Gaius 1);
- (xxi) SC Tertullianum group (BK Ordo 239, 243) two books (Paul 1, Gaius 1);
- (xxii) SC Orfitianum group (BK Ordo 240, 244) two books (Paul 1, Gaius 1);
- (xxiii) historical group (BK Ordo 247–249) nine books (Gaius 6, Pomponius 3);
- (xxiv) *praefectus vigilum* group (BK Ordo 256–257) two books (Paul 1, Ulpian 1);

Maecianus 1 *ex lege Rhodia*. In my view five of the seven *libri singulares* of Paul belong to the Sabinian mass: above, nn. 268–79.

[322] BK Ordo 32; above, nn. 74–80.

[323] Above, nn. 58–84.

(xxv) *praefectus urbi* group (BK Ordo 258–259) two books (Ulpian 1, Paul 1).

In all 240 books fall in these 14 groups. As before the larger groups come first, the smaller later, and the mass ends with a number of short works, mainly *libri singulares*. The total of books in the Papinian mass, excluding the Appendix, which is not part of it,[324] may be estimated as follows. From the 291 listed in our earlier study[325] subtract 11 of the *libri singulares* (Paul 5, Ulpian 3, Arcadius 2[326]) whose mass is doubted by Mantovani.[327] Add, however, 13 *libri singulares* of Paul to make up the total of 30 notionally assigned to each of the Sabinian and Papinian masses. One *liber singularis* of Papinian should be added, assuming it belongs to this mass rather than the Appendix.[328] The revised total is therefore 294 books. The 238 grouped works amount to 81 per cent of this total, the 97 in genre-groups (xiii, xiv, xvi, xxiii) to 33 per cent, the 85 in author-groups (xii, xviii) to 29 per cent, and the 56 in subject-groups (xv, xvii, xix, xx, xxi, xxii, xxiv) to 19 per cent. The tendency to group works by subject-matter is less in the Papinian than in the Sabinian mass. This is because the Papinian mass has a higher proportion of case-law collections such as *quaestiones* and *responsa*.

(3) Groups in the Edictal Mass

This mass yields 10 groups:

(xxvi) early edictal commentaries group (BK Ordo 95–100) 68½ books (Ulpian 25, Paul 27 + 5, Gaius 8½ +1, Callistratus 2);
(xxvii) later edictal commentaries group (BK Ordo 101–107) 73½ books (Ulpian 26, Paul 26 + 10?, Gaius 9½ + 2);
(xxviii) edict of the curule aediles group (BK Ordo 108–110) six books (Ulpian 2, Paul 2, Gaius 2);

[324] Mantovani (above n. 4) 112; Osler (above n. 115), 144–6; above chapter 5 nn. 59–107 contra Bluhme (above n. 1) 309–10 = *Labeo*, 6 (1960), 73–4.

[325] Honoré and Rodger (above n. 9) 314.

[326] Mantovani (above n. 4) 99–101, doubts Paul 1 *de poenis omnium legum*, 1 *ad regulam Catonianam*, 1 *de inofficioso testamento*, 1 *de tacitis fideicommissis*, 1 *de instrumenti significatione*, 1 *de gradibus et adfinibus*, 1 *de officio praefecti urbi*; Ulpian 1 *officio praefecti vigilum*, 1 *officio praefecti urbi*, 1 *officio quaestoris*; Arcadius 1 *de muneribus civilibus*, 1 *de officio praefecti praetorio*, Marcianus 1 *ad SC Turpillianum*, and Gaius 1 *regularum*. In my view two of these seven *libri singulares* of Paul, one of Ulpian and those of Gaius and Marcianus belong to the Papinian mass: above nn. 160–1, 280–7, 323–4.

[327] Above n. 4.

[328] αστυνομικος: above n. 7.

(xxix) transferred edictal commentaries group (BK Ordo 112–123) 12 books (Ulpian 3½, Paul 4½, Gaius 4);

(xxx) commentaries *ad Plautium* group (BK Ordo 124–131) 30 books (Paul 18, Iavolenus 5, Pomponius 7);

(xxxi) Celsus-Marcellus group (BK Ordo 134–135) 70 books (Celsus 39, Marcellus 31);

(xxxii) Modestinus group (BK Ordo 136–144, 146–151 + *Index auctorum* XXXI 10–11) 70 books (Modestinus 63 + 2, Ulpian 2 +3);

(xxxiii) Iavolenus group (BK Ordo 152–153) 29 books (Iavolenus 15 + 14);

(xxxiv) commentaries *ad legem Iuliam et Papiam* group (BK Ordo 162–167) 77 books (Ulpian 20, Paul 10, Clemens 20, Gaius 15, Mauricianus 6, Marcellus 6);

(xxxv) military law group (BK Ordo 171–172) eight books (Menander 4, Tarrutienus 4).

In this mass the size of the groups (except xxviii and xxxv) does not decline as the reading progresses. Five of the eight major groups in the edictal mass comprise between 65 and 77 books, so that group size remains steady. The total number of grouped books is 429. Our earlier estimate of the total for the mass was 573,[329] from which should be deducted 12 books of edictal commentary transferred from the Sabinian mass and 12 of those (Papinian 1, Modestinus 2, Callistratus 4, Paul 3, Gallus 1, Aquila 1) whose mass is doubted by Mantovani.[330] However Modestinus' two *libri singulares* can be restored to the edictal mass in view of the fact that it is Modestinus' basic mass; and two more of his *libri singulares* from the *Index auctorum* can be added to group (xxxii).[331] The case for adding three books of Ulpian *de officio consulis* to this group was argued earlier.[332] Taking the initial mass total, then, as 556 books, the grouped books form 77 per cent of the mass. Those in subject-groups (xxvi, xxvii, xxviii, xxix, xxx, xxxiv, xxxv) come to 263 books (47 per cent), those in author-groups (xxxii, xxxiii) to 96 (17 per cent) and those in genre-groups (xxxi) to 70 (13 per cent).

Combining the figures for the three masses, the initial assignment of 1,394 books consists of 1,134 arranged in groups (465 Sabinian, 240 Papinian, 429 edictal). Of these 555 are grouped according to

[329] Honoré and Rodger (above n. 9) 306.

[330] Mantovani (above n. 4) 94–7.

[331] Above nn. 175–7.

[332] Above nn. 25, 80, 180–4.

subject-matter (Sabinian 234, Papinian 58, edictal 263), 326 according to authorship (Sabinian 145, Papinian 85, edictal 96) and 253 according to genre (Sabinian 86, Papinian 97, edictal 70). Some 262 books are unattached. Of the total 81 per cent are in groups, 40 per cent grouped by subject-matter, 23 per cent by authorship, and 18 per cent by genre. The remaining 19 per cent are unattached.

Some 20 books of dubious mass[333] need to be added to these figures and distributed between the individual masses.[334] As between the three committees, the general picture is that of a roughly equal number of books to be read by the Sabinian and edictal committees (542 and 556 respectively) and little more than half that number (294) by the Papinian committee.

(4) Leading Works

Reading and excerpting works in groups related by subject-matter is more effective if one of them is taken as the leading work, so that it forms the basis of the excerpts to be taken. It can be supplemented by excerpts from other works on the same subject. It was an important decision, and one that only Tribonian could have taken, to treat Ulpian as the leading author for the Digest as a whole.[335] If we look at the 18 groups related by subject-matter and listed above[336] Ulpian is the leading author in nine of them, including the most important: the commentaries *ad Sabinum* (i), all the groups of commentary *ad edictum* (ii, xxvi, xxvii, xxviii, xxix), the appeals group (x), the commentaries *ad legem Iuliam et Papiam* (xxxiv) and probably, despite appearances, the *fideicommissa* group (xv).[337] Paul is the lead author in seven: one is substantial, the *ad Plautium* group in the edictal mass (xxx). The other six groups are small, the *lex Aelia Sentia* in the Sabinian mass (xi), and five groups of two books each in the Papinian mass (xix, xx, xxi, xxii, xxiv). His

[333] Mantovani (above n. 4) 90–103 but see nn. 6, 7, 322–3 above. Those of indeterminate mass that remain are: Paul 2 *de censibus*, 1 *de senatusconsultis*, 1 *ad legem Cinciam*, 1 *de poenis omnium legum*, 1 *ad regulam Catonianam.*, 1 *de inofficioso testamento*, 1 *de gradibus et adfinibus*, 1 *de officio praefecti urbi*; Callistratus 4 *de iure fisci*; Ulpian 1 *de officio praefecti urbi*, 1 *de officio quaestoris*; Arcadius 1 *de muneribus*, 1 *de officio praefecti praetorio*; Aquila 1 *responsorum*; Gallus 1 *de verborum significatione*; Maecianus 1 *ex lege Rhodia*.

[334] The Appendix of works not ultimately read by one of the committees comes to 110 books, excluding two each from Labeo's *posteriora* and Scaevola's *digesta* read by the Sabinian and Papinian committees respectively at the end of their initial masses: chapter 5 nn. 18–20.

[335] Above, nn. 83–4.

[336] Above, nn. 312–29.

[337] Mantovani (above n. 4) 98.

role is important but not comparable in scale to that of Ulpian. Ulpian leads groups amounting to 479 books, Paul to 58. Papinian rather than Ulpian may be the lead author in the adultery group (vi). Macer heads *iudicia publica* (viii), Menander military law (xxxv), Neratius his *responsa* group (xvii) and either Gaius or Marcianus the *formula hypothecaria* group (ix).

The author-groups are naturally headed by their respective authors: Ulpian (iii), Julian (iv), Papinian (xii), Tryphoninus (xviii), Modestinus (xxxii), Iavolenus (xxxiii). The genre-groups have a variety of leaders. Florentinus heads the institutional group (v), Neratius the *regulae* group (vii) in the Sabinian mass. Paul heads the *quaestiones*, *responsa* and *sententiae-iuris epitomae* groups (xiii, xiv, xvi) in the Papinian mass, Gaius the legal history group in that mass (xxii). Celsus leads the Celsus-Marcellus *digesta* group (xxxi) in the edictal mass. In groups of this type Paul is the most prominent author. He heads groups amounting to 88 books.

(5) Unattached Works

The 19 per cent of unattached works consist of those that do not appear to belong to a group constituted by subject-matter, authorship or genre. They include the codal sequences in the Sabinian and Papinian masses that consist largely of *libri singulares*. In the original BK Ordo *libri singulares* or shortish works, mainly by Gaius, Ulpian and especially Paul, ran in the Sabinian mass between BK Ordo 68 and 89 and in the Papinian mass between BK Ordo 224 and 244 and from 249 to 262. Even if some of these works are of indeterminate mass,[338] and a few belong to subject-groups,[339] long sequences of *libri singulares* remain, including some grouped by subject-matter. Thus, there are at least 10 *libri singulares* of Paul,[340] three of Ulpian[341] and one of Rutilius Maximus[342] between BK Ordo 68 and 89. There are at least 13 *libri* of Paul,[343] three

338 Above n. 333. 339 Above n. 258.

340 Paul 1 *ad legem Fufiam Caniniam*, 1 *de libertatibus dandis*, 1 *de liberali causa*, 1 *de iure codicillorum*, 1 *de centumviralibus iudiciis*, 1 *de adulteriis*, 1 *ad orationem divi Antonini et Commodi*, 1 *ad orationem divi Severi*, 1 *de variis lectionibus*, 1 *de poenis militum*.

341 Ulpian 1 *pandectarum*, 1 *de officio curatoris reipublicae*, 1 *de officio consularium* (BK Ordo 85, 88, 89). 342 Rutilius 1 *ad legem Falcidiam* (BK Ordo 68).

343 Paul 1 *de cognitionibus*, 1 *de concurrentibus actionibus*, 1 *de usuris*, 1 *ad SC Turpillianum*, 1 *ad SC Libonianum*, *ad SC Claudianum*, 1 *de poenis paganorum*, 1 *de forma testamenti*, 1 *de tacitis fideicommisis*, 1 *de instrumenti significatione*, 1 *ad SC Tertullianum*, 1 *ad SC Orfitianum*, 1 *ad legem Falcidiam* (BK Ordo 225, 226, 227, 228, 230, 231, 233, 235, 237, 238, 239, 240, 241) Mantovani (n. 4) 99–100.

of Gaius,[344] and one of Marcianus[345] between BK Ordo 224 and 244, and six of Paul[346] and one of Ulpian[347] between BK Ordo 249 and 262. The plan was to place minor works at the end of the Sabinian and Papinian masses. It is true that the *posteriora* of Labeo end the Sabinian mass, but this work was probably a late arrival, not part of the original assignment.[348]

On the other hand the edictal mass ends with an assortment of unattached works by a variety of authors, many represented by only one work. Does this coda to the edictal mass possess a structure? After the group *ad legem Iuliam et Papiam* (BK Ordo 162–167) we have, apart from two *libri singulares* that are clearly in the wrong mass,[349] 49 or 50 books in the last part of the edictal mass beginning at BK Ordo 168, omitting BK Ordo 169 and 170[350] and proceeding from BK Ordo 171 to 179 (Macer 2,[351] Menander 4, Tarrutienus Paternus 4, Tertullian 1, Modestinus 4, Rufinus 12 or 13, Callistratus 2, Papirius Iustus 20). This sequence includes the subject-group on military law by Menander and Tarrutienus, since in both cases their only surviving work was on military law. That makes 49 or 50 books, perhaps two more, since it is possible that Aelius Gallus and Iulius Aquila also belong here.[352] Like Menander, Papirius, Paternus and Rufinus they are one-work authors. The grouping, if any, was not by subject-matter, authorship, or genre, except in the sense that a number of one-work authors were grouped together. The Modestinus work does not fit this pattern, but given that his *de poenis* (between BK Ordo 165 and 177) is detached from the rest of his works, which come in the earlier sequence BK Ordo 137–151, it would not be surprising if it was a late arrival.

A number of unattached works come earlier in the Sabinian and Papinian masses. In the Sabinian mass Paul *de dotis repetitione*[353] comes

[344] Gaius 1 *de tacitis fideicommissis*, 1 *ad SC Tertullianum*; 1 *ad SC Orfitianum* (BK Ordo 242, 243, 244); Mantovani (above n. 4) 100.

[345] Marcianus 1 *ad SC Turpillianum*; (BK Ordo 229); above n. 310.

[346] Paul 1 *de iure libellorum*, 1 *de articulis liberalis causae*, 1 *de iuris et facti ignorantia*, 1 *de iure singulari*, 1 *de officio adsessorum*, 1 *de officio praefecti vigilum* (BK Ordo 250, 251, 252, 253, 255, 256); Mantovani (above n. 4) 101.

[347] Ulpian 1 *de officio praefecti vigilum* (BK Ordo 257); above nn. 322–3.

[348] Chapter 5 below nn. 72–95.

[349] Gaius 1 *ad legem Glitiam* (BK Ordo 169); Paul 1 *ad legem Cinciam* (BK Ordo 170); above nn. 157–8, 260.

[350] Above, n. 349.

[351] BK Ordo 168; above nn. 108–11.

[352] Above, nn. 232–6.

[353] BK Ordo 33; Mantovani (above n. 4) 91.

between the Julian group and Paul *de adsignatione libertorum.*[354] Paul *de adsignatione libertorum*, in turn, comes before Ulpian *de officio proconsulis.*[355] Paul *de portionibus quae liberis damnatorum conceduntur* and *de conceptione formularum*[356] come between the *regulae* group[357] and *iudicia publica.*[358] These insertions cannot be explained by subject-matter, authorship or genre. The explanation rests either with numerical balance,[359] or with filling a gap when one senior commissioner was waiting for a colleague to catch up and embark on the next group of works. If the 60 *libri singulares* of Paul were fairly evenly distributed between the Sabinian and Papinian masses, as seems likely,[360] these committees could have been free to insert one or more of these *libri* between groups in order not to waste time.

In the Papinian mass a similar insertion can be noted. Gaius *liber singularis de casibus*[361] is inserted between the *sententiae-iuris epitomae* group[362] and the Neratius *responsa* group.[363] Since the Papinian is Gaius' basic mass,[364] the Papinian committee may have been free to insert one of his *libri singulares* at a convenient point in their reading to avoid a gap or make up a numerical balance between the five books of Paul and the six of Hermogenianus in the *sententiae-iuris epitomae* group.

The edictal mass is different in that it contains no sequence of *libri singulares* and no unattached *libri singulares* whose position in the mass has been confirmed.[365] It consists, up to the commentaries *ad legem Iuliam et Papiam*, of a series of groups with no intermediate works other than Paul four *ad Vitellium* and two *de iure fisci*, between the group *ad Plautium* and the Celsus-Marcellus *digesta* group, and Ulpian three *de officio consulis*, between the Celsus-Marcellus *digesta* group and the Modestinus works. In both these cases I have argued that the explanation is numerical. These unrelated works were added at the end of one group and the beginning of another to make up an even number of books conveniently divisible between two commissioners.[366] But how are we to explain the sequence of works between the Iavolenus group

354 BK Ordo 34; Mantovani (above n. 4) 91.
355 BK Ordo 47.
356 BK Ordo 49, 51; Mantovani (n. 4) 91.
357 BK Ordo 36–46.
358 BK Ordo 52–56.
359 Above, nn. 22–6, 56–7, 80–4, 180–4, 294–5.
360 Above, nn. 249–87.
361 BK Ordo 215; Mantovani (above n. 4) 99.
362 BK Ordo 206–214.
363 BK Ordo 217–218.
364 Above, nn. 138–61.
365 Papinian 1 αστυνομικος, Gaius 1 *ad legem Glitiam* and Paul 1 *ad legem Cinciam* (BK Ordo 111, 169, 170) are of uncertain mass (Mantovani (n. 4) 94, 97) and should go in the Papinian mass (Papinian and Gaius) or in the Sabinian or Papinian mass (Paul).
366 Honoré (2004, above n. 2) 39–40; above nn. 180–4.

(BK Ordo 152–153) and the commentaries *ad legem Iuliam et Papiam* (BK Ordo 162–167)? The sequence begins with Pomponius' 39 books *ad Quintum Mucium* and includes his 15 books *variarum lectionum* besides Proculus' 11 books of *epistulae*, Callistratus' six *de cognitionibus* and Tertullian's eight books of *quaestiones.* Mantovani considers Callistratus' four books *de iure fisci* and Paul's two *de censibus* (BK Ordo 158–159) to be of uncertain mass.[367] The sequence cannot exactly be described as a Pomponius group, though his works dominate it and so justify treating the edictal mass as his basic mass. The various works in this group, if it is a group, are not related by subject-matter or genre. It is tempting to think of a numerical pattern by which, disregarding the works of uncertain mass,[368] the 39 books of Pomponius *ad Quintum Mucium* balance the 40 following books by him and others.

V. Conclusion

The thrust of this chapter has been to show that the distribution by Tribonian of authors and works to the three Digest masses and the consolidation of four-fifths or more of the books in groups within the masses formed part of a coherent and sophisticated scheme. The scheme was designed to ensure that the best texts were selected for inclusion in the Digest and that the work proceeded quickly, thus giving effect to the instruction in C. Deo Auctore 14 to the commissioners charged with the Digest project: *tam suptili quam celerrimo fini tradere.*

[367] Mantovani (above n. 4) 96.

[368] The unattached Paul 2 *de censibus*, of which we have only one text at the end of the title *de censibus*, is not likely to belong in the edictal mass. It should have been and perhaps was in a subject-group with Ulpian *de censibus* in the Sabinian mass.

4

Editing the Digest

I. Introduction

In 1973 I published an essay on the editing of the Digest titles.[1] It was concerned to quantify the extent to which in compiling the Digest the editors displaced texts that they received in the order in which they are thought to have been read and excerpted by the three committees appointed for the purpose, commonly known as the Sabinian, Papinian and edictal committees. That order is called the Bluhme-Krüger or BK order.[2] A further concern was to classify the displacements, and so to distinguish texts moved to form an introduction or code to a title or mass from those displaced within a mass or transferred to another mass. An ancillary aim was to list texts that Krüger had, according to his own criteria, mistakenly treated or failed to treat as displaced in the notes at the beginning of each title of the stereotype edition.

The time has come to review and supplement the essay in view of recent scholarship and fresh thoughts. There are, for example, some modifications to make to the BK order. An incisive study by Mantovani[3] and one of mine on the principles by which authors and works were allocated to the three committees[4] require some changes to be made or doubts to be expressed about the exact order in which the works were read. An updated version of the BK order that takes account of these developments was attached to my 2006 article on the distribution of authors and works and appears in this book as Addendum A.[5] In counting displaced texts I now adopt the view, in contrast with the 1973 article, that, when a group of texts has been displaced by way of introduction or coda, the number of texts forming the introduction or coda determines

[1] 'The Editing of the Digest Titles' 90 *SZ* (1973) 262–304.

[2] Based on F. Bluhme, 'Die Ordnung der Fragmente in den Pandecktentiteln' *ZGR* 4 (1820) 257–420.

[3] D. Mantovani, *Digesto e Masse Bluhmiane* (1987).

[4] Chapter 3 above.

[5] Below pp. 151–61.

the number of displacements, irrespective of whether the texts displaced remain in the BK order *inter se*. The reason for this change is that, when the editors decided to move a group of texts to form an introduction or coda, they were entitled to do so in the order that seemed to them most appropriate. Once the editors had decided to displace the texts, there was no special reason to keep them in the BK order.

Another change is that in certain groups of works read together (the commentaries on adultery, *fideicommissa*, and the *lex Iulia et Papia*), some doubt attaches to the subdivisions in the original BK order that are meant to present the sequence in which the texts were read. I have taken the liberty of omitting some alleged displacements recorded by Krüger that depend on accepting these questionable subdivisions of groups. In addition the present contribution analyses the titles and lists the displaced texts in more detail. For each book and title of the Digest it gives in Addendum B an updated analysis of the title according to the masses from which the texts are derived. The analysis includes a listing of the displaced texts with their inscription, and, when the displacements are from one mass to another or within a given mass, it also lists the preceding and following texts. After the analysis of each book the Schedule records the initial mass for each title and the number and types of displaced texts to be found in that book.

Complete agreement on the identification of displaced texts is not to be expected, but a reasonable approximation to the truth and, in particular, to the number and types of displacement, can throw light on the thinking of the compilers.

This review is supplemented by a study of the linking of texts. It analyses the sequences of linked texts created by the compilers, their resort to linking expressions, and their insertion in the Digest of short but largely authentic phrases taken from classical authors. These matters, which were not explored in 1973, throw light on the extent to which the compilers felt free to juxtapose and link classical texts. What changes of arrangement, balance and sequence did they think themselves entitled to make?

II. Character of the Digest

The Digest titles (*ius*) were designed to be read along with the corresponding titles of Justinian's Codex of legislative enactments (*lex*). Like them, they were edited with a view to presenting a coherent picture of a certain type of law: juristic law as opposed to imperial enactments. An overall view of juristic opinion had not previously existed because, in contrast with imperial enactments, later juristic opinions did not supplant earlier ones. The opinion of a highly regarded jurist did not, apart from the 426 Law of Citations,[6] displace that of one less highly regarded. Conflicts of juristic opinion persisted irrespective of priority in time and prestige. The Digest, building on the Fifty Decisions and other imperial enactments designed for the purpose, was meant to put an end to conflicts of juristic opinion. This was impossible so far as legislative enactments were concerned. However coherent Justinian's Codex might be, future legislation might and in fact did amend it.[7]

Our knowledge of how the Digest co-ordinated juristic law, to the extent that it did, is limited. Bluhme's analysis of 1820 remains important.[8] Among other insights he established that the compilers were content to list texts rather than to generalize them in the manner of a modern code. My earlier treatment of the subject[9] was in its time an advance and remains to some extent valid. Mantovani has since convincingly distinguished three stages in the editing of the texts selected for inclusion in the Digest.[10]

Though the Digest was not a codification in the modern sense, it possessed some elements of a code. For instance, the compilers intervened by shifting texts and linking them in sequence. On the other hand they often declined to intervene by adding even a few words to a text on their own initiative. In this contribution an effort is made to assess the balance between intervention and non-intervention. It lists in detail (a) the sequences that the editors seem to have linked together,[11] (b) the brief modifying phrases that they attributed to classical authors to ensure that the resulting sequence of texts ran smoothly[12] and (c) the texts that they displaced from their original position in the masses into which the books to be read were divided.[13] On what view of juristic law did the balance of intervention rest? That bears on the still controversial question of the extent to which the Digest commissioners altered the original texts, the problem of so-called 'interpolation'.

Bluhme pointed out that the compilers did not try to analyse the principles of the law in the manner of modern codes.[14] They were

[6] CTh. 1.4.3 (7 Nov 426). [7] C. Tanta 18. [8] Above n. 2.
[9] Above n. 1. [10] Above n. 3 at p. 115. [11] Below nn. 20–118.
[12] Below nn. 119–30. [13] Addendum B.
[14] Bluhme (above n. 2) 359–67.

content to present most of the texts in the order (the BK order)[15] in which they had been excerpted as part of the Sabinian, Papinian and edictal masses and the late arrivals known as the Appendix.[16] That is true of over four-fifths of the texts. The total number of Digest texts is on my count 9,139, arranged in 50 books and 432 titles. In each title all the texts but one could have been moved by the editors from their position in the BK order. There were therefore potentially 8,707 movable texts. The number of texts actually displaced from the BK order comes on a careful recount to 1,532.[17] The exact number clearly depends on what is taken to the have been the original Bluhme-Krüger order and which texts are in positions that are not consistent with that order. That is to some extent a matter of scholarly judgment. To help scholars to assess the evidence an updated version of the BK order is attached in Addendum A. On a considered view the number of displaced texts is just over a sixth of the total possible.[18] Most texts remained in the order in which they had originally been excerpted.

The role of the excerpting committees was vital both to the preservation of each text and, in most cases, to its position in relation to other texts. Only a twentieth of the material read was excerpted. A text that was not excerpted was lost to the Digest. Indeed, in the conception of Justinian and Tribonian, it was lost for ever. Nearly five-sixths of the texts that were preserved were kept in the position in which they were excerpted. The position of these texts in the Digest depended on the assignment of authors and works to the committees charged with excerpting texts, and the order in which they were read,[19] rather than on their relationship to the substance of the law or its historical development.

At the excerpting stage the members of the Sabinian, Papinian and edictal committees selected texts for inclusion in the Digest. These texts were each assigned to a title. The editorial process followed when the excerpting stage was complete, apart from the excerpting of texts from works that belong to the Appendix. The excerpting stage played a part in

[15] There are updated versions of this in Mantovani (above n. 3) 90–103 and Addendum A below.

[16] On the Appendix see below chapter 5.

[17] This figure is arrived at by counting the displacements in the 50 individual books of the Digest, listed in Addendum B below. This makes an increase of over 8 per cent on the figure of 1,416 out of 8,695 given in the 1973 article. The increase consists mainly of texts introducing a title, which on the system of counting explained above turn out to be more frequent than seemed originally to be the case.

[18] 17.6 per cent against 16.2 per cent in the 1973 study.

[19] On which see chapter 3 above.

the editorial process not merely by eliminating 95 per cent of the original material but by the choice of texts which, it was envisaged, the editors might later link in sequence.

III. Linking Texts: the Excerpting Stage

About 409 passages seem to have been chosen at the excerpting stage with a view to being linked later by the editors in the titles to which the texts were assigned.[20] The excerpters appear to have taken the view that not only individual texts but some combinations of texts were needed in order to present an accurate picture of the law. The combinations envisaged were drawn from the texts of different authors, apart from six sequences confined to two works of a single author that were read together. These six came from certain books of Gaius *ad edictum provinciale* and *ad edictum urbanum*[21] and of Paul *ad edictum praetoris* and *brevia.*[22]

The sequences were drawn from texts that dealt with the same subject-matter. To read them together was the key to selecting the best texts on the subject. Brackets in the BK Ordo indicate texts that were read together. The brackets are broadly reliable, but there are exceptions, especially in the Papinian mass. Thus *Pauli sententiae* and *Hermogeniani iuris epitomae* should have been bracketed, since they were read in sequence in five successive sections,[23] and so should the earlier books on *fideicommissa*,[24] and the works by Gaius and Pomponius on legal history.[25] Authors writing on the same topic often copied one another, and legal authors were no exception. But though the texts of two or more authors might run parallel most of the way, the excerpters were on the lookout for variations, which could be significant even if they amounted only to a few words.

The linked sequences usually link the whole or part of just two texts. When only the beginning or end of a text is part of a sequence, I have indicated this in the footnote citation with pr., fin. etc. Sometimes, however, a sequence runs to more than two texts. The second or later members of a sequence appear (and are meant to appear) in the edited version

[20] Below nn. 21–2, 54–76.
[21] D. 19.1.19–20; 29.4.13–16; 35.2.73.5–74.; 35.2.77–78; 35.2.80–81 pr.
[22] D. 16.1.11–12. [23] BK Ordo 205–214. [24] BK Ordo 194–198.
[25] BK Ordo 247–249.

of the Digest as a comment on or modification of the first. The second text is sometimes intercalated between two separated parts of the first, the inscription to which returns in the third member of the sequence. These excerpts were mostly made with a view to their being combined later by the editors of the Digest titles. From the excerpters' point of view, there was little point in excerpting the second or later text except to serve as a comment on or modification of the first. But the linking words were nearly always added at the editorial stage. To make the intended link clear the editors inserted words and phrases such as *at,*[26] *dummodo,*[27] *eadem dicemus,*[28] *ergo,*[29] *haec ita si,*[30] *hoc est,*[31] *id est,*[32] *idem est,*[33] *itaque,*[34] *(et) ideo,*[35] *inde,*[36] *item,*[37] *nam,*[38] *nec,*[39] *nisi,*[40] *plane,*[41] *proinde,*[42] *quia,*[43] *quin etiam,*[44] *quod si,*[45] *quoniam,*[46] *sed et,*[47] *sed et si,*[48] *sed si,*[49] other *sed* expressions,[50] and *veluti.*[51] Sometimes the link word or expression is inappropriate to the author to whom it is attributed.[52] The above incomplete list of links resembles the linking terms inserted between texts that belong to sequences created by the editors of the titles from the texts assigned to the title but which were not read together at the excerpting stage.[53] That gives us a reason to think that the words and phrases linking books read together and those not read together were generally added at the editorial stage.

The number of links cited above (409) is not an exact figure. Potential links may have been noted at the excerpting stage that were not in fact linked when the Digest was edited. Sometimes the editor of a title will have linked texts that the excerpters had not seen as a potential

[26] D. 37.5.11. [27] D. 3.3.2. [28] D. 45.1 4. [29] D. 4.6.22; 14.6.5.
[30] D. 23.1.5. [31] D. 38.10.2.
[32] D. 4.3.10; 6.1.74; 23.4.15; 35.1.88; 40.12.15.
[33] D. 7.9.6; 9.4.25; 17.1.13. [34] D. 21.1.32; 28.8.2. [35] D. 8.5.5.
[36] D. 50.16.184. [37] D. 2.6.2; 3.1.4; 3.4.6; 41.1.6; 44.4.3.
[38] D. 3.5.20; 4.3.22; 4.8.4; 7.9.2; 10.2.6; 15.1.20; 32.48; 38.2.7; 39.1.4; 47.2.51.
[39] D. 6.1.70; 11.7.25; 16.1.5; 37.15.6; 39.4.2; 43.19.2.
[40] D. 3.3.26; 4.4.10; 41.1.4; 42.5.10. [41] D. 3.4.4; 4.4.14.
[42] D. 9.2.22.
[43] D. 2.14.11; 3.5.14–6; 11.1.3; 11.3.12; 12.2.10; 14.6.10; 18.1.5.
[44] D. 3.6.2. [45] D. 4.4.26; 5.3.26; 6.1.14; 11.7.11; 47.10.2.
[46] D. 3.2.5; 40.12.2. [47] D. 4.6.24; 14.3.6; 46.4.10.
[48] D. 13.5.4; 29.4.9; 32.6; 36.1.9; 37.5.9; 37.9.2; 39.2.29; 41.2.7; 42.8.5.
[49] D. 2.9.6; 4.8.24; 29.3.7; 49.1.2.
[50] D. 1.14.2; 13.1.11; 15.3.4; 30.31; 46.3.42. [51] D. 11.7.23; 43.26.3.
[52] Even when the link word is inappropriate to the author to whom it is attributed. Thus *proinde*, which in the sense 'hence' is specifically Ulpianic (Honoré, *Ulpian*, 2002, p. 46 nn. 42–7), is inserted in a Paul text in D. 9.2.22.1 to link it to a preceding Ulpian text.
[53] Below nn. 80–116.

combination. Moreover judgements sometimes differ about whether texts that follow one another in the Digest and come from works that were read together are meant to be linked. But the suggested figure is not likely to be far from the truth. Most texts that were read together at the excerpting stage and later linked in the Digest were excerpted because of that possibility.

Even when combinations potentially noted at the excerpting stage unite texts from different authors, as is usual, they do not count as texts displaced from the BK Ordo. The combinations arise from the fact that at the excerpting stage a number of works, including the commentaries *ad Sabinum* and *ad edictum*, were read together or in parallel. This enabled the excerpters to link passages from different authors relating to the same subject. Thus the commentaries *ad Sabinum* yield 90 linked sequences of passages read together at the excerpting stage. In 56 a text from Paul *ad Sabinum* follows on and adds to or modifies one from Ulpian *ad Sabinum*.[54] There are just seven in which an Ulpian *ad Sabinum* text follows and adds to or modifies a text from Paul *ad Sabinum*.[55] In 14 sequences Pomponius *ad Sabinum* follows and is linked to Ulpian *ad Sabinum*.[56] There is one reverse sequence.[57] The linked sequence Paul *ad Sabinum*–Pomponius *ad Sabinum* is found 10 times,[58] and the reverse Pomponius–Paul *ad Sabinum* twice.[59] Since the chronological order is Pomponius–Paul–Ulpian there are 80 sequences in reverse chronological order against 10 in chronological order. This shows that the texts *ad Sabinum* were normally read in reverse chronological order. The same is true of the commentaries *ad edictum*.[60]

[54] D. 1.14.1–2; 2.9.5–6; 2.11.11–12 pr.; 7.1.13.8–15 pr.; 7.1.15.7–17 pr.; 7.4.5–6; 7.4.8–10 pr.; 7.4.10.8–11; 7.8.4.1–8 pr.; 9.2.44.1–45 pr.; 13.6.10.1–12 pr.; 17.2.7–9; 17.2.9–13; 17.2.16.1–17 pr.; 17.2.35–37; 17.2.45–47 pr.; 17.2.55–57; 18.1.9–11 pr.; 18.1.14–15; 18.1.22–24; 18.1.47–49; 18.2.2–3; 18.2.6.1–8; 21.2.17–19 pr.; 21.2.25–26; 23.3.10.6–11; 23.3.21–22; 23.3.36–38; 24.1.1–2; 24.1.11–13 pr.; 24.3.12–13; 25.1.1.3–3 pr.; 25.1.5.3–6; 29.2.13–14; 30.30.7–31; 32.47.1–49 pr.; 32.71–73 pr.; 33.6.11–12; 33.9.3.11–4 pr.; 34.2.23.3–25 pr.; 36.1.19–20; 36.3.8–9; 37.3.9.7–10; 39.1.10–11; 39.2.33–34; 39.2.35–37; 45.1.3–4; 45.1.26–27; 45.1.43–44; 47.2.3.2–5 pr.; 47.2.5.1–6; 47.2.11–12 pr.; 47.2.23–24; 47.2.27–31 pr.; 47.7.7.7–8 pr.; 47.10.30.1–31.

[55] D. 7.1.24–25 pr.; 28.5.12–13; 29.2.1–2; 30.52.1–53; 36.1.20.2–21; 36.2.1–2; 45.1.2.6–3 pr.

[56] D. 7.1.68.2–70 pr.; 7.8.6–7; 13.7.4–5; 17.2.14–16 pr.; 18.2.4.6–5; 18.2.11.1–13 pr.; 23.1.4–5; 23.3.4–5; 23.3.14–15; 26.2.12–15; 33.8.6–7; 45.1.26–27 pr.; 45.3.5–7 pr.; 46.2.6–7.

[57] D. 45.1.12–13.

[58] D. 6.1.69–71; 8.2.26–27; 8.3.21–22; 12.6.13–14; 21.1.47–48 pr.; 24.3.15.2–17 pr.; 25.2.3.4–4; 41.1.29–30 pr.; 43.26.14–15; 46.4.9–10.

[59] D. 18.1.4–6 pr.; 45.1.23–24.

[60] 241 antichronological to 47 chronological: below nn. 63–75.

This was a wise policy, since the most recent writing is likely to be the most complete. The compilers were not ignorant of the historical order of the writings they read but, though obsolete laws were to be omitted,[61] they were not concerned to record the historical development of the law. They were told not to be selective in their assessment of lawyers' opinions,[62] so that an excerpt from Paul might properly be linked to a text of Ulpian, though Paul, as the author of the earlier commentary *ad Sabinum* or on the edict, could not have taken account of what Ulpian was later to say. On the other hand Ulpian could have taken account of what Paul had said and decided to omit the passage restored by the compilers. If the Digest text returned to Ulpian's commentary after the excerpt from Paul, that was not because the passage as a whole represented Ulpian's view (or Paul's or any other jurist's), but because it presented what the compilers judged to be a correct statement of the law, drawn from reading the works together irrespective of their historical sequence. One of the contrasts between *ius* and *lex* was that a later enactment (*lex*) would override an earlier to the extent of any inconsistency, while a later juristic opinion (*ius*) would not. The task of the compilers was to record correct opinions or combinations of opinion, not necessarily the most recent.

For the edictal commentaries it is convenient to take the sequences excerpted by the Sabinian and edictal committees separately. The Sabinian committee excerpted 61 sequences of texts read together that are linked in the Digest. In 36 a Paul text is linked to a preceding Ulpian text.[63] There is one reverse linkage.[64] In 18 a Gaius text is linked to a preceding Ulpian text.[65] There is one counter-example.[66] Five Gaius texts are linked to a preceding Paul text,[67] with no reverse linkage.

[61] C. Deo auctore 10: *sed si quae leges in veteribus libris positae in desuetudinem abierunt, nullo modo vobis easdem ponere permittimus.*

[62] C. Deo auctore 6: *sed neque ex multitudine auctorum quod melius et aequius est iudicatote, cum possit unius forsitan et deterioris sententia et multos et maiores in aliqua parte superare.*

[63] D. 12.2.23–25; 13.1.10.3–12; 13.4.3–4 pr.; 13.5.3.2–4; 13.5.5.10–7; 13.5.14.3–15; 13.5.16.4–18 pr.; 13.6.1.2–3 pr.; 13.6.10.1–12 pr.; 13.7.13.1–14; 14.3.3–5 pr. ; 14.3.5.18–7 pr.; 14.4.1.5–3 pr.; 14.4.5.19–6; 14.5.18–7 pr.; 14.6.7.16–9 pr.; 14.6.9.4–11; 15.1.19.2–21 pr.; 15.1.30–31; 15.3.3.10–4; 15.3.7.5–8; 16.1.2.5–4 pr.; 16.3.1.47–4; 17.1.8.10–10 pr.; 18.4.4–5; 22.1.21–23 pr.; 24.3.22.13–23; 25.2.11.3–13; 27.3.9.7–10; 29.4.8–9; 37.5.8.6–10 pr.; 37.5.10.2–12 pr.; 37.9.1.28–3; 38.7.2.4–3; 47.7.7.7–8 pr.; 50.16.183–184.

[64] D. 12.2.17.3–18.

[65] D. 13.4.2.8–4 pr.; 13.7.9.5–10; 13.7.11.7–12; 14.1.1.25–4 pr.; 14.3.1–2; 14.3.7.2–10 pr.; 15.1.9.8–10; 15.3.3.10–4; 16.1.4.1–5; 17.1.12.17–13; 18.4.11–12; 21.1.25.10–27; 29.3.2–3; 29.3.6–7; 37.4.8.14–9; 38.2.6.4–8 pr.; 39.4.12.2–13 pr.; 47.2.50.4–51.

[66] D. 38.10.1.7–2.

[67] D. 17.2.1–3 pr.; 17.2.65.6–66; 18.4.14.1–15; 23.4.14–16; 38.1.18–20 pr.

The edictal committee excerpted about 223 combinations of texts read together that are linked in sequence in the Digest. In 123 a Paul text is linked to a preceding Ulpian text[68] and in 24 the reverse is true.[69] There are 42 in which an Ulpian text is linked to a following Gaius text,[70] with 14 contrary examples.[71] A Gaius text is linked to a preceding Paul text in 13 cases.[72] The order is reversed in five.[73] There is one Paul-Callistratus[74] and one Callistratus-Ulpian edictal link.[75]

[68] D. 2.4.4.3–5; 2.4.8.2–10 pr.; 2.7.1.2–2 pr.; 2.7.3.2- 4 pr.; 2.8.12–13; 2.9.1.1–2 pr.; 2.11.2.9–4 pr.; 2.13.4.5–5; 2.13.6.10–7 pr.; 2.14.10.2–13 pr.; 2.14.17.7–21 pr.; 3.1.3.3–6 pr.; 3.2.4.4–5; 3.2.15–17; 3.3.1.3–2 pr ; 3.3.3–4; 3.3.5–7; 3.3.19–24; 3.3.25–26; 3.3.35.3–36; 3.3.51.2–53; 3.4.3–4; 3.4.5–6 pr.; 3.5.5.14–7 pr.; 3.5.19–20 pr.; 3.6.1.4–3 pr.; 4.2.3.1–4; 4.2.14.15–15; 4.3.1.8–6; 4.3.9.5–11 pr.; 4.3.11.1–12; 4.3.13.1–15 pr.; 4.3.21–22; 4.4.9.6–10; 4.4.13.1–15; 4.6.5.1–7; 4.6.21.3–22 pr.; 4.6.23.4–26 pr.; 4.6.26.9–28 pr.; 4.7.4.6–7; 4.8.3.3–6; 4.8.7.1–9 pr.; 4.8.9.5–11 pr.; 4.8.11.5–12; 4.8.15–16 pr.; 4.8.21.12–22; 4.8.23.3–24; 4.8.25.2–26; 4.8.27.7–28; 4.9.3.5–4 pr.; 5.3.13.15–16 pr.; 5.3.18.1–19 pr.; 5.3.23.1–25 pr.; 5.3.25.20–26; 5.3.27.1–28; 5.6.1–3 pr.; 6.1.1.3–2; 6.1.3.2–4; 6.1.13–15; 6.1.15.3–16 pr.; 6.1.73–75; 6.2.1.2–3 pr.; 6.2.3.1–7 pr.; 6.2.9.6–10; 7.9.1.7–2; 7.9.5.3–6; 8.5.4.8–6 pr.; 9.2.5.3–7 pr.; 9.2.9.4–11 pr.; 9.2.13.3–15 pr.; 9.2.21.2- 22 pr.; 9.2.23.11–25 pr.; 9.2.25.2–26; 10.2.14.1–15; 10.2.20.9–22 pr.; 10.2.22.5–24 pr.; 11.1.2–3; 11.3.1.5–2; 11.3.3.1–4; 11.3.5.4–8; 11.3.11.2–12; 11.3.13–14 pr.; 11.5.1.4–2 pr.; 11.6.1.2–2 pr.; 11.6.5.2–7 pr.; 11.7.2.9–3; 11.7.10–11; 11.7.22–23; 11.7.24–27 pr.; 12.2.3.4–5 pr.; 12.2.7–9 pr.; 12.2.9.7–11 pr.; 13.5.3.2–4; 15.1.44–45; 20.1.6–8; 21.1.1.11–4 pr.; 21.1.38.14–42; 27.6.1–3; 27.6.7.4–8; 28.8.1–3; 35.3.1.15–3 pr.; 35.3.3.10–4 pr.; 36.1.38.2–40; 37.15.5–7 pr.; 39.1.3.4–4; 40.12.14.2–16 pr.; 40.12.18–20 pr.; 41.2.6–7; 42.4.3.-5 pr.; 42.4.8–9 pr.; 42.5.9.8–11; 42.5.17–19 pr.; 42.5.19.1–22 pr.; 43.3.1.18–2; 43.5.1.11–3 pr.; 43.16.1.48–3 pr.; 43.17.1.9–2; 43.19.1.12–3 pr.; 44.4.2.7–3; 47.10.1.9–2; 47.10.7.8–9 pr.; 47.10.9.4–10; 47.10.15.49–17 pr.

[69] D. 2.7.2.1–3 pr.; 2.14.13.1–15; 2.14.21.5–23; 2.14.25.2–26; 3.2.12–13 pr.; 4.3.20–22; 4.3.29–30; 4.8.16.1–17 pr.; 5.3.22–23 pr.; 5.3.32–33 pr.; 5.3.36.5–37; 6.1.10–11; 6.1.21–22; 9.2.22.1–23 pr.; 10.2.9–12 pr.; 10.4.10–11 pr.; 21.1.30.1–31 pr.; 27.9.3.6–5 pr.; 39.3.9.3–10 pr.; 41.2.1.22–2; 44.2.12–14 pr.; 44.4.1.3–2 pr.; 47.10.8–9 pr.; 47.23.2–3 pr.

[70] D. 2.1.7.5–8; 3.1.1–3 pr.; 3.2.2.5–4 pr.; 3.3.8.3–13; 3.6.5.1–6; 4.2.5–7 pr.; 4.3.5–6; 4.3.7.10–8; 4.9.1.8–3 pr.; 5.3.9–10 pr.; 5.3.16.7–17; 5.3.20.21–21; 5.5.1–2; 6.1.39.1–40; 6.2.7.17–9 pr.; 8.2.5–6; 9.2.3–4 pr.; 9.2.7.8–8 pr.; 9.3.1.10–4; 10.1.2.1–4 pr.; 10.2.2.5–4 pr.; 10.2.18.7–19; 11.7.12.6–13; 20.1.8–9 pr.; 21.1.12–13; 21.1.19.6–20; 21.1.21.3–23 pr.; 21.1.23.9–24; 21.1.25.10–27; 21.1.31.25–32; 28.8.5.1–6; 39.2.7.2–8; 39.2.28–29; 39.4.1.6–3 pr.; 40.12.1.2–3 pr.; 40.12.3.3–5 pr.; 40.12.5.1–6; 40.12.10–12 pr.; 43.26.2–3; 47.9.1.5–3 pr.; 50.16.10–12 pr.; 50.16.43–44.

[71] D. 2.14.28.2–29; 3.2.18–19; 3.3.12–13; 3.3.34–35 pr.; 3.6.4–5 pr.; 4.7.1.1–3 pr.; 5.3.1–3; 9.2.4.1–5 pr.; 10.2.5–6; 10.2.17–18; 11.1.5–6 pr.; 11.7.5–6 pr.; 21.1.18.2–19 pr.; 45.1.74–75 pr.

[72] D. 2.8.4–5; 2.11.7–8; 2.14.17.7–19 pr.; 2.14.19.1–21 pr.; 4.4.14–15; 4.8.19.2–21 pr.; 5.3.34–35; 9.4.22.4–23; 9.4.24–25; 10.2.25.22–26; 10.3.1–2 pr.; 12.2.20–21; 42.8.4–6 pr.

[73] D. 4.3.26–28; 4.4.25–26 pr.; 4.5.8–9; 10.1.3–4 pr.; 42.5.1–3.

[74] D. 2.6.1–3.

[75] D. 4.7.1.1–3 pr.

Some 32 other linked texts seem to have their origin in books read together at the excerpting stage.[76]

The combinations were unevenly distributed among the committees. The Sabinian committee was responsible for about 169, the Papinian committee 17, and the edictal committee 226. No doubt the figures are uneven partly because the edictal committee read more edictal commentary than the Sabinian committee. But 90 combinations come from commentaries *ad Sabinum*, which were read by the Sabinian committee. Perhaps the Sabinian committee was somewhat less keen to link texts than the edictal committee. The same is true of texts duplicated at the excerpting stage. Of the 59 duplicates that may go back to the excerpting stage, 42 were excerpted by the edictal committee, 11 by the Sabinian committee, five by the Papinian committee and one as part of the Appendix.[77] These differences at the excerpting stage may reflect the fact that, as I have suggested,[78] the edictal committee was headed by a law professor. Law teaching called for the techniques of combining and repeating texts more than did practice.

IV. Linking Texts: the Editorial Stage

An important activity of the editors was to combine texts. They did this both by inserting links into the 409 sequences that the excerpters had selected as potentially suitable for combination,[79] and by linking texts in another 487 sequences that were not drawn from texts on the same topic originally read together. In this way they could introduce in the second or later text a phrase that made it read as a comment on the preceding text, though it was not so in the original.

As regards the second group of sequences, it can be argued that all 1,532 texts moved from their BK Ordo position were moved so as to

[76] Sabinian mass (15): D. 1.6.3–4; 1.8.2.1–4 pr.; 1.8.5.1–6 pr.; 5.1.68–70; 39.6.4–5; 40.9.12.7–14 pr.; 41.1.1.1–3 pr.; 41.1.3.2–5 pr.; 41.1.5.7–7 pr.; 41.1.7.13–8; 46.3.41–42; 48.5.9.1–10 pr.; 48.5.21–23 pr.; 49.1.1–2; 49.11.1.4–2. Papinian (16) 1.2.1–2 pr.; 1.15.1–3 pr.; 17.1.23–25; 32.5.1–6 pr.; 34.5.5.1–7 pr.; 35.1.87–89; 36.1.3.5–5; 36.1.6.6–7; 36.1.8–9 pr.; 36.1.9.3–10 pr.; 36.1.15.8–17 pr.; 40.5.25–26 pr.; 40.5.26.11–27; 40.5.31.4–32 pr.; 42.1.49–50; 48.2.9–10. Edictal (1) 2.6.2–3.

[77] Bluhme, who counts fewer duplications, gives figures of 34 for the edictal mass, 12 for the Sabinian and three for the Papinian: above n. 2 at p. 345.

[78] Above ch. 2 nn. 77–8.

[79] Above nn. 20–78.

make a point of law by juxtaposing two or more texts that were not originally related to one another. In a sense that is true. Here, however, we focus attention on the 487 cases in which texts not originally read together were not merely displaced from their BK Ordo position but linked by expressions showing that they were meant to be read as modifying or supplementing one another.

The following list of linking expressions relates to texts not originally read together, but includes mixed sequences of three or more texts, two of which were originally read together but at least one of which was not. When there is a sequence of three or more texts the list records only the introductory words of the second text. I have taken phrases of this sort to include the following: *cui consequens est,*[80] *ergo,*[81] *hoc est,*[82] *id est,*[83] *idem et si,*[84] *idem(que) est/erit/fiet/esse,*[85] *(et) ideo,*[86] *ideoque,*[87] *immo,*[88] *ita tamen si/ut,*[89] *item,*[90] *longe magis,*[91] *et magis,*[92] *nam,*[93] *nec,*[94] *nisi,*[95] *non tamen,*[96] *plane,*[97] *proinde,*[98] *quare,*[99] *quemadmodum,*[100]

[80] D. 15.1.17–19 pr. [81] D. 1.3.39–40; 7.5.2–4 pr.; 8.3.4–5 pr.; 38.5.6–8.

[82] D. 38.10.1.7–3 pr.

[83] D. 19.1.13.31–16; 28.5.38.5–40; 33.10.1–2; 47.6.1.3–2.

[84] D. 16.1.17.2–18; 29.1.22–23.

[85] D. 1.5.15–16; 6.1.33–35 pr.; 8.2.36–37; 12.2.11.3–12; 13.5.5.10–7; 14.3.13.2–14; 16.2.11–12; 20.4.6.2–7 pr.; 24.1.13–14; 26.2.26.2–27; 28.2.14.2–15; 28.6.18.1–19; 29.1.7–8; 29.5.10–11; 34.3.13–14; 34.5.16–18 pr.; 37.4.1.9–2; 38.2.14.11–15; 42.8.1.2–3 pr.; 45.1.59–60.

[86] D. 1.3.10–11; 1.3.20–21; 1.3.26–28; 1.16.7.2–8; 3.3.77–78 pr.; 14.3.11.8–12; 17.2.25–26; 19.2.22.3–23; 37.5.1.3–3 pr.; 39.1.5.20–6; 45.1.14–15.

[87] D. 7.2.1.4–2; 23.2.6–7; 28.2.4–6 pr.; 40.3.33–34.

[88] D. 33.5.6–7; 43.30.1.5–2. [89] D. 6.1.1.1–3; 36.1.27–28 pr.

[90] D. 8.3.2.2–3; 19.2.21–22 pr.; 20.6.5.3–6 pr.; 33.7.16–17; 44.2.7.5–8; 44.2.9.2–10; 45.3.7.1–8; 49.15.2.2–3. [91] D. 27.4.1.8–3 pr.

[92] D. 46.3.3–5 pr.

[93] D. 1.1.7.1–8; 1.3.3.1–2; 1.3.4–6; 1.3.12–14; 1.3.37–38; 1.7.20–21; 1.7.38–39; 4.5.5.2–6; 5.2.14–15 pr.; 6.1.25–27 pr.; 8.6.5–6 pr.; 10.4.3.15–4; 12.1.12–13 pr.; 12.2.8–9; 12.6.8–9; 12.6.16–18; 15.3.5.3–7 pr.; 17.2.31–33; 18.3.2–3; 18.4.10–11; 19.5.1.2–4; 20.4.5–6 pr.; 24.1.40–41; 25.2.1–3 pr.; 28.3.4–5; 28.5.15–17; 29.1.29.3–30; 30.88–89; 33.8.1–2; 35.2.1.19–2; 35.2.50–51; 36.1.13.5–15 pr.; 36.2.2–3; 36.2.7.6–8; 37.5.6–7; 38.2.6.4–8 pr.; 39.5.29.2–30; 43.24.1.1–2; 43.24.7.10–9 pr.; 43.24.13.7–14; 45.3.11–12; 50.16.148–149.

[94] D. 1.16.2.1–3; 4.6.19–20; 13.5.19.2–20; 13.7.22.4–23; 16.3.9–10; 26.5.15–16; 33.5.4–5; 36.3.1.20–3; 37.7.6–7; 38.1.16.1–17; 46.3.5.3–6; 48.7.2–3 pr.; 50.10.3–4.

[95] D. 18.4.14.1–15; 34.1.6–7; 41.1.24–26 pr.; 42.8.15–16; 48.5.2.9–3.

[96] D. 21.2.23–24.

[97] D. 12.6.20–22; 17.2.23.1–24; 27.1.28.1–29 pr.; 27.1.41.3–45; 30.33–34; 35.2.34–36 pr.; 36.4.3.6–4; 38.1.13.5–14; 46.1.11–12. [98] D. 13.1.5–6.

[99] D. 15.1.27.8–28; 40.3.1–2. [100] D. 9.2.28.1–29 pr.

quia,[101] *quin etiam,*[102] *quod si,*[103] *quoniam,*[104] *sane,*[105] *sed et,*[106] *sed et si,*[107] *sed si,*[108] other *sed* links,[109] *si(n) autem,*[110] *si tamen,*[111] *si vero,*[112] *unde,*[113] *utique,*[114] *veluti*[115] and *videlicet.*[116] These introductory expressions usually point to a linkage, but the reader must be satisfied in each case that that is intended. On this point judgements may differ. In other instances the combination of the second or later text with the first in a sentence makes clear an intention to link them whatever the precise words used.[117] For instance initial *itaque* and *enim* in the second text points to a linkage, while *autem* less often does so.

[101] D. 2.1.5–6; 7.1.38–40; 9.2.15.1–16; 9.2.34–36 pr.; 10.1.4.11–5; 14.4.7.5–8; 14.6.3.4–5; 15 1.11.9–14 pr.; 24.1.5.18–7 pr.; 24.1.9.2–11 pr.; 24.3.12–13; 26.10.5–7 pr.; 28.5.24–26; 28.7.21–22; 37.5.18–19; 43.24.9.3–10.

[102] D. 23.2.54–55 pr.

[103] D. 4.4.23–24 pr.; 6.1.31–32; 7.1.46–47; 11.7.27.2–28; 12.1.9.9–10; 12.28.10–29; 12.6.17–18; 13.5.1.8–3 pr.; 15.3.2–3 pr.; 17.2.41- 42; 18.4.12–13; 19.2.27.1–28 pr.; 23.3.14–15; 23.3.26–27; 23.3.30–31; 23.3.44.1–45 pr.; 24.3.61–64 pr.; 25.1.9–11 pr.; 26.2.17.2–18; 27.8.2–3; 28.5.79.3–81; 29.2.32.2–34 pr.; 30.58–60; 30.75.4–76; 34.4.3.4–4; 34.4.6.2–8; 38.2.10.1–11; 46.3.13–14 pr.; 49.15.10.1–11.

[104] D. 7.5.9–10 pr.

[105] D. 13.7.16.2–17; 17.1.22.11–25; 46.4.6–7; 47.10.13.7–14.

[106] D. 3.3.58–59; 9.4.5–7 pr.; 9.4.9–10; 13.3.1.1–2; 13.5.3.2–4; 14.3.5.18–11 pr.; 25.2.17.3–19; 27.10.1.1–2; 36.3.2–3.

[107] D. 7.1.21–23; 8.5.2.3–3; 9.2.11.10–12; 9.2.17–20; 10.2.13–14 pr.; 12.4.1–2; 12.6.21–22 pr.; 13.5.11.1–14 pr.; 16.3.3–4; 19.2.11.4–12; 21.2.22.1–24; 24.1.24–25; 24.3.20–21; 33.8.3–4; 34.5.16–18 pr.; 34.7.1.2–2; 37.4.4.3–5; 37.5.2–3 pr.; 38.4.1.8–3 pr.; 40.5.54–55 pr.; 41.2.6.1–7; 43.26.6.4–7; 45.3.9.1–13; 46.1.19–20.

[108] D. 7.1.10–11; 9.2.46–47; 10.1.5–6; 10.3.4.4–5; 11.7.16–19; 15.1.8–9 pr.; 15.1.14–15; 15.1.32.2–35; 16.1.8.15–9; 18.1.12–14; 18.2.9–10; 21.2.27–28; 27.9.5.16–6; 28.5.5–6 pr.; 28.6.9–10 pr.; 30.39.10–40; 30.50.3–51; 30.87–90 pr.; 35.1.61–62 pr.; 35.2.34–36 pr.; 35.2.74–75; 37.10.4–5 pr.; 38.5.6–8; 41.1.24–26 pr.; 43.16.13–14; 43.26.4–5; 44.1.16–17; 45.3.9–11; 47.3.1.3–2; 47.7.10–11; 47.17.1–2; 49.14.31–32; 49.17.19.5–20; 50.1.15.3–16.

[109] D. 1.3.34–36; 1.7.13–14; 1.8.6.5–7; 3.5.3.11–5 pr.; 3.5.8–9 pr.; 3.5.14–15; 5.1.13–14; 7.1.64–65 pr.; 10.3.8.4–10 pr.; 14.5.2.1–4 pr.; 18.1.29–31; 19.2.40–41; 20.1.11.3–12; 23.1.11–12 pr.; 23.3.7.3–8; 23.5.5–6; 27.1.32–33; 27.9.1.4–3 pr.; 28.3.9–10; 31.4–5 pr.; 31.70.3–72; 36.1.11.2–12; 37.10.15–16; 39.3.12–13; 39.3.14.4–15; 39.3.19–20; 41.2.1.22–2; 46.3.41–42; 48.22.7.22–8.

[110] D. 3.5.18.5–20 pr.; 13.7.6.1–7; 21.1.6.2–7; 30.28.1–29; 36.4.1.4–2; 39.1.1.20–2.

[111] D. 4.4.4–5; 30.58–60; 31.24–25.

[112] D. 2.8.4–5 pr.; 13.5.7.1–8; 15.3.8–9; 17.1.11–12 pr.; 29.1.17.4–18 pr.

[113] D. 23.1.2–3.

[114] D. 40.12.20.4–21 pr.

[115] D. 1.1.1.4–3; 8.3.5.1–6; 17.2.76–80; 37.1.3.9–6 pr.; 48.19.6.2–8 pr.

[116] D. 4.6.28.6–29.

[117] D. 1.3.29–30; 1.5.1–3; 1.7.1.1–2 pr.; 1.7.15.3–17 pr.; 1.7.17.5–18; 1.18.10–12; 1.19.1.2–2; 2.4.2–4 pr.; 2.4.18–22 pr.; 3.3.17.2–24; 3.3.37.1–39; 3.3.43.6–45 pr.; 3.3.47–48; 3.5.17–18; 4.1.1–2; 4.2.1–3 pr.; 4.4.1.3–2; 4.5.3–4; 4.4.16.5–18 pr.; 4.4.18.5–19; 4.4.20.1–21; 4.7.8.5–10; 4.8.13.4–16 pr.; 4.8.17.7–18; 4.8.47–49; 5.1.1–2 pr.; 5.1.15–16; 5.1.26–28 pr.; 5.1.50.3–52; 5.1.68–72; 5.1.77–78; 5.2.3–5; 5.3.11–13 pr.; 5.4.3–4; 5.6.77–78; 6.1.27.5–30; 6.1.46–47; 7.1.1–2; 7.1.7.3–9 pr.; 7.2.4–6 pr.;

The listed group of initial phrases are mostly also found in the 409 instances mentioned earlier[118] in which the excerpters, reading works on the same subject together, combined texts from different works.

V. Linking Texts: Short Insertions from Classical Authors

The editors were free to insert suitable phrases to combine texts that were originally independent, especially by linking later with earlier authors. But they were not free to add even short insertions to a text on their own initiative. Short insertions were permissible but only if attributed to the author from whom they purported to be taken. There is therefore a paradox as regards the power of the compilers to change the classical texts. They could and did add linking words and phrases in the 896 sequences listed in this chapter, but they could not and did not add short phrases of their own to ensure that their personal view of the state of the law prevailed. On what was this distinction between permissible and impermissible changes based? The most obvious explanation is that changes

7.2.11–12; 7.4.5.3–7; 7.5.1–2 pr.; 7.8.2–4 pr.; 7.8.10.4–11; 7.8.12.6–13; 8.1.2–3; 8.2.28–29; 8.2.38–39; 8.3.34.1–35; 8.6.20–24; 9.4.33–35; 9.4.37–38 pr.; 11.1.10–11 pr.; 11.5.2.1–3; 12.1.38–39; 12.2.17.3–19; 12.2.20–21; 12.3.5.4–6; 12.5.1.2–2 pr.; 12.5.2.2–4; 13.4.5–6; 13.5.7.1–10; 13.6.5.15–7 pr.; 13.6.8–9; 13.6.15–16; 14.6.1.3–2; 14.6.3.4–7 pr.; 15.1.6–7.1; 15.3.8–9; 16.1.6–7; 16.3.7.2–8; 17.1.3.1–4; 17.1.11–12 pr.; 17.1.35–36 pr.; 17.2.19–21; 17.2.47.1–50; 17.2.52.15–54; 17.2.60.1–61; 17.2.63.10–64; 18.1.16–18 pr.; 18.6.1.2–4 pr.; 18.6.13–15 pr.; 19.1.13.31–16; 19.1.19–20; 19.1.43–45; 19.2.9.6–10; 19.2.15.9–19 pr.; 19.2.33–34; 20.4.5–6 pr.; 21.2.13–15 pr.; 23.2.28–29; 23.4.18–19; 23.5.9.3–11; 24.1.15–16; 24.1.29–31 pr.; 24.1.60.1–62 pr.; 25.2.8.1–10; 25.3.1.16–3 pr.; 26.2.12–15; 26.3.8–10; 26.4.3.10–4; 26.4.6–7; 26.5.5–6; 26.7.3.9–4; 26.7.28–29; 27.1.10.8–11; 27.1.34–35; 27.3.7.1–8; 27.9.3.6–5 pr.; 28.3.1–2; 28.5.21.1–22; 28.5.41–42; 28.5.43–44; 29.1.11.2–13 pr.; 29.2.15–17; 29.2.64–65; 29.3.4–7; 29.5.6.3–7; 29.7.11–13 pr.; 30.17.2–18; 30.41.16–43 pr.; 30.46.1–47; 30.92.2–94 pr.; 33.5.2–3; 33.6.9.4–12; 33.7.10–11; 33.7.13.1–14; 33.8.12–13; 33.8.19.2–20; 34.3.3.5–4; 34.3.16–17; 34.4.11–12; 34.5.5.1–7 pr.; 36.1.24–25; 36.1.41.2–43 pr.; 36.2.10–12 pr.; 36.4.1.4–2; 37.1.1–2; 37.1.7.2–8; 37.5.3.7–4; 37.14.10–11; 38.1.10–12; 38.1.20.1–21; 38.4.3.7–5 pr.; 38.10.3.2–4 pr.; 38.16.6–7; 39.6.3–6; 39.6.14–15; 39.6.42.1–43; 40.2.11–13; 40.3.1–2; 40.5.2–4 pr.; 41.1.14–15; 41.2.44.2–46; 41.8.2–3; 41.8.5–6; 41.2.16–18; 41.2.49.8–50; 42.1.21–22 pr.; 42.1.49–50; 43.19.4.1–5; 43.24.1.11–2; 43.24.4–5 pr.; 43.29.11.-2 pr.; 44.2.15–16; 46.1.6.2–7; 46.2.2–4 pr.; 46.3.1–3 pr.; 46.3.3.1–5 pr.; 46.3.4–5; 46.7.3.10–4; 46.8.10–12 pr.; 47.2.69–71; 47.7.1–2; 47.7.3.8–4; 48.2.8–11 pr.; 48.4.1.1–2; 48.4.3–4 pr.; 48.5.18.7–20 pr.; 48.6.3.6–5 pr.; 48.9.3–4; 48.11.3–4; 48.16.8–10; 48.17.2–3; 48.20.3–5 pr.; 50.1.3–4; 50.1.11–12; 50.16.229–230; 50.17.86–87.

[118] Above nn. 26–51.

of grammar and style to make the Digest read smoothly were allowed, and indeed required.[119] On the other hand the compilers were not in general authorized to change the law except on imperial authority. They were to select the best statement of the law, eliminate what was obsolete, to give effect to imperial legislation, and improve the style when necessary but not to insert their own views. There was a distinction between changes of form and of substance, the former being allowed and the latter, in the absence of official authority for making the change, discouraged. Especially after the Nika rising, however, Justinian's attention was diverted from reforming constitutions. In general, some changes for what seemed better (often presented as *benignius*, *humanius* or *commodius*) were made without the enactment of a constitution, presumably on Tribonian's authority but with Justinian's concurrence.[120]

I list here 147 short insertions, all of which were assigned to their original author as separate texts. The list is confined to phrases of less than ten words, and to phrases that cannot be treated as independent sentences. As edited they rather form part of the preceding sentence by the author of the initial text. They may of course include a linking word or phrase put in by the editors. Short phrases that resume the initial text are omitted, since once the initial text has been interrupted no special significance attaches to the fact that when it is resumed only a short phrase is left. Here is an example. If an oath is offered it must be taken in the terms in which it is offered:

D 12.2.3.4 (Ulp. 22 ed.) Iurari autem oportet, ut delatum est iusiurandum: ceterum si ego detuli ut per deum iurares, tu per caput tuum iurasti

12.2.4 (Paul 18 ed.) vel filiorum tuorum

12.2.5 pr. (Ulp. 22 ed.) non erit ratum habendum iusiurandum

Here D. 12.2.4 counts as a short insertion, in which *vel* may be a linking word put in by the editors, but *filiorum tuorum* comes from Paul's edictal commentary. D. 12.2.5 is not counted as a short insertion since it resumes the text from Ulpian's commentary with which the sequence begins. The reason for selecting phrases that satisfy these conditions is to be sure that the compilers have chosen not merely to ensure that the

[119] Implicit in C. Deo auctore 5: *pulcherrimo opere extruere*; 7: *et omne opus moderatum et quam pulcherrimum ostendatis*.

[120] D. Liebs, *Die Klagenkonkurrenz im römischen Recht* (1972) 32 f, 38–76; Honoré, 'Some suggestions for the study of interpolations' *TR* 49 (1981) 225–49; 'Techniques of interpolations: D. 33.4.15–17' *Sodalitas* 6 (1984) 2723–8.

short insertion is read in conjunction with the preceding text but to incorporate it in that text.

As has often been noticed, some insertions are only of two or three words: *vel filiorum tuorum*;[121] *vel fratres*;[122] *vel fatuo*;[123] *eo loco*;[124] *et clientes*;[125] *item vestis*;[126] *vel omnia sua*;[127] *vel solvendi causa*.[128] That such short texts should be inserted with an inscription giving the name of the classical author and book from which they are taken (or taken subject to a linking word or phrase) shows respect for authority. This applies both to the sequences taken from books read together and those taken from books not so read.

Of these 147 short insertions 79 came from books read together,[129] 62 from works not read together,[130] and six from sequences made up of both.[131] As with other editorial interventions there are more in the early books of the Digest than the later. The insertions are fairly evenly distributed and are consistent with other aspects of editing such as sequences and displacements, as the table below in the Overview section shows.

VI. Three Editorial Stages

At the editorial stage of the compilation, the texts assigned to a given title from the three masses were assembled. The masses were first arranged, Mantovani has shown,[132] in a settled order, which varied from title to title. At a second editorial stage the texts in each title were edited. Now some texts were displaced from the Bluhme-Krüger order, in which they had

[121] D. 12.2.3.4. above. [122] D. 21.1.39. [123] D. 21.1.39.
[124] D. 47.9.2. [125] D. 7.8.3. [126] D. 49.15.3. [127] D. 36.1.16.
[128] D.6.2.4.
[129] D. 2.1.8; 2.6.3; 2.13.5; 2.14.11; 3.1.2; 3.1.4; 3.2.5; 3.2.16; 3.3.4; 3.3.7; 3.3.9; 3.3.11; 3.3.21; 3.3.26; 3.3.52; 4.3.2; 4.3.4; 4.3.10; 4.3.12; 4.3.27; 4.4.10; 4.5.9; 4.6.6; 4.7.2; 4.7.5; 4.8.10; 4.8.22; 4.9.2; 5.6.2; 6.1.40; 6.2.4; 6.2.10; 7.1.14; 7.4.11; 9.3.2; 10.2.21; 11.1.3; 11.3.12; 11.7.13; 12.2.4; 12.2.8; 14.1.2; 14.4.2; 14.6.10; 15.1.20; 17.1.24; 17.2.48; 18.1.5; 18.1.48; 18.2.3; 18.4.15; 20.1.7; 21.1.39; 22.1.22; 23.3.22; 23.4.15; 24.3.13; 24.3.16; 25.1.2; 25.2.4; 28.8.2; 34.2.24; 35.1.88; 35.3.2; 36.1.16; 37.15.6; 39.4.2; 40.12.2; 41.1.2; 41.1.4; 42.5.2; 42.5.10; 42.5.20; 42.5.21; 43.5.2; 43.16.2; 44.2.13; 47.2.30; 47.9.2.
[130] D. 1.1.2; 3.3.18; 4.1.2; 5.1.69; 6.3.2; 7.1.8; 7.2.12; 7.8.3; 8.2.37; 8.6.21; 8.6.23; 9.2.20; 9.2.35; 11.7.19; 13.6.6; 15.1.34; 18.1.17; 18.4.9; 19.1.14; 19.2.16; 19.2.34; 21.2.14; 23.1.3; 24.1.30; 25.2.2; 25.3.2; 26.3.9; 26.5.6; 27.3.8; 27.9.4; 28.5.25; 28.5.39; 28.5.44; 28.8.4; 29.7.12; 30.42; 30.59; 33.7.14; 33.8.13; 34.1.7; 34.3.17; 34.4.12; 38.4.4; 39.5.30; 40.2.12; 40.3.2; 40.5.3; 41.2.45; 41.8.6; 42.1.50; 42.8.16; 46.6.3; 46.8.11; 47.2.70; 47.6.2; 48.5.19; 48.6.4; 48.16.9; 48.19.7; 48.20.9; 48.22.10; 49.15.3.
[131] D. 11.7.25; 11.7.26; 26.2.13; 26.2.14; 39.64; 39.6.5.
[132] Mantovani (above n. 3) 115.

originally been excerpted by the Sabinian, Papinian or edictal committees, and moved within a mass or to another mass or made into introductory or codal texts. At a third editorial stage, up to about Digest book 30, the Appendix texts were added at the end of each title.[133] Up to this point the titles had already been fully edited when the Appendix texts became available and there was no possibility of putting them earlier in the title. From about book 30 there was no third editorial stage because, when the Appendix texts arrived, the titles had been through only the first editorial stage, in which the three main masses were settled in order but not fully edited. Now the Appendix texts were sometimes added before the codal texts, if there were any, as part of a second editorial operation.[134] From book 40 onwards the Appendix texts became available when the first editorial stage had not yet been completed, so that the order of the masses was unsettled. The Appendix could then be placed in whatever position seemed most convenient, even if it preceded one or more of the three original masses.[135] In the eight titles in the last 10 books of the Digest in which the Appendix precedes another mass[136] this is not because it contains more texts than the succeeding mass, which is generally the Papinian.[137] Even at this stage the Appendix is never placed in the first position. From the point of view of the order of the masses the Appendix in some ways remains more like a chance collection of texts than a mass.

The Appendix texts were therefore incorporated in the Digest titles in three different ways,[138] as part of the third, second or first editorial stages, according to how far the editing of the books and titles, into which they were to be inserted, had gone. Moreover there may have been a fourth editorial stage, when the fully edited texts were read over or at least presented to the emperor and, if necessary, corrected before the promulgation of the Digest.

VII. Displacement of Texts

The number of texts that were displaced from their original BK Ordo position, about a sixth of the total, is not negligible. Some were moved from one mass to another, others within a given mass. Some were shifted

133 Up to book 33 (or perhaps 23.3 or 29.5): Mantovani (above n. 3) 114.
134 From book 33 (or perhaps 23.3 or 29.5) onwards: Mantovani (above n. 3) 114–15.
135 From book 40 onwards: Mantovani (above n. 3) 115.
136 D. 40.5,14; 44.1; 46.1,3; 48.10; 49.14; 50.17.
137 In every case except D. 48.10, where it precedes the edictal mass.
138 Mantovani (above n. 3) 109–24.

to form the introduction or coda to a title; others to form the first or last texts of a particular mass. So not only the titles but the masses that composed them could be edited as part of the second editorial operation, probably by the same person or team. A large number of texts, 438, were moved from one mass to another, to the Sabinian,[139] Papinian[140] or edictal[141] masses, or the Appendix,[142] or were put between two masses.[143] A further 345 were moved within a given mass (the Sabinian,[144]

[139] 249 displaced texts: D. 1.1.2,5,7; 1.3.9; 1.5.2; 1.7.13,16,18,20,21,32; 1.8.7; 1.16.5; 1.18.9,10,12; 2.14.60; 2.15.5; 3.3.77; 3.5.42; 4.8.48; 5.1.78; 6.2.16; 7.1.33,39; 7.2.5; 7.4.2; 7.5.2,4; 7.8.3,13; 8.2.29; 8.6.21,23; 9.4.37; 11.7.40; 12.1.8,10,12; 12.4.2; 12.6.9,17,21; 13.5.6,9,12,20; 13.6.9,16; 13.7.7,23; 14.3.14; 14.6.2,4,5,6; 15.3.2,6,9; 16.1.7,18,25; 17.1.23,24,25,28,36; 17.2.28,32,64; 18.1.12,19; 18.4.6,7,8,10,13; 19.1.12,14,16,18,19,20; 19.2.8,12,13,14,21,23,28,37; 20.1.6,7,8,10,12,14; 20.2.3; 20.4.6; 20.5.6; 20.6.4,6; 21.2.14,22,28,35,41,42; 22.5.15,16; 23.2.7,15,57a; 23.3.8,13,26,31,45; 23.4.6,17; 23.5.10; 24.1.25,27,41; 25.2.2,5,14,16,18,20; 26.2.4,9,18; 26.4.4; 26.5.4,11; 26.8.10; 26.10.6; 27.1.24; 27.3.8; 28.1.19; 28.2.5; 28.3.10; 28.5.11,14,18,24,26,30,34,42; 28.6.12,15,23,29; 28.7.12,15; 29.1.8,12,14,18,23,27; 29.2.12,16,19,20,33,48,50,53,56,57; 29.3.5; 29.4.5,7,11; 29.5.2,4,11; 29.7.5; 30.11,27,29,40,42,46,51,58,61,63,83,85,87,90,93,95; 32.46,66; 33.2.2; 33.5.7; 33.6.10; 33.7.11,14; 33.8.13,17; 33.10.4; 34.2.3,4; 34.3.4,6; 34.4.6; 34.5.17; 36.1.25,33; 36.4.2,4; 37.1.8; 37.4.2; 37.5.7,13; 37.9.3; 38.1.14,21; 38.2.15; 38.4.2,4; 38.5.7; 38.16.7; 40.2.8; 40.5.54; 40.9.6; 40.12.21; 42.8.16; 44.1.17; 45.1.60; 45.3.8,12; 46.1.20; 47.7.2,4; 48.1.10; 48.2.9,10; 48.6.4; 48.19.7; 48.20.9; 50.10.4.

[140] 19 displaced texts: D. 1.5.10; 2.4.19,21; 5.1.51; 8.2.37; 8.3.35; 19.1.44; 22.3.2; 22.4.4; 24.1.61; 26.9.4; 27.3.19; 29.7.15; 33.8.20; 35.2.34,35; 39.5.30; 45.1.122; 45.3.23.

[141] 154 displaced texts: D. 1.3.15,16,20,21,22,26,29; 1.5.18,20,24; 1.19.2; 2.4.6; 2.11.6; 2.14.8; 3.3.28,30,38,44,47,60; 3.5.4,8,16,18; 4.2.2,11,17,18; 4.3.19; 4.4.4,8,17,24; 4.5.6; 4.6.19,20,29; 4.8.33; 5.1.14,25,27; 5.2.7; 6.1.34,46,48; 7.4.24; 7.9.4; 8.1.4; 8.2.3,4; 8.3.4,9; 9.2.12,16,18,20,28,31; 9.4.8,9,13,16,18,28; 10.1.5; 10.2.7,13; 10.3.3,5,9; 10.4.4,6,8; 11.1.10; 11.5.3; 1.7.15,17,18,19,26,28,30; 12.1.34; 12.2.18,23,24,25,29; 12.4.11; 16.2.11; 17.2.77,79; 18.1.58; 21.1.5,7,9,11,15,16,34,36; 23.2.28; 24.3.59,61,62; 27.1.11; 28.5.71; 28.7.22,24; 29.1.30; 31.5,6,24; 33.2.17; 34.3.17; 35.2.51; 36.1.42; 36.3.2; 38.10.2; 39.1.18,19; 39.2.3; 39.3.12,15,16,20; 40.4.33; 41.3.7; 41.8.3,6; 42.8.8,11; 43.19.4; 43.24.2,4,8,10,12,14; 43.26.5,7; 43.29.2; 43.30.2; 44.2.8,10,16; 46.6.3; 46.7.4; 46.8.11; 47.2.70; 50.16.89,90,91,92.

[142] 4 displaced texts: D. 23.3.81,82; 34.2.14,17.

[143] 12 displaced texts: D. 1.5.16; 3.5.29; 4.8.41; 26.5.13–14; 28.6.7; 29.7.9; 32.43; 34.3.14; 40.1.10; 40.4.29; 45.1.114.

[144] 207 displaced texts: D. 1.3.12,36; 1.5.4; 1.16.3,8; 2.14.59; 4.3.35,36; 5.1.65,69,71; 5.2.28; 6.1.52,60; 7.1.8,11,21,23,24; 7.2.2,4; 7.4.4,7; 7.8.11; 8.2.16,22; 9.2.42,47; 9.4.34; 12.1.5; 12.5.2,4,5,6; 12.6.16,18,20; 13.1.6; 13.4.6; 13.5.2; 13.7.17,19; 14.3.12; 14.4.8; 14.5.3; 15.1.28; 15.3.14; 16.1.9; 17.1.35; 17.2.13,20,22,24,26,33,34,40,41,42,43,44,49,52,58,59,61; 18.1.17,30; 18.2.8,10; 18.6.2,14; 19.1.5; 19.2.10,16,18,34; 19.5.21; 20.1.9; 20.2.4; 21.2.24; 22.5.17; 23.2.6,10,11,54,59; 23.4.13,18,19; 23.5.2,5,6; 24.1.30; 24.3.2,9,21,28; 25.1.4,10; 25.2.9; 25.3.2; 26.2.3,6,14,16; 26.4.7; 26.5.7; 26.10.2,4; 27.4.2; 27.8.3; 27.9.2,4,6; 27.10.2; 28.2.2,15; 28.3.4; 28.5.5,7,8,16,22,25,39,44; 28.6.9,19; 29.2.41,61,63; 29.5.7; 30.6,18,33,60,76,88,106; 33.2.11; 33.5.5; 33.8.2,4; 33.10.2; 34.4.4,5,8,12; 35.1.59; 35.2.75; 36.1.27; 36.2.3,8,11; 37.4.5; 37.5.2,4,6; 37.10.2,4; 38.1.11,17; 38.2.11,13,22; 38.5.2,4; 40.1.5; 40.2.12,14; 40.5.3; 41.1.25,34; 41.2.37; 43.7.2; 43.26.17; 45.1.15;

Papinian,[145] edictal[146] or the Appendix).[147] Some 438 texts were shifted to form the introduction to a title.[148] Fewer (147) were put at the end of a title or amalgamated title either as a coda or because they were left over by accident or did not fit elsewhere.[149] These include texts ending a title which also end a mass, but exclude 32 displaced texts that would have ended a title had one or more Appendix texts not been added.[150] A small number (24) were moved to introduce a mass rather than a title.[151] Rather more (108) were moved to end a mass[152] without at the same time ending a title.[153]

45.3.10; 46.1.7,12; 46.3.13; 46.4.7; 47.2.11; 47.10.40; 48.5.3,7,15,19,25,27,29; 48.6.2; 48.8.2,6; 48.9.2,4; 48.11.4,6; 48.13.3; 48.16.9; 48.17.3; 48.20.4; 48.22.2,8,10; 50.15.2.

145 27 displaced texts: D. 1.3.35; 2.14.47; 5.2.18; 8.2.39; 12.1.38; 13.7.41; 18.7.7; 22.1.18; 26.2.27; 26.3.9; 27.1.33,39,42; 28.5.80; 29.7.12; 31.68,71; 32.4; 35.1.93; 36.1.55; 37.7.7; 41.2.45; 45.3.25; 46.1.71; 50.1.12,16; 50.17.87.

146 109 displaced texts: D. 1.3.30; 2.4.3; 2.8.10; 2.13.3; 2.14.3,9,24; 3.1.5; 3.2.10; 3.3.18,41,54; 3.5.10,15; 4.1.3,4; 4.2.13; 4.4.2,6,19,21; 4.5.4; 4.6.2,4,9,11,14; 4.7.2,5,7,9; 4.8.14,18,21; 5.1.13,16,29; 5.2.9; 5.3.6,12; 5.4.4; 6.1.25,26,29,32,38; 7.1.47; 8.1.7; 8.2.7; 8.3.6; 8.5.3; 8.6.6; 9.2.35; 9.4.6,10,15; 10.4.2; 11.1.5,7,8; 12.1.33; 12.4.10; 17.1.45; 19.1.34; 19.2.40; 22.1.37; 23.3.61; 26.2.25; 26.5.16; 28.7.26; 28.8.4; 31.9,12,50; 34.5.22,23; 37.14.10,11; 38.10.5; 39.2.2,21,22; 39.3.7; 40.12.21; 41.2.2,7,10; 41.4.8; 42.1.17,20,22,25,26; 42.4.4; 42.5.2; 42.8.2,4,5; 44.1.2,5; 46.1.43; 46.7.9; 46.8.13; 47.2.72; 49.15.3,25; 49.16.2; 50.16.29,149.

147 Two displaced texts: D. 34.4.30; 46.3.90.

148 Below nn. 173–80.

149 80 titles: D. 1.1.11–12; 1.3.41; 1.5.26–27; 1.6.11; 1.16.16; 1.22.6; 2.1.20; 2.4.24–25; 2.8.16; 2.13.12–13; 2.15.17; 3.1.11; 3.2.23–25; 3.5.46–48; 5.1.79–82; 5.2.32; 7.1.64–74; 7.2.12; 7.4.28–31; 7.5.10–12; 7.7.6; 7.9.12; 8.6.25; 10.2.55–57; 11.7.46; 11.8.5; 12.1.41–42; 12.4.13–16; 19.5.26; 22.1.49; 22.3.29; 22.4.6; 22.5.25; 22.6.10; 23.1.18; 25.2.30; 25.3.9; 26.1.14–18; 26.4.11; 26.10.12; 27.5.5; 28.2.30–32; 29.1.42–44; 29.5.24–27; 30.128; 32.43; 33.1.22–25; 33.2.38–43; 33.4.15–17; 33.8.24–26; 33.10.13–14; 34.1.20–23; 34.3.29–31; 35.1.113; 36.1.82–83; 37.6.12; 37.10.16; 37.15.11; 39.2.47–48; 40.9.30–32; 40.10.6; 40.14.6; 42.2.8; 44.3.16; 46.1.73; 46.3.108; 47.2.93; 47.10.45; 47.15.7; 47.23.8; 48.4.11; 48.5.45; 48.18.22; 48.19.41–43; 49.14.50; 50.2.14; 50.12.15; 50.13.6; 50.15.8; 50.17.211. Cf. Mantovani (above n. 5) 60–64.

150 16 titles: D. 2.14.61; 4.3.39; 4.4.45–49; 9.2.42; 11.1.21; 12.6.65–66; 13.5.30; 16.3.32; 21.1.59–63; 22.2.7–8; 22.3.24–26; 23.4.31; 28.5.92; 34.9.24–25; 35.2.93; 36.3.14–17.

151 17 instances: D. 1.3.13; 1.9.8; 4.3.33; 5.2.13; 6.1.68; 12.3.6; 19.5.5–6; 22.5.8; 23.2.21; 24.3.65; 26.3.2; 29.2.68; 34.1.7; 36.1.50; 38.10.8; 46.1.45; 49.14.18–24.

152 64 instances: D. 4.3.38; 4.4.44; 6.1.50; 7.1.56; 7.4.18; 9.2.40; 9.4.32; 12.1.26; 13.4.9; 13.7.35; 15.1.41–43; 16.1.26; 18.1.47–49; 18.1.76; 20.1.27; 20.4.15; 22.1.46; 22.2.6; 22.3.17; 22.5.7; 22.5.23; 24.1.42–44; 27.1.27–29; 27.10.13; 28.2.29; 29.1.28; 29.2.65–67; 29.4.23; 32.70–76; 34.5.19; 35.1.41–42; 35.1.65–69; 35.1. 99–107; 36.3.4; 36.4.12; 37.4.16–17; 37.8.5; 37.9.9; 37.11.9; 38.1.39; 38.8.5–6; 39.6.39; 40.4.58; 40.5.39–42; 41.1.57–58; 42.1.36–39; 42.1.53–54; 42.5.36; 42.8.13; 43.24.19; 44.7.26; 44.7.59–60; 45.3.17; 46.3.50; 46.3.85–87; 46.5.7; 46.6.8; 46.7.11; 48.8.8–9; 48.9.7–8; 48.19.17; 48.19.32; 50.7.14; 50.16.158. On mass codas see 90 *SZ* (1973) 265–6.

153 In another 20 instances the coda of a mass and a title coincide: D. 1.16.16; 1.22.6; 2.13.12–13; 2.15.17; 7.7.6; 11.7.46; 11.8.5; 22.3.29; 22.6.10; 27.5.5; 30.128; 35.1.113; 37.15.11; 46.3.108; 47.15.7; 48.5.45; 48.18.22; 48.19.41–43; 49.14.50; 50.17.211.

The texts moved vary in length and importance, and how they should be classified is at times doubtful. But the general picture is clear. The order of the masses in each title was settled before the title was finally edited in a form that might include texts constituting a coda to the title.[154] So there were stages in the editorial process. The first settled the order of the masses, while at the second stage displacements could be introduced within each mass, or by transferring texts to one mass from another or by displacing introductory or codal texts. Appendix texts might be added at a third stage, or, for later books of the Digest, as part of the second or first.

In practice editorial intervention by way of displacement of texts was limited. In 163 titles out of 432[155] there was no displacement of texts at the second stage. The texts remain in their BK Ordo position, though the excerpters will already have changed them by shortening them and eliminating outdated terms like *mancipatio*. The editors may also have altered texts in the BK Ordo position to fit the context of the title they were editing, without moving them to a different position. In the 163 titles that lack displaced texts a decision was made at the first editorial stage to place the masses in a certain order, but no change in the order of the individual masses was made at the second stage and no texts were moved to form an introduction or coda. Most of these titles have only a few texts, but D.11.3 and 44.4 have 17 each. The texts in these titles were kept in a settled order that derived from the assignment of authors and texts to the masses at the excerpting stage. This was a striking example of the overall policy to make no consistent attempt to state the law in terms of general principles.

For each book or title an initial decision as to the order of masses must have been made by Tribonian or another commissioner or committee. For each title there was also a final editor or committee, which need not have been the same as the one deciding at the first stage. I now deal with the choice of the initial mass in each title.

154 Mantovani (above n. 3) 115.

155 Titles 1.2; 1.4; 1.10; 1.11; 1.12; 1.13; 1.14; 1.15; 1.17; 1.18; 1.20; 1.21; 2.2; 2.3; 2.5; 2.6; 2.7; 2.9; 2.10; 3.4; 3.6; 4.9; 5.5; 5.6; 6.3; 7.3; 7.6; 9.1; 9.3; 11.2; 11.3; 11.4; 11.6; 11.8; 12.7; 13.2; 14.1; 15.2; 15.4; 18.3; 18.5; 18.7; 19.3; 19.4; 20.3; 21.2; 21.3; 25.4; 25.5.; 25.6; 25.7; 26.4; 26.6; 27.2; 27.4; 27.6; 27.7; 28.4; 29.6; 33.3; 33.7; 34.2; 34.6; 34.8; 35.3; 37.2; 37.3; 37.12; 37.13; 38.3; 38.9; 38.11; 38.12; 38.13; 38.14; 38.17; 39.4; 40.3; 40.6; 40.8; 40.13; 40.15; 40.16; 41.5; 41.6; 41.7; 41.9; 41.10; 42.3; 42.6; 42.7; 43.1; 43.3; 43.4; 43.5; 43.6; 43.8; 43.9; 43.10; 43.11; 43.12; 43.13; 43.14; 43.15; 43.17; 43.18; 43.20; 43.21; 43.22; 43.23; 43.25; 43.27; 43.28; 43.31; 43.32; 43.33; 44.4; 44.5; 44.6; 47.1; 47.4; 47.5; 47.8; 47.9; 47.12; 47.13; 47.14; 47.15; 47.16; 47.17; 47.18; 47.19; 47.20; 47.21; 47.22; 48.7; 48.12; 48.14; 48.15; 48.21; 48.23; 48.24; 49.2; 49.3; 49.4; 49.5; 49.6; 49.7; 49.8; 49.9; 49.10; 49.11; 49.12; 49.13; 49.17; 49.18; 50.3; 50.5; 50.6; 50.8; 50.9; 50.11; 50.14.

VIII. The Initial Mass

By the initial mass is meant the first mass in the title, which may be the Sabinian, the Papinian or the edictal but, even in the last 10 books of the Digest, is never the Appendix. A mass is taken to begin with the text or texts that come earliest in the BK order in that mass. The first mass may, however, be preceded by introductory texts from the same or another mass.[156]

In general the initial mass is chosen because its texts exceed the other masses in number, volume or both. When the number of texts in two masses is equal or nearly equal the volume may determine the initial mass,[157] or the Sabinian mass may be put first by way of default.[158] Sometimes the initial mass is fixed by putting the most important text on the subject first.[159] As between two masses, one of which has more texts and the other a larger volume of texts, volume may, again, settle the initial mass.[160]

Titles are mostly arranged in a way that keeps to the general practice of putting the mass with most texts first. Rarely does a mass with a smaller number and lesser volume of texts come first. I have found only 35 titles out of 432 in which this occurs.[161] One reason for the exceptions is that the Papinian mass sometimes comes later although it has a greater number or volume of texts. This is partly because texts from the Papinian mass often concern particular cases (e.g. *quaestiones, responsa*). Some compilers seem to have felt that these would appropriately come after texts that state more general principles.[162] For other exceptions the apparent reason is to put the most important text or texts first in the title, but without treating them as merely introductory.[163] Sometimes the introductory text, once chosen, is followed by the mass to which it belongs,[164] or is the sole text from that mass, which therefore counts

[156] Nn. 173–98 below.

[157] E.g. D. 11.2,11.4; 19.4; 25.7; 26.6; 37.3; 37.12; 38.9; 40.11; 41.4; 41.5; 41.9; 43.8; 43.9; 43.27; 43.23; 47.18; 47.19; .49.9; 49.10; 49.16; 50.2; 50.4; 50.15; Bluhme (above n. 2) 350–1.

[158] D. 20.2,4; 29.7; 38.12; 47.16; 48.10,15,23; 50.5,6.

[159] E.g. D. 42.2; 44.3.

[160] D. 1.4; 11.8; 27.5; 37.8,15; 42.6; 43.6,12,20; 48.16; 50.8.

[161] D. 1.22; 8.2,3,4; 14.2; 18.7; 19.5; 20.1,3; 22.3; 26.3,9; 28.6; 33.1,3; 34.1,9; 37.7,14; 40.5,13,14; 41.7,8,10; 44.6; 45.2; 47.15,20; 48.7,20; 49.15,17,18; 50.1,17.

[162] E.g. D. 18.7; 20.3; 26.9; 33.1; 34.1,9; 37.7; 40.5,13; 44.6; 45.2; 49.17; 50.1.

[163] E.g. D. 20.1; 48.20; 49.15.17.

[164] E.g. D. 14.2; 19.5; 22.3; 28.6; 37.14; 41.7,8,10; 48.7.

as the initial mass.[165] On the whole, however, the editors regularly put the mass with most texts first. It must have been settled policy to do so unless there was a good reason not to.

To fix the initial mass was important, because in a work like the Digest that is not indexed the reader who wants to find the law on a topic has to read the title that deals with that topic from the beginning. It therefore helps if the most important texts come at the beginning or form part of the initial mass. The importance of the first mass is shown by another practice of the Digest editors. Of the 269 titles[166] that were edited by moving one or more texts at the second editorial stage, it is often only the initial mass that is edited by transposing texts within it or adding to it relevant texts from other masses.[167] There are some 129 titles in which only the first mass is edited in this way,[168] and another 33 in which this is true apart from one or more introductory[169] and/or codal texts.[170] Even when the second or third mass is edited by displacing a text, in 28 cases only one text is moved to or within the second or third mass.[171] In these 190 titles, therefore, the initial mass as edited contains the compilers' considered statement of the law on the subject covered by the title, including the exceptions and qualifications they wish to stress. The second and third masses are treated as less important.[172] The texts from the other masses that have not been transferred to the first mass are largely left in the order in which they were excerpted. Of the 432 Digest titles, therefore, in 163 no texts are displaced at the second editorial stage, while in another 190 only the first mass is effectively edited. The

165 E.g. D. 33.3; 40.14; 42.6; 47.15,20; 49.18; 50.1.

166 432 less 163 where there were no displacements at the second stage (above n. 155).

167 Bluhme (above n. 2) 349–50.

168 D. 1.1; 1.7; 1.16; 1.19; 2.4; 2.8; 2.11; 2.15; 3.1; 3.3; 4.1; 4.2; 4.3; 4.5; 4.7; 5.3; 5.4; 6.1; 7.2; 7.5; 7.8; 7.9; 8.1; 8.5; 10.1; 10.2; 10.3; 10.4; 11.1; 12.2; 12.3; 12.4; 12.5; 12.6; 13.1; 13.4; 13.5; 13.6; 14.3; 14.5; 14.6; 15.1; 15.3; 16.1; 16.2; 16.3; 18.2; 18.4; 18.6; 19.2; 20.2; 20.5; 20.6; 21.2 (second part); 22.4; 23.4; 23.5; 24.2; 25.2; 25.3; 26.3; 26.8; 26.10; 27.3; 27.8; 27.9; 28.1; 28.2; 28.3; 28.8; 29.3; 29.4; 29.5; 32 (first and second parts); 33.5; 33.6; 33.7 (second part); 33.8; 33.10; 36.2; 36.3; 37.1; 37.4; 37.5; 37.7; 37.9; 37.10; 37.11; 38.2; 38.4; 38.5; 38.8; 38.16; 39.2; 39.3; 40.1; 40.9; 40.12; 41.3; 41.4; 41.8; 42.4; 43.24; 43.26; 43.29; 43.30; 44.1; 44.2; 44.7; 46.4; 46.5; 46.6; 46.7; 46.8; 47.6; 47.7; 48.1; 48.2; 48.5; 48.6; 48.8; 48.9; 48.11; 48.13; 48.17; 48.22; 49.15; 49.16; 50.4; 50.16.

169 22 titles: D. 1.6; 2.12; 8.4; 14.2; 26.7; 33.9; 34.7; 38.6; 38.7; 38.15; 40.7; 40.11; 43.2; 43.16; 45.2; 46.2; 47.3; 48.3; 48.10; 49.1; 50.4; 50.17.

170 11 titles: D. 1.22; 2.1; 22.6; 23.1; 26.1; 47.23; 48.4,18; 50.2,12,15.

171 28 titles: D. 2.14; 4.4,6,8; 7.1,4; 8.3; 11.7;13.7; 17.1,2; 18.1; 19.1,5; 20.1; 21.1; 23.3; 24.1; 28.5; 29.1,2; 34.3; 38.10; 39.6; 42.5,8; 45.3; 47.10.

172 Bluhme (above n. 2) 368; below nn. 211–16.

view that the Digest is not primarily a codification is specially pertinent as regards the editing of the second and third masses in a title.

IX. Introductory Texts

Sometimes the initial mass does not come at the beginning of the title but after one or more texts that are displaced from their BK Ordo position. This happens in 117 titles,[173] including the 33 mentioned above,[174] in which the editor has moved one or more texts, in view of their importance, to the beginning of the title. In 62 titles the displaced texts come from the immediately following mass, which obviously remains the first mass.[175] Sometimes the introductory text or texts are detached from another mass,[176] the main body of which is not part of the first mass, but constitutes the second or third mass in the title. Even so, the introductory texts are not treated as changing the identity of the first mass. Even if the introductory texts come from two or more masses,[177] this still does not alter the identity of the first mass.

Usually there are only one or a few introductory texts, but in some titles there are six or more,[178] and in one title 21.[179] Even if there are several introductory texts, and they mostly come from a particular mass, they are not treated as constituting the initial mass, which is taken to begin with the text that comes earliest in the BK order for that mass.[180]

[173] Listed in nn. 175–7. [174] Above nn. 169–70.

[175] 62 titles (174 texts): 1.6.1–5; 1.16.1; 1.18.1; 2.8.1; 3.3.1–4; 5.3.1–3; 6.1.1–5; 9.4.1–2; 11.1.1; 12.1.1–2; 13.3.1; 13.7.1; 18.1.1; 19.2.1–2; 22.2.1; 22.4.1–2; 22.6.1–2; 23.1.1–3; 26.1.1; 26.2.1; 27.3.1; 29.1.1–3; 29.2.1–4; 29.4.1; 33.9.1–2; 34.7.1; 37.14.1; 38.1.1–3; 38.2.1; 38.6.1–2; 38.7.1; 39.6.1–7; 40.7.1; 40.11.1; 41.1.1–16; 41.3.1–5; 42.1.1; 42.4.1; 43.2.1; 43.16.1–3; 44.7.1–5; 45.1.1–5; 45.3.1; 46.2.1–2; 46.3.1–8; 47.2.1–8; 47.3.1; 47.10.1–21; 47.23.1; 48.3.1; 48.4.1; 48.5.1; 48.10.1; 48.16.1–3; 48.17.1; 48.18.1; 48.19.1–2; 49.1.1–9; 49.14.1–3; 50.2.1; 50.3.1; 50.12.1.

[176] 23 titles (34 texts): D.1.22.1; 7.8.1; 8.1.1; 8.3.1–2; 8.4.1; 20.1.1–3; 20.2.1; 20.4.1–3; 20.5.1–4; 20.6.1; 22.5.1; 23.4.1; 24.2.1–3; 28.3.1; 31.1; 35.1.1; 38.15.1; 43.26.1; 45.2.1–2; 46.4.1; 47.11.1; 50.4.1; 50.17.1.

[177] 32 titles (230 texts): 1.3.1–7; 1.7.1–8; 2.1.1–6; 2.12.1–2; 2.15.1–3; 4.1.1–2; 5.2.1–5; 7.1.1–6; 12.2.1–13; 12.6.1–3; 13.6.1–7; 14.2.1–2; 15.1.1–21; 16.2.1–2; 16.3.1–10; 17.1.1–16; 17.2.1–5; 19.5.1–4; 23.2.1–2; 23.3.1–3; 24.1.1–21; 26.7.1–15; 28.1.1–17; 28.6.1–2; 30.1–2; 35.2.1–6; 36.1.1–18; 37.1.1–6; 39.1.1–9; 39.5.1–3; 48.1.1–2; 50.1.1–2.

[178] D.1.3; 1.7; 2.1; 7.1; 13.6; 15.1; 16.3; 17.1; 26.7; 28.1; 35.2; 36.1; 37.1; 39.1.

[179] D. 24.1.

[180] In adopting this procedure I differ at times from the practice of Krüger and Mommsen not to asterisk introductory texts in titles when the editor has, for instance, put texts in Sabinian mass taken from commentaries *ad edictum* before texts from

The reason for taking this view is that the editors started with texts presented to them in the BK order.

In the Digest as a whole about 42 per cent of the texts come from the Sabinian mass, 35 per cent from the edictal and 19 per cent from the Papinian. The remainder belong to the Appendix or are of uncertain assignment.[181] In many titles, as one might expect, most texts come from the Sabinian mass, and that mass comes first in the title. Indeed the Sabinian mass comes first in nearly 58 per cent of the titles,[182] the edictal in nearly 38 per cent[183] and the Papinian in just under 4 per cent.[184] The Sabinian mass predominates partly because it is the default choice. No title starts with the Appendix, even when the Appendix texts are most in number or volume.[185] Up to about book 40 the Appendix texts were always introduced after the order of the other masses had been settled.[186]

In some titles the mass with the greatest number of texts does not come first.[187] For instance in D. 8.2, 8.3, and 8.4 the edictal mass comes first, although the Sabinian mass provides more texts. In this and some other books it was decided, presumably at the first editorial stage, that all or nearly all the titles in the book should have the same initial mass, even if that mass did not have the most texts in all the titles.[188] It seems that

commentaries *ad Sabinum* that come earlier in the BK order: D. 13.6.1–7; 15.1.1–21; 16.3.1–10; 17.1.1–16; 26.7.1–15; 28.1.1–17; 38.15.1; 39.1.1–9; 47.10.1–21; 47.11.1. See also T. Honoré (1973), above n. 1, 271–3. My reason is that the editors must always have started with texts arranged in the BK order.

181 On my count Sabinian 3,857/9,147 = 42.17 per cent; Papinian 1,727/9,147 = 18.88 per cent; edictal 3,239/9,147 = 35.41 per cent; Appendix 298/9,147 = 3.26 per cent; uncertain 28/9147 = 0.31 per cent.

182 Sabinian 249/432 = 57.6 per cent: D. 1.1,3–8,14,16,18,20,22; 2.15; 7.1–6,8; 11.2; 12.1,3–7; 13.1,3–7; 14.1,3–6; 15.1–4; 16.1–3; 17.1–2; 18.1–7; 19.1–4; 20.1–6; 21.2; 22.6; 23.1,2 first part, 3–5; 24.1–3; 25.1–6; 26.1–2,4–5,7–10; 27.2–5,7–10; 28.1–5, 7; 29.1–7; 30; 32 second part; 33.1–10; 34.1–2,3–6,8–9; 35.1; 36.1–2,4; 37.1–2, 4–15; 38.1–9,11–17; 39.1,5–6; 40.1–4,7,9,11,13,15; 41.1,5,8–9; 43.7,33; 44.7; 45.1–3; 46.1–3; 47.1–7,11,13–14,16–19,22; 48.1–13,15,17–19,21–24; 49.1–9. 11–13; 50.1–10, 12–15,17.

183 Edictal 163½ /432 = 37.6 per cent: D. 1.9,10,17,19; 2.1–14; 3.1–6; 4.1–9; 5.1–6; 6.1–3; 7.7,9; 8.1–6; 9.1–4; 10.1–4; 11.1,3–8; 12.2; 13.2; 21.1,3; 22.2,5; 23.2 second part; 25.7; 26.3,6; 27.1,6; 28.6,8; 31; 34.7; 35.3; 36.3; 38.10; 39.2–4; 40.5–6, 8,12,14,16; 41.2–4,6–7,10; 42.1–8; 43.1–6, 8–9,11–32; 44.1–6; 46.4–7; 47.8–10, 12,15,21,23; 48.14,20; 49.10,14–18; 50.11,16.

184 Papinian 16½ /432 = 3.8 per cent (D. 1.2,15,21; 14.2; 19.5; 22.1,3,4; 32 first part; 34.5; 35.2; 37.3; 40.10; 43.10; 46.8; 47.20; 48.16); doubtful 3/432 = 0.7 per cent (D. 1.11; 1.12; 1.13).

185 E.g. D. 33.1.17–21; 33.7.5–7 (first part); 44.3.14–15.

186 Mantovani (above n. 3) 109–24.

187 Above nn. 161–5.

188 In books 20, 33 and 45 the Sabinian forms the initial mass in all the titles, although in 20.1, 20.3, 33.1, 33.3 and 45.2 it does not have the most texts.

the order of masses was sometimes decided book by book rather than title by title. For example in book 8 the edictal mass is the initial mass in all six titles. It is true that in 8.1, 8.3, and 8.4 there are one or two introductory texts from the Sabinian mass, but the decision to put them there must belong to the second stage of the editorial process, and so does not make the Sabinian the initial mass. Introductory texts were expressly treated as significant in book 20, where the compilers were instructed to begin the titles with texts of Papinian.[189] The editors have in D. 20.1, 20.2, 20.4, 20.5 and 20.6 moved texts of Papinian to the beginning of the title,[190] while leaving the rest of the Papinian mass to come towards the end. The result is that in all six titles of book 20, despite the introductory texts of Papinian, the Sabinian is the initial mass.

D. 50.17, *De diversis regulis iuris antiqui*, is an unusual title. It was presumably the last to be edited and, perhaps for that reason, not only have very few texts been moved from their original BK order,[191] but the edictal mass, though it has the most texts,[192] comes last.[193] Perhaps texts from the three main masses were originally arranged in the hierarchical order Sabinian-Papinian-edictal, which is the order adopted in D. 50.17, and the person or persons deciding the order of the masses had to rearrange them if he wished them to come in a different order.

The Papinian mass leads off in disproportionately few titles.[194] In about 20, though it has the most or bulkiest texts, it is not put first.[195] The reason varies. Sometimes the most important text in the title,[196] for example an excerpt from the edictal commentary, is put first.[197] In other titles texts from the Papinian mass, many of them turning on an analysis of the facts, are put after more general texts.[198] This was presumably as a matter of editorial policy.

In sum the mass with the most or bulkiest texts is generally put first in a title. A few apparent exceptions are exceptions only if texts that are

[189] C. Omnem s.4. [190] D. 20.1.1–3; 20.2.1; 20.4.1–3; 20.5.1–4; 20.6.1.

[191] Only 50.17.1, 87 and 211.

[192] Sabinian mass 72 texts (50.17.2–72); Appendix 2 (72–73); Papinian 28 (74–101); edictal 111 (102–211); Bluhme (above n. 2) 349. [193] Above nn. 160–4.

[194] Sixteen and a half: D. 1.2,15,21; 14.2; 19.5; 22.1,3,4; 32 first part; 34.5; 35.2; 37.3; 40.10; 43.10; 46.8; 47.20; 48.16.

[195] D. 1.22 (though with one initial Pap. mass text); 18.7; 20.3; 26.3,9; 31; 33.1; 34.1; 34.9; 36.1 (but with 17 initial Pap. mass texts); 37.7; 40.5; 40.13; 42.6; 43.6; 44.6; 45.2; 46.1; 49.17; 50.1. [196] E.g. D. 42.6; 43.6.

[197] E.g. D. 44.6. [198] Above n. 162.

displaced to form an introduction are included in the count.[199] A long text that dominates the discussion of the topic may reasonably be put first. Problems that depend for their solution on special facts are not usually put early in a title. Given the overall aim of providing a collection of texts that in each title runs from the more important and more general to the more specific, the choice of the initial mass in the 432 titles of the Digest can nearly always be defended.

Another way of analysing how the 432 titles begin is to note that nearly 60 per cent of them start with a text of Ulpian. This is hardly a matter of chance. Ulpian was consciously selected as the lead author for most topics. As Soubie hinted,[200] the contribution of Ulpian to the Digest in terms of the volume of texts from his work (over 40 per cent), the number of texts that introduce titles (nearly 60 per cent), the rubrics adopted as title headings, and the precedent that his oeuvre afforded for the project as a whole, is not acknowledged in the constitutions composed by Tribonian. If anything really counted as a 'predigest' it would be Ulpian's oeuvre. Of the 258 titles[201] in which he provides the first text, many come from his Sabinian[202] or edictal commentaries, the latter excerpted either by the Sabinian[203] or the edictal[204] committee. Most of the initial texts from his other works, apart from those on fideicommissa,[205] the lex Iulia et Papia,[206] the office of consul,[207] and perhaps the urban prefect and quaestor[208] come from works assigned to the Sabinian committee.[209] Not

[199] E.g. D. 39.1, where the order of masses, leaving aside introductory texts, is Sabinian-edictal, but the nine introductory texts include seven from the edictal mass, which gives it a majority for the title as a whole.

[200] A. Soubie, *Recherches sur les origines des rubriques du Digeste* (1964) 100–1.

[201] 59.7 per cent of the total of 432.

[202] 46 titles: D. 1.14,16,20; 7.3,4,5,6; 12.3,7; 13.1; 18.3,6; 19.1; 21.2; 24.1; 25.1; 26.4,5,8; 27.10; 28.2,4,5,6; 31; 33.4,5,6,9; 34.3; 38.4,16,17; 40.1,3,4,9; 41.9; 45.1; 46.1,2,3; 47.1; 48.13; 50.7,14.

[203] 66 titles: D. 2.15; 12.1,4,6; 13.3,5,6,7; 14.1,3,4,6; 15.1,2,3,4; 16.3; 18.7; 19.3; 25.3,4,5,6; 26.7; 26.10; 27.2,3,4,5,7,8,9; 29.1,4,5,6; 36.4; 37.1,4,5,6,7,8,9,10,11,12,13; 38.2,3,5,6,8,9,11,14; 40.5; 41.10; 42.3,4; 46.5; 47.3,4,5; 48.23; 49.5.

[204] 97 titles: D. 1.9,17,19; 2.2,3,5,7,9,10,13,14; 3.1,3,5,6; 4.1,2,3,4,6,9; 5.1,2,4,5,6; 6.1,2; 7.2,8; 8.5; 9.1,2,3; 10.4; 11.3,4,5,6,7,8; 21.1,3; 27.6; 28.7; 30; 35.3; 39.1,2,3,4; 40.12; 41.7; 42.6,8; 43.1,2,3,4,5,6,9,11,12,13,14,15,16,17,18,19,20,21,22,23,24,25,26,27,28,29,30,31,32; 44.1,2,3,5,6; 47.9,10,12,15; 49.16,17; 50.1,16.

[205] Three titles: D. 32; 36.1,3.

[206] One title: D. 25.7.

[207] One title: D. 49.10.

[208] Two titles: D. 1.12,13.

[209] 42 titles: De adulteriis 48.5; De appellationibus 49.1,2,3,4,7,9,11; De censibus 50.15; De officio curatoris rei publicae 50.12; De officio proconsulis 37.14; 40.13; 47.14,17,18; 48.3,4,18,24; 50.3; De omnibus tribunalibus 2.12; 34.1; 50.13; Disputationes 28.7; 41.8; 48.19,21; 50.8; Institutiones D. 1.1,4; 8.3,4; Opiniones 37.15; 47.13; 50.2,5,6,9,10; Regulae 2.1; 48.15; Responsa 40.11.

surprisingly, an initial text taken from Ulpian is sometimes an introductory text rather than the start of a mass.[210]

X. Second and Third Masses

The second and third masses were usually arranged so that the number or volume of texts in the second mass was greater than in the third. But there is some vacillation as regards the position of the Papinian mass, which had an ambiguous status. In rank it was the second mass, but as regards number and volume of texts it was usually the third, and the policy of putting case law towards the end of each title supported relegation to the third position even when the number or volume of texts from the Papinian mass was considerable. There are, however, six books (1 to 5, 50) in which the Papinian mass more often comes in the second position. In these the order Sabinian-Papinian-edictal (SPE)[211] or edictal-Papinian-Sabinian (EPS)[212] occurs in 25½ titles and the order SEP (Sabinian-edictal-Papinian)[213] or ESP (edictal-Sabinian-Papinian) in only 10,[214] though overall in the Digest the order SEP occurs in 111 titles against 24 with SPE and ESP in 51 titles against 27 with EPS. In some of the titles in these six books where the Papinian mass often comes second it has fewer texts[215] or is less voluminous[216] than the third mass. At the beginning and end of the editorial process the editors seem to have taken a more hierarchical view of when it was appropriate to put the Papinian mass second in a title.

XI. The Consistency of the Editorial Process

As suggested, the unit for editing seems to have been a book rather than a title or titles. This is expressly stated as regards the book on mortgage and pledge (*liber hypothecariae*).[217] In books 8, 20, 33 and 45 the initial mass is the same in all the titles, although these books include titles in which it is not the mass with most texts.[218] Some books are more highly

210 E.g. D. 1.12; 8.3; 8.4.
211 D. 1.3, second part,4,7; 50.1,2,5,7,8,15,17.
212 D. 1.9; 2.4,8,14; 3.1,2,3,5; 4.2,3,4,6,8; 5.1,2,3.
213 D. 1.18; 2.15; 50.4,9.
214 D. 2.1,10,11; 3.4; 5.4; 50.11.
215 D. 1.9; 4.3,6; 5.1,3; 50.8,15,17.
216 D. 2.7; 4.2.
217 C. Omnem 4, referring to Digest book 20.
218 Above nn. 187–9.

edited as regards the displacement of texts than others. As one might expect, the percentage of texts shifted falls off as the editing proceeds,[219] since the later books have more texts than the earlier ones.[220] But there is no more than a slight decline in the total number of texts shifted as the editing proceeds.[221] Perhaps a time limit was prescribed for editing each book.

The level of editing remains fairly consistent throughout. Book 1, with 22 titles, has six titles with introductory[222] and six with codal texts.[223] Book 50, with 17 titles, has six with introductory and five with codal texts. The pattern set from the start by which the longer titles and many shorter titles have introductory and/or codal texts persists with few exceptions[224] throughout the Digest. But this does not exclude some variation between books. As mentioned above there was unevenness in the treatment of the Papinian mass.[225] The Appendix was not really treated as a mass.

So far as the editors shifted texts, they concentrated on shifting them within or into the first mass or the introduction to a title. As mentioned 438 texts were shifted to introduce titles.[226] From other masses 316 were moved into the first mass.[227] Another 273 texts were moved within the first mass.[228] Thus, of the 1,532 texts displaced by the editors in all, 1,027, or two-thirds of the total, were shifted within or moved to the first mass or formed an introduction to it. The editing of the first mass

[219] Books with percentage of displacements in brackets: 1 (33), 2 (18), 3 (18), 4 (20), 5 (18), 6 (19), 7 (31), 8 (15), 9 (23), 10 (12), 11 (17), 12 (29), 13 (21), 14 (14), 15 (39), 16 (22), 17 (35), 18 (12), 19 (22), 20 (29), 21 (14), 22 (24), 23 (18), 24 (28), 25 (20), 26 (24), 27 (14), 28 (24), 29 (22), 30 (20), 31 (10), 32 (11), 33 (18), 34 (16), 35 (14), 36 (21), 37 (18), 38 (15), 39 (18), 40 (8), 41 (16), 42 (15), 4 (16), 44 (10), 45 (9), 46 (11), 47 (19) , 48 (18), 49 (14), 50 (4).

[220] The lowest number of texts are in books 14 (77 texts), 15 (87 texts), 16 (90 texts), 25 (67 texts), and 31 (89 texts), the highest in books 40 (330 texts), 46 (308 texts), 48 (349 texts), and 50 (628 texts).

[221] Number of displaced texts: book 1 (69), 2 (35), 3 (31), 4 (49), 5 (32), 6 (18), 7 (51), 8 (23), 9 (25), 10 (13), 11 (17), 12 (53), 13 (26), 14 (10), 15 (32), 16(19), 17 (50), 18 (20), 19(32), 20 (27), 21 (20), 22 (29), 23 (38), 24 (40), 25 (12), 26 (48), 27 (19), 28 (62), 29 (53), 30 (26), 31 (9), 32 (11), 33 (35), 34 (29), 35 (31), 36 (38), 37 (29), 38 (28), 39 (34), 40 (23), 41 (34), 42 (24), 43 (19), 44 (15), 45 (18), 46 (34), 47(42), 48 (52), 49 (23), 50 (25). There are 346 displacements in books 1–10; 286 in books 11–20; 347 in books 21–30; 267 in books 31–40; 286 in books 41–50.

[222] D. 1.3,6,7,16,18,21.

[223] D. 1.1,3,5,6,16,22.

[224] An exception is book 43 with 33 titles, three of which have introductory and none codal texts.

[225] Above nn. 161–5, 188–9.

[226] Above nn. 172–209.

[227] Into the Sabinian mass 195 texts, edictal 118, Papinian 3.

[228] Sabinian 156, Papinian 4, edictal 113.

dominated the editorial process. The editing of the later masses, and the provision of codal texts to titles and masses, were secondary.

XII. Overview

It may be relevant to compare the linked sequences of books read together and those not read together with the number of displaced texts and short insertions in each five books of the Digest. The figures per five books are on my calculation as follows:

	Sequences read together	*Not read together*	*Total linked sequences*	*Displacements*	*Short insertions*
1–5	109	67	176	216	33
6–10	55	50	105	130	16
11–15	55	55	110	138	14
16–20	31	50	81	148	12
21–25	31	34	65	139	13
26–30	16	64	80	208	14
31–35	14	32	46	115	8
36–40	39	57	96	152	11
41–45	33	38	71	110	13
46–50	26	40	66	176	13
1–50	409	487	896	1,532	147

Tentative conclusions can be drawn from this table. More combinations of texts not originally read together were introduced at the editorial stage than of texts read together at the excerpting stage, but not greatly more. The variation in linkages between series of books is, as one would expect, greater for the combinations from books read together than from books not read together. The latter proceed rather evenly, apart from a modest increase in books 26 to 30 and 36 to 40. But a deeper significance attaches to the fact that the compilers constructed not merely short insertions but many sequences of texts that are not derived from any single classical author. They clearly thought that the sequences they created were accurate statements of the law, but that the true state of the law was to be arrived at by co-ordinating classical texts, or parts of them. This co-ordination amounts to a partial codification of the law of juristic opinion.

The displacements, also, are intended to co-ordinate juristic opinion by placing some texts in a more prominent position than others and by juxtaposing a text, even without linking words, that the compilers regarded as qualifying or supplementing a previous text. Taking these forms of activity together, about a quarter of the Digest texts are subjected to some form of co-ordination.

The activity of the compilers was greatest in the first five books. In these the number of linked sequences drawn from books read together at the excerpting stage, of linked sequences put together at the editorial stage from books not read together, of text displacements and of short insertions, is highest. Although the number of linked sequences declines as the editing proceeds, this is not primarily because the editors' enthusiasm for linkage falls off, but because the sequences from books read together, especially in the edictal commentaries, come mainly in the earlier Digest books. In fact the editing, apart from the first five books, proceeds rather evenly so far as the other linked sequences, displacements and short insertions are concerned, though the number of displacements increases in books 26 to 30.

Can we estimate the scale of editorial intervention? As mentioned above, the number of texts displaced from their BK Ordo position is, at 1,532, just over a sixth. The number of linked sequences created is not dissimilar, though the number of linked texts cannot directly be compared with the number of displacements. The number of linked texts is not simply twice the number of linkages (1,798 = 2 × 899) because often only the beginning or end of a text is linked to another. This fact tends to reduce the total number of linked texts. On the other hand there are a number of linkages of three or more texts. Making allowances for these factors, the number of linked texts must, like the number of displaced texts, be about a sixth. Linkages involve making minor changes to texts in order to link them, which in a sense are 'interpolations'. That conventional but misleading expression covers many different sorts of change in the classical texts: omissions, shortening of texts, the substitution of new for obsolete terms, the incorporation of imperial constitutions, improvements of style, and informal changes approved by Tribonian with Justinian's concurrence. Terms introduced by way of linkage changed the classical texts in a way that has to some extent been quantified in this chapter. The overall subject of interpolation however involves too many complex issues to be dealt with here except in broad terms. Important changes to the classical law were made by omitting 95 per cent of the texts read. The changes sometimes included generalizing a text either by omitting a qualification or by shifting it to a different context from that which it occupied originally. But the scale of changes made must have been consistent with the degree of intervention that we have been able to quantify, with the compilers' concern for adhering to a time scale and with the serious effort they made to find textual authority for the statements of law they endorsed, even when by transposing and rearranging classical propositions of law they in effect changed the law.

XIII. The Editors

It is not possible to determine the identity of the editors of the various Digest books and titles. There were at least two and often three operations in relation to each title—to determine the order of the masses, to edit the title by deciding whether to displace texts from their BK Ordo position and to add material from the late arrivals that make up the Appendix.

At the excerpting stage different patterns of work were exhibited by the edictal as opposed to the Sabinian and Papinian committees in matters such as the linkage of texts[229] and their duplication. In contrast the editorial work seems to have proceeded rather steadily, in a way that does not point to different editorial teams. In an earlier essay I argued that there were three editors or teams of editors and suggested that these be identified with the three committees set up to read and excerpt the texts.[230] But on reconsideration this cannot have been the case. Mantovani has shown that the Appendix works were read at a time when the editorial stage of the enterprise had already begun.[231] So some commissioners must have been assigned to the reading of the Appendix works, others to the editorial task. The existing committee structure cannot have been retained unaltered. The editorial work cannot have been entrusted to the three committees charged with reading and excerpting the various authors and works incorporated in the Digest. A reallocation of tasks was called for, by which some commissioners read and excerpted the Appendix works, until that task was finished, while others concentrated on editing titles and books. Perhaps the most senior commissioners, including the three who were later charged with compiling the Institutes, Tribonian,

[229] Above nn. 76–8. [230] *SZ* 90 (1973) 282–3.
[231] Above n. 3 at p. 115.

Dorotheus and Theophilus, were among those playing a regular part in the editing. There may have been a time-limit for editing a book, and an arrangement by which an editor or editorial team which finished a book early proceeded to edit a later book in advance of the other editors. Further research may lead to greater precision as regards the identification of the individual editors.

5

Late Arrivals. The Appendix Reconsidered

This chapter was written originally as an essay in tribute to my immediate successor in the Oxford chair of Roman law, Peter Birks. Peter owed much to John Kelly, who taught him Roman law, and to Herbert Hart, who commissioned the book on restitution for the Clarendon Law Series and made, he told me, some 500 comments on Peter's first draft. As time went on, Peter's historical and analytical interests dovetailed. He appreciated how Roman texts and classifications could be used not merely as a teaching tool but to build up a branch of modern law. His commitment to the value of law as an intellectual discipline was total.

We were mutually supportive. But the paths of the 26th and 27th holders of the Regius Chair of Civil Law in Oxford ran parallel rather than converged. Peter's Roman-related modern interest was restitution/unjust enrichment, to which he made a fundamental contribution. Mine concerned trusts in the civil law. His classical focus was on early Roman law and the institutional tradition, mine on palingenetic studies and the later Empire. He had, before his sudden exodus, found my renewed attack on the compilation of Justinian's Digest exciting,[1] and the present tribute to the genius of Justinian's minister Tribonian would not come to him as a surprise.

In the course of a complex enterprise such as the compilation of Justinian's Digest in AD 530–533 changes of plan, to meet unexpected snags, are inevitable. This chapter deals with a change of plan on the part of Tribonian, who was in charge of the operation, to confront the fact that there were more works to be read and excerpted by the Digest

[1] P. Birks, 'Roman Law in Twentieth-Century Britain' in J. Beatson and R. Zimmermann (eds), *Jurists Uprooted. German-Speaking Emigré Lawyers in Twentieth-Century Britain* (2004) 257 n. 20.

commissioners than originally envisaged. It concerns the works known as the Appendix and proposes a new theory as to their character.

The term Appendix refers to a group of writings that seemed to fall outside the three main groups of work, termed the Sabinian, edictal and Papinian masses, detected by Bluhme in 1820.[2] Like the three main masses these writings appear in the Digest titles in a regular sequence. That suggests that they were read, excerpted and edited for inclusion in the Digest as an ordered group. In that sense, but only in that sense, they constitute a fourth mass, as Gustav Hugo, who invented the term Appendix to describe them, stressed.[3] But the number of works,[4] books[5] and excerpts[6] in this group is less than for the other masses, and in over three-quarters of the titles in which texts from them occur they come at the end of the title.[7] This explains why the term 'Appendix' has gained currency.

I argue that the Appendix is a composite collection of texts, drawn from all three main masses. It consists, as has long been believed,[8] of works that became available to Justinian's compilers after the reading and excerpting of the main masses had begun. The late arrivals were each allotted to their appropriate main mass, according to a rational system.[9] The committees charged with reading the main masses were however to read these books only when they had finished reading the works originally assigned to them. Through pressure of time, the three committees made only a modest start on the late arrivals. It was then decided to collect the works as yet unread from all three masses and entrust them to an ad hoc committee

[2] F. Bluhme, *ZGR* 4 (1920) 257–420; reprint in *Labeo* 6 (1960) 5096, 235–77, 368–404.

[3] G. Hugo, 'Der von Bluhme entdeckten Reihen sind vier' *Civilistisches Magazin* 6.4 (1837) 512–23 at 514–15; but see D. Mantovani, *Digesto e masse Bluhmiane* (1987) 1–3,16–19,109–24; 'Le masse Bluhmiane sono tre' *Seminarios Complutenses de Derecho Romano* 4 (1993) 87–119. I am much indebted to Mantovani's study but draw different conclusions from it. He comments on and replies to some suggestions in the present essay in 'Postilla 1, Indagini recenti sull'Appendix', annexed to the text of his intervention in our debate in San Ginesio of 17 September 2004 and published in *Alberico Gentili. L'uso della forza nel diritto internazionale* (2006) pp. 275–395 at 343–65.

[4] At least 11 or 12, listed below at nn. 18–20.

[5] Of a Digest total of 1,522 at least 101 or 110, depending on the view taken of the two series of inscriptions for Labeo's *posteriora*, belong to the Appendix: below nn. 18–19.

[6] About 299 out of a Digest total of 9,139 (3.27 per cent).

[7] On my count in 102 out of 127 titles in which there are Appendix texts. There are also 10 to 13 titles in which the Appendix is the last mass but is succeeded by codal texts: below n. 156.

[8] Bluhme (above n. 2) 317.

[9] The works of Pomponius to the edictal committee, to which his works were in principle assigned; those of Scaevola to the Papinian committee for the same reason; those of Venuleius to the Sabinian committee; below nn. 113–17.

to read and excerpt. At the same time commissioners other than those charged with reading the Appendix began to edit the Digest titles. This they did methodically from book 1 onwards, title by title (50 books and 432 titles in all), combining the texts from all three masses. When the ad hoc committee had finished reading the Appendix the editors of the Digest titles inserted the excerpts from them in each title at a point that depended on the progress that had been made in editing that title.[10] In the first half of the Digest, which had by then been fully edited, they inserted the Appendix excerpts at the end of the title. From about the middle, when the editors had settled the order of masses but had not decided how to introduce or end each title, they put the Appendix texts in the penultimate position, before whatever texts were chosen to end the title. From book 40 onwards the Appendix was treated as a fourth mass on a level with the other three. The editors then placed it wherever seemed best in relation to the other masses—not necessarily at or near the end of the title.

A number of problems need to be addressed. What works make up the Appendix? In what internal order do they come? What is their general character? How do the works that constitute the Appendix relate to the main masses? Were there late arrivals that are not part of the Appendix? In which titles of the Digest do Appendix texts appear? In what position, and in what order, have the editors placed them in each title?

I. What Works Constitute the Appendix and in what Internal Order do they Come?

The Bluhme-Krüger *Ordo librorum iuris veteris in compilandis Digestis observatus* (BK Ordo)[11] lists 13 Appendix works, which Krüger put after the Sabinian, edictal and Papinian masses and numbered from 263 to 275. Two, it is generally agreed, should be removed because their listing rests on a single text with a false inscription.[12] These are no. 266 (*Proculi libri III ex posterioribus Labeonis*) and no. 272 (*Valentis libri VII actionum*). As to the first, in D. 33.6.16, '*Idem* [*Proculi*]' is probably a mistake for '*Iavoleni*'. For the second, in D. 36.4.15, '*Valens*' should be '*Venuleius*'. The hypothetical Proculus and Valens works are not listed in the so-called Florentine *Index auctorum*,[13] whereas the existence of

[10] What follows essentially adopts the theory proposed by Mantovani (above n. 3, 1987) 114–16, 123.

[11] Corpus Iuris Civilis (T. Mommsens and P. Krüger (eds) stereotype ed.) I.927–31.

[12] Mantovani (above n. 3, 1987) 109.

[13] Above n. 11 at I.26–28.

the suggested alternatives by Iavolenus and Venuleius is confirmed by inscriptions to 44 and eight Digest texts respectively.[14] That leaves a list of 11 works, about four of which Mantovani expresses doubt.[15] All four can, however, plausibly be defended as members of the Appendix. In the table that follows this list of 11 (or, if the two versions of Labeo's *posteriora* are treated as separate works, 12) defensible works are set out, in accordance with the conclusions I have reached, along with the number of books,[16] texts and lines[17] from each that appear in the Digest. They are set out in the order in which I think they were presented for incorporation in the Digest, with the Bluhme-Krüger number in brackets. The order is marginally uncertain in that the relative position of items 2 and 3 and of 10 and 11 is debatable.[18]

	Work and number of books	*Texts*	*Lines*
1 (BK Ordo 263)	Pauli imperialium sententiarum 2 (out of 6)	6	27
2 (BK Ordo 265)	Labeonis posteriorum a Iavoleno epit. books 2–10 (1–2 in Sabinian mass)	25	328
(BK Ordo 94)	Iavoleni ex posterioribus Labeonis books 2–10 (1–2 in Sabinian mass)	38	419
3 (BK Ordo 264)	Quinti Mucii Scaevolae ορων 1	4	20
4 (BK Ordo 267)	Scaevolae digestorum books 3–40 (1–2 in Papinian mass)	120	3072
5 (BK Ordo 268)	Labeonis pithanon a Paulo epitomatorum 8	34	299
6 (BK Ordo 269)	Pomponii epistularum 20[19]	24	258
7 (BK Ordo 270)	Pomponii senatusconsultorum 5	9	103
8 (BK Ordo 271)	Scaevolae quaestionum publice tractatarum 1	9	158
9 (BK Ordo 273)	Venuleii Saturninii actionum 10	7	57
10 (BK Ordo 274)	Venuleii Saturnini de interdictis 6	20	246
11(BK Ordo 275)	Furii Anthiani ad edictum 1	3	15

[14] Above n. 11 at I.935, 946; Lenel *Palingenesia* 1.299–315.

[15] Mantovani (above n. 3, 1987) 109–12.

[16] 101 or 110 books out of 1,522.

[17] As printed in Lenel's *Palingenesia Iuris Civilis* (1889).

[18] Below nn. 30–7, 47–55. The Table to some extent agrees with that set out by Hugo (above n. 3) 520–1.

[19] Of the texts inscribed to Pomponius epistularum et variarum lectionum, instead of just epistularum, some seem to belong to the edictal mass, where his variae lectiones come at BK Ordo 155. I have not attempted to assign them all to the correct mass, but see Mantovani (above n. 3, 1993) 112–13.

The table serves to bring out the weight that, within the Appendix list, attaches to items 2, 4 and 5, especially to Scaevola's *digesta*, which provides over half the lines from these works: 3,072 out of 5,002 (61.4 per cent).

I deal first with the four works (items 1, 3, 10 and 11) doubted by Mantovani[20] and then with the two (items 2 and 4) the first books of which seem to have been read by the Sabinian and Papinian committees respectively. Then I turn to those works that may belong to the Appendix though they are not listed as such.

The first suspect work is Paul's *imperiales sententiae in cognitionibus prolatae*, an account of cases heard by the emperor Severus in which Paul participated.[21] Of the six books attributed to this work, which is not recorded in the *Index auctorum*, the Digest has only an epitome in two books. It can be assumed that only two were available to the compilers.[22]

Mantovani's reason for doubting whether this work belongs to the Appendix is that of the six texts from it in the Digest, three come at the end of the Papinian mass,[23] and so might be thought to belong to that mass rather than to the Appendix. Two other texts come at the end of the Appendix mass.[24] But Kaiser points out[25] that one of these last two appears in a series of texts that are plainly out of order, and there is reason to suppose that the text is not really the last in the title but was followed by two others the source of which is unknown.[26] The conflict between the remaining *imperiales sententiae* text that comes at the end of the Appendix, D. 35.1.113, and D. 50.16.240, which comes at the beginning should be solved, he argues, in favour of D. 50.16.240. The title 50.16 *De Verborum Significatione* has suffered little editorial intervention, whereas 35.1 has about 20 displaced texts. The sixth text from *imperiales sententiae* (D. 40.1.10) seems more likely to be an insertion in an earlier mass than to constitute the Appendix, since in the title in question there is another Appendix text in its normal position at the end of the title.[27] The case for moving this work to the Papinian mass is therefore weak.[28]

[20] The position of the first two is also doubted by H. Krüger, *Studi Bonfante* (1930) 2.234f.

[21] Mantovani (above n. 3, 1987) 109–10; (1993) 103.

[22] D. Liebs in *HLL* 4 (1997) § 423 no. 79.

[23] D. 28.5.93; 37.14.24; 50.16.240.

[24] D. 35.1.113; 36.1.83.

[25] W. Kaiser, 'Digestenentstehung und Digestenüberlieferung' 108 *SZ* (1991) 330–50 at 339–40.

[26] D. 36.1.84, 85 (Bas. 35.1.84,85).

[27] D. 40.1.26 (Iav. 4 post. Lab.) is the final text in the title.

[28] So also Kaiser (above n. 25) 339–40. Osler thinks that the texts are consistent with the work coming either at the end of the Papinian mass or at the beginning

In any case Paul's *imperiales sententiae* is closely related to his *decreta* in three books, which was excerpted as part of the Papinian mass at no. 222 in the Bluhme-Krüger Ordo. There seem to have been two summaries of his original six-book collection of cases.[29] Had both been available from the outset, they would have been read together as a group, rather than separated by 40 works in the BK Ordo (nos. 222 and 263 respectively). That they were not read together is therefore evidence that the second summary of *imperiales sententiae* became available only later. This conclusion holds even if Mantovani is right in thinking that this work may belong to the end of the Papinian mass or was read separately from any mass rather than the beginning of the Appendix. In general the works of the five authors honoured in the Valentinian Law of Citations (Papinian, Gaius, Ulpian, Paul and Modestinus) will have been available to the Digest commission from the start, but this need not apply to a summary of a work by one of these writers, such as the summaries of Paul's *imperiales sententiae*. It looks like a later arrival and, if it was assigned on arrival to the Papinian committee, it was assigned on the basis that it was not to be read until the reading of the works originally assigned to that committee had been completed.

The next suspect work is Quintus Mucius Scaevola's one book of ορων,[30] from which four texts survive. One of these comes at the end of a title after the Papinian mass.[31] Another follows the Papinian mass but precedes a text from Labeo's *pithana*, item no. 5 in the Appendix list.[32] A third comes after the text from Paul's *imperiales sententiae* in D. 50.16 just discussed and is followed by five Appendix texts.[33] The fourth[34] comes from the most regular of all titles, D. 50.17, after a text from Iavolenus *ex posterioribus Labeonis*, a work which is for good reason to be listed in the Appendix table.[35] There is little doubt that Quintus Mucius' monograph belongs to the Appendix.[36] Osler, on the basis of this fourth text, would place it after Labeo's *posteriora*.[37] This involves holding that the third text, D. 50.16.241, is displaced within the Appendix mass, since it comes before 50.16.242 from Iavolenus *ex posterioribus Labeonis*. Such internal displacements with Appendix texts are not unknown.[38] I have with some hesitation adopted the suggested change of position in the above table.

of the Appendix: 'Following Bluhme: a note on Dario Mantovani, "Digesto e masse Bluhmiane"' *IVRA* 38 (1988) 137–58 at 147.

[29] Liebs (above n. 22). [30] Mantovani (above n. 3, 1987) 110; (1993) 103–4.
[31] D. 43.20.8. [32] D. 41.1.64. [33] D. 50.16.241.
[34] D. 50.17.73. [35] Below nn. 39–53. [36] Kaiser (above n. 25) 340.
[37] Osler (above n. 28) 149–50. [38] Below nn. 168–72.

The third work doubted by Mantovani is Venuleius' six books *de interdictis*.[39] He thinks that it is not possible to know where in the Bluhme-Krüger Ordo this work was read. This view is not persuasive. Of the texts from this work D. 41.2.52 and 53 come after a text from Iavolenus' *posteriora Labeonis* book 5. D. 41.1.66 comes after a text from Quintus Mucius' ορων and two from Labeo's *pithana*; D. 44.3.15 after a text from Scaevola's *quaestiones publice tractatae*; 43.26.22 after one from Venuleius' *actiones*. Together these texts point to a position for Venuleius' *interdicta* after items 2, 3, 4, 5 and 8 in the Appendix table, either just before or after Furius Anthianus. I have followed the Bluhme-Krüger Ordo in placing it before, but the precise order is not really important.

Mantovani draws attention to the fact that excerpts from Venuleius' work are found only in books 41 to 44 of the Digest, whereas one might expect the 20 texts from it to be more widely distributed. Thirteen texts come in book 43, which concerns interdicts.[40] Seven appear in neighbouring Digest books.[41] At this very late stage in the process of reading and excerpting when, on Mantovani's plausible view, the editors had finished their work up to about book 40,[42] the committee reading this work may have been encouraged to confine its attention to titles that were to appear in the last 10 books of the Digest. Mantovani also notes that a number of texts are either interwoven with excerpts from Ulpian's books 70,[43] 71,[44] and 73[45] *ad edictum*, or come at the end of a title after an Ulpian text from these books.[46] Given that the Appendix excerpts were now available to the editors before they began to edit each title, it was easy for them to interweave the Appendix texts with texts from other masses. When they did not, it was normal to place Appendix texts at the end of a title. In sum, I see no reason to doubt that Venuleius' *de interdictis* was read in the ordinary way toward the end of the Appendix mass, but that the commissioners reading it took account of its place near the end of the long-drawn-out programme of reading and excerpting for the Digest.

The last work to be listed in the Appendix is Furius Anthianus's one book *ad edictum*, the only one of five books to which the compilers

39 Mantovani (above n. 3, 1987) 111–12.

40 D. 43.19.4; 43.21.4; 43.23.2; 43.24.2,4,8,10,12,22; 43.26.7,22; 43.29.2,4; 43.30.5.

41 D. 41.2.52,53; 41.1.66; 42.8.8,11,25; 44.3.15.

42 Mantovani (above n. 3, 1987); below nn. 155–61.

43 D. 43.19.4.

44 D. 43.24.2,4,8,10,12; 43.26.7; 43.29.2.

45 D. 42.8.11.

46 D. 43.21.4; 43.23.2; 43.29.4.

had access,[47] from which we have three fragments.[48] All come at the end of their respective titles and Mantovani doubts whether this work can securely be attributed to the Appendix.[49] But one of these texts comes after two Appendix texts from Labeo's *pithana*.[50] Moreover the texts that he cites from the second book of Scaevola's *digesta* in titles 2.14[51] and 4.3[52] have been shown by Osler, convincingly, to belong to the Papinian mass.[53] Hence they do not show that the Appendix was placed in an earlier position in these titles. In that case there is no reason why the Furius Anthianus texts at the end of these two titles (D. 2.14.47 and 4.3.32) should not belong to the Appendix, the end being the usual position for Appendix texts. It is likely that Furius Anthianus' book belongs to the Appendix[54] and comes at or near the end of that mass. If it does, the fact that it was incomplete and likely to have been found at a late stage is not, pace Mantovani,[55] an argument against the thesis that the Appendix consisted of works found after the reading and excerpting of the main masses had begun.

II. The General Character of the Appendix Works

Various views have been held about the character of the Appendix. Hugo Krüger thought that it consisted of works destined for students to read in the fifth year of study, a 'constitution-mass'.[56] But the works do not form a coherent object of study, and are by no means confined to constitutions. I adhere to the traditional view that these works were late arrivals. Moreover they were assigned to one of the three masses as they arrived—the mass to whom the works of the author in question were in principle assigned—but were to be read by each committee after its main assignment. The assumption that the Appendix works were late arrivals has been challenged by Mantovani.[57] He thinks that they were in the main parallel editions of works which formed part of the main masses. Thus Pomponius' *epistulae* in the Appendix (BK Ordo 269) were parallel to his *variae lectiones* in the edictal mass (BK Ordo 153). The parallel

[47] Index auctorum XXXVI Ανθου ητοι Φωριου Ανθιανου μερος edictu βιβλιων πεντε; D. Liebs, 'Variae Lectiones' (Zwei Juristenschriften), *Studi Volterra* V (1971) 65 n. 59 in fine.

[48] D. 2.14.62; 4.3.40; 6.1.80.

[49] Mantovani (above n. 3) 112.

[50] D. 6.1.80.

[51] D. 2.14.47.

[52] D. 4.3.32.

[53] Osler (above n. 28) 154–7.

[54] Kaiser (above n. 25) 338 n. 53.

[55] Mantovani (above n. 3), 1987) 112.

[56] H. Krüger, *Die Herstellung der Digesten Justinians und der Gang der Exzerption* (1922).

[57] Mantovani (above n. 3, 1993) 114–19.

works may have been available from the beginning but were left on one side until, if ever, there was time for them to be read. But would this arrangement be sensible? At least in the Sabinian mass similar works by an author could be read together as part of a group. Papinian's *libri 2 de adulteriis* and his *liber singularis* on the same subject were read together (BK Ordo 31). So there was no ban on reading similar works by the same author as part of a group. Indeed, that was essential if the best texts were to be discovered and excerpted for the Digest. On the other hand if works previously not available arrived after the committees had begun reading those that were available from the start, they would be overburdened by having to add the new works to their load. It was then rational to postpone reading them until the programme of reading already agreed and calculated according to a timetable had been finished. Mantovani's observation explains rather why, when these parallel works arrived, they were either not incorporated in the reading programme for the main masses or were put towards the end of the mass. This happened in the case of Scaevola's *digesta* of which the first two books were read towards the end of the Papinian mass rather than along with his other works, which come near the beginning of the mass (BK Ordo 184, 187, 189, 191, 193).[58]

III. How do the Works that Constitute the Appendix Relate to the Main Masses?

Bluhme considered that the Appendix works were assigned to the Papinian committee, since the Appendix normally follows the Papinian mass.[59] Mantovani rightly disputes this assignment.[60] One reason for doubting it is that the Appendix does not always follow the Papinian mass. It should be stressed that the position of the masses in each title does not depend on the ranking of the various committees,[61] with the possible exception of D. 50.17, where in this largely unedited title the order is Sabinian, Appendix, Papinian, edictal. In my view, as the order in this title suggests, the senior committee was the Sabinian, the second the Papinian, the third the edictal.[62]

[58] Below nn. 96–110.
[59] Bluhme (above n. 2) 309f.
[60] Mantovani (above n. 3, 1987) 112, 116, 123–4; cf. Osler (above n. 28) 144–6.
[61] As suggested by Mantovani (above n. 3, 1987) 114.
[62] Honoré, 'How Tribonian Organised the Compilation of Justinian's Digest' in *SZ* 121 (2004) 1–43 at 12–13; cf. Kaiser (above n. 25) 338. The position of the Appendix in D. 50.17 would be explained if the single Appendix text, from Quintus Mucius ορων,

Normally however the titles were edited in a way that took account not so much of the ranking of the committees as of the relative character and bulk of the materials provided by each mass, and particularly of the convenience of treating Ulpian, whose work mainly falls in the Sabinian mass, as the lead author for most topics.[63] In the upshot the Sabinian mass is chosen as the first mass in 249 of the 431 titles, the edictal in 163 and the Papinian in 19.[64] The Papinian mass usually falls in the third position not because it ranks as the third mass or because this is its 'natural position' but because it is less bulky than the others and consists largely of case law.

Although the Appendix usually follows the Papinian mass there are 20 titles with both a Papinian mass and an Appendix where the Appendix comes at the end of a title but after another mass.[65] There are also eight titles where the Appendix precedes another mass. In seven of these it precedes the Papinian mass; in the eighth it follows it.[66] We can disregard six titles where the only Appendix text is inserted in another mass,[67] and 14 where there is no Papinian mass.[68] In the upshot the Appendix follows the Sabinian mass in 15 titles, the edictal mass in 12.[69] That leaves 80 titles in which the Appendix follows the Papinian mass, including 10 or 12 where it is in turn followed by one or more codal texts.[70]

was placed there because, when his sole surviving work was discovered, the author was initially assigned to the Sabinian committee.

63 Honoré (above n. 62) 21.

64 The order of the masses in a title, and whether a text counts as part of a mass or as a detached text, is sometimes debatable. I have generally followed Krüger's views except where, as discussed above, he seems to have placed texts in the wrong mass.

65 D 2.14 (after Sab.), 4.4 (after Sab.), 5.3 (after Sab.), 6.1 (after ed.), 9.4 (after Sab.), 13.5 (after ed.), 14.2 (after Sab.), 14.6 (after ed.), 22.1 (after ed.), 22.3 (after Sab.), 23.5 (after ed.), 24.3 (after ed.), 34.5 (after ed.), 35.2 (after Sab.), 36.3 (after Sab.), 36.4 (after ed.), 42.1 (after Sab.), 44.7 (after ed.), 46.5 (after Sab.), 49.15 (after Sab.). My list does not entirely coincide with Osler's list of titles in which the Papinian mass does not appear in the third position (above n. 28 at 145–6 n. 31). In my view in D. 15.3 the Appendix (15.3.21) follows the Papinian mass (15.3.19–20). In D. 43.30 there is no Papinian mass, only a displaced text (43.30.2). Osler rightly doubts D. 33.4 and he was not bound to list D. 50.1, since on his view Scaevola's *digesta* books 1 and 2 belong to the Papinian mass. Mantovani (above n. 2, 1987) 114 n. 43 lists 19 titles to which I would add 8 (D. 2.14, 4.4, 9.4, 13.5, 14.6, 22.3, 35.2, 36.3).

66 D. 40.5 (after ed.), 40.14 (after Sab.), 44.1 (after Sab.), 46.1 (after ed.), 46.3 (after ed.), 49.14 (after Sab.), and 50.17 (after Sab.). The only exception is D. 48.10, where it comes between the Papinian and edictal masses.

67 D. 3.5 (Sab.); 4.8 (ed.), 7.4 (ed.); 40.13 (between ed. and Pap.); 43.19 (ed.), 45.1 (Pap.).

68 D. 4.3, 8.5, 12.2, 25.4, 28.8, 33.6, 41.9, 43.21, 43.23, 43.24, 43.26, 43.29, 43.30, 50.12.

69 Above nn. 66–7.

70 Below nn. 156–61.

The Appendix very often follows the Papinian mass because from an editorial point of view it was sensible to put the more bulky general material first and to leave the *quaestiones* and *responsa* of Papinian, Scaevola and Paul, essentially case law, to the end. The normal position of the Appendix, which contains less material than the other masses, is at the end of a title, either because it was not available to the editors earlier or, if it was, because of its slender character. It is found there in 102 of the 127 titles in which a text from it occurs.[71] So it is not surprising that it often, though by no means always, comes straight after the Papinian mass. This does not make it part of the Papinian mass. The Appendix is not part of one of the main masses.

There was, however, a connection between the Appendix and the main masses. Two works that belong mainly to the Appendix were, it seems, read in part by one of the main committees. The evidence suggests that the first books in Labeo's *posteriora* and Scaevola's *digesta* were read as part of the Sabinian and Papinian masses respectively.

To begin with Labeo's *posteriora*, this appears in the Digest in two sets of texts, one inscribed Iavolenus *ex posterioribus Labeonis* or the like, the other Labeo *posteriorum a Iavoleno epitomatorum*. Both refer to a summary of Labeo's posthumous works in 10 books. Whether the compilers had two different manuscripts in their hands and, if so, whether these came from different summaries of Labeo's *posteriora* is disputed.[72] The two series of inscriptions occur in both the Sabinian and the Appendix masses. Neither is confined to a particular book or books. To Bluhme the different inscriptions represented separate works[73] and the BK Ordo accordingly puts the Iavolenus texts at the end of the Sabinian mass at no. 94 and the Labeo texts in the Appendix at no. 265. The *Index auctorum* VII.2, however, does not support the existence of two different works. It attributes 10 books of *posteriorum* to Labeo and nothing comparable to Iavolenus, who is instead assigned epistolon βιβλια δεκατεσσερα (BK Ordo 153). Had the compilers regarded the *posteriora* as a single work by Iavolenus, it should have been assigned to the edictal mass, to which his 15 books *ex Cassio*, 14 of *epistulae*, and 5 *ex Plautio* belong.[74] But if the compilers considered that there were two different summaries of Labeo's manuscripts by Iavolenus, one

[71] Below nn. 137–8.

[72] In 1974 (below n. 78) I took the view that there were two different manuscripts, but not necessarily two different works. This still seems plausible cf. Mantovani (above n. 3, 1987) 117 n. 49.

[73] Bluhme (above n. 2) 320–3.

[74] BK Ordo 152,153.

predominantly of Labeo texts, the other in the nature of a commentary by Iavolenus, the two had obviously to be read together as a group. In that case, if they assigned the works of Labeo to the Sabinian committee, the Iavolenus work would be grouped with it in the Sabinian rather than the edictal mass.[75] This was the procedure with Paul's epitomarum Alfeni Digestorum libri VIII.[76] Though the *Index auctorum* is often unreliable it suggests that to the compilers the *posteriora* was a single work of Labeo. Lenel also treated it as a single work but assigned it to Iavolenus.[77]

Even if there were separate works, the BK Ordo assignment of the Iavolenus work to the Sabinian mass and the Labeo work to the Appendix was a mistake. The excerpts from book 1 and some from book 2 of the *posteriora* in both the Labeo and the Iavolenus series of inscriptions belong to the end of the Sabinian mass, while a larger number of excerpts from book 2 and all those from books 3 to 10, again from both series, belong to the Appendix.[78] It is not necessary to review the evidence for this conclusion, which is now, despite some apparent exceptions,[79] well established.[80] But what conclusion should we draw? At least in this instance, what began as part of the Sabinian mass ended as an item in the Appendix. Mantovani has suggested, to my mind convincingly, that the transfer occurred because at a certain stage in the Digest project the compilers in the interests of speed began assembling the texts already excerpted from the three main masses into titles and books without waiting until the reading of the remaining works was ended.[81] The Appendix therefore consists of the works that had not yet been read when that decision was taken. Mantovani goes on to suggest that the Appendix is a continuation of the Sabinian mass and that the *posteriora* were consequently read without interruption by the Sabinian

[75] Honoré (1974) 162.

[76] BK Ordo 16 (Paulus 89 epitomatorum Alfeni digestorum, read next to BK Ordo 15 Alfeni Vari libri XL digestorum (really 7), since both were available.

[77] Lenel, *Palingenesia* I .299 n. 1.

[78] Honoré, 'Labeo's *posteriora* and the Digest Commission' in A. Watson (ed.), *Daube Noster* (1974) 161–81; Mantovani (above n. 3, 1987) 117 n. 48.

[79] Mantovani (above n. 3, 1987) 17–121; (1993) 99. In D. 28.1.25 (Iav. 5 post. Lab.) the inscription is a mistake for 1 post. Lab (Lenel, *Palingenesia* I. 312 n. 2) so that the text is the last in the Sabinian mass. D. 49.15.27 falls between the Sabinian mass and an Appendix text from Labeo's *pithana*. D. 50.17.72 (Iav. 3 post. Lab.) falls between the Sabinian mass and a text, already cited, from Quintus Mucius' *ορων*. So none of these falls unambiguously in the Sabinian mass: Kaiser (above n. 25) 153.

[80] Mantovani (above n. 3, 1987) 116–20; Kaiser (above n. 25) 338; Osler (above n. 28) 150–3.

[81] Mantovani (above n. 3, 1987) 115–23.

committee.[82] This last conclusion is rejected by two scholars[83] and is in my view wrong.

It is true that if the summary of Paul's *imperiales sententiae* really belongs to the Papinian mass, and if Quintus Mucius' ορων comes after Labeo's *posteriora* in the Appendix table, Labeo's *posteriora* from book 2 to book 10 could have been the first work in the Appendix list and have been read by the Sabinian committee without interruption. But Osler has pointed to an objection to this hypothesis.[84] In the article that first highlighted the different masses in which texts from the early and later books of the *posteriora* occurred, I suggested that the five texts from book 2 that form part of the Sabinian mass, however inscribed, come from the first part of that book, but the 14 in the Appendix position come from the later part of that book.[85] But the subject-matter of these texts does not perhaps fit that hypothesis. The five texts in the Sabinian position come from titles 28.7 (*de condicionibus institutionum*),[86] 29.2 (*de acquirenda vel omittenda hereditate*),[87] 33.4 (*de dote praelegata*),[88] 34.2 (*de auro argento etc. legatis*),[89] and 35.1 (*de condicionibus et demonstrationibus*).[90] The 14 texts in the Appendix position come from books 32, 33, 34, 36 and 50 of the Digest,[91] so that there is a good deal of overlap with the first five. Title 34.2, admittedly a title in which the various masses appear twice, has one text from book 2 of the *posteriora* in the Sabinian, another in the Appendix position.[92] There are also two titles in which displaced texts from book 2 come between texts from the edictal mass.[93] It may be that further analysis will show that the fragments in the two masses relate respectively to topics that came earlier or later in that book.[94] Or may the committee charged with reading the

[82] Mantovani (above n. 3, 1987) 121, 124; (1993) 98–100, 107–8.

[83] Osler (above n. 28) 146; Kaiser (above n. 25) 341, citing the adding of codal texts to the Sabinian mass in 35.1.41–2 following on the excerpts from Labeo's *posteriora* books 1 and 2 at 39–40. This shows that the Sabinian mass was edited as a mass after the reading of these two books. It is inconsistent with *uninterrupted* reading of the *posteriora* but not necessarily with continued reading after an interval of time.

[84] Osler (above n. 28) 153–4. Mantovani (above n. 3, 1993) 106 points out that Lenel *Palingenesia* I.299f. simply arranged the fragments of this work in the order in which they appear in the Digest.

[85] Above n. 78.

[86] D. 28.7.20.

[87] D. 29.2.64.

[88] D. 33.4.6.

[89] D. 34.2.31.

[90] D. 35.1.40.

[91] D. 32.29,30,100; 33.1.17; 33.2.30; 33.2.31; 33.2.41; 33.5.20; 33.7.4,25; 33.8.22; 34.2.39; 36.4.14; 50.16.242.

[92] D. 34.2.31,39.

[93] D. 33.6.7; D. 34.3.17, also between two edictal texts. There are Appendix texts in a normal end position at 33.6.16 and 34.3.28.

[94] Mantovani (above n. 3, 1987, 120 n. 55; Mantovani (above n. 3, 1993) 106,107.[88]

Appendix works have read book 2 again and taken a fresh, more copious series of excerpts from it than the Sabinian committee had done: 14 texts against the previous five? In that case the Appendix committee cannot have consisted of the same commissioners as the Sabinian committee, and the Appendix cannot be a continuation of the Sabinian mass. Between the two there was an interval of time and a change of personnel. It may even be that the plan of reading the Appendix works was left aside until it became clear that there would be time enough to read them.[95] Moreover, the *posteriora* need not have been the first work to be read by the Appendix committee. Paul's *imperiales sententiae* could have been the first.

Another objection to the supposed continuity between the Sabinian mass and the Appendix is Osler's thesis that the texts from Scaevola's *digesta*, like those from Labeo's *posteriora*, belong partly to the Papinian mass and partly to the Appendix.[96] Those from the first two books, he argues, belong to the Papinian mass, the rest to the Appendix. From the first two books we have eight fragments. In D. 2.14.47 (1 dig.) the Scaevola text comes near the end of the Papinian mass after a text from Tryphoninus' *disputationes*. It is followed by another text from the Papinian mass, 2.14.48 from Gaius *ad legem XII tabularum*. Then, after the Sabinian mass from 2.14.49 onwards, the title ends with an Appendix text, 2.14.62, from Furius Anthianus.[97] D. 4.3 is similar in that 4.3.32 (2 dig.) follows the edictal mass and is followed by the Sabinian mass. The final text of the title, 4.3.40, presumably constituting the Appendix, again comes from Furius Anthianus.[98] There are no other texts from the Papinian mass in this title apart from one insertion in the edictal mass.[99] Much the same is true of D. 4.4.39 (2 dig.) where the preceding Papinian mass text is from Paul's *decreta*, and, after the Sabinian mass from 4.4.40 onwards, the title ends with an Appendix text, 4.4.50, from Pomponius' *epistulae*.[100] In D. 4.8.44 the Scaevola text from 2 dig. comes between the Papinian and Sabinian masses. At this early stage of the editorial process it would be unique for the Appendix to appear before another mass, something that does not happen until book 40,[101] whereas the position of the text fits the end of the Papinian

[95] Mantovani (above n. 3, 1987) 122.
[96] Osler (above n. 28) 154–8; Mantovani (above n. 3, 1993) 104.
[97] D. 2.14.62. [98] D. 4.3.40. [99] D. 4.3.19 (Pap. 37 quaest.).
[100] D. 4.4.50.
[101] Below n. 163.

mass. D. 50.1 and 50.7 are less strong cases, because here, though the Scaevola texts (50.1.24 and 50.7.13) come between the Papinian and edictal masses, at this stage in the editorial process the editors were free to put the Appendix in whatever position they thought best.[102] But since in both titles the Scaevola texts come at the end of the Papinian mass, after texts from Hermogenianus *iuris epitomae* (BK Ordo 206) and Paul *de iure libellorum* (BK Ordo 250) respectively, and are not followed by Appendix texts, they are inconclusive. In D. 2.15 the Scaevola text (2.15.3) is part of a trio of introductory texts all of which are displaced from their normal position. In D. 50.9 the Scaevola text (50.9.6) comes at the end of the title but, as there is no other text from either the Papinian mass or the Appendix, we cannot tell to which mass it belongs.

In all eight cases the position of the text from books 1 and 2 of Scaevola's *digesta* is consistent with its coming near the end of the Papinian mass and in the first four listed it fits that position better than the Appendix. But D. 2.14.48 (BK Ordo 247) shows that the first two books of the *digesta* may not have been read as the last of the Papinian mass but shortly before the last, since a number of *libri singulares* come after Gaius on the XII Tables.[103] On the other hand it must have been read after BK Ordo 221 (Tryphoninus 12 disputationes) in view of D. 2.14.46, which precedes 2.14.47 (Scae. 1 dig.). It also appears to have been read after Paul 1 *de iure libellorum* (BK Ordo 250) in view of D. 50.7.12 from that work which precedes 50.7.13 (Scae. 1 dig.). It is true that the exact position of Paul's *de iure libellorum* in the Papinian mass is uncertain,[104] but in general *libri singulares* come towards the end of that mass, at any rate after the Tryphoninus group at BK Ordo 219–222.[105] If we suppose that the first two books were read a week or two before the end and the rest detached to be read later, that would show that the idea of detaching Appendix works from the main masses was contemplated, as it should have been, in advance.

Osler makes the further point about the relation of the Appendix to the Papinian mass that, in the 32 titles he lists in which both the Papinian mass and the Appendix appear but the Papinian mass is not

[102] Below nn. 163–7. [103] Mantovani (above n. 3, 1993) 108.

[104] Mantovani (above n. 3, 1987) 100.

[105] Mantovani (above n. 3, 1987) 100 places Paul *de iure singulari* after BK Ordo 219 and Paul *de officio adsessorum* after BK Ordo 220.

in its usual third position,[106] the Appendix seems to come immediately after it in only seven or eight cases. These at first sight include the six titles 2.14, 4.3, 4.4, 4.8, 50.1 and 50.7 just discussed, in all of which the Appendix does not in fact follow the Papinian mass if the first two books of Scaevola are taken to belong to the Papinian mass rather than the Appendix.[107] This is an extra argument against the view that the Appendix forms part of the Papinian mass. It would be odd if the Appendix followed the Papinian mass in just those few cases in which the Appendix text came from these two books of Scaevola's *digesta*.

We may, I think, safely assign the first two books of Scaevola's *digesta* to the Papinian mass and the remaining 38 to the Appendix. That has important implications. The Appendix cannot be both part of the Sabinian mass because Labeo's *posteriora* formed part of that mass and was read by the Sabinian committee and also part of the Papinian mass because Scaevola's *digesta* formed part of the Papinian mass and was read by the Papinian committee. The Appendix cannot, in fact, be part of either, but must be a collection of books drawn from both and also, probably, from the edictal mass. The case of Scaevola's *digesta* is particularly revealing, if we assume that it was treated as part of the Papinian mass before its transfer to the Appendix. For it cannot have been available to the compilers at the outset of their work. Such a substantial work, in 40 books, would in that case have been read earlier in the operations of the Papinian committee. From the BK Ordo it is clear that the programme of all three main committees required them to read the most substantial works first, in particular the Sabinian and edictal commentaries and the works of Papinian. In all three masses the number of lines per book declines towards the end.[108] In the Sabinian (BK Ordo 69–92) and Papinian (BK Ordo 224–261) masses there is a long list of minor works read towards the end of the mass. Many of these are *libri singulares* of Paul, of which the compilers read 60, none of which can be confirmed as part of the edictal mass.[109] Although it is often

[106] Osler (above n. 28) 145–6 n. 31.

[107] Only in D. 47.10.24 does the Appendix follow the Papinian mass when the latter is in the second position in the title. D. 33.4 is not an exception, because there the text from Labeo's *posteriora* at 33.4.6 is part of the Sabinian mass, and the Appendix at 33.4.13–14 appears after the Papinian mass at 33.4.11–12, but is followed by three displaced texts at 33.4.15–17.

[108] Honoré (above n. 62) p. 7.

[109] Paul *ad legem Cinciam* is his only *liber singularis* allotted to the edictal mass (BK Ordo 170) but its real mass is uncertain (Mantovani, above n. 3, 1987, 97).

doubtful whether a *liber singularis* should be assigned to the Sabinian or Papinian mass or where within the mass it should be placed, there are enough whose position is secure to show that the general scheme was for the minor works to be read towards the end of these two masses.[110] The *posteriora* of Labeo and the *digesta* of Scaevola do not fit this scheme. That is a reason for regarding them, and also Paul's *imperiales sententiae*, if it belongs to the Appendix,[111] as late arrivals that had to be fitted in after the initial assignment of works to the three committees had been made. Mantovani's scepticism about whether the Appendix consists of late arrivals, and whether the *digesta* of Scaevola was a late arrival,[112] therefore seems unjustified.

How was it decided to which committee to assign each work? The system by which Tribonian allotted works to the committees has been explained elsewhere.[113] Each author was assigned to a particular mass, but some of his works could be hived off to another mass to form an interrelated group, for example a group of works on adultery or of commentaries on Plautius. Papinian provides a convenient example. His *quaestiones*, *responsa* and *definitiones*, 58 books in all, were assigned to the Papinian mass, but his three books *de adulteriis* went to the Sabinian mass to be combined with the works of Ulpian and Paul on that subject at BK Ordo 28–31. One *liber singularis*, *αστυνομικος*, appears in the BK Ordo in the edictal mass at 111, but its real mass is indeterminate.[114] It should be moved, in my view, to the Papinian mass which inherits Papinian's works except those required to form a group in another mass, or to the Appendix.

How does this apply to the Appendix works? In the case of Labeo's *posteriora* there was no previous Labeo work to go by. The choice of committee was open and the Sabinian was selected. In the case of Scaevola, however, his *quaestiones* and *responsa* had already been assigned to the Papinian mass, his four books of *regulae* to the *regulae* group in the Sabinian mass.[115] The Papinian mass was therefore the appropriate one for his *digesta* unless this work was to be allocated to a

[110] Mantovani's analysis (above n. 3, 1987, at 90–103) confirms the existence of 17 *libri singulares* of Paul in the Sabinian and 17 in the Papinian mass but leaves 26 doubtful, including 11 which have left no excerpts in the Digest.

[111] Above nn. 20–8.

[112] Mantovani (above n. 3, 1987) 116.

[113] Ch. 3 and Honoré (2004) 18–25.

[114] Mantovani (above n. 3, 1987) 111.

[115] BK Ordo 36–46. One ought probably to add to this group as 46 bis Marcellus, *responsorum* 1 (BK Ordo 59): Mantovani (above n. 3, 1987) 104–5.

group of works similar in point of subject-matter or genre. The *digesta*, had they been available from the start, might (but would not necessarily) have been combined with the *digesta* of Celsus and Marcellus in the edictal mass. In fact, as Osler shows,[116] it went to the Papinian mass. Applying the same principles to the other Appendix works, Venuleius' *actiones* and *interdicta* went to the Papinian committee, given his 19 books of *stipulationes* at BK Ordo 216. Pomponius' *epistulae* and *senatusconsulta* went to the edictal committee in view of his books *ad Quintum Mucium* and *variae lectiones* at BK Ordo 154 and 156. The summary of Paul's *imperiales sententiae* went to the Papinian committee not because Paul's works were assigned to this committee (on the contrary, they were divided more or less equally between the three masses) but because the other summary, Paul's *decreta*, had already been assigned to that mass at BK Ordo 222. The *quaestiones publice tractatae* of Scaevola, assuming the compilers regarded this as a work of Cervidius Scaevola, would also go to the Papinian committee. The monographs by Quintus Mucius and the only available part of the commentary by Furius Anthianus might have been placed in any of the masses, since these were the only works of theirs available to the compilers. Given the allocation to the Sabinian committee of Labeo's *posteriora*, his *pithana* would also be allotted to it.

The extra works, especially Scaevola's *digesta*, would impose a heavier burden on the Papinian committee (57 books) than on the other committees (17 or 26 for the Sabinian committee, 25 for the edictal). This may have been one reason for reorganizing the programme of reading and excerpting.

We do not know how the Appendix committee was composed. It is not likely to have consisted of any of the committees charged with reading the original three masses. The Sabinian and Papinian committees were the two senior committees and must have been headed by Tribonian and Constantinus,[117] who would be needed for the editorial work that, as Mantovani convincingly argues, went on at the same time. The same is, I think, true of Theophilus, who as the senior law professor must have been in charge of the edictal committee.[118] Those charged with reading and excerpting the Appendix are likely to have been chosen from among the three more junior law professors, Dorotheus, Anatolius and Cratinus.

[116] Above nn. 28, 53, 83. [117] Honoré (2004) 12–13. [118] Ibid.

IV. Were there Late Arrivals that are not Part of the Appendix?

It is possible that there were late arrivals that are not listed as part of the Appendix since the only text or texts from them come at the end of a title. An example is Callistratus 4 *de iure fisci* (BK Ordo 158) which Mantovani lists as possibly belonging to the Appendix since the two texts from it each come at the end of a title.[119] D. 29.5.27 comes after 29.5.26 (Scae. 34 dig.) and 40.15.4 (Call. 1 iur. fisc.) comes after two Papinian mass texts. If this were so, it would clear up a difficulty about the editing of D. 29.5,[120] which would then end in two Appendix texts rather than an Appendix text and a codal text.

There may be other works of this sort that belong to the Appendix but are not easy to detect as such. In particular it is worth inquiring whether works not listed in the *Index auctorum* of which we have excerpts in the Digest belong to the Appendix and were not listed because the compiler of the Index had an incomplete list of these late arrivals. A possible example of an Appendix work is Maecianus' *ex lege Rhodia*,[121] the only excerpt from which comes just before an Appendix text at the end of a title. Four *libri singulares* of Gaius (the Index does not list his μονοβιβλια) are also possible candidates. The single texts from Gaius *ad sc. Tertullianum*[122] and *ad sc. Orfitianum*[123] each precede an Appendix text at the end of D. 38.17.[124] The single text from *de tacitis fideicommissis*[125] comes before two displaced Papinian mass texts[126] and a final Appendix text.[127] At this point in the process of editing Appendix texts can be placed before codal texts,[128] and this may be an example. The single text from the mysterious *lex Glitia*,[129] which appears in the title *de inofficoso testamento*, is in a group of introductory texts from at least the Sabinian and edictal masses and could have been an Appendix text inserted by the title editor like some others in these early books.[130] On the other hand Papinian's αστυνομικος[131] which provides the only text

[119] D. 14.2.9 (Maec. 1 ex leg. Rhod.) before 14.2.10 (Lab. 1 pith.).
[120] Kaiser (1991) 341[64]; Mantovani (above n. 3, 1993) 105; below nn. 156–9.
[121] BK Ordo 93. Mantovani (above n. 3, 1993) 109 also suggests this possibility.
[122] D. 38.17.8. [123] D. 38.17.9. [124] D. 38.17. 10 (Pomp. 2 SCC).
[125] D. 34.9.23. [126] D. 34.9.24 (Pap. 18 quaest.), 25 (id. 14 resp.).
[127] D. 34.9.26 (Scae. 30 dig.).
[128] Mantovani (above n. 3, 1987) 14–15; below nn. 155–60. [129] D. 5.2.4.
[130] Below nn. 146–8. [131] D. 38.10.1 (Pap. 1 astu.).

in a title,[132] Arcadius Charisius *de muneribus civilibus*[133] and Paul *de gradibus et adfinibus et nominibus eorum,*[134] which provide a single, long text at the end of a title[135] and from that point of view could belong to the Appendix, are all listed in the Index.[136]

V. In which Titles of the Digest do Appendix Texts Appear?

On the basis of the works identified above as belonging to the Appendix an Appendix text or texts appears in 127 titles of the Digest.[137] These are: D. 2.14.62* (Furius Anth. 1 ed.), 3.5.42 (Labeo 6 post.), 4.3.40* (Furius Anth. 1 ed.), 4.4.50* (Pomp. 9 epist.), 4.8.18 (Pomp. 17 epist.), 5.3 58* (Scae. 3 dig.), 6.1.78–80* (Lab. 4 pith., 6 pith., Furius Anth. 1 ed.), 7.4.24 (Iav. 3 post. Lab.), 8.1 19–20* (Lab. 4 post., Iav. 5 post. Lab.), 8.5.20–1* (Scae. 4 dig., Lab 1 pith.), 9.2 57* (Iav. 6 post. Lab.), 9.4 43* (Pomp. 8 epist.), 11.1.22* (Scae. 4 dig.), 12.2.42* (Pomp. 18 epist.), 12.6.67* (Scae. 5 dig.), 13.5.31* (Scae. 5 dig.), 13.7.31* (Scae. 5 dig.), 14.2.10* (Lab. 1 pith.), 14.3.20* (Scae. 5 dig), 14.6.20* (Pomp. 5 SCC), 15.1.58* (Scae. 5 dig.), 15.3.21* (Scae. 5 dig.), 16.1.32* (Pomp. 1 SCC), 16.3.33–4* (Lab. 6 post., 2 pith.), 17.1.62* (Scae. 6 dig.), 17.2.84* (Lab. 6 post.), 18.1.77–81* (Iav. 4 post. Lab., Lab. 4 post., Iav. 5 post. Lab., Lab. 5 post., Scae. 7 dig.), 18.3.8* (Scae. 7 dig.), 18.4.24–25* (Lab. 4 post., 2 pith.), 18.5.9–10* (Scae. 4 dig., 7 dig.), 18.7.10* (Scae. 7 dig.), 19.1 50–55* (Lab. 4 post., 5 post., Scae. 7 dig., Lab. 1 pith., 2 pith., Pomp. 10 epist.), 19.2.28/57–62* (Lab. 4 post./ Iav. 4 post. Lab., Lab. 4 post., Iav. 5 post. Lab., Lab. 5 post., Scae. 7 dig., Lab. 1 pith.), 20.1.34–5* (Scae. 27 dig., Lab. 1 pith.), 20.2.10* (Scae. 6 dig.), 20.4.21* (Scae. 17 dig.), 20.5.14* (Scae. 6 dig.), 20.6.14–15* (Lab. 5 post., Scae 6 dig.), 21.1.64–65* (Pomp. 17 epist., Ven. 5 act.), 22.1.47–49* (Scae. 9 dig., 22 dig., Iav. 3 post. Lab.), 22.2.9* (Lab. 5 pith.), 22.3.27–29* (Scae. 33 dig., Lab. 7 pith., Scae. 9 dig.),

[132] BK Ordo 111. [133] BK Ordo 260. [134] BK Ordo 254.

[135] D. 38.10.10 (Paul 1 grad. et adfin.); 50.4.18 (Arc. Char. 1 mun. civ.).

[136] Index auctorum II 6; XXXIV 3; XXV 29.

[137] Mantovani (above n. 3,1987) lists 131 titles. D. 28.7 should be removed because of the assignment to the Sabinian mass of Labeo's *posteriora* in the Labeo inscribed series book 1 and some texts from book 2. The assignment of Scaevola's *digesta* books 1 and 2 to the Papinian mass leads to the removal of D. 2.15, 50.1, 50.7 and 50.9. D. 40.13 should in my view be added.

23.3.79–80/83–85* (Lab. 6 post., Iav. 6 post. Lab./Iav. 6 post. Lab., Lab. 6 pith., Scae. 8 dig.), 23.4.32* (Iav. 6 post. Lab.), 23.5.18* (Iav. 6 post. Lab.), 24.1.64–67* (Iav. 6 post. Lab., Lab. 6 post., Scae. 9 dig., Lab. 2 pith.), 24.3.65–67* (Scae. 1 quaest. pub. tract., Iav. 6 post. Lab., Pomp. 20 epist.), 25.4.4* (Scae. 20 dig.), 26.2.33–34* (Iav. 8 post. Lab., Scae. 10 dig.), 26.3.11* (Scae. 20 dig.), 26.7.56–61* (Scae. 4 dig., 10 dig., 11 dig., 26 dig., Pomp. 8 epist., 20 epist.), 26.8.20–22* (Scae. 10 dig., 26 dig., Lab. 5 pith.), 28.3.20* (Scae. 13 dig.), 28.5.93* (Paul. 2 imp. sent.), 28.6.48* (Scae. 1 quaest. pub. tract.), 28.8.11* (Iav. 4 post. Lab.), 29.2.98–99* (Scae. 26 dig., Pomp. 1 SCC), 29.5.26 (Scae. 34 dig.)*, 30.46 (Pomp. 9 epist.), 32.29–42*/100–103* (Lab. 2 post., 2 post., 1 pith., Scae. 14 dig., 15 dig., 16 dig., 17 dig., 18 dig., 18 dig., 19 dig., 20 dig., 21 dig., 22 dig., 33 dig./ Iav. 2 post. Lab., Scae. 16 dig., 17 dig., 1 quaest. pub. tract.), 33.1.17–21 (Lab. 2 post., Scae. 14 dig., 17 dig., 18 dig., 22 dig.), 33.2.30–37/41–43* (Iav. 2 post. Lab., Lab. 2 post., Scae. 15 dig., 17 dig., 18 dig., 22 dig., 25 dig., 33 dig./Iav. 2 post. Lab., 5 post. Lab., Ven. 10 act.), 33.4.13–14 (Lab. 1 pith., Scae. 15 dig.), 33.5.20–22* (Lab. 2 post., Scae. 22 dig., 17 dig.), 33.6.7–8*/16* (Iav. 2 post. Lab., Pomp. 6 epist./Iav. 3 post. Lab.), 33.7.4–7*/25–29* (Iav. 2 post. Lab., Lab.1 pith., Scae. 16 dig., Scae. 2 dig./Iav. 2 post. Lab., 5 post. Lab., Scae. 16 dig., 23 dig., Lab. 1 pith.), 33.8.22–23 (Lab. 2 post., Scae. 15 dig.), 33.10.10–12 (Iav. 3 post. Lab., 10 post. Lab., Lab. 4 pith.), 34.1.15–19 (Scae. 17 dig., 18 dig., 19 dig., 20 dig., 22 dig.), 34.2.13,15–16,18*/39–40* (Scae. 15 dig., 15 dig., 18 dig., 22 dig./Iav. 2 post. Lab., Scae. 17 dig.), 34.3.28 (Scae. 16 dig.), 34.4.30–32* (Scae. 20 dig., 14 dig., Ven. 10 act.), 34.5.28–29* (Iav. 3 post. Lab., Scae. 18 dig.), 34.9.26* (Scae. 30 dig.), 35.1.105, 108–113* (Pomp. 5 epist./Scae. 19 dig., 20 dig., Pomp. 9 epist., 11 epist., 12 epist., Paul 2 imp. sent.), 35.2.94–96* (Scae. 21 dig., 21 dig., 1 quaest. pub. tract.), 36.1.77–83* (Scae. 18 dig., 19 dig., 20 dig., 21 dig., 1 quaest. pub. tract., 15 dig., Paul 2 imp. sent.), 36.2.30–31* (Lab. 3 post., Scae. 14 dig.), 36.3.18* (Scae. 29 dig.), 36.4.14–15* (Lab. 2 post., Ven. 7 act.), 37.14.24* (Paul 1 imp. sent.), 38.2.51* (Lab. 1 pith.), 38.4.2,4,12–13* (Pomp. 4 SCC, 4 SCC/12 epist., 4 SCC), 38.17.10* (Pomp. 2 SCC), 39.5.35* (Scae. 31 dig.), 40.1.10,26* (Paul 2 imp. sent., Iav. 4 post. Lab.), 40.4.29/59–61* (Scae. 13 dig./23 dig., 24 dig., Pomp. 11 epist.), 40.5.17–20 (Scae. 21 dig., 23 dig., 24 dig., Pomp. 7 epist.), 40.7.39–42* (Iav. 4 post. Lab., Scae. 24 dig., Lab. 1 pith., 3 pith.), 40.12.42–44* (Lab. 4 post., Pomp. 3 SCC, Ven. 7 act.), 40.13.3 (Pomp. 11 epist.), 40.14.3 (Pomp. 5 SCC), 41.1.64–66* (Quintus Mucius 1 ορων, Lab. 6 pith., Ven. 6 interdict.),

41.2.51–53* (Iav. 5 post. Lab., Ven. 1 interdict., 5 interdict.), 41.3.49* (Lab. 5 pith.), 41.4.14* (Scae. 25 dig.), 41.9.3* (Scae. 25 dig.), 42.1.64* (Scae. 25 dig.), 42.8.8,11/23–25* (Ven. 6 interdict., 6 interdict./Scae. 32 dig., 1 quaest. pub. tract., Ven. 6 interdict.), 43.16.20* (Lab. 3 pith.), 43.19.4 (Ven. 1 interdict.), 43.20.8* (Quintus Mucius 1 ορων), 43.21.4* (Ven. 1 interdict.), 43.23.2* (Ven. 1 interdict.), 43.24.2,4,8,10,12 /22* (Ven. 2 interdict., 2 interdict., 2 interdict., 2 interdict., 2 interdict./2 interdict.), 43.26.7/21–22* (Ven. 3 interdict./ 4 act., 3 interdict.), 43.29.2,4* (Ven. 4 interdict., 4 interdict.), 43.30.5* (Ven. 4 interdict.), 44.1.23 (Lab. 6 pith.), 44.3.14–15 (Scae. 1 quaest. pub. tract., Ven. 5 interdict.), 44.4.17* (Scae. 17 dig.), 44.7.61* (Scae. 28 dig.), 45.1.122 (Scae. 28 dig.), 46.1.45–46 (Scae. 6 dig., Iav. 10 post. Lab.), 46.3.88–93 (Scae. 5 dig., 29 dig., 26 dig., Lab. 6 pith., Pomp. 9 epist., Scae. 1 quaest. pub. tract.), 46.4.23* (Lab. 5 pith.), 46.5.11* (Ven. 8 act.), 46.7.20–21* (Scae. 29 dig., 1 quaest. pub. tract.), 47.2.91–92 (Iav. 9 post. Lab., Lab. 2 pith.), 47.10.44 (Iav. 9 post. Lab.), 48.10.24 (Scae. 22 dig.), 49.1.28* (Scae. 25 dig.), 49.14.35 (Pomp. 11 epist.), 49.15.27–30* (Iav. 9 post. Lab., Lab. 4 pith., 6 pith., 8 pith.), 50.12.14 (Pomp., 6 epist.), 50.16.240–246* (Paul 1 imp. sent., Quintus Mucius 1 ορων, Iav. 2 post. Lab., Scae. 18 dig., Lab. 4 pith., Pomp. 10 epist.), 50.17.72–73 (Iav. 3 post Lab., Quintus Mucius 1 ορων).

An asterisk indicates one of the 102 titles that end with the Appendix.[138] In the complex titles 32, 33.6, 33.7 and 34.2 two asterisks are inserted to indicate that the Appendix comes at the end of both cycles of masses. On my count there are 25 titles with an Appendix text that do not end with the Appendix, but this includes six titles with only a single displaced Appendix text.[139] In some 10 to 13 titles the Appendix is in the penultimate position followed by one or more codal texts.[140] In eight titles, all in the last 10 books of the Digest, the Appendix precedes another mass.[141] Six titles recorded in the stereotype edition of the Digest as containing one or more Appendix texts are not in the above list,[142] because books 1 and 2 of Scaevola's *digesta* and books 1 and some texts from book 2 of Labeo's *posteriora* both with the Labeo and

[138] Including D. 36.1 and 36.4 which are doubtful in view of the hypothetical codal texts 36.1.84–5 and 36.4 16–7. D. 29.5 also possibly ends with the Appendix: above n. 120.

[139] D. 3.5, 4.8, 7.4, 30, 43.19, 45.1.

[140] D. (29.5?), 33.1, 33.4, 33.8, 33.10, 34.1, 34.3, (36.1, 36.4?), 44.3, 47.2, 47.10, 50.12.

[141] D. 40.5, 40.14, 44.1, 46.1, 46.3, 48.10, 49.14 and 50.17.

[142] D. 2.15 (2.15.3, Scae. 1 dig.); 28.1 (28.1.2, Lab. 1 post.); 28.7 (28.7.20, Lab. 2 post.); 50.1 (50.1.24, Scae. 2 dig.); 50.7 (50.7.13, Scae. 1 dig.); 50.9 (50.9.6, Scae. 1 dig.).

the Iavolenus inscriptions are now taken to belong to the Papinian or Sabinian mass rather than the Appendix.[143]

VI. In what Position did the Editors Place the Appendix Texts in the Digest Titles?

The list just set out enables us to see how the Appendix texts were edited by the Digest compilers. It supports, and indeed strengthens, Mantovani's analysis. In the early books of the Digest the titles seem to have been fully edited before the Appendix texts became available. The editors had already, when appropriate, added codal texts.[144] By a codal text is meant one either chosen as suitable to end a mass or title or one that has become detached from the main mass to which it originally belonged and is then added at the end in a sort of tidying operation. At least up to D. 22.3 the Appendix excerpts were added at the end, if necessary after the intended codal texts.[145] There were very few insertions of Appendix texts in the first four books of the Digest.[146]

Five titles present difficulties: D. 3.5, 4.8, 7.4, 19.2 and 23.3. In the first three a single Appendix text is inserted in the Sabinian or edictal mass. How was this possible if these titles had been fully edited? In D. 4.8 the apparent insertion, inscribed Pomponius 17 *epistularum et variarum lectionum*, may be not an Appendix text but, as treated by Krüger,[147] one from Pomponius' *variae lectiones* in the edictal mass (BK Ordo 156), but displaced within that mass. In D. 3.5 and 7.4 the insertions in the Sabinian mass, both relevant, come from Labeo's *posteriora* books 6 and 3.[148] Was the editor of these titles keeping track of how the excerpting of the *posteriora*, read early on in the Appendix operation,[149] was progressing? Since the work was taking place in the imperial palace and the texts excerpted had to be assigned to a title, presumably at once, this would have been possible. The title editor could then discover which Appendix texts were marked for his title and perhaps pre-empt a relevant text. In D. 19.2 an apposite text from

[143] Above nn. 72–104.

[144] Mantovani (above n. 3, 1987) 104–6.

[145] The Appendix comes after one or more codal texts in eight titles: D. 2.14, 4.4, 11.1, 12.6, 13.5, 16.3, 21.1 and 22.3: Mantovani (above n. 3, 1987) 115 n. 47. I do not share M.'s doubts about 2.14 and 4.4.

[146] Mantovani (above n. 3, 1993) 110–13 argues that there were none.

[147] *Corpus Iuris*, Stereotype ed. I.96 n. 14; also Mantovani (above n. 3, 1993) 112.

[148] D. 3.5.42 (Lab. 6 post.); 7.4 24 (Iav. 3 post. Lab.).

[149] Above nn. 18–38.

Labeo's *posteriora* book 4[150] is again inserted in the Sabinian mass, though the bulk of the Appendix consists of six texts at the end of the title. In D. 23.3 there are five Appendix texts at the end of the title, the first two separated from the last three by two insertions, a text of Papinian from the Papinian mass[151] and one of Proculus from the edictal mass.[152] Neither insertion really fits the position in which it occurs, and they seem more like texts that have become detached. But, as Kaiser suggests,[153] in that case the last two Appendix texts in this title, which invert the order of Scaevola's *digesta* and Labeo's *pithana*,[154] may form part not of the regular Appendix but of a detached group of codal texts. It might follow that the phase of the editorial process in which the Appendix comes in principle before the codal texts had already begun at D. 23.3. Whatever the truth about D. 23.3, the conclusion is that Mantovani's theory about the placing of the Appendix in the earlier books of the Digest is sound, but that texts from Labeo's *posteriora* in both series of inscriptions seem to have been available before the process of reading and excerpting the Appendix works was complete.

From D. 33.1, and perhaps as early as 23.3, a change in editing takes place.[155] In some titles Appendix texts appear in a penultimate position, before the codal texts that are meant to end the title. The title editors apparently had access to the Appendix texts after they had settled the order of the three main masses but before they had finished editing the title. This is true in D. 33.1, 33.4, 33.8, 33.10, 34.1, 34.3, 35.1 and perhaps 29.5, 36.1 and 36.4.[156] In most of these titles the codal texts look as if they had become detached from the main mass or masses.[157] D. 29.5, where the codal text has been chosen to end the title, presents a problem. There, although in the Florentine MS the apparent codal text

150 D. 19.2.28 (Lab. 4 post.).

151 D. 23.3.51 (Pap. 8 quaest.).

152 D. 23.3.52 (Proc. 5 epist.).

153 Kaiser (above n. 25) 340 n. 60.

154 D. 23.3.84 (Lab. 6 pith.), 23.3.85 (Scae. 8 dig.).

155 Mantovani (above n. 3, 1987) 115; (1993) 104–6.

156 It continues in the later titles 44.3, 47.2, 47.10, and 50.12: below nn. 163–7. Mantovani (above n. 3, 1987) 115 n. 47 regards 7.4 as an exception but there the Appendix text is an insertion in the edictal mass. D. 35.2 really is an exception (below n. 161). D. 29.5 may not contain any codal text but merely end with two Appendix texts (above n. 120). D. 23.3 (above nn. 151–4) perhaps belongs to a transitional phase and shows that the change in editing took place earlier than book 33.

157 D. 33.1.22–24 (from the Sabinian mass); 33.4.15–17 (from all three masses); 33.8.24–26 (all three masses); 33.10.13–14 (edictal mass); 34.1.20–23 (Papinian mass); 34.3.29–31 (edictal and Papinian masses); 35.1 105–7 (perhaps from all three masses).

follows the Appendix,[158] Kaiser stresses that it has been shifted by the Florentine editor from the end of D. 29.6, where the text he was copying had mistakenly placed it.[159] Hence in 29.5 the Appendix text originally ended the title. But it may be that 29.5.27 (Call. 1 iur fisc.) is not really a codal text but part of the Appendix.[160] In D. 35.2 three Appendix texts end the title but come after a codal text from the Papinian mass. Here the title editor seems to have inserted before the Appendix a detached Papinian text that either did not fit the main Papinian mass or had been overlooked.[161] Editorial practice was evidently not uniform. The Appendix texts were now available to be inserted after the main masses and before any codal texts. Most editors seem to have put the Appendix before the codal texts but perhaps some left them to the end where they would previously have gone.

There are in these books where the Appendix appears before the codal texts also titles in which the Appendix ends the title, as before, and follows directly on one of the three main masses.[162] Moreover some Appendix texts are inserted in other masses. D. 30.46 (Pomp. 9 epist.) is inserted in the Sabinian mass at a relevant point. The same is true of D. 38.4.2 and 4 (Pomp. 4 SCC), also in the Sabinian mass. But D. 35.1.105 (Pomp. 5 epist.) comes after a series of Papinian mass texts that are out of order, and before two Sabinian mass texts, also out of order. There is no obvious reason why it should come where it does. It seems to belong to a group of texts detached from their masses. In D. 40.1 an Appendix text comes at the end of the title and another Appendix text is inserted between the Sabinian and edictal masses. In 40.4 three Appendix texts come at the end but one is inserted between the Sabinian and edictal masses. In neither case is the reason for the insertion obvious.

The pattern detected by Mantovani for these books in the 30s of the Digest is convincing, but allowance must be made for some editorial discretion when there are both codal and Appendix texts.

Towards the end of book 40 a fresh approach to editing is seen.[163] In D. 40.5 the Appendix for the first time comes before the Sabinian

[158] D. 29.5.26 (Scae. 34 dig.), 29.5.27 (Call. 1 iur. fisc.).

[159] Kaiser (above n. 25) 340–1; Mantovani (above n. 3, 1993) 105.

[160] Above nn. 119–20.

[161] Kaiser (above n. 25) 340; Mantovani (above n. 3, 1993) 105. There is an earlier text from the same book of Papinian at D. 35.2.10 (Pap. 20 quaest.).

[162] D. 32 (two cycles); 33.5; 33.6 (two cycles); 33.7 (two cycles); 34.2 (two cycles); 34.4; 34.5; 34.9; 35.1; 35.2; 36.2; 36.3; 37.14; 38.2; 38.4; 38.17; 39.5; 40.1; 40.4.

[163] Mantovani (above n. 3, 1987) 115–16.

and Papinian masses. This pattern is repeated in 40.14, 44.1, 46.1, 46.3 and 49.14, in all of which the Appendix precedes the Papinian mass and 48.10, where the single Appendix text precedes the edictal mass. In 50.17 the Appendix comes before both the Papinian and edictal masses. It has become possible, as Mantovani stresses, for the Appendix to be treated like the other masses and to come before another mass when the title editors think it convenient. Editing is now more flexible. There are three titles (44.3, 47.2, 47.10) in which the Appendix comes before a carefully chosen codal text[164] and one (50.12) in which it precedes a detached Sabinian text that has been put at the end of the title because it does not cohere with the first text in the title.[165] There are also titles in which, as before, Appendix texts have been inserted in other masses.[166] In some cases the Appendix appears both as a mass of its own and as an insertion in other masses.[167]

VII. Did the Editors Insert the Appendix Works Strictly in Order?

Anyone who reads the Digest inscriptions with the Bluhme-Krüger Ordo in mind must be impressed by the discipline with which the order, set out above,[168] is in general observed. There are some exceptions. If the *posteriora* texts inscribed Labeo and Iavolenus are treated as equivalent, the following sequences appear to be in the wrong order:

D 22.3.27–29: Scae. 33 dig., Lab. 7 pith, Scae 9 dig.
D 23.3.84–85: Lab. 6 pith., Scae. 8 dig.
D 24.3.65–67: Scae. 1 quaest. pub. tract., Iav. 6 post. Lab., Pomp. 20 epist.
D 32.31–32: Lab. 1 pith., Scae. 14 dig.
D 33.4.13–14: Lab. 1 pith., Scae. 15 dig.
D 33.5.20–22: Lab. 2 post., Scae. 22 dig., Scae. 17 dig.
D 33.7.4–7, 28–29: Iav. 2 post. Lab., Lab. 1 pith., Scae. 16 dig., Scae. 22 dig./ Scae. 23 dig., Lab. 1 pith.
D 34.4.30–32: Scae. 20 dig., Scae 14 dig., Ven. 10 act.

164 D. 44.3.16 (Paul 3 Sab.); 47.2.93 (Ulp. 38 ed.); 47.10.45 (Herm. 5 epit.).

165 D. 50.12.1,15 (Ulp. 1 de off. cur. reip.).

166 D. 43.19.4 (in the edictal mass); 45.1.122 (one text in the Papinian mass).

167 D. 42.8.23–5 but also 42.8.8,11; 43.24.22 but also 43.24.2,4,8,10,12; 43.26.7; 43.26.21–2; 43.29.4; 43.29.2. All these instances involve Venuleius' *de interdictis*, but in principle the technique is not confined to this work. It occurred earlier in D. 19.2.

168 Above nn. 18–20.

D 36.1.80–83: Scae. 21 dig., Scae 1 quaest. pub. tract., Scae. 5/?15 dig., Paul 2 imp. sent.

D 46.1.45–46: Scae. 6 dig., Iav. 10 post. Lab.

D 50.16.241–242: Quintus Mucius 1 ορων, Iav. 2 post. Lab.

It is difficult to say whether the inversions of the normal order are unusually many, except perhaps in the case of Labeo's *pithana* and Scaevola's *digesta*. Labeo comes after Scaevola in 10 instances,[169] but precedes him in four.[170] In D. 22.3 Labeo both follows and precedes Scaevola. A curious feature of D. 33.7, a composite title, is that Labeo precedes Scaevola in the first cycle at 33.7.5–6 and follows him in the second at 33.7.28–29. What this suggests is that the titles that go to make up 33.7 *De instructo vel instrumento legato* were edited separately by different commissioners before they were amalgamated.[171]

In the upshot the explanation of the irregular sequence of these works of Scaevola and Labeo is obscure, but it may be relevant, as I have argued elsewhere,[172] that both belong to a group of 48 books excerpted as a whole but divided into two lots of 24 books each.

[169] D. 8.5, 19.1, 19.2, 20.1, 24.1, 26.8, 33.7, 40.7, 46.3, 50.16.

[170] D. 23.3, 32, 33.4, 33.7.

[171] The first cycle runs from 33.7.1–7 and the second from 33.7.8–29.

[172] A. M. Honoré and A. Rodger (1970) 246–314, at 312; Honoré (2002) 36–37.

6

Some Digest Texts of Ulpian Attributed to Paul

This chapter concerns some texts attributed in the Digest to Paul but which seem really to be texts of Ulpian. The reason for thinking that these texts are wrongly inscribed is mainly the difference in style between the two writers, but also turns in part on the way in which Digest titles were constructed. Moreover differences of style are not ultimately distinct from differences in legal outlook.

In *Ulpian* I suggested that Paul had a more conservative outlook than Ulpian.[1] His style was also more restrained in that, though they write in ways that closely resemble each other, Paul keeps to a more conventional word order and avoids unusual words. Ulpian's, on the other hand, was an oral style. He dictated most of his work, and more readily embraced expressions that were unusual, or at any rate commoner in speech than in writing. Whether or not this is a correct assessment, the writings of these two contemporary authors are relatively easy to distinguish. And the detection of misattributed texts throws light either on mistakes made by scribes in copying the Digest or on the detailed supervision of the compilers' work.

I list nine texts that seem to be wrongly attributed to Paul, and one in which Paul has cited Ulpian without acknowledgement. The texts themselves, or the relevant part of them, are set out in footnotes. In each there is a case for supposing that these texts, or part of them, have been attributed to the wrong author. The strength of the case however varies. No doubt there are other examples of misattribution that I have overlooked.[2]

[1] T. Honoré, *Ulpian. Pioneer of Human Rights* (2nd edn, Oxford 2002) 37, 74–5, 136–8: henceforth *Ulpian* (2002).

[2] These include cases where the Ulpian text is followed e.g. by one of Gaius: D. 18.6.2 (Gai. 2 *rer. cott.*) where 18.6.2.1 is from Ulpian 28 *ad Sab.*, as noted by W. Kalb, *Roms Juristen nach ihrer Sprache dargestellt* (Leipzig 1890) 131. Eight more texts which seem to have been wrongly attributed to Paul rather than Ulpian are dealt with below.

(a) **D. 47.2.21.** To begin with a text that is agreed to be misattributed, F1 and B inscribe this text to Paul 40 Sab., but F2 and most editors, including Lenel, opt for Ulpian 40 Sab. The text fits Ulpian's book 40, which is about *tutela* and *furtum*. Paul *ad Sabinum* runs to only 16 books and *furtum* comes in book 9. D. 47.2.20 is a text from book 9 of Paul and so is D. 47.2.22. So the attribution of D. 47.2.21 to Paul seems to reflect a mistake by a scribe who repeated the previous inscription. In it Ulpian, for it is really he, argues that a person who handles (*contrectat*) part of a whole steals only the part that he handles and could carry away, not the whole cupboard, heap of corn, ship's cargo etc. This is true even if he intended to take more.

There is another mistaken attribution in D. 47.2.21.2, where the received text reads:

Si quis aes subripuit, dum aurum se subripere putat, vel contra, ex libro octavo Pomponii ad Sabinum aut minus esse, cum plus esset: eius quod subripuit furtum committit: idem Ulpianus.

According to a plausible reconstruction the compilers intended the following sequence:

Ulpianus *libro quadragesimo ad Sabinum*. . . .Si quis aes subripuit, dum aurum se subripere putat, vel contra,

Pomponius *libro octavo* [add *decimo*, Lenel)] *ad Sabinum* aut minus esse, cum plus esset

Ulpianus *libro quadragesimo ad Sabinum* eius quod subripuit, furtum committit.

The thief makes a mistake as to substance or amount. The reference to Ulpian at this point seems to be a distorted version of the fact that, after the short text of Pomponius, the compilers returned to Ulpian's commentary on Sabinus. The text as a whole contains a number of words and expressions characteristic of Ulpian: *proinde*;[3] *utrum . . . an vero*;[4] *et magis est*;[5] *proinde si*;[6] *et ita et Sabinus ait*;[7] *et ita utimur*;[8]

[3] D. 47.2.21 pr.; *Ulpian* (2002) 43 nn. 30–1; 44 nn. 38–9; 46 nn. 42–7: 65 of 68 texts in which *proinde* is a conjunction on its own. There is no text from Paul.

[4] D. 47.2.21.5; *Ulpian* (2002) 51 n. 142; 21 of 25 texts, of which one from Paul (D. 44.7.44.6).

[5] D. 47.2.21.2; *Ulpian* (2002) 47 n. 70: 84 of 104 texts, including 7 from Paul, of which D. 11.3.14.2 is really Ulpian.

[6] D. 47.2.21.8; Ulpian (2002) 44, 46 nn. 43–4; 85 of 88 texts, with two from Paul, of which D. 9.2.22 pr. is editorial, 47.2.21.8 is part of this text, really of Ulpian, as is 13.7.16.1 (below nn. 55–8).

[7] D. 47.2.21.8; *Ulpian* (2002) 48 n. 100–2: 118 texts of 123, with two from Paul, of which 23.2.60.4 is a citation from Ulpian: below n. 69.

[8] D. 47.2.21.9; *Ulpian* (2002) 55 n. 199: all six texts.

quamvis... attamen.[9] His authorship is not in doubt, but there is one feature, insufficiently noticed in my *Ulpian*, which is important from the point of view of the writer's outlook, the use of *si proponas* in D. 47.2.21.6.[10]

Si mihi proponas is found only in Ulpian.[11] But that is not the whole picture. *Proponere* and the form *si proponas* are primarily used in the legal sources of a petitioner putting forward a view of the facts to which a legal response is requested. The response may take the form of a formal reply (*responsum*), an imperial ruling (*rescriptum*) or an answer to a question put (*quaestio*). This is true of the two texts, apart from the spurious D. 47.2.21, in which Paul used the form *sed* or *si proponas*. In one he is answering a petitioner who has stated in his petition that the creditor was absent.[12] The other is the celebrated case of Arecusa, about which Nörr has written a delightful study.[13] This text consists of Paul's answer to an inquiry by a correspondent who presents him with a legal problem.[14]

Ulpian has one text of this sort, in which he cites from a rescript of Antoninus and Severus that refers to a fact asserted by the petitioner.[15] But he has another 34 texts, including the 10 already mentioned,[16] in which *si proponas* is used not of a view of the facts put forward by a petitioner but of a version that someone might put forward and that demands a legal answer.[17] In only one of these 34 texts, from Ulpian's *disputationes*,[18] can we suppose that there was really an interlocutor. In

[9] D. 4.2.21.10; *Ulpian* (2002) 50 n. 117; 16 of 18 texts, and the one attributed to Paul (D. 47.2.21.10) is part of this text of Ulpian.

[10] *Certe si proponas in apotheca amphoras esse vini easque subtractas, singularum furtum fit, non totius apothecae, quemadmodum si ex pluribus rebus moventibus in horreo reclusis unam tulerit.*

[11] *Ulpian* (2002) s. 44 mentions nine such texts, but there are 10: D. 28.6.10.5 (4 Sab.); 49.17.6 (6 Sab.); 32.52.7a (24 Sab.); 17.2.55 (30 Sab.); 46.3.12.3 (30 Sab.); 47.3.2 (42 Sab.); 40.4.13.3 (5 disp.); 16.1.8.13 (29 ed.); 44.2.7(75 ed.); 44.4.4.23 (76 ed.).

[12] D. 17.1.58.1 (Paul 4 qu.: *cum proponas eum afuisse...*).

[13] D. Nörr, *Römisches Recht: Geschichte und Geschichten. Der Fall Arecusa et alii (Dig. 19.1.43 sq.)* (Munich 2005).

[14] D. 19.1.43 (Paul 5 quest.: *plane si... proponas*).

[15] D. 19.2.19.9 (Ulp. 32 ad ed.: *cum per te non stetisse proponas*).

[16] Above n. 11.

[17] Above n. 11 and D. 28.3.3.6 (3 ad Sab.); 29.2.30.2,6 (8 ad Sab.); 7.1.25.6 (18 ad Sab.); 33.8.6.1 (25 ad Sab.); 19.1.1.1 (28 ad Sab.); 23.3.5.4 (31 ad Sab.); 24.1.5.14 (32 ad Sab.); 26.2.10.2 (ad 36 Sab.); 47.3.2 (42 ad Sab.); 47.2.46.5 (42 ad Sab.); 11.4.1.8a (1 ad ed.); 10.4.11.1 (24 ad ed.); 26.10.3.7 (35 ad ed.); 37.11.1.11 (39 ad ed.); 37.5.3.5 (40 ad ed.); 38.5.1.1 (44 ad ed.); 38.2.16.8 (45 ad ed.); 29.4.1.9 (50 ad ed.); 47.8.2.7 (56 ad ed.); 42.5.17 pr. (63 ad ed.); 29.2.24.1 (81 ad ed.); 36.1.17.9 (4 fid.); 5.1.52.2 (6 fid.).

[18] D. 40.4.13.3 (Ulp. 5 disp.).

the 17 texts from *ad Sabinum*, the 14 *ad edictum* and the two on *fideicommissa* there cannot have been. Take as an example Ulpian's discussion of fraud on a patron. If the freedman does not alienate *dolo malo*, the patron must prove that the alienation was on death (*mortis causa*). For if you allege (*si enim proponas*) that it was on death we do not ask whether it was alienated *dolo malo*. Liability is automatic.[19]

'You' is here not an actual petitioner but stands for anyone interested in the law on the subject. Ulpian imagines an interlocutor who suggests a certain set of facts or interpretation of the facts. He thinks of law as emerging from a dialogue, and in that way comes closest of the Roman jurists to the common law tradition by which the law emerges from a dialogue between judge and advocate.

I. Ulpian Inscription Omitted

Some attributions that seem wrong come after texts of Ulpian to which a brief comment by Paul is added.[20] The Digest then returns to the Ulpian text but does not repeat the Ulpian inscription. The latter part of the text looks like part of Paul's text, not Ulpian's.

(b) D. 2.7.3–4. In this title on the praetor's edict against removing one summoned to court by force ([*qui*] *vi eximat*) or fraud (*neve facit dolo malo quo magis eximeretur*) there is a discussion about whether both force and fraud are needed or whether one will suffice.[21] In D. 2.7.3 Ulpian says that force is enough without fraud. A text of Paul is then inserted which makes the point that removing (*eximere*) is a general term, and covers any form of removal. The text goes on to give examples of non-forcible removal, for instance causing a delay so that the action is lost. *Ut puta*, which introduces the examples, is markedly Ulpianic: he has the phrase 298 times in the Digest out

[19] D. 38.5.1.1 (Ulp. 44 ad ed.).

[20] Below (b) to (h).

[21] D. 2.7.3.2 (Ulpianus *libro quinto ad edictum*) Quod praetor praecepit 'vi eximat': vi an et dolo malo? Sufficit vi, quamvis dolus malus cesset. 2.7.4 (Paulus *libro quarto ad edictum*) Sed eximendi verbum generale est, ut Pomponius ait. Eripere enim est de manibus auferre per raptum: eximere quoque modo auferre.// <Ulp. 5 *ad ed.*> Ut puta si quis non rapuerit quem, sed moram fecerit quo minus in ius veniret, ut actionis dies exiret vel res tempore amitteretur: videbitur exemisse, quamvis corpus non exemerit. Sed et si eo loci retinuerit, non abduxit, his verbis tenetur. 1. Item si quis eum, qui per calumniam vocabatur, exemerit: constat eum hoc edicto teneri. Praetor ait 'neve faciat dolo malo, quo magis eximeretur': nam potest sine dolo malo id fieri, veluti cum iusta causa est exemptionis.

of 317.[22] Other phrases in the rest of this text (*eo loci*,[23] *praetor ait*[24]) also point to Ulpian.

One may reasonably conclude that D. 2.7.4, after the first two sentences (or one sentence) from Paul, returns to the text of Ulpian book 5 on the edict. But this was overlooked by the scribe copying the Digest title. The phrase *praetor ait* is particularly significant, since this phrase is found in 53 Ulpian texts and only once in Paul,[25] in this very text. Moreover *ait praetor* is found in 117 Ulpian texts and only twice in Paul.[26] It is not that the use of *ait* was foreign to Paul, especially when he quotes jurists.[27] But only Ulpian is cited as using *ait/aiunt* to give the words of the edict of the praetor or curule aediles.[28] The few other texts that give the words of part of the edict do so with a formula such as *verba autem edicti haec/talia sunt.*[29] The three instances of *ait praetor/praetor ait* attributed to Paul, though not doubted by Lenel,[30] are all in my view spurious.[31] The closest Paul comes to using *ait* of a clause of the edict is in D. 9.4.31, but this text is concerned to interpret edictal words rather than to record them.[32]

[22] *Ulpian* (2002) 65 n. 433.

[23] D. 2.4.7. pr.; *Ulpian* (2002) 71 n. 723 lists 19 of 20 texts: the other is D. 14.2.10.1 (Labeo 1 *pith. Paul epit*).

[24] D. 2.4.7.1; *Vocabularium Iurisprudentiae Romanae* (Berlin 1903–1985 = *VIR*) I 326.16–43.

[25] *VIR* I 326.16–25.

[26] *VIR* I 326.25–41; The Paul texts are D. 4.7.8.1 (Paul 12 *ad ed.*); 43.3.2.1 (Paul 63 *ad ed.*), both in texts attributable to Ulpian: below nn. 49, 60.

[27] T. Honoré and J. Menner, *Concordance to the Digest Jurists* (Oxford 1980) lists 216 instances of *ait*, all relating to jurists, *e.g.* D. 44.4.5.1 (Paul 71 *ad ed.*: *Marcellus ait*), apart from the three which refer to the praetor but which I argue are Ulpianic or editorial (above n. 26, below n. 31).

[28] *VIR* IV.I s.1092.5–29 lists 177 Ulpian texts for *praetor ait* and *ait praetor*. VIR I 332.37–39 lists four texts for the curule aediles: 21.1.1.1; 21.1.19.5 (Ulp. 1 *ad ed. aed. cur.*) 21.1.38 pr., 21.1.40 (Ulp. 2 *ad ed. aed. cur.*). D. 28.8.10 (Marc. 28 *dig.*) gives the effect rather than the wording of an edict: *per singulos observaturum se ait praetor id quod praefiniendo tempore deliberationis edicit....*

[29] D. 4.6.1.1 (Ulp. 1 *ad ed.*); 4.3.1.1 (Ulp. 11 *ad ed.*); 15.1.1.2 (Ulp. 29 *ad ed.*); 27.6.1.1 (Ulp. 12 *ad ed.*); 4.4.1.1 (Ulp. 11 *ad ed.*: *praetor edicit*); 39.4.12.1 (Ulp. 38 *ad ed.*; *praetor hoc edictum proposuit*); 2.6.1 (Paul 1 *ad ed.*: *edicto cavetur ut...*); 13.5.17 (Paul 29 *ad ed.*: *ut illa verba 'neque fecisset* [fecisse *S*]' *hoc significent, ut neque in diem in quem constituit fecerit neque postea.*); 50.16.8 pr. (Paul 3 *ad ed.*: *verbum 'oportebit' tam praesens quam futurum tempus significat*); 50.16.227 (Paul 2 *man.*: *ex illa parte edicti 'cum quem ei heredem esse oportet'*).

[30] O. Lenel, *Das Edictum Perpetuum* (Leipzig 1927) 74 (D. 2.7.4.2); 125 (D. 4.7.8.1); 453 (D. 43.3.2.1).

[31] This text and below nn. 48–50, 59–60.

[32] D. 9.4.31 (Paul 7 *ad Plaut.*): *Quod ait praetor, cum familia furtum faciat, ad eum modum se actionem daturum, ut tantum actor consequatur, quantum si liber fecisset consequeretur, quaeritur, utrum....*

Ulpian also uses *ait* to give the text of a *lex*,[33] *senatus consultum*,[34] *oratio principalis*,[35] or enactment of a particular emperor (Traianus,[36] Antoninus Augustus[37]). But his practice in this regard is not consistent. He and other writers have a variety of ways, for example, of introducing the text of a rescript.[38]

The consistent formula employed for the words of the praetor's edict and that of the curule aediles throws light on the organization of the Digest project. It must have been an instruction to the excerpters and editors that the texts of these edicts were to be taken from Ulpian's commentaries, not, for example, Paul's. According to Lenel, Paul put the edict in a different, though historically more correct, order from that adopted in Julian's *Digesta* and by Ulpian.[39] It cannot be supposed that in his 78 book commentary Paul did not cite the words of the edict on which he was commenting. But only Ulpian's citations have survived. This is one aspect of Tribonian's reliance on Ulpian, never expressly acknowledged. And Ulpian, with few exceptions,[40] introduced his citations of the edict's *ipsissima verba* with *ait* or *aiunt*.

(c) **D. 3.4.5–6.**[41] In book 3 of the Digest we have a longer passage mistakenly attributed to Paul in much the same way.[42] In the title dealing with persons who may sue or be sued on behalf of the *universitas*, Ulpian deals with rule that the representative be appointed by a two-thirds majority of those voting. A father's vote, he says, benefits a son and a son's the father. There is then a sentence of Paul which extends this principle to persons in the same *potestas*, since they vote as decurions (members of the council), not in their domestic capacity. The text attributed

[33] *VIR* I 326.44–47; 9 texts: D. 5.1.2.1 (Ulp. 3 *ad ed.*); 9.2.21 pr., 9.2.27.5 (Ulp 18 *ad ed.*); 23.2.45.4 (Ulp. 3 *ad leg. Iul. Pap.*); 24.2.11 pr.,1 (Ulp. 3 *ad leg. Iul. Pap.*) 24.3.64.10 (Ulp. 7 *ad leg. Iul .Pap.*); 48.5.24 pr.,4 (Ulp. 1 *adult.*).

[34] *VIR* I 326.47–49; 7 texts: D. 5.3.20.7,17; 5.3.25.2,3 (Ulp. 15 *ad ed.*); 14.6.7.3 (Ulp. 29 *ad ed.*); 38.17.1.12; 38.17. 2.23 (Ulp. 1 *ad Sab.*).

[35] *VIR* I 326.49–50; 3 texts: D. 24.1.32.9, 14 (Ulp. 33 *ad Sab.*); 49.4.1.7 (Ulp. 1 *appell.*).

[36] *VIR* I 326.50–51; D. 49.14.16 (Ulp. 8 *ad leg. Iul. Pap.*).

[37] *VIR* I 326.51: D. 24.2.3 pr. (Ulp. 32 *ad Sab.*).

[38] E.g. D. 22.6.9.5 (Paul 1 *de iur. fact. ignor.*: *rescripsise in haec verba*); 27.9.13 pr. (Paul 1 *ad or. d. Sev.*: *et imperator Antoninus et divus pater eius in haec verba rescripserunt*); 47.21.2 (Call. 3 cogn.: *in haec verba rescripsit*).

[39] O. Lenel, *Das Edictum Perpetuum*, above n. 30, 3–13.

[40] Above n. 27.

[41] *Ulpian* (2002) 74.

[42] D. 3.4.5 (Ulpianus *libro octavo* <Lenel *nono*> *ad edictum*) Illud notandum Pomponius ait, quod et patris suffragium filio proderit et filii patri 3.4.6 (Paulus *libro nono ad edictum*) pr. item eorum, qui in eiusdem potestate sunt: quasi decurio enim hoc dedit, non quasi domestica persona. // [Ulp. 8 *ad ed.*] Quod et in honorum petitione erit servandum, nisi lex municipii vel perpetua consuetudo prohibeat... 1... 2... 3.

to Paul goes on to say that the same principle applies to elections to office (*honores*). But this sentence contains the phrase *erit servandum*, a future tense with an inversion of word order, which is a common feature of Ulpian's writing, and also appears in an earlier text of Ulpian.[43] In D. 3.4.6.1 and 2 the text continues with other Ulpianic phrases: *parvi enim refert*;[44] *et puto sic hoc accipiendum*.[45] The discussion of the procedure for appointing an agent to sue or be sued and the comparison between the agent and the procurator of a private person seems, then, to be taken from Ulpian's edictal commentary, apart from Paul's remark about councillors in the same *potestas*.

(d) D. 2.14.12–13. In the title on pacts we have what looks like another example of the phenomenon.[46] In D. 2.14.12 Ulpian says that a pact made by the principal's procurator can operate either in his favour or against him. In D. 2.14.13 pr. a text attributed to Paul by S and B but to Ulpian by F says that, if a procurator is appointed only to bring or defend an action, the pact that he makes does not prejudice the principal because payment cannot validly be made to the procurator. D. 2.14.13.1 goes on to say that if the procurator is appointed to act on his own behalf, he takes the place of the principal and so the pact must be observed. The text as it stands in the Digest is awkward, because both sentences in D. 2.14.13 begin *sed si*, and neither Ulpian nor Paul is likely to have begun two successive sentences in this way. The most likely explanation is that the first sentence is Paul's and the second, which qualifies the first, Ulpian's. Moreover *servandum erit* in the second sentence points more to Ulpian, who has *erit servandum* in D. 3.2.19 (Ulp. 8 [Lenel 9] ed.) and, as we saw, the same phrase in a text wrongly attributed to Paul.[47] Perhaps in copying the text one scribe has inscribed Paul's name, another Ulpian's, though both inscriptions occurred in the original.

[43] D. 3.2.19 (Ulp. 8 *ad ed.*).

[44] *Ulpian* (2002) 39, 48 n. 72, 55 n. 201, 74 nn. 826–7: 28 of 30 texts, with this the only Digest text attributed to Paul.

[45] *Ulpian* (2002) 47 nn. 53–55, 65 n. 432, 74 n. 828. *Et puto* is Ulpian's 112 times out of 126. There are seven texts of Paul, including this spurious text.

[46] D. 2.14.12 (Ulpianus *libro quarto ad edictum*) Nam et nocere constat, sive ei mandavi ut pacisceretur, sive omnium rerum mearum procurator fuit: ut et Puteolanus libro primo adesessoriorum scribit: cum placuit eum etiam rem in iudicium deducere 2.14.13 pr. (Paulus *libro tertio ad edictum*) Sed si tantum ad actionem procurator factus sit, conventio facta domino non nocet, quia nec solvi ei possit. // [Ulp. 4 *ad ed.*] 1. Sed si in rem suam datus sit procurator, loco domini habetur: et ideo servandum erit pactum conventum.

[47] D. 3.4.6 pr. (Paul 9 *ad ed.*); *Ulpian* (2002) cit. 74.

(e) **D. 4.7.4–8.** At first sight this sequence does not appear to be one in which a passage from Paul that modifies one from Ulpian continues to be attributed to Paul after the text has returned to Ulpian. But in reality it is similar. In the title on alienation by a defendant in bad faith which prejudices the plaintiff in litigation[48] Ulpian, at the end of a long passage, says that the action is not penal but compensatory and is not given after a year.[49] Gaius in the next text points out that the action is compensatory but resembles a delict. Paul then says that to produce the object sued for (*exhibere*) does not prevent the edict applying, if in the judge's opinion the previous position is not restored by its production. In 4.7.8.1 we find the actual words of the edict introduced by the phrase *Ait praetor.* As mentioned earlier,[50] though there are 91 Ulpian texts with this formula, this is the only one attributed to Paul. The attribution is clearly wrong, as is confirmed by the fact that D. 4.7.8 and 4.7.9 are both inscribed to Paul, whereas if D. 4.7.8 had been entirely Paul's the next inscription should read *Idem.* One possible reason for duplicated inscriptions is that an intermediate text by another author has dropped out between the two. The intermediate text of Ulpian has been overlooked by the scribe copying the Digest text, and this has resulted in a duplication of the Paul inscriptions.

(f) **D. 11.3.13–14.** There is another example in the title on the corruption of a slave. This title is mainly composed of texts from Ulpian on the edict with short interventions by Paul. But towards the end of the title there is apparently a change. A short text of Ulpian is followed by a long text of Paul on the edict.[51] According to Ulpian the action for corrupting a slave includes the case in which the slave belongs to

[48] *De alienatione iudicii mutandi causa facta.*

[49] D. 4.7.4.6 Ulpianus *libro terto decimo ad edictum* Haec actio non est poenalis, sed rei persecutionem arbitrio iudicis continet, quare et heredi dabitur: in heredem autem 4.7.5 Paulus *libro undecimo ad edictum* vel similem 4.7.6 Ulpianus *libro tertio decimo ad edictum* vel post annum non dabitur 4.7.7 Gaius *libro quarto ad edictum provinciale* quia pertinet quidem ad rei persecutionem, videtur autem ex delicto dari 4.7.8 pr. Paulus *libro duodecimo ad edictum* Ex hoc edicto tenetur et qui rem exhibet, si arbitratu iudicis pristinam iudicii causam non restituit. // [Ulp. 13 *ad ed.*] 1. Ait praetor 'quaeve alienatio iudicii mutandi causa facta erit': id est si futuri iudicii causa, non eius quod iam sit... 2...3...4...5...

[50] Above nn. 26–27.

[51] D. 11.3.13 (Ulpianus *libro vicesimo tertio ad edictum*) 1. Sed et si quis servum hereditarium corruperit, hac actione tenebitur: sed et petitione hereditatis quasi praedo tenebitur D. 11.3.14 pr. (Paulus *libro non decimo ad edictum*) ut tantum veniat in hereditatis petitionem quantum in hanc actionem. // [Ulp. 23 *ad ed.*] 1. De filio filiave familias corruptis huic edicto locus non est, quia servi corrupti constituta actio est, qui in patrimonio nostro esset, (ubi insert *B*) et pauperiorem se factum esse dominus probare potest dignitate et fama domus integra manente....2...3...4...5...6...7...8...9.

an inheritance, and damages for corruption can be claimed in a suit for the inheritance. Paul adds that in a suit for the inheritance the damages are the same as in the action for corrupting a slave. The text attributed to Paul then goes on to discuss the corruption of a *filius familias*, which will not lie because the action presupposes patrimonial loss. There is a further discussion of corrupting a slave owned by plaintiff and defendant in common, and of the case where a slave owned in common corrupts another slave. There is reason to believe that this extensive discussion comes from Ulpian's edictal commentary. Phrases such as: *et magis est*;[52] *interdum tamen*;[53] and *utrum... an vero*;[54] point to him. Moreover there is no reason why the structure of the title should change towards the end, with Ulpian's edictal commentary being replaced by Paul's.

(g) D. 13.7.15–16 falls in the title on mortgage and pledge.[55] In it Ulpian's edictal commentary is prominent. In lex 15 he considers the duty of the creditor of mortgaged land, and in lex 16 pr. Paul turns to the tutor or curator who pledges his pupil, minor or insane person's property.[56] 16.1 begins with a compilatorial sentence giving the creditor a right to sue the debtor by contrary action. It continues with examples of a debtor who pledged the property of another or property already pledged to another or liable to the state, whose claim takes priority. The examples are introduced with *proinde si*, a phrase that is strongly Ulpianic. He has 214 texts in which it means 'hence', and there are only six others in the Digest, two attributed to Paul.[57] Neither is genuine Paul, but both are interesting in their way. In D. 9.2.22 pr. the phrase introduces an example by Paul of the principle stated by Ulpian in D. 9.2.21 that in the lex Aquilia actual loss (*id quod interest*) must be paid for. The link is

[52] D. 11.3.14.2: *Ulpian* (2002) cit. 44, 47 n. 70; 88 out of 104 texts. There are seven texts of Paul, including this one and D 47.2.21.5, both of which are really Ulpian's (above n. 5).

[53] D. 11.3.14.9; *Ulpian* (2002) 51 n. 147: 11 of 13 texts. The only text attributed to Paul is this one.

[54] D. 11.3.14.9; above n. 4.

[55] *De pigernaticia actione vel contra.*

[56] D. 13.7.16 pr. (Paulus *libro vicensimo nono ad edictum*) Tutor lege non refragante si dederit rem pupilli pignori, tuendum erit, scilicet si in rem pupilli pecuniam accipiat. Idem est et in curatore adulescentis vel furiosi.//[Ulp. 28 *ad ed.*] [Contrariam pigneraticiam creditori actionem competere certum est.] proinde si rem alienam vel alii pigneratam vel in publicum obligatum dedit, tenebitur, quamvis et stellionatus crimencommittat. Sed utrum ita demum, si scit, an et si ignoravit? Et quantum ad crimen pertinet, excusat ignorantia: quantum ad contrarium iudicium, ignorantia eum non excusat, ut Marcellus libro sexto digestorum scribit. Sed si sciens creditor accipiat vel alienum vel obligatum vel morbosum, contrarium ei non competit... 2.

[57] Honoré, *Ulpian* (2002) 46 nn. 43–7.

editorial, and shows that the editor of the title was influenced by reading Ulpian, who was fond of *proinde*.

The present text conceals, I think, a reversion by the title editor to Ulpian's commentary. This is confirmed by the reference in the text to Marcellus *libro sexto digestorum*. Ulpian often cites Marcellus, to whom he refers 193 times as against 18 references by Paul. But the crucial difference is that 53 of Ulpian's references to Marcellus are by book (*libro* ..)[58] whereas the only such reference attributed to Paul is in this text, which has in my view been misallocated from *proinde si* onwards, at least to the end of D. 13.7.16.1.

(h) D. 43.3.1–2. Much the same applies to the title *Quod legatorum*, dealing with an interdict that protects the heir or *bonorum possessor* against a legatee who takes possession of the property bequeathed without the heir or possessor's consent. It contains only two texts, the first a long text of Ulpian, the second a shorter but still substantial text inscribed to Paul. The end of the long Ulpian text deals with the giving of security by the *bonorum possessor* to a legatee to whom a legacy is due. The *bonorum possessor* can bring an interdict only for property for which he has given security.[59] The Paul text begins with the point that giving security for a legacy includes security for anything that later accrues to it. The text attributed to Paul then goes on to another part of the edict, the text of which is introduced with *ait praetor*. It deals with the position of the *bonorum possessor* if it is not his fault that security has not been given. This means that he must be willing to give security and must not delay unduly when security is demanded. The phrases *ait praetor*[60] and *accipimus*[61] are typical of Ulpian and there is no reason, again, why the title editor should have shifted from Ulpian's commentary to Paul's when he introduced a fresh part of the edict *quod legatorum*.

(i) D. 2.14.9. So far we have examined sequences in which the text of Ulpian was followed by a short text of Paul which appears to be longer

[58] T. Honoré and J. Menner (above n. 27) fiche 63.

[59] D. 43.3.1.18 (Ulpianus *libro sexagesimo septimo ad edictum*) Si quarumdam rerum nomine satisdatum sit, quarundam non sit satisdatum, earum rerum nomine sine impedimento agi poterit, de quibus satisdatum est, ceterarum non poterit. 43.3.2 pr. (Paulus *libro sexagesimo tertio ad edictum*) pr. Diversum est, si postea pars legato adcreverit: nam hoc nomine tenentur fideiussores in totum. // [Ulp. 67 *ad ed.*] 43.3.2.1. Quod ait praetor 'si per bonorum possessorem non stat, ut satisdetur', sic accipimus, si paratus sit satisdare; non ergo offerre debet satisdationem, sed petenti moram non facere...2...3...4.

[60] Above nn. 24–32.

[61] D. 43.3.2.1; *Ulpian* (2002) cit. 64 n. 430: 60 texts out of 62, with two of Paul including this one wrongly attributed to him.

than it really is, because the inscription returning to Ulpian's commentary has been omitted. The converse can also happen. Sometimes a text of Paul contains an insertion from Ulpian. There is perhaps an instance of this in title 2.14. The discussion is about a pact by an heir with creditors of the deceased. If the majority of the creditors agree on the proportion of the debts to be paid, the praetor issues a decree adopting their wishes. According to Ulpian this means the wishes of those who are owed most of the debt. But if the amount owed by those who agree and those who do not is equal, Papinian says that the view of the greater number of creditors prevails. A Paul text[62] then makes the point that if several creditors have the same action they are regarded, for purposes of counting creditors, as one. Some examples are then given which, to judge by the drafting, come from Ulpian rather than Paul. The examples are introduced by *ut puta*,[63] and one of them begins *nec non et*,[64] which is also Ulpianic.[65] *Difficile est, ut...* also points to him.[66]

The text returns again in my view from Ulpian to Paul in the next sentence, which takes up his original point, by asserting that a creditor who has several actions is not treated as several persons in relation to a creditor who has only one action. Another reason for thinking that the Paul text has resumed is that the sentence begins *nam nec is*, whereas the previous sentence began *nam difficile est*. It is not likely that two successive sentences by the same author began with the same introductory word. The rest of the text (D. 2.14.9.1) concerns how to calculate the amount of debt, and is in my view also Paul's.

(j) **D. 23.2.60.** A different text, in which the attribution is not mistaken, but Paul incorporates in his own work some sentences from Ulpian, comes towards the end of the title on marriage.[67] It is

62 D. 2.14.9 pr. (*Paulus sexagesimo secundo ad edictum*) Si plures sint qui eandem actionem habent, unius loco habentur. // [Ulp. 4 ad ed.] Ut puta plures sunt rei stipulandi vel plures argentarii, quorum nomina simul facta sunt: unius loco numerabuntur, quia unum debitum est. et cum tutores pupilli creditoris plures convenissent, unius loco numerantur, qui unius pupilli nomine convenerant. nec non et unus tutor plurium pupillorum nomine unum debitum praetendentium si convenerit, placuit unius loco esse. nam difficile est, ut unus homo duorum vicem sustineat. // [Paul. 62 ad ed.] nam nec is, qui plures actiones habet, adversus eum, qui unum actionem habet, plurium personarum loco accipitur. 1. Cumulum debiti et ad plures summas referemus......

63 Above n. 22.

64 *Ulpian* (2002) 49 n. 104: nine of 11 texts: this is the only one supposedly of Paul.

65 D. 2.14.9 pr.; *Ulpian* (2002) 49 nn. 104: 9 of 11 texts, the only one of Paul being this text.

66 *VIR* II s. 5–7: D. 18.6.4.1 (Ulp. 28 ad Sab.); 21.1.38.4 (Ulp 1 ad ed. cur.); 49.4.1.15 (Ulp. 1 appell.) and this text 2.14.9 pr (Paul. 62 ad ed.?).

67 *De ritu nuptiarum.*

the only text from Paul's book on the oration of Marcus Antoninus and Commodus.[68] There is no doubt that this is a text of Paul, but he seems to have excerpted in s. 4 at least two sentences of Ulpian, who must therefore have written on the same subject.[69] The topic discussed is whether a tutor who wished to be excused from office but has not yet assembled the evidence to be excused could marry a *pupilla* who had in the meantime reached puberty so that the tutor's office was at an end. That these sentences are Ulpian's appears from the phrase *quaestio in eo est*[70] and the sentence beginning *et ait Papinianus*.[71] But though Ulpian raises the question he does not expressly answer it, and Paul differs from Papinian,[72] and perhaps by implication from Ulpian, in that he thinks that the tutor can be excused if he marries the ward in these circumstances.

That Paul here cited Ulpian without naming him does not show that there were bad relations, as opposed to differences of outlook on legal issues, between the two. Ulpian seems also to have cited Paul without naming him. To avoid citing the opinion of a contemporary by name could save embarrassment.[73]

Reading through the Digest texts again I find another instance of what appears to be an Ulpian text wrongly attributed by the compilers or a copyist to Paul. The Digest title 38.17 concerns two *senatus consulta* (the Tertullianum of 133 AD and the Orfitianum of 178 AD) that dealt

[68] *Libro singulari ad orationem divi Antonini et Commodi*; Honoré, *Ulpian* (2002) 123, 186, 202, 205; D. Liebs, in *HLL* 4 (1997) §423.17.

[69] D. 23.2.60 *Idem (Paulus) libro singulari ad orationem divi Antonini et Commodi.* 3 Quin autem ille, qui, cum datus est tutor, cessat in administratione, pertineat ad orationem, non est dubitandum, quia perinde tenetur ex sacris constitutionibus atque si gessisset. 4. Quid ergo si, cum se vellet excusare aliquo titulo nec in promptu probationes haberet, excusationis negotium fuerit dilatum et inter moras pupilla adolvererit, an ad senatus consultum pertineat? [Ulp. Quaestio in eo est, an et post pubertatem officio finito excusationem eius recipi oporteat: nam si recipitur et excusaverit <excusatus erit Mommsen> impune potest ducere: si vero non debeat recipi post officium finitum, non recte ducit. et ait Papinianus libro quinto responsorum officio finito excusationem recipi non oportere et ideo exacti temporis periculum ad eum pertinere.] sed mihi hoc nequaquam placet; iniquum enim est propter dilationem, quae forte non dolo, sed quae ex necessitate contingit, non excusari vel nuptias impediri excusatione recepta...5... 6...7...8.

[70] Honoré, *Ulpian* (2002) 52 n. 155 : four texts: D. 37.6.1.21 (Ulp. 40 ed.); 43.26.6.4 (Ulp. 71 ed.); 47.2.43.14 (Ulp. 41 Sab); 41.1.23.1 (Ulp. 43 Sab.) and the present text attributed to Paul.

[71] Above n. 7.

[72] Cf. D. 20.4.16 (Paul 3 qu.: *mihi nequaquam hoc iustum esse videbatur*).

[73] *Ulpian* (2002) 137–8. There are other examples: Julian citing his teacher Iavolenus (H. Buhl, *Salvius Julianus*, 1886), Paul his teacher Cervidius Scaevola (D. 32.78 pr.,2,3; 32.93.2; 32.101.1; 33.7.20.6).

with the succession on intestacy of a mother to her children. It is constructed from two long texts from Ulpian *ad Sabinum* followed by some shorter texts. Five of these from D. 38.17.5–9 are inscribed successively to Paul on the SC Tertullianum, Paul on the SC Orfitianum, Paul on the SCC Tertullianum and Orfitianum, Gaius on the SC Tertullianum and Gaius on the SC Orfitianum. There is evidently something wrong with these inscriptions, since Paul can hardly have written three monographs, one on the Tertullianum, one on the Orfitianum and a third devoted to both. Mommsen dealt with this problem by suggesting that the third of these texts should be inscribed to Paul on the Tertullianum alone, the reference to the Orfitianum being eliminated. Hence D. 38.17.7, inscribed *Idem* (Paulus) *libro singulari ad senatus consultum Tertullianum et Orphitianum* is correctly inscribed to Paul, but 'et Orphitianum' should be deleted.

I think this is right, and would take the suggestion further. The first of these texts (D. 38.17.5 inscribed *Paulus ad SC Tertullianum*) should be attributed to Ulpian rather than Paul.[74] In other words either Ulpian, like Paul, wrote a monograph on this SC, and D. 38.17.5 was taken from his monograph, or the text comes from his thirteenth book *ad Sabinum*, from which D. 38.17.2 is also taken. In this book Ulpian seems to have commented on the SC Tertullianum.[75] But D. 38.17.7 and two other texts inscribed to Paul in other Digest titles will have come from Paul, not Ulpian.[76] The order of texts in D. 38.17.5–9 would therefore be: (5) Ulpian *libro tertio decimo ad Sabinum* or *libro singulari ad SC Tertullianum*, (6) Paul ad Orfitianum, (7) Paul ad Tertullianum, (8) Gaius ad Tertullianum, (9) Gaius ad Orfitianum. The sequence of Paul texts would then agree with that in D. 50.16.230–231 where text 230 is inscribed *Idem (*Paulus*) libro singulari ad senatus consultum Orfitianum* and text 231 *Idem libro singulari ad senatus consultum Tertullianum.* The order set out in D. 50.16, which is generally reliable, is confirmed if my suggestion is correct. It is true that the order listed for Gaius is chronologically more correct than that for Paul, but

[74] D. 38.17.5 (*Paulus [Ulpianus] libro singulari ad senatus consultum Tertullianum*) Aequissimum visum est omnes filios matri praeferri, etiamsi per adoptionem in familiam relicti essent. Sed et nepos ex adoptivo natus ex verbis senatus consulti matri obstabit. Si ex filio nepotem avus manumiserit isque patre et avo et matre superstitibus decesserit, potest quaeri, quis potior esse debeat. Nam si mater excluserit avum manumissorem, qui patre anteponitur, edicto praetoris inducetur pater defuncti, quo admisso desinit senatus consulto locus esse et rursus avus vocabitur. Itaque rectius est avo ius suum conservare, qui et contra scriptos heredes bonorum possesionem accipere solet.

[75] O. Lenel, *Palingenesia* II 1046.

[76] D. 38.17.7; 50.16.231; 32.28.

that consideration may not have determined the order in which Paul's *libri singulares* were read by the compilers of the Papinian mass from which these texts are taken. The writers themselves are often excerpted in anti-chronological order, as in the edictal commentaries, so that Ulpian comes before Paul, and Paul before Gaius. The reason for the anti-chronological sequence may be that the most recent author is likely to be the most comprehensive and up to date. But my reconstruction assumes that the attribution of D. 38.17.5 to Paul is mistaken, and it is to the reasons for supposing this that I now turn.

D 38.17.5 begins *aequissimum visum est. Aequissimus* in its various inflections accounts for 80 Ulpian texts in the Digest out of 86,[77] and though there are four Paul texts, including this doubtful one,[78] Paul nowhere else uses *aequissimus videri* or begins a sentence with *aequissimus*. Ulpian on the other hand has nine texts with *aequissimum visum est*[79] or *videtur*.[80] Some of these may pick up a phrase in the original enactment, as is the case with his citation of the senatus consultum Trebellianum.[81] The present text may also echo the original senatusconsultum, but whereas *aequissimum praetori visum est* is in order,[82] *aequissimum senatui visum est* would be presumptuous, since one must assume that what the senate prescribes is equitable.

Moreover the futures *obstabit*[83] and *vocabitur* fit Ulpian's liking for future tenses.[84] So it is likely that this article has uncovered one or possibly two hitherto unknown monographs of Ulpian that ran parallel to those of Paul. This latter *liber singularis* of Ulpian, if it existed, would appear in the Papinian mass, contrary to the general assignment of such works to the Sabinian mass, because they were naturally grouped with the similar commentaries of Paul and Gaius on these two *senatus consulta*.

[77] *Ulpian* (2002) 71 n. 721.

[78] D. 17.1.22.4 (Paul 32 ed.); 14.2.2 pr. (Paul 35 ed.); 48.20.7 pr. (Paul 1 port. lib. damn.).

[79] D. 7.9.1 pr. (79 ed.); 11.7.16 (25 ed.); 36.2.8 (34 Sab.); 37.12.1 pr. (45 ed.); 43.3.1.2 (67 ed.); 43.20.1.39 (70 ed.); 44.4.4.27 (76 ed.); 46.3.1 (43 Sab.).

[80] D. 18.4.2.18 (49 Sab.).

[81] D. 36.1.1.2 (Ulp. 3 fid: cuius verba haec sunt: 'Cum esset aequissimum...).

[82] D. 7.9.1 pr. (79 ed.).

[83] 10 Ulpian texts: T. Honoré and J. Menner (above n. 27) fiche 65.

[84] *Ulpian* (2002) 59–62.

Addendum A

Bluhme-Krüger Ordo Librorum Iuris Veteris in Compilandis Digestis Observatus (Updated in the Light of Modern Scholarship)

In this list of the order in which the works read in compiling the Digest were perused, commonly known as the BK Ordo, Krüger's numbering of the works is retained in the interests of convenience. Authors' names are given in the nominative case.

A	=	group based on authorship
S	=	group based on subject-matter
G	=	group based on literary genre
N	=	work added or inserted to achieve numerical balance
Sab.	=	Sabinian mass
Ed.	=	edictal mass
Pap.	=	Papinian mass
App.	=	Appendix
ID	=	mass indeterminate
IA	=	Index auctorum veterum
H	=	according to Honoré
M	=	according to Mantovani
O	=	according to Osler

Sabinian mass

(i) *ad Sabinum* group. S.
1. Ulpianus 51 ad Sabinum
2. Pomponius 36 ad Sabinum
3. Paulus 16 ad Sabinum

(ii) middle edictal commentaries group. S.

4. Ulpianus 81 ad edictum lib. 26-51 init.
5. Paulus 78 ad edictum lib. 28-48 init.
6. Paulus 23 brevium lib. 6-8
7. Gaius 30 ad edictum provinciale lib. 9-18
8. Gaius ad edictum urbanum 2 lib. de testamentis
9. Gaius ad edictum urbanum 3 lib. de legatis

(iii) Ulpian group. A.

10. Ulpianus 10 disputationum
11. Ulpianus 10 de omnibus tribunalibus

Unattached

12. Ulpianus 6 opinionum
13. Ulpianus 6 de censibus (position in mass doubted by **M**)

(iv) Julian group. A.

14. Iulianus 90 digestorum
15. Alfenus Varus 7 dig. (40 dig. **IA**.)
16. Paulus 8 epitomatorum Alfeni digestorum
17. Iulianus de ambiguitatibus
18. Iulianus 4 ad Urseium Ferocem
19. Iulianus 6 ex Minicio
20. Africanus 9 quaestionum

(v) institutions group. G.

21. Florentinus 12 institutionum
22. Marcianus 16 institutionum
23. Ulpianus 2 institutionum
24. Gaius 3 rerum cottidianum (7 rer. cott. **IA**.)
25. Gaius 4 institutionum
26. Callistratus 3 institutionum
27. Paulus 2 institutionum

(vi) adultery group. S.

28. Ulpianus 5 de adulteriis
29. Papinianus 2 de adulteriis
30. Papinianus 1 de adulteriis
31. Paulus 3 de adulteriis

Unattached

32. Ulpianus 1 de sponsalibus (ID, **M**; Sab., **H**)
33. Paulus 1 de dotis repetitione
34. Paulus 1 de adsignatione libertorum
35. Paulus 1 de iure patronatus (ID, **M**; Sab., **H**)

(vii) *regulae* group. G.

36. Neratius 15 regularum
37. Ulpianus 7 regularum
38. Scaevola 4 regularum
39. Paulus 1 regularum
40. Marcianus 5 regularum lib. 1-2
41. Ulpianus 2 responsorum
42. Marcianus 5 regularum lib. 3-4
43. Paulus 7 regularum
44. Marcianus 5 regularum lib. 5
45. Pomponius 1 regularum
46. Ulpianus 1 regularum

46 bis. (from BK 59) ? Marcellus 1 responsorum (repositioned, **M**; N, **H**)

Unattached

47. Ulpianus 10 de officio proconsulis
48. Paulus 1 ad SC Silanianum (ID, **M**; Sab., H)
49. Paulus 1 de portionibus quae liberis damnatorum conceduntur
50. Paulus 2 ad legem Iuniam
51. Paulus 1 de conceptione formularum

(viii) *iudicia publica* group. S.

52. Macer 2 publicorum iudiciorum
53. Venuleius 3 de iudiciis publicis
54. Paulus 1 de iudiciis publicis
55. Marcianus 2 de iudiciis publicis
56. Maecianus 14 de iudiciis publicis

(ix) *formula hypothecaria* group. S.

57. Marcianus 1 ad formulam hypothecariam
58. Gaius 1 de formula hypothecaria

Unattached

59. Marcellus 1 responsorum (to BK 46 bis)
60. Neratius 7 membranarum
61. Macer 2 de officio praesidis
62. Arcadius Charisius 1 de testibus
63. Marcianus 1 de delatoribus

(x) appeals group. S.

64. Ulpianus 4 de appellationibus
65. Macer 2 de appellationibus

66. Marcianus 2 de appellationibus
67. Paulus 1 de appellationibus
Unattached
68. Rutilius 1 ad legem Falcidiam
69. Paulus 1 ad legem Fufiam Caniniam

(xi) *lex Aelia Sentia* group. S.

70. Paulus 3 ad legem Aeliam Sentiam
71. Ulpianus 4 ad legem Aeliam Sentiam
Unattached
72. Paulus 1 de libertatibus dandis
73. Paulus 1 de liberali causa
74. Paulus 1 de secundis tabulis
75. Paulus 1 de iure codicillorum
76. Paulus 1 de centumviralibus iudiciis
77. Paulus 1 de adulteriis
78. Paulus 1 de senatusconsultis (ID, **M**; S or P, **H**)
79. Paulus 1 ad SC Velleianum (ID, **M**; S or P, **H**)
80. Paulus 1 de intercessionbus feminarum (ID, **M**; S or P, **H**)
81. Paulus 1 ad orationem divi Antonini et Commodi
82. Paulus 1 de excusationibus tutelarum (ID, **M**; S or P, **H**)
83. Paulus 1 ad orationem divi Severi
84. Paulus 1 de variis lectionibus
85. Ulpianus 1 pandectarum
86. Macer 2 de re militari
87. Paulus 1 de poenis militum
88. Ulpianus 1 de officio curatoris reipublicae
89. Ulpianus 1 de officio consularium
90. Paulus 2 de officio consulis
91. Venuleius Saturninus 4 de officio proconsulis
92. Claudius Saturninus 1 de poenis paganorum
93. Volusius Macianus 1 ex lege Rhodia (ID, **M**)

(xi bis ?) Labeo *posteriora* group probably formed from late arrivals. S.

93 bis. (from BK 265). Labeo 10 posteriorum a Iavoleno epitomatarum lib. 1-2 (S, **M**, **O**; for later books see BK 265)
94. Iavolenus 10 ex posterioribus Labeonis lib. 1-2 (S, **M**, **O**; for later books see BK 265 bis)

Papinian mass

(xii) Papinian group. A.
- 180. Papinianus 37 quaestionum
- 181. Papinianus 19 responsorum
- 182. Papinianus 2 definitionum

(xiii) *quaestiones* group. G.
- 183. Paulus 26 quaestionum
- 184. Scaevola 20 quaestionum
- 185. Callistratus 2 quaestionum

(xiv) *responsa* group. G.
- 186. Paulus 23 responsorum lib. 1-7
- 187. Scaevola 6 responsorum lib. 1
- 188. Paulus 23 responsorum lib. 8-15
- 189. Scaevola 6 responsorum lib. 2-4
- 190. Paulus 23 responsorum lib. 16-19
- 191. Scaevola 6 responsorum lib. 5
- 192. Paulus 23 responsorum lib. 20-23
- 193. Scaevola 6 responsorum lib. 6

(xv) *fideicommissa* group. S.
- 195. Ulpianus 6 fideicommissorum lib. 1-4
- 194. Valens 7 fideicommissorum lib. 1-4
- 196. Maecianus 16 fideicommissorum lib. 1-8
- 197. Gaius 2 fideicommissorum
- 198. Paulus 3 fideicommissorum lib. 1-2
- 199. Pomponius 5 fideicommissorum lib. 1-2
- 203. Ulpianus 6 fideicommissorum lib. 5-6
- 200. Maecianus 16 fideicommisssorum lib. 9-16
- 201. Valens 7 fideicommissorum lib. 5-7
- 202. Pomponius 5 fideicommissorum lib. 3-5
- 204. Paulus 3 fideicommissorum lib. 3.

(xvi) *sententiae/iuris epitomae* group. G.
- 205. Paulus 5 sententiarum lib. 1 init.
- 206. Hermogenianus 6 iuris epitomarum lib. 1
- 207. Paulus 5 sententiarum lib.1 fin.- 2
- 208. Hermogenianus 6 iuris epitomarum lib. 2
- 209. Paulus 5 sententiarum lib. 3
- 210. Hermogenianus 6 iuris epitomarum lib. 3

211. Paulus 5 sententiarum lib. 4
212. Hermogenianus 6 iuris epitomarum lib. 4
213. Paulus 5 sententiarum lib. 5
214. Hermogenianus 6 iuris epitomarum lib. 5-6

Unattached

215. Gaius 1 de casibus
216. Venuleius Saturninus 19 stipulationum

(xvii) Neratius *responsa* group. S.

217. Neratius 3 responsorum
218. Paulus 4 ad Neratium

(xviii) Tryphoninus group. A.

219. Tryphoninus 21 disputationum lib. 1-12
220. Paulus 3 manualium
221. Tryphoninus 21 disputationum lib. 13-21
222. Paulus 3 decretorum

(According to Mantovani (1987) 219-222 form a group of works read together, but the exact arrangement cannot be settled)

Unattached

223. Gaius 3 regularum
224. Gaius 1 regularum (ID, **M**; P, **H**)
225. Paulus 1 de cognitionibus
226. Paulus 1 de concurrentibus actionibus
227. Paulus 1 de usuris

(xix) *SC Turpillianum* group. S.

228. Paulus 1 ad SC Turpillianum
229. Marcianus 1 ad SC Turpillianum

Unattached

230. Paulus 1 ad SC Libonianum
231. Paulus 1 ad SC Claudianum
232. Paulus 1 de poenis omnium legum (ID, **M**; S or P, **H**)
233. Paulus 1 de poenis paganorum
234. Paulus 1 ad regulam Catonianam (ID, **M**; S or P, **H**)
235. Paulus 1 de forma testamenti (ID, **M**; S or P, **H**)
236. Paulus 1 de inofficioso testamento (ID, **M**; S or P, **H**)

(xx) *tacita fideicommissa* group. S.

237. Paulus 1 de tacitis fideicommissis (ID, **M**; P, **H**)
242. Gaius 1 de tacitis fideicommissis

Unattached

238. Paulus 1 de instrumenti significatione (ID, **M**; P, **H**)

241. Paulus 1 ad legem Falcidiam

(xxi) *SC Tertullianum* group. S.

239. Paulus 1 ad SC Tertullianum

243. Gaius 1 ad SC Tertullianum

(xxii) *SC Orfitianum* group. S.

240. Paulus 1 ad SC Orfitianum

244. Gaius 1 ad SC Orfitianum

Unattached

245. Gaius 3 de manumissionibus

246. Gaius 3 de verborum obligationibus

(xxiii) historical group. G.

247. Gaius 6 ad legem XII tabularum

248. Pomponius 1 enchiridii

249. Pomponius 2 enchiridii

Unattached

250. Paulus 1 de iure libellorum

251. Paulus 1 de articulis liberalis causae

252. Paulus 1 de iuris et facti ignorantia

253. Paulus 1 de iure singulari

254. Paulus 1 de gradibus et adfinibus et nominibus eorum (ID, **M**; S or P, **H**)

255. Paulus 1 de officio adsessorum

(xxiv) *praefectus vigilum* group. S.

256. Paulus 1 de officio praefecti vigilum

257. Ulpianus 1 de officio praefecti vigilum

(xxv) *praefectus urbi* group. S.

258. Ulpianus 1 de officio praefecti urbi (ID, **M**; S or P, **H**)

259. Paulus 1 de officio praefecti urbi (ID, **M**; S or P, **H**)
(BK 258 and 259 form a group but whether in the Sabinian or Papinian mass is uncertain)

Unattached

260. Arcadius Charisius 1 de muneribus civilibus (ID, **M**; S or P, **H**)

261. Arcadius Charisius 1 de officio praefecti praetorio (ID, **M**; S or P, **H**)

262. Ulpianus 1 de officio quaestoris (ID, **M**; S or P, **H**)

262 bis. Scaevola 40 digestorum lib. 1-2 (P, **M**, **H**, **O**)

Edictal mass

(xxvi) early edictal commentaries group. S.
95. Ulpianus 81 ad edictum lib. 1-25.
96. Paulus 78 ad edictum lib. 1-27
97. Paulus 23 brevium lib. 1-5
98. Gaius 30 ad edictum provinciale lib. 1-8, 19
99. Gaius ad edictum praetoris urbani
Unattached
100. Callistratus 4 edicti monitorii lib. 1-2 (see BK 176)

(xxvii) later edictal commentaries group. S.
101. Ulpianus 81 ad edictum lib. 56-81
102. Paulus 78 ad edictum lib. 53-78
103. Paulus 23 brevium lib. 16
104. Gaius 30 ad edictum provinciale lib. 21 fin.- 30
105. Gaius ad edictum praetoris urbani tit. de praediatoribus
106. Gaius ad edictum praetoris urbani tit. qui neque sequantur neque ducantur
107. Gaius ad edictum praetoris urbani tit. de re iudicata

(xxviii) edict of the curule aediles group. S.
108. Ulpianus 2 ad edictum aedilium curulium
109. Paulus 2 ad edictum aedilium curulium
110. Gaius 2 ad edictum aedilium curulium
Unattached
111. Papinianus 1 αστυνομικὸς (ID, M; P or Appendix, H)

(xxix) transferred edictal commentaries group. S.
112. Ulpianus 81 ad edictum lib. 54-55 init.
113. Paulus 78 ad edictum lib. 50-51
114. Gaius 30 ad edictum provinciale lib. 20
115. Gaius ad edictum praetoris urbani de liberali causa
116. Ulpianus 81 ad edictum lib. 55 fin.
117. Paulus 78 ad edictum lib. 52
118. Gaius ad edictum provinciale lib. 21
119. Gaius ad edictum praetoris urbani tit. de publicanis
120. Ulpianus 81 ad edictum lib. 52 fin.- 53
121. Paulus 78 ad edictum lib. 48 fin.- 49
122. Gaius ad edictum provinciale lib. 19
123. Gaius ad edictum praetoris urbani tit. de operis novi nuntiatione, de damno infecto, de aquae pluviae arcendae

(xxx) commentaries *ad Plautium* group. S.

124. Paulus 18 ad Plautium lib. 1-14
125. Iavolenus 5 ad Plautium lib. 1
126. Pomponius 7 ad Plautium lib. 1
127. Iavolenus 5 ad Plautium lib. 2
128. Pomponius 7 ad Plautium lib. 2-3 (2, H)
129. Paulus 18 ad Plautium lib. 15-18
130. Iavolenus 5 ad Plautium lib. 3-5
131. Pomponius 7 ad Plautium lib. 4-7 (3-7, H)
132. Paulus 4 ad Vitellium (N, H)
133. Paulus 2 de iure fisci (N, H)

(xxxi) Celsus-Marcellus *digesta* group. G.

134. Celsus 39 digestorum
135. Marcellus 31 digestorum

(xxxii) Modestinus group. A.

136. Ulpianus 3 de officio consulis (N, H)
137. Modestinus 1 de manumissionibus
138. Modestinus 9 differentiarum
139. Modestinus 10 regularum
140. Modestinus 1 de ritu nuptiarum
141. Modestinus 1 de differentia dotis
142. Modestinus 6 excusationum
143. Ulpianus 1 de officio praetoris tutelaris
144. Ulpianus 1 excusationum
145. Modestinus 4 de praescriptionibus (non-existent, the sole text so inscribed coming from his pandectarum lib. 4, BK Ordo 149)
146. Modestinus 19 responsorum
147. Modestinus 1 de enucleatis casibus
148. Modestinus 1 de praescriptionibus
149. Modestinus 1 pandectarum
150. Modestinus 1 de heurematicis
151. Modestinus 1 de inofficioso testamento

(xxxiii) Iavolenus group. A.

152. Iavolenus 15 ex Cassio
153. Iavolenus 14 epistularum

Unattached

154. Pomponius 39 ad Quintum Mucium
155. Proculus 11 epistularum lib. 1-6
156. Pomponius 15 variarum lectionum

157. Proculus 11 epistularum lib. 7-11
158. Callistratus 4 de iure fisci (ID, **M**)
159. Paulus 3 de censibus (ID, **M**; S or P, **H**)
160. Callistratus 6 de cognitionibus
161. Tertullianus 8 quaestionum

(xxxiv) commentaries on *lex Iulia et Papia* group. S.

162. Ulpianus 20 ad legem Iuliam et Papiam
163. Paulus 10 ad legem Iuliam et Papiam
164. Terentius Clemens 20 ad legem Iuliam et Papiam
165. Gaius 15 ad legem Iuliam et Papiam
166. Mauricianus 6 ad legem Iuliam et Papiam
167. Macellus 6 ad legem Iuliam et Papiam

Unattached

168. Macer 2 ad legem vicensimam hereditatis
169. Gaius 1 ad legem Glitiam (ID, **M**; P, **H**)
170. Paulus 1 ad legem Cinciam (ID, **M**; S or P, **H**)

(xxxv) military law group. S.

171. Arrius Menander 4 de re militari
172. Tarrutienus Paternus 4 de re militari

Unattached

173. Tertullianus 1 de castrensi peculio
174. Modestinus 4 de poenis
175. Licinius Rufinus 12 or 13 regularum (**IA** 12)
176. Callistratus 4 edicti monitorii (including lib. 1-2 from BK 100)
177. Papirius Iustus 20 constitionum
178. Aelius Gallus 1 de verborum quae ad ius pertinent significatione
179. Iulius Aquila 1 responsorum

Appendix

263. Paul 2 (6 **IA**) imperialium sententiarum in cognitionibus prolatarum (ID, **M**; App., **H**, **O**)
264. Quintus Mucius Scaevola 1 ορων (ID, **M**; App., **H**, **O**)
265. Labeo 10 posteriorum a Iavoleno epitomatorum lib. 2 fin.-10 (for earlier books see BK 93 bis)

265 bis. Iavolenus 10 posteriorum lib. 2 fin.–10 (for earlier books see BK 94)

266. Proculus 3 ex posterioribus Labeonis
(This work is non-existent, the sole text, inscribed IDEM, referring rather to 265 bis)
267. Scaevola 40 digestorum lib. 3-40
268. Labeo 8 πιθανων a Paulo epitomatorum
269. Pomponius 20 epistularum
270. Pomponius 5 de senatusconsultis
271. Scaevola 1 quaestionum publice tractatarum
272. Valens 7 actionum
(This work is non-existent, the sole text so inscribed referring rather to BK 273)
273. Venuleius Saturninus 10 actionum
274. Venuleius Saturninus 6 de interdictis
275. Furius Anthianus 1 (5 **IA**) ad edictum (ID, **M**; App., **H**)

Addendum B

Analysis of Digest Texts Displaced from the BK Ordo According to the Masses from which they were Taken and how they have been Displaced

Abbreviations:

S = Sabinian mass
P = Papinian mass
E = edictal mass
A = Appendix
Q = mass dubious
initial mass = the first mass of a title
<intro.> = displaced text or texts introducing a title. They include texts that are displaced from the initial mass
<mass intro.> = displaced text or texts introducing a mass
<codal> = displaced text or texts forming the coda of a title. They include displaced texts that also form the coda of the last mass of the title.
<codal apart from Appendix> = displaced text or texts which formed the coda of a title before a text or texts from the Appendix were added
<mass codal> = displaced text or texts forming the coda of a mass
/// = when two draft titles have been combined in one, this marks the transition from the first to the second
* = displaced text, other than introductory or codal

1.1. S 1 (Ulp. 1 inst.), P 2 (Pomp. 1 enchir.)*, S 3 (Flor. 1 inst.), 4 (Ulp. 1 inst.), P 5 (Hermogen. 1 iur. epit.)*, S 6 (Ulp. inst.), P 7 (Pap. 2 def.)*, S 8 (Marcian. 1 inst.)-10 (Ulp. 1 reg.) <codal S 11 (Paul 14 Sab.), 12 (Marcian. 1 inst.)>.

1.2. P 1-2.

1.3. <intro. P 1 (Pap. 1 def.), S 2 (Marcian. 1 inst.), 3 (Pomp. 25 Sab.), E 4 (Cels. 5 dig.), 5 (Cels. 17 dig.), 6 (Paul 17 Plaut.), 7 (Mod. 1 reg.)> S 8 (Ulp. 3 Sab.), E 9 (Ulp. 16 ed.)*, S 10 (Iul. 59 dig.)-11 (Iul. 90 dig.), 12 (Iul. 15 dig.)*, <mass intro. E 13 (Ulp. 1 ed. cur. aed.)>, 14 (Paul 54 ed.), S 15 (Iul. 27 dig.)*, P 16 (Paul 1 iur. sing.)*, E 17 (Paul 26 dig.)-19 S 20 (Iul. 55 dig.)*, 21 (Nerat. 6 membr.)*, 22 (Ulp. 35 ed.)* E 23 (Paul 4 Plaut.)-25 (Mod. 8 resp.), P 26 (Paul 4 quaest.)*, E 27 (Tertull. 1 quaest.)-28 (Paul 5 leg. Iul.Pap.), S or P 29 (Paul 1 leg. Cinc.)*, E 30 (Ulp. 4 ed.)*-31 (Ulp. 13 Iul.Pap.) /// S 32 (Iul. 84 dig.)-34 P 35 (Hermogen. 1 iur. epit.)*, S 36 (Paul 7 Sab.)* P 37 (Paul 1 quaest.)-38 E 39 (Cels. 2 dig.)-40 <codal S 41 (Ulp. 2 inst.)>.

1.4. S 1 P 2 E 3-4.

1.5. S 1 (Gai. 1 inst.), P 2 (Hermogen. 1 iur. epit.)*, S 3 (Gai. 1 inst.), 4 (Flor. 9 inst.)*, 5 (Marcian. 1 inst.)-7 P 8 –9 (Pap. 31 quaest.), S 10 (Ulp. 1 Sab.)*, P 11 (Paul 18 resp.)-15 S between P and E 16 (Ulp. 6 disp.* E 17 (Ulp. 22 ed.), S 18 (Ulp. 27 Sab.)*, E 19 (Cels. 9 dig.), S 20 (Ulp. 38 Sab.)*, E 21 (Mod. 7 reg.)-23 (Mod. 1 pand.), S 24 (Ulp. 27 Sab.)*, E 25 (Ulp. 1 Iul. Pap.) <codal S 26 (Iul. 69 dig.), 27 (Ulp. 5 opin.)>.

1.6. <intro. S 1 (Gai. 1 inst.), 2 (Ulp. 8 off. proc.), 3 (Gai. 1 inst.), 4 (Ulp. 1 inst.), 5 (Ulp. 36 Sab.) > S 6 (Ulp. 9 Sab.)-8 E 9-10 (Ulp. 4 Iul. Pap.) <codal E 11 (Mod. 1 pand.)>.

1.7. <intro. E 1 (Mod. 2 reg.), S 2 (Gai. 1 inst.), 3 (Paul 3 Sab.), E 4 (Mod. 2 reg.), 5 (Cels. 18 dig.), S 6 (Paul 35 ed.), E 7 (Cels. 29 dig.), 8 (Mod. 2 reg.)> S 9 (Ulp. 1 Sab.)-12 (Ulp. 14 Sab.), P 13 (Pap. 36 quaest.)*, S 14 (Pomp. 5 Sab.), 15 (Ulp. 26 Sab.), E 16 (Iavolen. 6 Cass.)*, S 17 (Ulp. 26 Sab.), E 18 (Marcell. 26 dig.)*, S 19 (Ulp. 26 Sab.), E 20 (Marcell. 26 dig.)*, P 21 (Gai. 1 reg.)*, S 22 (Ulp. 26 Sab.)-31 (Marcian. 5 reg.), P 32 (Pap. 31 quaest.)*, S 33 (Marcian. 5 reg.) P 34 –37 E 38-46.

1.8. S 1-6 (Marcian. 3 inst.), E 7 (Ulp. 25 ed.)*, S 8 (Marcian. 4 reg.) E 9-11.

1.9. E 1-7 P <mass intro. 8 (Ulp. 6 fid.)>, 9 (Pap. 4 resp.) S 10-12.

1.10. E 1.

1.11. Q 1.

1.12. S or P 1-2 E 3.

1.13. S or P 1.

1.14. S 1-4.

1.15. P 1-4.

1.16. <intro. S 1 (Ulp. 1 disp.)> S 2 (Marcian. 1 inst.), 3 (Ulp. 26 Sab.)*, 4 (Ulp. 1 off. proc.), P 5 (Pap. 1 quaest.)*, S 6 (Ulp. 1 off.

proc.)-7 (Ulp. 2 off. proc.), 8 (Ulp. 39 ed.)*, 9 (Ulp. 2 off. proc.)-11 E 12-15 (Ruf. 3 reg.), <codal 16 (Ulp. 2 ed.)>.

1.17. E 1.

1.18. <intro. S 1 (Macer 1 off. praes.)> S 2 (Ulp. 26 Sab.)-8 (Iul. 1 dig.), E 9 (Callist. 1 cogn.)*, P 10 (Hermogen. 2 iur. epit.)*, S 11 (Marcian. 3 inst.), E 12 (Proc. 4 epist.)*, S 13-16 E 17-19 P 20-21.

1.19. E 1 (Ulp. 16 ed.), P 2 (Paul 2 sent.)*, E 3 (Callist. 6 cogn.).

1.20. S 1-2.

1.21. P 1 S 2-4 E 5.

1.22. <intro. P 1 (Paul 1 off. adsess.)>, S 2-3 P 4 (Pap. 4 resp.), 5 (Paul 1 sent.), <codal 6 (Pap. 1 resp.)>.

Total texts 234 S 112 P 44 E 73 A 0 S or P 4 Q 1

Initial masses S 12 (1.1,3-8,14,16,18,20,22: S,SE/SPE,SPE,SE,SE, SPE,SE,S or PE,S or P,S,SE,SEP,S,SP) P 3 (1.2,15,21: P,P,PSE) E 4 (1.9,10,17,19: EPS,E,E,E) S or P 2 (1.12,13) Q 1(1.11)

Insertions in other masses 29: S in P 1 (1.5.10) S in E 7 (1.3.15, 20,21,22; 1.5.18.20,24) S between P and E 1 (1.5.16) S or P in E 1 (1.3.29) P in S 9 (1.1.2,5,7; 1.5.2; 1.7.13,21,32; 1.16.5; 1.18.10) P in E 3 (1.3.16,26; 1.19.2) E in S 7 (1.3.9; 1.7.16,18,20; 1.8.7; 1.18.9,12)

Displacements within masses 7: S 5 (1.3.12,36; 1.5.4; 1.16.3,8) P 1 (1.3.35) E 1 (1.3.30)

Texts introducing titles 23: S 2 P 1 E 4 (1.3.1-7) S 5 (1.6.1-5) S 3 E 5 (1.7.1-8) S 2 (1.16.1; 1.18.1) P 1 (1.22.1)

Codal title texts 8: S 2 (1.1.11-12); S 3 (1.3.41, 1.5.26-27) E 2 (1.6.11; 1.16.16) P 1 (1.22.6)

Texts introducing masses 2: P 1 (1.9.8) E 1 (1.3.13)

Total displacements 69/212 = 33 per cent

2.1. <intro. S 1 (Ulp. 1 reg.), E 2 (Iavolen. 6 Cass.), S 3 (Ulp. 1 off. quaest.), E 4 (Ulp. 1 ed.), S 5 (Iul. 1 dig.), E 6 (Paul 2 ed.)> E 7 (Ulp. 3 ed.)-12 S 13-18 P 19 <codal E 20 (Paul 1 ed.)>.

2.2. E 1-4.

2.3. E 1.

2.4. E 1-2 (Ulp. 5 ed.), 3 (Callist. 1 cogn.)*, 4 (Ulp. 5 ed.), 5 (Paul 4 ed.), P 6 (Paul 1 sent.)*, E 7 (Paul 4 ed.)-13 P 14-18 (Gai. 1 XII Tab.), E 19 (Paul 1 ed.)*, P 20 (Gai. 1 XII tab.), E 21 (Paul 1 ed.)*, P 22 (Gai. 1 XII Tab.) S 23 <codal E 24 (Ulp. 5 ed.), 25 (Mod. 1 poen.)>.

2.5. E 1-2 S 3.

2.6. E 1-4.

2.7. E 1-5 S 6.

2.8. <intro. E 1 (Gai. 5 ed. prov.)> E 2 (Ulp. 5 ed.)-9 (Gai. 5 ed. prov.), 10 (Paul 75 ed.)*, 11 (Ulp. 75 ed.)-13 P 14 S 15 <codal E 16 (Paul 6 ed.)>.

2.9. E 1-4 S 5-6.

2.10. E 1-2 S 3.

2.11. E 1-5 (Paul 69 ed.), P 6 (Gai. 1 XII Tab.)*, E 7-10 S 11-14 P 15.

2.12. <intro. S 1 (Ulp. 4 omn. trib.), E 2 (Ulp. 5 ed.)> E 3 (Ulp. 2 ed.)-7 (Ulp. 1 off. cons.) S 8-9 P 10.

2.13. E 1-2 (Paul 3 ed.), 3 (Mod. 2 poen.)*, 4 (Ulp. 4 ed.)-10 (Gai. 1 ed. prov.), 11 (Mod. 3 reg.) <codal 12 (Callist. 1 ed. mon.), 13 (Ulp. 4 ed.)>.

2.14. E 1-2 (Paul 3 ed.), 3 (Mod. 3 reg.)*, 4 (Paul 3 ed.)-7 (Ulp. 4 ed.), P 8 (Pap. 10 resp.)*, E 9 (Paul 62 ed.)*, 10 (Ulp. 4 ed.)-23 (Paul 3 ed.), 24 (Paul 3 Plaut.)*, 25 (Paul 3 ed.)-37 P 38-46 (Tryph. 2 disp.), 47 (Scae. 1 dig. not A)*, 48 (Gai. 3 XII Tab.) S 49-58 (Nerat. 3 membr.), 59 (Paul 3 reg.)*, E 60 (Iust. 8 const.)*, S 61 (Pomp. 9 Sab.)*, A 62 (Anth. 1 ed.).

2.15. <intro. E 1 (Ulp. 50 ed.), E 2 (Ulp. 74 ed.), P 3 (Scae. 1 dig. not A)> S 4 (Ulp. 46 Sab.), P 5 (Pap. 1 def.)*, S 6 (Gai. 17 ed. prov.)-10 E 11-13 P 14-16 (Hermogen. 1 iur. epit.), <codal 17 (Pap 2 quaest.)>.

Total texts 205 S 41 P 31 E 132 A 1

Initial masses S 1 (2.15: SEP) E 14 (2.1-14: ESP,E,E,EPS,ES,E,ES,EPS,ES,ES, ESP,ESP,E,EPSA)

Insertions in other masses 7: P in S 1 (2.15.5) P in E 3 (2.4.6; 2.11.6; 2.14.8) E in S 1 (2.14.60) E in P 2 (2.4.19,21)

Displacement within masses 8: S 1 (2.14.59) E 6 (2.4.3; 2.8.10; 2.13.3; 2.14.3,9,24) P 1 (2.14.47)

Texts introducing titles 12: S 3 E 3 (2.1.1-6) E 1 (2.8.1) S 1 E 1 (2.12.1-2) P 1 E 2 (2.15.1-3)

Codal title texts 7: E 4 (2.1.20; 2.4.24-25; 2.8.16); E 2 (2.13.12-13) P 1 (2.15.17)

Codal text apart from Appendix 1: S 1 (2.14.61).

Total displacements 35/190 = 18 per cent

3.1. E 1-4 (Paul 5 ed.), 5 (Ulp.9 ed.)*, 6 (Ulp. 6 ed.)-7 P 8-9 (Pap. 1 resp.), S 10 (Paul 1 reg.), <codal P 11 (Tryph. 5 disp.)>.

3.2. E 1-9 (Paul 5 ed.), 10 (Paul 8 ed.)*, 11 (Ulp. 6 ed.)-19 P 20-21 S 22 (Marcian. 2 pub.) <codal E 23 (Ulp. 8 ed.), 24 (Ulp. 6 ed.), P 25 (Pap. 2 quaest.)>.

3.3. <intro. E 1 (Ulp. 9 ed.), 2 (Paul 8 ed.), 3 (Ulp. 9 ed.), 4 (Paul 8 ed.)> E 5 (Ulp. 7 ed.), 6 (Paul 6 ed.), 7 (Ulp. 7 ed.), 8 (Ulp. 8 ed.)-17 (Ulp.

9 ed.), 18 (Mod. 10 pand.)*, 19 (Ulp. 9 ed.)-27 (Ulp. 9 ed.), S 28 (Ulp. 1 disp.)*, E 29 (Ulp. 9 ed.), P 30 (Paul 1 sent.)*, E 31 (Ulp. 9 ed.)-37 (Ulp.9 ed.), S 38 (Ulp. 40 ed.)*, E 39 (Ulp. 9 ed.)- 40 (Ulp. 9 ed.), 41 (Paul 9 ed.)*, 43 (Ulp. 9 ed.), S 44 (Ulp. 7 disp.)*, E 45 (Paul 9 ed.), 46 (Gai. 3 ed. prov.), S 47 (Iul. 4 Urs. Fer.)*, E 48 (Gai. 3 ed. prov.)-53 (Ulp. 60 ed.), 54 (Paul 50 ed.)*, 55 (Ulp. 65 ed.)-59 P 60 (Paul 4 resp.)*, E 61 (Paul 1 Plaut.)-65 P 66-73 S 74-76, E 77 (Paul 57 ed.)*, S 78 (Afr. 6 quaest.)

3.4. E 1-8 S 9 P 10.

3.5. E 1-3 (Ulp. 10 ed.), S 4 (Ulp. 45 Sab.)*, E 5 (Ulp. 10 ed.), -7 (Ulp. 10 ed.), P 8 (Scae. 1 quaest.)*, E 9 (Ulp. 10 ed.), 10 (Pomp. 21 QM)*, 11 (Ulp. 10 ed.)-14 (Paul 9 ed.), 15 (Paul 7 Plaut.)*, S 16 (Ulp. 35 ed.)*, E 17 (Paul 9 ed.), P 18 (Paul 2 Nerat.)*, E 19 (Ulp. 10 ed.)-28 S between E and P 29 (Iul. 3 dig.)* P 30-38 S 39-41 (Paul 32 ed.), A 42 (Lab. 6 post. Iav. epit.)*, S 43 (Ulp. 6 disp.)-45 (Afr. 7 quaest.) <codal P 46 (Paul 1 sent.), 47 (Pap. 3 quaest.), S 48 (Afr. 8 quaest.)>.

3.6. E 1-7 S 8-9.

Total texts 181 S 22 P 30 E 128 A 1

Initial masses E 6 (3.1-6: EPS,EPS,EPS,ESP,EPS,ES)

Insertions in other masses 13: S in E 6 (3.3.28,38,44,47; 3.5.4,16) S between E and P 1 (3.5.29) E in S 1 (3.3.77) P in E 4 (3.3.30,60; 3.5.8,18) A in S 1 (3.5.42)

Displacements within masses 7: E 7 (3.1.5; 3.2.10; 3.3.18,41,54; 3.5.10,15)

Texts introducing titles 4: E 4 (3.3.1-4)

Codal title texts 7: S 1 P 2 (3.5.46-48) 1 P 2 E (3.2.23-25) P 1 (3.1.11)

Total displacements 31/175 = 18 per cent

4.1. <intro. E 1 (Ulp. 11 ed.), P 2 (Paul 1 sent.)>, E 3 (Mod. 8 pand.)*, E 4 (Callist. 1 ed. mon.)*, E 5 (Paul 7 ed.), 6 (Ulp. 13 ed.)-7 S 8.

4.2. E 1 (Ulp. 11 ed.), P 2 (Paul 1 sent.)*, E 3 (Ulp. 11 ed.)-10, S 11 (Iul. 4 dig.)*, E 12 (Ulp. 11 ed.), 13 (Callist. 5 cogn.)*, 14 (Ulp. 11 ed.)-16 (Ulp. 11 ed.) P 17 (Paul 1 quaest.)*, S 18 (Iul. 64 dig.)*, E 19 (Gai. 4 ed. prov.)-21 P 22 S 23.

4.3. E 1-18 (Paul 11 ed.), P 19 (Pap. 37 ed.)*, E 20 (Paul 11 ed.)-31 P 32 (Scae. 2 dig. not A), <mass intro. S 33 (Ulp. 4 opin.)> S 34 (Ulp. 42 Sab.), 35 (Ulp. 30 ed.)*, 36 (Marcian. 2 reg.)*, 37 (Ulp. 44 Sab.), <mass codal 38 (Ulp. 4 opin.)>, <codal apart from Appendix E 39 (Gai. 27 ed. prov.)>, A 40 (Fur. Anth. 1 ed.).

4.4. E 1 (Ulp. 11 ed.), 2 (Ulp. 9 Iul. Pap.)*, 3 (Ulp. 11 ed.), S 4 (Afr. 7 quaest.)*, E 5 (Ulp. 11 ed.), 6 (Ulp. 10 ed.)*, 7 (Ulp. 11 ed.),

P 8 (Hermogen. 1 iur. epit.)*, E 9 (Ulp. 1 ed.)-16, P 17 (Hermogen. 1 iur. epit.)*, E 18 (Ulp. 11 ed.), 19 (Ulp. 13 ed.)*, 20 (Ulp. 11 ed.), 21 (Ulp. 10 ed.)*, 22 (Ulp. 11 ed.)-23 (Paul 11 ed.), P 24 (Paul 1 sent.)*, E 25 (Gai. 4 ed. prov.)-29 P 30 –39 (Scae. 2 dig. not A) S 40-43 (Afr. 7 quaest.), <mass codal S 44 (Ulp. 5 opin.)>, <codal apart from Appendix E 45 (Callist. 1 ed. mon.), P 46 (Paul 2 resp.), 47 (Scae. 1 resp.), 48 (Paul sent.), S 49 (Ulp. 35 ed.)> A 50 (Pomp. 9 epist. et var. lect.).

4.5. E 1-3 (Paul 11 ed.), 4 (Mod. 1 pand.)*, 5 (Paul 11 ed.), S 6 (Ulp. 51 Sab.)*, E 7 (Paul 11 ed.)-10 S 11.

4.6. E 1 (Ulp.. 12 ed.), 2 (Callist. 2 ed. mon.)*, 3 (Ulp. 12 ed.), 4 (Callist. 2 ed. mon.)*, 5 (Ulp. 12 ed.)-8 (Paul 3 brev.), 9 (Callist. 2 ed. mon.)*, 10 (Ulp. 12 ed.), 11 (Callist. 2 ed. mon.)*, 12 (Ulp. 1 ed.)-13 (Paul 1 ed.), 14 (Callist. 2 ed. mon.)* , 15 (Ulp. 12 ed.)-18 (Paul 12 ed.), P 19 (Pap. 3 quaest.)*, 20 (Pap. 23 quaest.)*,21 (Ulp. 21 ed.)-28 (Ulp. 11ed.), S 29 (Afr. 7 quaest.)*, 30 (Paul 12 ed.)-38 P 39 S 40-44 (Afr. 7 quaest.), 44 (Paul 2 Sab.)*, 45 (Scae. 1 reg.)-46.

4.7. E 1 (Gai. 4 ed. prov.), 2 (Ulp. 13 ed.)*, 3 Gai. (4 ed. prov.)-4 (Ulp. 13 ed.), 5 (Paul 11 ed.)*, 6 (Ulp. 13 ed.), 7 (Gai. 4 ed. prov.)*, 8 (Paul 12 ed.), 9 (Paul 1 ed. aed. cur.)*, 10 (Ulp. 13 ed.) S 11-12.

4.8. E 1-13 (Ulp. 13 ed.), 14 (Pomp. 11 QM)*, 15 (Ulp. 13 ed.)-17 (Ulp. 13 ed.), 18 (Pomp. 17 epist. et var. lect.)*, E 19 (Paul 13 ed.)-32 (Paul 13 ed.), P 33 (Pap. 1 quaest.)*, E 34 (Paul 13 ed.)-40 (Pomp. 11 var. lect.), S between E and P 41 (Callist. 1 ed. mon.)* P 42-44 (Scae. 2 dig. not A) S 45-47 (Iul. 4 dig.), E 48 (Mod. 4 reg.)*, S 49 (Iul. 4 dig.)-52.

4.9. E 1-7.

Total texts 249 S 37 P 30 E 179 A 3

Initial masses E 9 (4.1-9: ES,EPS,EPSA,EPS,ES,EPS,ES,EPS,E)

Insertions in other masses 16: S in E 5 (4.2.11,18; 4.4.4; 4.5.6; 4.6.29) S between E and P 1 (4.8.41) P in E 10 (4.2.2,17; 4.3.19; 4.4.8,17,24; 4.6.19,20; 4.8.33) E in S 1 (4.8.48)

Displacements within masses 22: E 19 (4.1.3,4; 4.2.13; 4.4.2,6,19,21; 4.5.4; 4.6.2,4,9,11,14; 4.7.2,5,7,9; 4.8.14,18,21) S 2 (4.3.35,36)

Texts introducing titles 2: E 1 P 1 (4.1.1-2)

Codal apart from Appendix 6: S 1 P 3 E 2 (4.3.39; 4.4.45-49)

Text introducing masses 1: S 1 (4.3.33)

Codal mass texts 2: S 2 (4.3.38; 4.4.44)

Total displacements 49/240 = 20 per cent

5.1. E 1-12 (Paul 12 ed.), 13 (Gai. 7 ed. prov.)*, S 14 (Ulp. 2 disp.)*, E 15 (Ulp. 21 ed.), 16 (Ulp. 5 ed.)*, 17 (Ulp. 22 ed.)-24 (Paul 17 Plaut.),

S 25 (Iul. 1 dig.)*, 26 (Paul 17 Plaut.), S 27 (Iul. 1 dig.)*, E 28 (Paul 17 Plaut.), 29 (Paul 8 Plaut.)*, 30 (Marcell. 1 dig.)-38 P 39 –50 (Ulp. 6 fid.), S 51 (Marcian. 8 inst.)*, P 52 (Ulp. 6 fid.)-55 S 56-64 (Ulp. 1 disp.), 65 (Ulp. 35 ed.)*, 66 (Ulp. 2 disp.)-68 (Ulp. 8 disp.), 69 (Ulp. 4 omn. trib.)*, 70 (Ulp. 8 disp.), 71 (Ulp. 4 omn. trib.)*, 72 (Ulp. 8 disp.)-77 (Afr. 3 quaest.), E 78 (Paul 16 Plaut.)* <codal S 79 (Ulp. 5 off. proc.), 80 (Pomp. 2 Sab.), 81 (Ulp. 5 opin.), E 82 (Ulp. 1 off. cons.)>.

5.2. <intro. E 1 (Ulp. 14 ed.), S 2 (Marcian. 4 inst.), E 3 (Marcell. 3 dig.), P 4 (Gai. 1 leg. Glit.), E 5 (Marcell. 3 dig.)> E 6 (Ulp. 14 ed.), S 7 (Paul 1 septemvir.)*, E 8 (Ulp. 14 ed.), 9 (Mod. 1 inoff. test.)*, 10 (Marcell. 3 dig.), 11 (Mod. 3 resp.)-12 <mass intro. P 13 (Scae. 3 resp.)>, 14 (Pap. 5 quaest.)-17 (Paul 2 quaest.), 18 (Paul 1 inoff. test.)*, 19 (Paul 2 quaest.)-23 S 24-27 (Ulp. 6 opin.), 28 (Paul 1 septemvir.)*, 29 (Ulp. 6 opin.), 30 (Marcian. 4 inst.), 31 (Paul 1 septemvir.) <codal P 32 (Paul 1 inoff. test.)>.

5.3. <intro. E 1 (Gai. 6 ed. prov.), 2 (Ulp. 15 ed.), 3 (Gai. 6 ed. prov.)> E 4 (Paul 1 ed.), 5 (Ulp. 14 ed.), 6 (Ulp. 75 ed.)*, 7 (Ulp. 14 ed.)-11 (Ulp. 15 ed.), 12 (Ulp. 77 ed.)*, 13 (Ulp. 15 ed.)-48 P 49-52 S 53-57 A 58.

5.4. E 1-3 ((Paul 17 Plaut.), 4 (Ulp. 15 ed.)*, 5 (Paul 17 Plaut.) S 6-9 P 10.

5.5. E 1-2.

5.6. E 1-3.

Total texts 187 S 48 P 34 E 104 A 1

Initial masses E 6 (5.1-6: EPS,EPS,EPSA,ESP,E,E)

Insertions in other masses 6: S in P 1 (5.1.51) S in E 4 (5.1.14,25,27; 5.2.7) E in S 1 (5.1.78)

Displacement within masses 12: S 4 (5.1.65,69,71; 5.2.28) E 7 (5.1.13,16,29; 5.2.9; 5.3.6,12; 5.4.4) P 1 (5.2.18)

Texts introducing titles 8: S 1 P 1 E 3 (5.2.1-5) E 3 (5.3.1-3)

Codal title texts 5: P 1 (5.2.32) S 3 E 1 (5.1.79-82)

Text introducing masses 1: P 1 (5.2.13)

Total displacements 32/181 = 18 per cent

6.1. <intro. E 1 (Ulp. 16 ed.), 2 (Paul 21 d.), 3 (Ulp. 16 ed.), 4 (Paul 21 ed.), 5 (Ulp. 21 ed.)>.

E 6 (Paul 6 ed.)-24 (Gai. 7 ed. prov.), 25 (Ulp. 70 ed.)*, 26 (Paul 2 Plaut.)*, 27 (Paul 21 ed.)-28 (Gai. 7 ed. prov.), 29 (Pomp. 21 QM)*, 30 (Gai. 7 ed. prov.)-31 (Paul 21 ed.), 32 (Mod. 8 diff.)*, 33 (Paul 21 ed.), S 34 (Iul. 7 dig.)*, E 35 (Paul 21 ed.)-37 (Ulp. 17 ed.), 38 (Cels. 3 dig.)*,

39 (Ulp. 17 ed.)-45 (Ulp. 69 ed.), S 46 (Paul 13 Sab.)*, E 47 (Paul 17 Plaut.), P 48 (Pap. 2 resp.)* E 49 (Cels. 18 dig.), <mass codal E 50 (Callist. 2 ed. mon.)> S 51 (Pomp. 16 Sab.), 52 (Iul. 55 dig.)*, 53 (Pomp. 31 Sab.), 54 (Ulp. 6 opin.), 55 (Iul. 55 dig.)-59 (Iul. 6 Minic.), 60 (Pomp. 29 Sab.)*, 61 (Iul. 6 Minic.) P 62-67/// <mass intro. S 68 (Ulp. 51 ed.)>, 69 (Paul 13 Sab.)-71 E 72 (Ulp. 16 ed.)-77 A 78-80 (Anth. 1 ed.).

6.2. E 1-14 S 15 (Pomp. 3 Sab.), P 16* (Pap. 10 quaest.) S 17 (Nerat. 3 membr.).

6.3. E 1-3.

Total texts 100 S 19 P 8 E 70 A 3

Initial masses E 3 (6.1-3: ESP/SEA,ES,E)

Insertions in other masses 4: S in E 2 (6.1.34,46) P in E 1 (6.1.48) P in S (6.2.16)

Displacements within masses 7: S 2 (6.1.52,60) E 5 (6.1.25,26,29,32,38)

Texts introducing titles 5: E 5 (6.1.1-5)

Text introducing masses 1: S 1 (6.1.68)

Codal mass text 1: E 1 (6.1.50)

Total displacements 18/97 = 19 per cent

7.1. <intro. E 1 (Paul 3 Vitell.), 2 (Cels. 18 dig.), S 3 (Gai. 2 rer. cott.), E 4 (Paul 2 ed.), P 5 (Pap. 7 quaest.), E 6 (Gai. 7 ed. prov.)> S 7 (Ulp. 17 Sab.), 8 (Ulp. 40 ed.)*, S 9 (Ulp. 17 Sab.)-10 (Pomp. 5 Sab.), 11 (Paul 2 epit. Alfen.)*, 12 (Ulp. 17 Sab.)-20 (Ulp. 18 Sab.), 21 (Ulp. 17 Sab.)*, 22 (Ulp. 18 Sab.), 23 (Ulp. 17 Sab.)*, 24 (Paul 10 Sab.)*, 25 (Ulp. 18 Sab.)-32 (Pomp. 33 Sab.), P 33 (Pap. 17 quaest.)*, S 34 (Iul. 35 dig.)-38 (Marcian. 3 inst.), E 39 (Gai. 7 ed. prov.)*, S 40 (Marcian. 3 inst.)-44 E 45-46 (Paul 9 Plaut.), 47 (Pomp. 5 Plaut.)*, 48 (Paul 9 Plaut.)-55 (Pomp. 26 QM), <mass codal E 56 (Gai. 17 ed. prov.)> P 57-63 <codal S 64 (Ulp. 51 ed.), E 65 (Pomp. 5 Plaut.), S 66 (Paul 47 ed.), 67 (Iul. 1 Minic.), 68 (Ulp. 17 Sab.), 69 (Pomp. 5 Sab.), 70 (Ulp.17 Sab.), E 71 (Marcell. 17 dig.), S 72 (Ulp. 17 Sab.), 73 (Pomp. 5 Sab.), E 74 (Gai. 7 ed. prov.).>

7.2. S 1 (Ulp. 17 Sab.), 2 (Afr. 5 quaest.)*, 3 (Ulp. 17 Sab.), 4 (Iul. 35 dig.)*, E 5 (Gai. 7 ed. prov.)*, 6 (Ulp. 17 Sab.)-8 (Ulp. 17 Sab.), 9 (Afr. 5 quaest.), E 10 (Ulp. 17 ed.) P 11 <codal S 12 (Ulp. 17 Sab.)>.

7.3. S 1.

7.4. S 1 (Ulp. 17 Sab.), P 2 (Pap.17 quaest.)*, S 3 (Ulp. 17 Sab.), 4 (Marcian. 3 inst.)*, 5 (Ulp. 17 Sab.), 6 (Pomp. 5 Sab.), 7 (Iul. 35 dig.)*,

8 (Ulp. 17 Sab.)-17 (Iul. 35 dig.), <mass codal 18 (Pomp. 3 Sab.)> E 19-23 (Pomp. 26 QM), A 24 (Iavolen. 3 post.Lab.)*, 25 (Pomp. 11 var. lect.) P 26-27 <codal E 28 (Paul 13 Plaut.), S 29 (Ulp. 17 Sab.), E 30 (Gai. 7 ed. prov.), 31 (Pomp. 4 QM)>.

7.5. S 1 (Ulp. 18 Sab.), E 2 (Gai. 7 ed. prov.)*, S 3 (Ulp. 18 Sab.), P 4 (Paul 1 Nerat.)*, S 5 (Ulp. 18 Sab.), 6 (Iul. 35 ed.) E 7 (Gai. 7 ed. prov.) P 8-9, <codal E 10 (Ulp. 79 ed.), 11 (Ulp. 18 Sab.), 12 (Marcian. 7 inst.)>.

7.6. S 1-4 E 5-6.

7.7. E 1-5 (Terent. Clem. 18 Iul. Pap.), <codal 6 (Ulp. 55 ed.)>.

7.8. <intro. E 1 (Gai. 7 ed. prov.)>, S 2 (Ulp. 17 Sab.), E 3 (Paul 3 Vitell.)*, S 4 (Ulp. 17 Sab.)-10 (Ulp. 17 Sab.), 11 (Gai. 2 rer. cott.)*, 12 (Ulp. 17 Sab.), E 13 (Gai. 7 ed. prov.)*, 14 (Ulp. 17 Sab.)-17 E 18-22 P 23.

7.9. E 1-3 (Ulp. 79 ed.), P 4 (Venul. 1 stip.)*, E 5 (Ulp. 79 ed.)-8 S 9-10 P 11 <codal S 12 (Sab. 18 Sab.)>.

Total texts 177 S 99 P 19 E 58 A 1

Initial masses S 7 (7.1-6,8: SEP,SP,S,SEP,SEP,SE,SEP) E 2 (7.7,9: E,ESP)

Insertions in other masses 10: P in S 3 (7.1.33; 7.4.2; 7.5.4) P in E 1 (7.9.4) E in S 5 (7.1.39; 7.2.5; 7.5.2; 7.8.3,13) A in E 1 (7.4.24)

Displacements within masses 11: S 10 (7.1.8,11,21,23,24; 7.2.2,4; 7.4.4,7; 7.8.11) E 1 (7.1.47)

Texts introducing titles 7: S 1 P 1 E 4 (7.1.1-6) E 1 (7.8.1)

Codal title texts 21: S 2 (7.2.12; 7.9.12) E 1 (7.7.6) S 1 E 3 (7.4.28-31) S 1 E 2 (7.5.10-12) S 8 E 3 (7.1.64-74)

Codal mass texts 2: E 1 (7.1.56) S 1 (7.4.18)

Total displacements 51/168 = 31 per cent

8.1. <intro. S 1 (Marcian. 3 reg.)>, E 2 (Ulp. 17 ed.)-3 (Paul 21 ed.), P 4 (Pap. 7 quaest.)*, E 5 (Gai. 7 ed. prov.), 6 (Paul 21 ed.), 7 (Ulp. 13 Iul. Pap.)*, 8 (Paul 14 Plaut.)-13 S 14-17 P 18 A 19-20 (Iavolen. 5 post. Lab., not S.).

8.2. E 1-2 S 3 (Ulp. 9 Sab.)*, 4 (Paul 2 inst.)*, E 5 (Ulp. 17 ed.)-6 (Gai. 7 ed. prov.), 7 (Pomp. 26 QM)*, 8 (Gai. 7 ed. prov.)-14 S 15 (Ulp. 29 Sab.), 16 (Paul 2 epit. Alfen.)*, 17 (Ulp. 29 Sab.)-21 (Pomp. 33 Sab.), 22 (Iul. 2 Minic.)*, 23 (Pomp. 33 Sab.)-28 (Paul 15 Sab.), E 29 (Pomp. 32 QM)*, S 30 (Paul 15 Sab.)-35 P 36 (Pap. 7 quaest.), S 37 (Iul. 7 dig.)*, P 38 (Paul 2 quaest.), 39 (Paul 1 manual.)*, 40 (Paul 3 resp.)-41.

8.3. <intro. S 1 (Ulp. 2 inst.), 2 (Nerat. 4 reg.)>, E 3 (Ulp. 17 ed.), P 4 (Pap. 2 resp.)*, E 5 (Ulp. 17 ed.), 6 (Paul 15 Plaut.)*, 7 (Ulp. 21 ed.)-8

(Gai. 7 ed. prov.), P 9 (Paul 1 sent.)*, E 10 (Paul 49 ed.)-17 S 18-33 P 34 (Pap. 7 quaest.), E 35 (Paul 15 Plaut.)*, P 36 (Paul 2 quaest.)-38.

8.4. <intro. S (Ulp. 2 inst.)>, E 2 (Ulp. 17 ed.)-5 S 6-16 P 17-18.

8.5. E 1-2 (Ulp. 17 ed.), 3 (Ulp. 70 ed.)*, 4 (Ulp. 17 ed.)-13 S 14-19 A 20-21.

8.6. E 1-5 (Paul 66 ed.), 6 (Cels. 5 dig.)*, 7 (Paul 13 Plaut.)-17 S 18-20 (Scae. 1 reg.), P 21 (Paul 5 sent.)*, S 22 (Scae. 1 reg.), P 23 (Paul 5 sent.)*, S 24 (Scae. 1 reg.) <codal P 25 (Paul 5 sent.)>.

Total texts 163 S 69 P 16 E 74 A 4

Initial masses E 6 (8.1-6: ESPA,ESP,ESP,ESP,ESA,ES)

Insertions in other masses 10: S in P 1 (8.2.37) S in E 2 (8.2.3-4) P in S 2 (8.6.21,23) P in E 3 (8.1.4; 8.3.4,9) E in S 1 (8.2.29) E in P 1 (8.3.35)

Displacements within masses 8: S 2 (8.2.16,22) P 1 (8.2.39) E 5 (8.1.7; 8.2.7; 8.3.6; 8.5.3; 8.6.6)

Texts introducing titles 4: S 4 (8.1.1; 8.3.1-2; 8.4.1)

Codal title text 1: P 1 (8.6.25)

Total displacements 23/157 = 15 per cent

9.1. E 1-4 S 5.

9.2. E 1-11 (Ulp. 18 ed.), S 12 (Paul 10 Sab.)*, 13 (Ulp. 13 ed.)-15 (Ulp. 18 ed.), S 16 (Marcian. 4 reg.)*, E 17 (Ulp. 18 ed.), S 18 (Paul 10 Sab.)*, E 19 (Ulp. 18 ed.), 20 (Ulp. 42 Sab.)*, E 21 (Ulp. 18 ed.)-27 (Ulp. 18 ed.), 28 (Paul 10 Sab.)*, E 29 (Ulp. 18 ed.)-30 (Paul 22 ed.), S 31 (Paul 10 Sab.)*, E 32 (Gai. 7 ed. prov.)-34 (Marcell. 21 dig.), 35 (Ulp. 18 ed.)*, 36 (Marcell. 21 dig.)-39 (Pomp. 17 QM), <mass codal 40 (Paul 3 ed.)> S 41 (Ulp. 41 Sab.), 42 (Iul. 48 dig.)*, 43 (Pomp. 19 Sab.)-46 (Ulp. 50 Sab.), 47 (Iul. 86 dig.)*, 48 (Paul 39 ed.)-53 P 54-56 A 57 (not S.).

9.3. E 1-7.

9.4. <intro. E 1 (Gai. 2 ed. prov.), 2 (Ulp. 18 ed.)>, E 3 (Ulp. 3 ed.)-5 (Ulp. 3 ed.), 6 (Ulp. 18 ed.)*, 7 (Ulp. 3 ed.), S 8 (Ulp. 37 ed.)*, 9 (Paul 39 ed.)*, E 10 (Paul 22 ed.)*, 11 (Ulp. 7 ed.)-12 (Paul 6 ed.), S 13 (Gai. 13 ed. prov.)*, E 14 (Ulp. 18 ed.), 15 (Gai. 6 ed. prov.)*, S 16 (Iul. 22 dig.)*, E 17 (Paul 22 ed.), S 18 (Pomp. 18 Sab.)*, E 19 (Paul 22 ed.)-27 (Gai. 6 ed. prov.), S 28 (Afr. 6 quaest.)*, E 29 (Gai. 6 ed. prov.)-31 (Paul 7 Plaut.), <mass codal 32 (Callist. 2 ed. mon.)> S 33 (Pomp. 19 Sab.), 34 (Iul. 4 Urs. Fer.),* 35 (Ulp. 41 Sab.), 36 (Ulp. 37 ed.), P 37 (Tryph. 15 disp.)*, 38 (Ulp. 37 ed.)-41 (Iul. 2 Urs. Fer.), <codal apart from Appendix S 42 (Ulp. 37 ed.)> A 43.

Total texts 112 S 35 P 4 E 71 A 2

Initial masses E 4 (9.1-4: ES,ESPA,E,ESA)

Insertions in other masses 13: S in E 12 (9.2.12,16,18,20,28,31; 9.4.8,9,13,16,18,28) P in S 1 (9.4.37)

Displacement within masses 7: S 3 (9.2.42,47; 9.4.34) E 4 (9.2.35; 9.4.6,10,15)

Texts introducing titles 2: E 2 (9.4.1-2)

Codal text apart from Appendix 1: S 1 (9.4.42)

Codal mass texts 2: E 2 (9.2.40; 9.4.32)

Total displacements 25/108 = 23 per cent

10.1. E 1-4 ((Paul 33 ed.), S 5 (Paul 15 Sab.)*, 6 (Paul 23 ed.)-7 S 8-10 P 11-13.

10.2. E 1-6 (Ulp. 19 ed.), P 7 (Venul. 7 stip.)*, E 8 (Ulp. 10 ed.)-12 (Ulp. 19 ed.), P 13 (Pap. 7 quaest.)*, E 14 (Ulp. 19 ed.)-30 P 31-36 (Paul 2 quaest. 37 (Scae. 1 quaest.)-41 S 42-54 <codal E 55 (Ulp. 2 ed.), 56 (Paul 23 ed.), P 57 (Pap. 2 resp.)>.

10.3. E 1 (Paul 23 ed.), 2 (Gai. 7 ed. prov.), S 3 (Ulp. 30 Sab.)*, E 4 (Ulp. 19 ed.), S 5 (Iul. 2 Urs. Fer.)*, E 6 (Ulp. 19 ed.), 7 (Ulp. 20 ed.), 8 (Paul 23 ed.), S 9 (Afr. 7 quaest.)*, 10 (Paul 23 ed.)-18 S 19 (Paul 6 Sab.)-27 P 28-31.

10.4. E 1 (Ulp. 24 ed.), 2 (Paul 21 ed.)*, 3 (Ulp. 24 ed.), S 4 (Pomp. 6 Sab.)*, E 5 (Ulp. 24 ed.), S 6 (Paul 14 Sab.)*, E 7 (Ulp. 24 ed.), S 8 (Iul. 9 dig.)*, E 9 (Ulp. 24 ed.)-13 S 14 (Pomp. 14 Sab.)-20.

Total texts 121 S 39 P 21 E 61 A 0

Initial masses E 4 (10.1-4: ESP,EPS,ESP,ES)

Insertions in other masses 9: S in E 7 (10.1.5; 10.3.3,5,9; 10.4.4,6,8) P in E 2 (10.2.7,13)

Displacements within masses 1: E 1 (10.4.2)

Codal title texts 3: E 2 P 1 (10.2.55-57)

Total displacements 13/117 = 12 per cent

11.1. <intro. E 1 (Callist. 2 ed. mon.)>, E 2 (Ulp. 2 ed.)-4 (Ulp. 22 ed.), 5 (Gai. 3 ed. prov.)*, 6 (Ulp. 22 ed.), 7 (Ulp. 18 ed.)*, 8 (Paul 2 ed.)*, 9 (Ulp. 22 ed.), S 10 (Paul 48 ed.),* E (Ulp. 22 ed.)-14 S 15-18 P 19-20 <codal apart from Appendix E 21 (Ulp. 22 ed.)>, A 22.

11.2. S 1 P 2.

11.3. E 1-15 S 16-17.

11.4. E 1-2 S 3 P 4-5.

11.5. E 1-2 (Paul 19 ed.), S 3 (Marcian. 5 reg.)*, E 4 (Paul 19 ed.).

11.6. E 1-7.

11.7. E 1-14 (Ulp. 25 ed.), S 15 (Pomp. 5 Sab.)*, E 16 (Ulp. 25 ed.), P 17 (Pap. 3 resp.)*, S 18 (Iul. 10 dig.)*, S 19 (Ulp. 15 Sab.)*, E 20 (Ulp. 25 ed.)-25 (Paul 27 ed.), S 26 (Pomp. 5 Sab.)*, E 27 (Ulp. 25 ed.), S 28 (Pomp. 15 Sab.)*, E 29 (Gai. 9 ed. prov.), S 30 (Pomp. 15 Sab.)*, E 31 (Ulp. 25 ed.)-37 S 38-39 (Marcian. 3 inst.), P 40 (Paul 3 quaest.)*, S 41 (Callist. 2 inst.)-42 P 43-45 (Maeci. 8 fid.), <codal P 46 (Scae. 2 quaest.)>.

11.8. E 1-2 S 3-4 (Ulp. 2 resp.) <codal S 5 (Ulp. 1 opin.)>.

Total texts 108 S 23 P 11 E 73 A 1

Initial masses S 1 (11.2: SP) E 7 (11.1,3-8: ESPA,ES,ESP,E,E,ESP,,ES)

Insertions in other masses 10: S in E 8 (11.1.10; 11.5.3; 11.7.15,18,19,26,28,30) P in S 1 (11.7.40) P in E 1 (11.7.17)

Displacements within masses 3: E 4 (11.1.5,7,8)

Text introducing title 1: E 1 (11.1.1)

Codal title texts 2: S 1 (11.8.5) P 1 (11.7.46)

Codal text apart from Appendix E 1: 1 (11.1.21)

Total displacements 17/100 = 17 per cent

12.1. <intro. S 1 (Ulp. 26 ed.), 2 (Paul 28 ed.)>, S 3 (Pomp. 27 Sab.), 4 (Ulp.34 = 43? Sab.), 5 (Pomp. 22 Sab.)*, 6 (Paul 28 ed.), 7 (Ulp. 26 ed.), E 8 (Pomp. 6 Plaut.)*, S 9 (Ulp. 26 ed.), E 10 (Ulp. 2 ed.)*, S 11 (Ulp. 26 ed.), E 12 (Pomp. 6 Plaut.)*, S 13 (Ulp. 26 ed.)-25 (Ulp. 1 off. consular.), <mass codal 26 (Ulp. 5 opin.)>, E 27-32 (Cels. 6 dig.) 33 (Mod. 10 pand.)*, P 34 (Paul 2 sent.)*, E 35 (Mod. 3 resp.)-36 P 37 (Pap. 1 def.), 38 (Scae. 1 quaest.)*, 39 (Pap. 1 def.)-40 <codal S 41 (Afr. 8 quaest.), E 42 (Cels. 6 dig.)>.

12.2. <intro. E 1 (Gai. 5 ed. prov.), 2 Paul 18 ed.), 3 (Ulp. 22 ed.), 4 Paul 18 ed.), 5 (Ulp.22 ed.), 6 (Paul 18 ed.), 7 (Ulp. 22 ed.), 8 (Paul 18 ed.), 9 (Ulp. 22 ed.), 10 (Paul 18 ed.), 11 (Ulp. 22 ed.), S 12 (Iul. 9 dig.), E 13 (Ulp. 22 ed.)> E 14 (Paul 3 ed.)- 17 (Paul 18 ed.), S 18 (Ulp. 26 ed.)*, E 19 (Ulp. 22 ed.)-22 (Paul 18 ed.), S 23 (Ulp. 26 ed.)*, 24 (Paul 28 ed.)*, 25 (Ulp. 26 ed.)*, E 26 (Paul 18 ed.)-28 (Paul 18 ed.), P 29 (Tryph. 6 disp.)*, E 30 (Paul 30 ed.)-32 S 33 (Ulp. 28 Sab.)-41 A 42.

12.3. S 1-5 (Marcian. 4 reg.) <mass intro. E 6 (Paul 26 ed.)>, 7 (Ulp. 7 ed.)-9 P 10-11.

12.4. S 1 (Ulp. 26 ed.), P 2 (Hermogen. 2 iur. epit.)*, S 3 (Ulp. 26 ed.)-8 E 9 (Paul 17 Plaut.), 10 (Iavolen. 1 Plaut.)*, S 11 (Iul. 10 dig.)*, E 12 (Paul 6 Iul. Pap.), <codal S 13 (Marcian. 3 reg.), 14 Paul 3 Sab.), 15 (Pomp. 22 Sab.), E 16 (Cels. 8 dig.)>.

12.5. S 1 (Paul 10 Sab.), 2 (Ulp. 26 ed.)*, 3 (Paul 10 Sab.), 4 (Ulp. 26 ed.)*, 5 (Iul. 3 Urs. Fer.)*, 6 (Ulp. 18 Sab.)*, 7 (Pomp. 22 Sab.) P 8 E 9.

12.6. <intro. E 1 (Ulp. 26 ed.), S 2 (Ulp. 16 Sab.), P 3 (Pap. 28 quaest.)>, S 4 (Paul 3 Sab.)-8, E 9 (Ulp. 66 ed.)*, S 10 (Paul 7 Sab.)-15 (Paul 10 Sab.), 16 (Pomp. 17 Sab.)*, E 17(Ulp. 2 ed.)*, S 18 (Ulp. 47 Sab.)*, 19 (Pomp. 22 Sab.), 20 (Iul. 12 dig.)*, P 21 (Paul 3 quaest.)*, S 22 (Pomp. 22 Sab.)-41 E 42-53 P 54-64 <codal apart from Appendix E 65 (Paul 17 Plaut.), P 66 (Pap. 8 quaest.)> A 67.

12.7. S 1-4 P 5.

Total texts 192 S 101 P 25 E 64 A 2

Initial masses S 6 (12.1,3-7: SEP,SP,SE,SPE,SEPA,SP) E 1 (12.2: ESA)

Insertions in other masses 14: S in E 5 (12.2.18,23,24,25; 12.4.11) P in S 2 (12.4.2; 12.6.21) P in E 2 (12.1.34; 12.2.29) E in S 5 (12.1.8,10,12; 12.6.9,17)

Displacement within masses 11: S 8 (12.1.5; 12.5.2,4,5,6; 12.6.16,18,20) P 1 (12.1.38) E 2 (12.1.33; 12.4.10)

Texts introducing titles 18: S 2 (12.1.1-2) S 1 E 12 (12.2.1-13) S 1 P 1 E 1 (12.6.1-3)

Codal title texts 6: S 3 E 1 (12.4.13-16) S 1 E 1 (12.1.41-42)

Codal texts apart from Appendix 2: E 1 P 1 (12.6.65,66)

Text introducing mass 1: E 1 (12.3.6)

Codal mass text 1: S 1 (12.1.26)

Total displacements 53/185 = 29 per cent

13.1. S 1-5 (Paul 9 Sab.), 6 (Ulp. 38 ed.)*, 7 (Ulp. 42 Sab.)-14 E 15-16 P 17-20.

13.2. E 1.

13.3. <intro. S 1 (Ulp. 27 ed.)>, S 2 (Ulp. 28 Sab.), 3 (Ulp. 27 ed.)-4.

13.4. S 1–5 (Paul 28 ed.), 6 (Pomp. 22 Sab.)*, 7 (Paul 28 ed.)-8 (Afr. 3 quaest.), <mass codal 9 (Ulp. 47 Sab.)> P 10.

13.5. S 1 (Ulp. 27 ed.), 2 (Iul. 11 dig.)*, 3 (Ulp. 27 ed.)-5 (Ulp. 27 ed.), P 6 (Paul 2 sent.)*, S 7 (Ulp. 27 ed.)-8 (Paul 29 ed.), P 9 (Pap. 8 quaest.)*, S 10 (Paul 29 ed.)-11 (Ulp. 27 ed.), E 12 (Paul 13 ed.)*, S 13 (Paul 29 ed.)-19 (Paul 29 ed.), E 20 (Paul 4 Plaut.)*, S 21 (Paul 29 ed.)-24 P 25-26 (Scae. 1 resp.), E 27 (Ulp. 14 ed.)-29 (Paul 24 ed.) <codal apart from Appendix P 30 (Paul 2 sent.)> A 31.

13.6. <intro. S 1-3 (Ulp. 28 ed.), P 4 (Gai. 1 verb. obl.), S 5 (Ulp. 28 ed.)-6 (Pomp. 5 Sab.), 7 (Ulp. 28 ed.)> S 8 (Pomp. 5 Sab.), E 9 (Ulp. 2 ed.)*, S 10 (Ulp. 29 Sab.), 11 (Paul 5 Sab.), 12 (Ulp. 29 Sab.), 13

(Pomp. 11 Sab.), 14 (Ulp. 48 Sab.), 15 (Paul 29 ed.), E 16 (Marcell. 5 dig.)*, S 17 (Paul 29 ed.)-21 E 22 –23.

13.7. <intro. S 1 (Ulp. 40 Sab.)> S 2 (Pomp. 6 ? Sab.)-6 (Pomp. 35 Sab.), P 7 (Paul 2 sent.)*, 8 (Pomp. 35 Sab.)-16 (Paul 29 ed.), 17 (Marcian. 1 form. hyp.)*, 18 (Paul 29 ed.), 19 (Marcian. 1 form hyp.)*, 20 (Paul 29 ed.)-22 (Ulp. 30 ed.), P 23 (Tryph. 8 disp.)*, S 24 (Ulp. 30 ed.)-34 (Marcell. 1 resp.), <mass codal 35 (Flor. 8 inst.)> E 36 –39 P 40 (Pap. 3 resp.), 41 (Paul 3 quaest.)*, 42 (Pap. 3 resp.) A 43.

Total texts 132 S 98 P 16 E 16 A 2

Initial masses S 6 (13.1,3-7: SEP,S,SP,SPEA,SE,SEPA) E 1 (13.2: E)

Insertions in other masses 8: P in S 5 (13.5.6,9; 13.7.7,23) E in S 4 (13.5.12,20; 13.6.9,16)

Displacement within masses 6: S 5 (13.1.6; 13.4.6; 13.5.2; 13.7.17,19) P 1 (13.7.41)

Texts introducing titles 9: S 6 P 1 (13.6.1-7) S 2 (13.3.1; 13.7.1)

Codal text apart from Appendix 1: P 1 (13.5.30)

Codal mass texts 2: S 2 (13.4.9; 13.7.35)

Total displacements 26/125 = 21 per cent

14.1. S 1-7.

14.2. <intro. P (Paul 2 sent.), S 2 (Paul 34 ed.)>, P 3-5 S 6-8 (Iul. 2 Minic.), S or P 9 (Maec. leg. Rhod.) A 10.

14.3. S 1-11 (Ulp. 28 ed.), 12 (Iul. 11 dig.)*, 13 (Ulp. 28 ed.), E 14 (Paul Plaut.)*, S 15 (Ulp. 28 ed.)-18 P 19 A 20.

14.4. S 1-7 (Ulp. 29 ed.), 8 (Iul. 22 dig.)*, 9 (Ulp.29 ed.)-12.

14.5. S 1-2 (Ulp. 29 ed.), 3 (Ulp. 3 disp.)*, 4 (Ulp. 29 ed.)-6 P 7-8.

14.6. S 1 (Ulp. 29 ed.), E 2 (Ulp. 64 ed.)*, S 3 (Ulp. 29 ed.), P 4 (Scae. 2 quaest.)*, 5 (Paul 3 quaest.)*, 6 (Scae. 2 quaest.)*, S 7 (Ulp. 29 ed.)-15 P 16-18 E 19 (Pomp. 7 var. lect.), A 20 (Pomp. 5 SCC).

Total texts 77 S 59 P 11 E 3 A 3 S or P 1

Initial masses S 5 (14.1,3-6: S,SPA,S,SP,SPEA) P1 (14.2: PSA)

Insertions in other masses 5: P in S 3 (14.6.4,5,6) E in S 2 (14.3.14; 14.6.2)

Displacements within masses 3: S 3 (14.3.12; 14.4.8; 14.5.3)

Texts introducing titles 2: P 1 S 1 (14.2.1-2)

Total displacements 10/71 = 14 per cent

15.1. <intro. S 1 (Ulp. 29 ed.), 2 (Pomp. 5 Sab.), 3 (Ulp. 29 ed.), 4 (Pomp. 7 Sab.), 5 (Ulp. 29 ed.) E 6 (Cels. 6 dig.), S 7 (Ulp. 29 ed.), 8 (Paul 8 Sab.), 9 (Ulp. 29 ed.), 10 (Gai. 9 ed. prov.), 11 (Ulp. 29 ed.) 12

(Iul. 12 dig.), 13 (Ulp. 29 ed.), 14 (Iul. 12 dig.), 15 (Ulp. 29 ed.), 16 (Iul. 12 dig.), 17 (Ulp. 29 ed.), P 18 (Paul 4 quaest. S 19 (Ulp. 29 ed.), 20 (Paul 30 ed.), 21 (Ulp. 29 ed.)> S 22 (Pomp. 7 Sab.)-27 (Gai. 9 ed. prov.), 28 (Iul. 12 dig.)*, 29 (Gai. 9 ed. prov.)-32 (Ulp. 2 disp.), E 33 (Iavolen. 1 Cass.)*, 34 (Pomp. 12 var. lect.)*, 35 (Iavolen. 1 Cass.)*, S 36 (Ulp. 2 disp.)-40 (Marcian. 5 reg.), <mass codal S 41 (Ulp. 43 Sab.), E 42 (Ulp. 12 ed.), S 43 (Paul 30 ed.)> E 44-49 P 50-57 A 58.

15.2. S 1-2 E 3.

15.3. S 1 (Ulp. 29 ed.), E 2 (Iavolen. 12 Cass.)*, S 3 (Ulp. 29 ed.)-5 (Ulp. 29 ed.), P 6 (Tryph. 1 disp.)*, S 7 (Ulp. 29 ed.)-8 (Paul 30 ed.), E 9 (Iav. 12 Cass.)*, S 10 (Ulp. 29 ed.)- Ulp. 13 (Ulp. 29 ed.), 14 (Iul. 11 dig.)*, 15 (Ulp.2 disp.)-18 P 19-20 A 21.

15.4. S 1-3 E 4-5.

Total texts 87 S 54 P 12 E 18 A 2

Initial masses S 4 (15.1-4: SEPA,SE,SPA,SE)

Insertions in other masses 6: P in S 1 (15.3.6) E in S 5 (15.1.33-35; 15.3.2,9)

Displacement within masses 2: S 2 (15.1.28; 15.3.14)

Texts introducing titles 21: S 19 P1 E 1 (15.1.1-21)

Mass codal texts 3: S 3 (15.1.41-43)

Total displacements 32/83 = 39 per cent

16.1. S 1-6 (Ulp. 29 ed.), P 7 (Pap. 9 quaest.)*, S 8 (Ulp. 29. ed.), 9 (Paul 6 reg.)*, 10 (Ulp. 29 ed.)-17 (Afr. 4 quaest.), E 18 (Paul 8 Plaut.)*, S 19 (Afr. 4 quaest.)-22 (Paul 6 reg.), S or P 23 (Paul 1 SC Vell.), 24 (Paul 1 intercess. fem.) E 25 (Mod. 1 heur.)*, < mass codal S 26 (Ulp. 37 ed.)> P 27-31 A 32.

16.2. <intro. E 1 (Mod. 6 pand.), S 2 (Iul. 90 dig.)>, S 3 (Pomp. 25 Sab.)-9 E 10 (Ulp. 63 ed.), S 11 (Ulp. 32 ed.)*, E 12 (Ulp. 64 ed.)-15 P 16-24.

16.3. <intro. S 1-3 (Ulp. 30 ed.), E 4 (Paul 5 Plaut.), S 5 (Ulp. 30 ed.), E 6 (Paul 2 ed.), S 7 (Ulp. 30 ed.), P 8 (Pap. 9 quaest.), E 9 (Paul 17 ed.), S 10 (Iul. 2 Minic.)> S 11 (Ulp. 41 Sab.), 12 (Pomp. 22 Sab.)-18 (Nerat. 2 membr.), E 19 (Paul 17 ed.)-23 P 24-31 (Tryph. 9 disp.), <codal apart from Appendix E 32 (Cels. 11 dig.)>, A 33 (Lab. 6 post. Iav. epit.)-34.

Total texts 90 S 46 P 24 E 17 A 3

Initial masses S 3 (16.1-3: SPA,SEP,SEPA)

Insertions in other masses 4: P in S 1 (16.1.7) S in E 1 (16.2.11) E in S 2 (16.1.18,25)

Displacements within masses 1: S 1 (16.1.9)
Texts introducing titles 12: E 1 S 1 (16.2.1-2) S 6 E 3 P 1 (16.3.1-10)
Codal text apart from Appendix 1: E 1 (16.3.32)
Codal mass text 1: S 1 (16.1.26)
Total displacements 19/87 = 22 per cent

17.1. <intro. S 1 (Paul 32 ed.), 2 (Gai. 2 rer. cott.), 3 (Paul 32 ed.), 4 (Gai. 2 rer. cott.), 5 (Paul 32 ed.), 6 (Ulp. 31 ed.), P 7 (Pap. 3 resp.), 8 (Ulp. 31 ed.)-10 (Ulp. 31 ed.), E 11 (Pomp. 3 Plaut.), 12 (Ulp. 31 ed.)-14 (Ulp. 31 ed.), 15 (Paul 2 Sab.), 16 (Ulp. 31 ed.)> S 17 (Paul 7 Sab.)-22 (Paul 32 ed.), P 23 (Hermogen. 2 iur. epit.)*, 24 (Paul 2 sent.)*, 25 (Hermogen. 2 iur. epit.)*, S 26 (Paul 32 ed.)-27 (Gai. 10 ed. prov.), E 28 (Ulp. 14 ed.)*, 29 (Ulp. 7 disp.)-34 (Afr. 8 quaest.), 35 (Nerat. 5 membr.)*, E 36 (Iavolen. 7 Cass.)*, S 37 (Afr. 8 quaest.)-39 (Nerat. 7 membr.) E 40-44 (Ulp. 62 ed.), 45 (Plaut. 5 Plaut.)*, 46 (Ulp. 74 ed.), 47 (Pomp. 3 Plaut.)-52 P 53-61 A 62.

17.2. <intro. S 1 (Paul 32 ed.), 2 (Gai. 10 ed. prov.), 3 (Paul 32 ed.), E 4 (Mod. 3 reg.), S 5 (Ulp. 31 ed.)> S 6 (Pomp. 9 Sab.)-12 (Paul 6 Sab.), 13 (Paul 32 ed.)*, 14 (Ulp. 30 Sab.)-19 (Ulp. 30 Sab.), 20 (Ulp. 31 ed.)*, 21 (Ulp. 30 Sab.), 22 (Gai. 10 ed. prov.)*, 23 (Ulp. 30 Sab.), 24 (Ulp. 31 ed.)*, 25 (Paul 6 Sab.), 26 (Ulp. 31 ed.)*, 27 (Paul 6 Sab.), E 28 (Paul 60 ed.)*, S 29 (Ulp. 30 Sab.)-31, E 32 (Ulp. 2 ed.)*, S 33 (Ulp. 31 ed.)*, 34 (Gai. 10 ed. prov.)*, 35 (Ulp. 30 Sab.)-39 (Pomp. 13 Sab.), 40 (Pomp. 17 Sab.)*, 41 (Ulp. 20 ed.)*, 42 (Ulp. 45 Sab.)*, 43 (Ulp. 28 ed.)*, 44 (Ulp. 30 ed.)*, 45 (Ulp. 30 Sab.)-48 (Paul 6 Sab.), 49 (Ulp. 31 ed.)*, 50 (Paul 6 Sab.), 51 (Ulp. 30 Sab.), 52 (Ulp. 31 ed.)*, 53 (Ulp. 30 Sab.)-57 (Ulp. 30 Sab.), 58 (Ulp. 31 ed.)*, 59 (Pomp. 12 Sab.)*, 60 (Pomp. 13 Sab.), 61 (Ulp. 31 ed.)*, 62 (Pomp. 13 Sab.), 63 (Ulp. 31 ed.), P 64 (Callist. 1 quaest.)*, S 65 (Paul 32 ed.)-73 E 74-76 (Proc. 5 epist.), P 77 (Paul 4 quaest.)*, E 78 (Proc. 5 epist.), P 79 (Paul 4 quaest.)*, E 80 (Proc. 5 epist.), P 81-83 A 84.

Total texts 146 S 101 P 19 E 24 A 2

Initial masses S 2 (17.1-2: SEPA,SEPA)
Insertions in other masses 10: P in S 4 (17.1.23-25; 17.2.64) P in E 2 (17.2.77,79) E in S 4 (17.1.28,36; 17.2.28,32)
Displacements within masses 19: S 18 (17.1.35; 17.2.13,20,22,24,26, 33,34,40-44,49,52,58,59,61) E 1 (17.1.45)
Texts introducing titles 21: S 14 P 1 E 1 (17.1.1-16) S 4 E 1 (17.2.1-5)
Total displacements 50/144 = 35 per cent

18.1. <intro. S 1 (Paul 33 Ed.)>, S 2 (Ulp. 1 Sab.)-11 (Ulp. 28 Sab.), E 12 (Pomp. 31 QM)*, S 13 (Pomp. 9 Sab.)-16 (Pomp. 9 Sab.), 17 (Paul 33 ed.)*, 18 (Pomp. 9 Sab.), E 19 (Pomp. 31 QM)*, S 20 (Pomp. 9 Sab.)-29 (Ulp. 43 Sab.), 30 (Ulp. 32 ed.)*, 31 (Pomp. 22 Sab.)-46 (Marcian. 1 delat.), <mass codal S 47 (Ulp. 29 Sab.), 48 (Paul 5 Sab.), 49 (Ulp. 29 Sab.)> E 50-57 (Paul 5 Plaut.), P 58 (Pap. 10 quaest.)*, E 59 (Cels. 8 Dig.)-71 P 72-75 (Hermogen. 2 iur. epit.), <mass codal P 76 (Paul 6 resp.)> 76 A 77 (Iavolen. 4 post. Lab., not S)-79 (Iavolen. 5 post. Lab., not S)-81.

18.2. S 1-7 (Paul 5 Sab.), 8 (Paul 33 ed.)*, 9 (Ulp. 28 Sab.), 10 (Iul. 13 dig.)*, 11 (Ulp. 28 Sab.)-18 E 19 P 20.

18.3. S 1-5 P 6-7 A 8.

18.4. S 1-5 (Paul 33 ed.), P 6 (Paul 5 quaest.)*, E 7 (Paul 14 Plaut.)*, 8 (Iavolen. 2 Plaut.)*, S 9 (Paul 33 ed.), E 10 (Iavolen. 2 Plaut.)*, S 11 (Ulp. 32 ed.), 12 (Gai. 10 ed. prov.), E 13 (Paul 14 Plaut.)*, S 14 (Paul 33 ed.)-20 P 21-23 A 24-25.

18.5. S 1-5 E 6 P 7-8 A 9-10.

18.6. S 1 (Ulp. 28 Sab.), 2 (Gai. 2 rer. cott.)*, 3 (Paul 5 Sab.)-13 (Paul 3 Alfen. epit.), 14 (Iul. 3 Urs. Fer.)*, 15 (Paul 3 Alfen. epit.)-16 E 17-18 P 19-20.

18.7. S 1-2 E 3-4 P 5-6 (Pap. 27 quaest.), 7 (Pap. 10 quaest.)*, 8 (Pap. 27 quaest.)-9 A 10.

Total texts 174 S 108 P 22 E 33 A 11

Initial masses S 7 (18.1-7: SEPA,SEP,SPA,SPA,SEPA,SEP,SEPA)

Insertions in other masses 8: P in S 1 (18.4.6) P in E 1 (18.1.58) E in S 6 (18.1.12,19; 18.4.7,8,10,13)

Displacements within masses 7: S 6 (18.1.17,30; 18.2.8,10; 18.6.2,14) P 1 (18.7.7)

Text introducing title 1: S 1 (18.1.1)

Codal mass texts 4: S 3 (18.1.47-49) P 1 (18.1.76)

Total displacements 20/167 = 12 per cent

19.1. S 1-4 (Paul 5 Sab.), 5 (Paul 3 Sab.)*, 6 (Pomp. 9 Sab.)-11 (Ulp. 32 ed.), E 12 (Cels. 27 dig.)*, S 13 (Ulp. 32 ed.), E 14 (Pomp. 31 QM)*, S 15 (Ulp. 32 ed.), E 16 (Pomp. 31 QM)*, S 17 (Ulp. 32 ed.), E 18 (Iavolen. 7 Cass.)*, 19 (Gai. ed. urb. publ.)* 20 (Gai. 21 ed. prov.)* S 21 (Paul 33 ed.)-31 E 32-33 (Ulp. 23 ed.), 34 (Ulp. 18 ed.)*, 35 (Ulp. 70 ed.)-40 P 41-43 (Paul 5 quaest.), S 44 (Afr. 8 quaest.)*, P 45 (Paul 5 quaest.)-49 A 50-55.

19.2. <intro. S 1 (Paul 34 ed.), 2 (Gai. 2 rer. cott.)> S 3 (Pomp. 9 Sab.)-7 (Ulp. 32 ed.), P 8 (Tryph. 9 disp.)*, S 9 (Ulp. 32 ed.), 10 (Iul.

Urs.Fer.)*, 11 (Ulp. 32 ed.), P 12 (Hermogen. 2 iur. epit.)*, E 13 (Ulp. 32 ed.)*, 14 (Ulp. 71 ed.)*, S 15 (Ulp. 32 ed.), 16 (Iul. 15 dig.)*, 17 (Ulp. 32 ed.), 18 (Iul. 15 dig.)*, 19 (Ulp. 32 ed.)-20 (Paul 34 ed.), E 21 (Iavolen. 11 epist.)*, S 22 (Paul 34 ed.), P 23 (Hermogen. 2 iur. epit.)*, S 24 (Paul 34 ed.)-27, A 28 (Lab. 4 post. Iav. epit.)*, S 29 (Alfen Var. 7 dig.)-33 (Afr. 8 quaest.), 34 (Gai. 10 ed. prov.)*, 35 (Afr. 8 quaest.)-36 (Flor. 7 inst.), E 37 (Iavolen. 8 Cass.)*, S 38 (Paul 1 reg.) E 39 (Ulp. 2 ed.), 40 (Gai. 5 ed. prov.)*, E 41 (Ulp. 5 ed.), 42 (Paul 13 ed.)- 52 P 53-56 A 57 (Iavolen. 9 post. Lab., not S)-58 (Lab. 4 post. Iav.epit.), 59 (Iavolen. 5 post Lab., not S)-62.

19.3. S 1-2.

19.4. S 1 E 2.

19.5. <intro. P 1 (Pap. 8 quaest.), E 2 (Cels. 8 dig.), S.3 (Iul. 14 dig.), 4 (Ulp. 30 Sab.)> <mass intro. P 5 (Paul 5 quaest.), 6 (Nerat. 1 resp.)>, 7 (Pap. 2 quaest.)-9 E 10-12 S 13-20 (Ulp. 32 ed.), 21 (Ulp. 2 disp.)*, 22 (Gai. 10 ed. prov.), 23 (Alfen. Var. 3 dig.)-25 (Marcian. 3 reg.), <codal S 26 (Pomp. 21 Sab.)>-Q 27.

Total texts 148 S 76 P 21 E 37 A 13 Q 1

Initial masses S 4 (19.1-4: SEPA,SEPA,S,SE) P 1 (19.5: PES)

Insertions in other masses 15: S in P 1 (19.1.44) P in S 3 (19.2.8,12,23) E in S 10 (19.1.12,14,16,18,19,20; 19.2.13,14,21,37) A in S 1 (19.2.28)

Displacements within masses 8: S 5 (19.1.5; 19.2.10,16,18,34; 19.5.21) E 2 (19.1.34; 19.2.40)

Texts introducing titles 6: S 2 (19.2.1-2) S 2 P 1 E 1 (19.5.1-4)

Codal text 1: S 1 (19.5.26)

Texts introducing masses 2: P 2 (19.5.5-6)

Total displacements 32/143 = 22 per cent

20.1. <intro. P 1 (Pap. 11 resp.), 2 (Pap. 3 resp.), 3 (Pap. 20 quaest.)> S 4 (Gai. 1 form. hyp.)-5 (Marcian. 1 form. hyp.) E 6 (Ulp. 73 ed.)*, 7 (Paul 68 ed.)*, 8 (Ulp. 73 ed.)*, S 9 (Gai. 9 ed. prov.)*, E 10 (Ulp. 73 ed.)*, S 11 (Marcian. 1 form. hyp.), E 12 (Paul 68 ed.)*, S 13 (Marcian. 1 form. hyp.), E 14 (Ulp. 73 ed.)*, S 15 (Gai. 1 form. hyp.)-16 E 17 (Ulp. 17 ed.)-26 (Mod. 4 resp.), <mass codal 27 (Marcell. 5 dig.)> P 28-33 A 34-35.

20.2. <intro. P 1 (Pap. 10 resp.)>, S 2 (Marcian. 1 form. hyp.), E 3 (Ulp. 73 ed.)*, S 4 (Ner. 1 membr.)*, 5 (Marcian. 1 form. hyp.) E 6 (Ulp. 73 ed.)-7 P 8-9 A 10.

20.3. S 1-2 P 3-5.

20.4. <intro. P 1 (Pap. 8 quaest.), 2 (Pap. 3 resp.), 3 (Pap. 1 resp.)>, S 4 (Pomp. 35 Sab.),-5 (Ulp. 3 disp.) E 6 (Ulp. 7 ed.)*, S 7 (Ulp. 3 disp.)-12 E 13-14 (Paul 14 Plaut.), <mass codal 15 (Paul 68 ed.)> P 16-20 A 21.

20.5. <intro. P 1 (Pap. 26 quaest.), 2 (Pap. 2 resp.), 3 (Pap. 3 resp.), 4 (Pap. 11 resp.)>, S 5 (Marcian. 1 form. hyp.), E 6 (Mod. 8 reg.)*, S 7 (Marcian. 1 form. hyp.), E 8 (Mod. 4 reg.), P 9 (Paul 3 quaest.)-13 A 14.

20.6. <intro. P 1 (Pap. 11 resp.)>, S 2 (Gai. 9 ed. prov.) 3 (Ulp. 8 disp.), E 4 (Ulp. 73 ed.)*, S 5 (Marcian. 1 form. hyp.), E 6 (Ulp. 73 ed.)*, S 7 (Gai. 1 form. hyp.)-8 (Marcian. 1 form. hyp.) E 9 (Mod. 4 resp.), P 10-13 A 14-15.

Total texts 100 S 27 P 37 E 29 A 7

Initial masses S 6 (20.1-6: SEPA,SEPA,SP,SEPA,SEPA,SEPA)

Insertions in other masses 11: E in S 11 (20.1.6-8,10,12,14; 20.2.3; 20.4.6; 20.5.6; 20.6.4,6)

Displacements within masses 2: S 2 (20.1.9; 20.2.4)

Texts introducing titles 12: P 12 (20.1.1-3; 20.2.1; 20.4.1-3; 20.5.1-4; 20.6.1)

Codal mass texts 2: E 2 (20.1.27; 20.4.15)

Total displacements 27/94 = 29 per cent

21.1. E 1-4 (Ulp. 1 ed. aed. cur.), S 5 (Paul 11 Sab.)*, E 6 (Ulp. 1 ed. aed. cur.), S 7 (Paul 11 Sab.)*, E 8 (Ulp. 1 ed. aed. cur.), S 9 (Ulp. 44 Sab.)*, E 10 (Ulp. 1 ed. aed. cur.), S 11 (Paul 11 Sab.)*, E 12 (Ulp. 1 ed. aed. cur.)-14 (Ulp. 1 ed. aed. cur.), S 15 (Paul 11 Sab.)*, 16 (Pomp. 2 Sab.)*, E 17 (Ulp. 1 ed. aed. cur.)-33 (Ulp. 1 ed. aed. cur.), S 34 (Afr. 6 quaest.)*, E 35 (Ulp. 1 ed. aed. cur.), S 36 (Pomp. 23 Sab.)*, E 37 (Ulp. 1 ed. aed. cur.)-40 (Ulp. 2 ed. aed. cur.), 41 (Paul 2 ed. aed. cur.), 42 (Ulp. 2 ed. aed. cur.), 43 (Paul 1 ed. aed. cur.)-45 (Gai. 1 ed. aed. cur.) S 46 (Pomp. 18 Sab.), 47 (Paul 11 Sab.)-53 P 54-58 <codal apart from Appendix E 59 (Ulp. 74 ed.), 60 (Paul 69 ed.), 61 (Ulp. 80 ed.), 62 (Mod. 8 diff.), 63 (Ulp. 1 ed. aed. cur.)> A 64-65.

21.2. S 1-8 E 9-10 P 11-12/// S 13 (Paul 5 Sab.), E 14 (Ulp. 18 ed.)*, S 15 (Paul 5 Sab.)-21 (Ulp. 29 Sab.), E 22 (Pomp. 1 Plaut.)*, S 23 (Ulp. 20 Sab.), 24 (Afr. 6 quaest.)*, 25 (Ulp. 29 Sab.)-27 (Pomp. 11 Sab.), E 28 (Ulp. 80 ed.)*, S 29 (Pomp. 11 Sab.)-34 (Pomp. 27 Sab.), E 35 (Paul 2 ed. aed. cur.)*, S 36 (Paul 29 ed.)-40 (Iul. 58 dig.), E 41 (Paul 2 ed. aed. cur.)*, 42 (Paul 53 ed.)*, S 43 (Iul. 58 ed.)-48 E 49-63 P 64-76.

21.3. E 1-2 P 3.

Total texts 144 S 54 P 21 E 67 A 2

Initial masses S ½ + ½ (21.2: SEP////SEP) E 2 (21.1,3: ESPA,EP)

Insertions in other masses 14: S in E 8 (21.1.5,7,9,11,15,16,34,36) E in S 6 (21.2.14,22,28,35,41,42)

Displacements within mass 1: S 1 (21.2.24)

Codal apart from appendix: E 5 (21.1.59-63)

Total displacements 20/141 = 14 per cent

22.1. P 1-17 (Paul 1 usur.), 18 (Paul 3 resp.)*, 19 (Gai. 6 XII tab.) S 20-33 E 34-36 (Ulp. 61 ed.), 37 (Ulp. 10 ed.)*, 38 (Paul 6 Plaut.)–45, <mass codal 46 (Ulp. 62 ed.)> A 47-48 (Scae. 22 dig.), <codal A 49 (Iavolen. 3 post. Lab., not S)>.

22.2. <intro. E 1 (Mod. 10 pand.)>, E 2 (Pomp. 3 Plaut.), 3 (Mod. 4 reg.) P 4 (Pap. 3 resp.)-5 (Scae. 6 resp.), <mass codal P 6 (Paul 25 quaest.)>, <codal apart from Appendix E 7 (Paul 3 ed.), E 8 (Ulp. 71 ed.)> A 9 (Lab. 5 pith.).

22.3. P 1 (Pap. 3 quaest.), E 2 (Paul 69 ed.)*, P 3 (Pap. 9 resp.)-7 (Paul 2 sent.) E 8 –16 (Terent. Clem. 3 Iul. Pap.), <mass codal 17 (Cels. 6 dig.)> S 18-23,<codal apart from Appendix E 24 (Mod. 4 reg.), P 25 (Paul 3 quaest.), 26 (Pap. 20 quaest.)> A 27 (Scae. 33 dig.), 28 (Lab. 7 pith.) <codal A 29 (Scae. 9 dig.)>.

22.4. <intro. P 1 (Paul 2 sent.), 2 (Paul 5 sent.)> P 3 (Paul 3 resp.), S 4 (Gai. 1 form. hyp.)*, P 5 (Callist. 2 quaest.), <codal S 6 (Ulp. 50 ed.)>.

22.5. <S 1 (Arcad. Char. 1 test.)> E 2 (Mod. 8 reg.)-6 (Ruf. 2 reg.), <mass codal 7 (Mod. 3 reg.)>, <mass intro. S 8 (Scae. 4 reg.)>, 9 (Paul 1 Sab.)-14 (Pap. 1 adult.), P 15 (Paul 3 sent.)* 16 (Paul 5 sent.)* S 17 (Ulp. 1 reg.)*, 18 (Paul 2 adult.)-22 (Venul. 2 off. proc.) <mass codal S 23 (Venul. 1 iud. pub.)>, P 24 (Paul 5 sent.), <codal S 25 (Arcad. Char. 1 test.)>.

22.6. <intro. S 1 (Paul 44 ed.), 2 (Nerat. 5 membr.)> S 3 (Pomp. 3 Sab.), 4 (Pomp. 13 Sab.), E 5-6 P 7-9 (Paul 1 iur. fact. ignor.), <codal P 10 (Pap 6 resp.)>.

Total texts 128 S 42 P 41 E 38 A 7

Initial masses S 1 (22.6: SEP) P 3 (22.1,3,4: PSEA,PESA,PS) E 2 (22.2,5: EPA,ESP)

Insertions in other masses 4: S in P 1 (22.4.4) E in P 1 (22.3.2) P in S 2 (22.5.15-16)

Displacements within masses 3: P 1 (22.1.18) E 1 (22.1.37) S 1 (22.5.17)

Texts introducing titles 6: E 1 (22.2.1) P 2 (22.4.1-2) S 3 (22.5.1; 22.6.1-2)

Codal title texts 5: A 2 (22.1.49; 22.3.29) S 2 (22.4.6; 22.5.25) P 1 (22.6.10)

Codal apart from Appendix 5: E 2 (22.2.7-8;) E 1 P 2 (22.3.24-26)

Text introducing mass 1: S 1 (22.5.8)

Codal mass texts 5: E 3 (22.1.46; 22.3.17; 22.5.7) P 1 (22.2.6) S 1 (22.5.23)

Total displacements 29/122 = 24 per cent

23.1. <intro. S. 1 (Flor. 3 inst.), 2 (Ulp. 1 spons.), 3 (Flor. 3 inst.)> S 4 (Ulp. 35 Sab.)-11 (Iul. 16 dig.), 12 (Ulp. 1 spons.) E 13-17 (Gai. 1 Iul. Pap.), <codal 18 (Ulp. 6 ed.)>.

23.2. <intro. E 1 (Mod. 1 reg.), S 2 (Paul 35 ed.)>, S 3 (Paul 1 Sab.)-5, 6 (Ulp. 35 Sab.)*, P 7 (Paul 1 leg. Falc.)*, 8 (Pomp. 5 Sab.)- 9 (Ulp. 26 Sab.), 10 (Paul 35 ed.)*, 11 (Iul. 62 dig.)*, 12 (Ulp. 26 Sab.)-14 (Paul 35 ed.), P 15 (Pap. 4 resp.)*, S 16 (Paul 35 ed.)-20 <mass intro. E 21 (Terent. Clem. 3 Iul.Pap.)>, 22 (Cels. 15 dig.)-27 (Ulp. 3 Iul. Pap.), S 28 (Marcian. 10 inst.)*, E 29 (Ulp. 3 Iul. Pap.)-33 P 34 –38 /// E 39-46, 47 (Paul 2 Iul. Pap.)*, 48-51 S 52-53 (Gai. 11 ed. prov.), 54 (Scae. 1 reg.)*, 55 (Gai. 11 ed. prov.)-57, P 57a (Pap. 2 adult. Marcian. not.)*, S 58 (Marcian. 4 reg.), 59 (Paul 1 de adsig. libert.)*, 60 Paul (1 ad orat. dd. Anton. et Comm.) P 61-68.

23.3. <intro. S 1 (Paul 14 Sab.), E 2 (Paul 60 ed.), 3 (Ulp. 63 ed.)> S 4 (Paul 4 Sab.)-7 (Ulp. 31 Sab.), P 8 (Callist. 2 quaest.)*, S 9 (Ulp. 31 Sab.)-12 (Ulp. 34 Sab.), E 13 (Mod. 1 diff. dot.)*, S 14 (Ulp. 34 Sab.)-25 (Paul 7 Sab.), E 26 (Mod. 1 reg.)*, S 27 (Ulp. 36 Sab.)-30 (Paul 7 Sab.), P 31 (Pap. 4 resp.)*, S 32 (Pomp. 16 Sab.)-44 (Iul. 16 dig.), P 45 (Tryph. 8 disp.)*, S 46 (Iul. 16 dig.)-53 E 54-60 (Cels. 11 dig.), 61 (Terent. Clem. 3 Iul.Pap.)*, 62 (Mod. 5 resp.)-67 P 68-78 A 79-80 (Iavolen. 6 post. Lab., not S) P 81 (Pap. 8 quaest.)*, E 82 (Proc. 5 epist.)* A 83-85.

23.4. <intro. E 1 (Iavolen. 4 Cass.)>, S 2 (Ulp. 19 Sab.)-5 (Paul 7 Sab.), E 6 (Ulp. 4 ed.)*, S 7 (Pomp. 15 Sab.)-12 (Paul 35 ed.), 13 (Iul. 17 dig.)*, 14 (Paul 35 ed.)-16 (Paul 35 ed.), E 17 (Proc. 11 epist.)*, S 18 (Iul. 18 dig.)*, 19 (Alfen. Var. 3 dig.)*, 20 (Paul 35 ed.), 21 (Iul. 17 dig.), 22 (Iul. 2 Urs.Fer.)-25 P 26-30 (Tryph. 10 disp.) <codal apart from Appendix P 31 (Scae. 3 quaest.)> A 32.

23.5. S 1 (Paul 36 ed.), 2 (Ulp. 4 adult.)*, 3 (Paul 36 ed.)- 4 Gai. 11 ed. prov., 5 (Ulp. 2 omn. trib.)*, 6 (Ulp. 5 adult.)*, 6 (Iul. 16 dig.)-9 (Afr. 8 quaest.), P 10 (Paul 5 quaest.)*, S 11 (Afr. 8 quaest.)- 14 (Paul 3 adult.), P 15-16 E 17 A 18 (Iavolen. 6 post. Lab., not S).

Total texts 221 S 120 P 39 E 55 A 7

Initial masses S 4 (23.1,3,4,5: SE,SEPA,SPA,SPEA) S 1 + E 1 (23.2:SEP/ESP)

Insertions in other masses 14: S in E 1 (23.2.28) P in S 7 (23.2.57a; 23.2.7,15; 23.3.8,31,45; 23.5.10) P in A 1 (23.3.81) E in S 4 (23.3.13,26; 23.4.6,17) E in A 1 (23.3.82)

Displacement within masses 12: S 12 (23.2.6,10,11,54,59; 23.4.13,18,19; 23.5.2,5,6) E 1 (23.3.61)

Texts introducing titles 9: S 3 (23.1.1-3) E 1 S 1 (23.2.1-2) S 1 E 2 (23.3.1-3) E 1 (23.4.1)

Codal title text 1: S 1 (23.1.18)

Codal text apart from Appendix 1: P 1 (23.4.31)

Text introducing mass 1: E 1 (23.2.21)

Total displacements 38/216 = 18 per cent

24.1. <intro. S 1-3 (Ulp. 32 Sab.), 4 (Iul. 17 dig.), 5 (Ulp. 32 Sab.), 6 (Gai. 11 ed. prov.), 7 (Ulp. 32 Sab.), 8 Gai. 11 ed. prov.), 9 (Ulp. 3 Sab.), 10 (Gai. 1 ed. prov.), 11 (Ulp. 32 Sab.)-13 (Ulp. 32 Sab.), E 14 (Paul 71 ed.), S 15 (Ulp. 32 Sab.), P 16 (Tryph, 10 disp.), S 17 (Ulp. 32 Sab.), E 18 (Pomp. 4 var. lect.), S 19 (Ulp. 32 Sab.), E 20 (Iavolen. 11 epist.), 21 (Ulp. 32 Sab.)> , S 22 (Ulp. 3 Sab.), 23 (Ulp. 6 Sab.), 24 (Paul 7 Sab.) E 25 (Terent. Clem. 5 Iul. Pap.)*, S 26 (Paul 7 Sab.), E 27 (Mod. 7 reg.)*, S 28 (Paul 7 Sab.)-29 (Pomp. 14 Sab.), 30 (Gai. 11 ed. prov.)*, 31 (Pomp. 14 Sab.)-40 (Ulp. 2 resp.), E 41 (Ruf. 6 reg.)*, <mass codal S 42 (Gai. 11 ed. prov.), 43 (Paul 1 reg.), 44 (Nerat. 5 membr.)> E 45-51 P 52-60 (Hermogen. 2 iur. epit.), S 61 (Gai. 11 ed. prov.)*, P 62 (Hermogen. 2 iur. epit.)-63 A 64 (Iavolen. 6 post. Lab, not S)-67.

24.2. <intro. S 1 (Paul 35 ed.), 2 (Gai. 11 ed. prov.), 3 (Paul 35 ed.)>, S 4 (Ulp. 26 Sab.), 5 (Ulp. 34 ed.)-9 E 10-11.

24.3. S 1 (Pomp. 15 Sab.), 2 (Ulp. 35 Sab.)*, 3 (Paul 7 Sab.)-5 (Ulp. 31 Sab.)- 8 (Paul 7 Sab.), 9 (Pomp. 14 Sab.)*, 10 (Pomp. 15 Sab.)-20 (Paul 7 Sab.), 21 (Ulp. 3 disp.)*, 22 (Ulp. 33 ed.)-27 (Gai. 11 ed. prov.), 28 (Ulp. 1 inst.)*, 29 (Ulp. 3 disp.)-38 P 39-54 E 55-58 (Mod. 1 heur.), S 59 (Iul. 2 Urs. Fer.)*, E 60 (Proc. 5 epist.), P 61 (Pap. 11 quaest.)*, S 62 (Ulp. 33 ed.)*, E 63 (Paul 2 Iul.Pap.)-64 A 65 <mass intro. (Scae. 1 quaest. pub. tract.)>, 66 (Iavolen. 2 post. Lab., not S)-67.

Total texts 145 S 87 P 29 E 22 A 7

Initial masses S 3 (24.1-3: SEPA,SE,SPEA)

Insertions in other masses 7: S in P 1 (24.1.61) S in E 2 (24.3.59,62) P in E 1 (24.3.61) E in S 3 (24.1.25,27,41)

Displacements within masses 5: S 5 (24.1.30; 24.3.2,9,21,28)

Texts introducing titles 24: S 17 P 1 E 3 (24.1.1-21) S 3 (24.2.1-3)

Text introducing mass 1: A 1 (24.3.65)

Codal mass texts 3: S 3 (24.1.42-44)

Total displacements 40/142 = 28 per cent

25.1. S 1-3 (Ulp. 36 Sab.), 4 (Paul 36 ed.)*, 5 (Ulp. 36 Sab.)-9 (Ulp. 36 Sab.), 10 (Paul 36 ed.)*, 11 (Ulp. 36 Sab.)-16.

25.2. S 1 (Paul 7 Sab.), E 2 (Gai. ed. urb. re iud.),* S 3 (Paul 7 Sab.)-4 (Pomp. 16 Sab.), P 5 (Pap. 11 quaest.)*, S 6 (Paul 7 Sab.)-8 (Pomp. 16 Sab.), 9 (Paul 37 ed.)*, 10 (Pomp. 16 Sab.)-13 (Ulp. 33 ed.), E 14 (Paul 18 ed.),* S 15 (Ulp. 34 ed.), P 16 (Hermogen. 2 iur. epit.)*, S 17 (Ulp. 34 ed.), P 18 (Paul 6 quaest.)*, S 19 (Ulp. 34 ed.), E 20 (Marcell. 7 dig.)*, S 21 (Paul 37 ed.)-25 E 26 (Gai. 4 ed. prov.) P 27 (Pap 4 resp.),-29 (Tryph. 11 disp.), <codal 30 (Pap. 1 quaest.)>.

25.3. S 1 (Ulp. 34 ed.), 2 (Iul. 19 dig.)*, 3 (Ulp. 34 ed.) P 4 (Paul 2 sent.) E 5-8 <codal S or P 9 (Paul 1 iur. patr.)>.

25.4. S 1 (Ulp. 34 ed.), 2 (Iul. 24 dig.) E 3 (Paul 14 Plaut.) A 4.

25.5. S 1-2.

25.6. S 1.

25.7. E 1-2 S 3 P 4-5.

Total texts 67 S 43 P 10 E 12 A 1 S or P 1

Initial masses S 6 (25.1-6: S,SEP,SPE,SEA,S,S) E 1 (25.7: ESP)

Insertions in other masses 6: P in S 3 (25.2.5,16,18) E in S 3 (25.2.2,14,20)

Displacement within masses 4: S 4 (25.1.4,10; 25.2.9; 25.3.2)

Codal title texts 2: P 1 (25.2.30) S or P 1 (25.3.9)

Total displacements 12/60 = 20 per cent

26.1. <intro. S 1 (Paul 38 ed.)>, S 2 (Pomp. 3 Sab.)-9 (Marcian. 2 inst.) E 10-11 P 12-13 S <codal 14 (Ulp. 37 Sab.), 15 (Ulp. 38 Sab.), 16 (Gai. 12 ed. prov.), 17 (Paul 8 Sab.), 18 (Nerat. 3 reg.)>.

26.2. <intro. S 1 (Gai. 10 ed. prov.)>,S 2 (Ulp. 2 Sab.), 3 (Ulp. 35 ed.)*, E 4 (Mod. 7 diff.)*, S 5 (Ulp. 15 Sab.), 6 (Ulp. 36 Sab.)*, 7 (Paul 3 Sab.)-8 (Ulp. 24 Sab.), E 9 (Pomp. 3 QM)*, S 10 (Ulp. 36 Sab.)-12 (Ulp. 38 Sab.), 13 (Pomp. 17 Sab.), 14 (Marcian. 2 inst.)* 15 (Ulp. 38 Sab.), 16 (Ulp. 36 Sab.)*, 17 (Ulp. 35 ed.), E 18 (Callist. 3 ed. mon.)*, S 19 (Ulp. 35 ed.)-23 (Afr. 8 quaest.) E 24 (Iavolen. 5 Cass.), 25 (Mod. 4 pand.)* P 26 (Pap. 4 resp.), 27 (Tryph. 8 disp.)*, 28 (Pap. 4 resp.)-32 A 33 (Iavolen. 8 post. Lab., not S)-34.

26.3. E 1 (Mod. 6 exc.), <mass intro. S 2 (Nerat. 3 reg.)>, 3 (Iul. 21 dig.), S or P 4 (Paul 1 excus. tut.) P 5-9 (Tryph. 14 disp.), 9 (Paul 1 cogn.)*, 10 (Tryph. 14 disp.) A 11.

26.4. S 1-3 (Ulp. 38 Sab.) E 4 (Mod. 4 diff.)*, 5 (Ulp. 35 ed.)-6 (Paul 38 ed.), 7 (Gai. 1 inst.)*, 8 (Paul 38 ed.)-9 P 10 <codal E 11 (Paul 16 Plaut.)>.

26.5. S 1 (Ulp. 39 Sab.), 2 (Ulp. 35 ed.), 3 (Ulp. 36 ed.), E 4 (Ulp. 9 Iul. Pap.)* S 5 (Gai. 12 ed. prov.), 6 (Ulp. 8 omn. trib.), 7 (Ulp. 1 omn. trib.)*, 8 (Ulp. 8 omn. trib.)-10, E 11 (Cels. 11 dig.)*, S 12 (Ulp. 3 off. proc.), P between S and E 13 (Pap 11 quaest.)*, 14 (Pap. 12 quaest.)* E 15 (Paul 2 ed.), 16 (Paul 73 ed.)*, 17 (Ulp. 9 ed.)-23 P 24 (Paul 9 resp.)-29.

26.6. E 1-2 P 3-4.

26.7. <intro. S 1 (Ulp. 35 ed.), E 2 (Ulp. 9 ed.), S 3 (Ulp. 35 ed.), E 4 (Ulp. 9 ed.), S 5 (Ulp. 35 ed.), 6 (Ulp. 36 ed.), 7 (Ulp. 35 ed.) , E 8 (Ulp. 23 ed.), S 9 (Ulp. 36 ed.), 10 (Ulp. 50 ed.), 11 (Ulp. 33 ed.), 12 (Paul 38 ed.), 13 (Gai. 12 ed. prov.), 14 (Paul 8 brev.), P 15 (Paul 2 sent.)> S 16 (Paul 6 Sab.)-21 (Marcell. 1 resp.) E 22 (Paul 3 ed.)-34 P 35-55 A 56-61.

26.8. S 1–9 (Gai. 10 ed. prov.), E 10 (Paul 24 ed.)*, S 11 (Iul. 21 dig.)-16 E 17-18 P 19 A 20-22.

26.9. S 1-2 P 3 (Pap 20 quaest.), E 4 (Ulp. 64 ed.)*, P 5 (Pap 5 resp.)-8.

26.10. S 1 (Ulp. 35 ed.), 2 (Ulp. 1 omn. trib.)*, 3 (Ulp. 35 ed.), 4 (Ulp. 1 omn. trib.)*, 5 (Ulp. 3 disp.), E 6 (Callist. 4 cogn.)*, S 7 (Ulp. 1 omn. trib.) E 8-9 P 10-11 <codal E 12 (Aquila 1 resp.)>.

Total texts 210 S 95 P 56 E 46 A 12 S or P 1

Initial masses S 8 (26.1-2,4-5,7-10: SEP,SEPA,SP,SE,SEPA,SEPA,SEP,S EP) E 2 (26.3,6: ES or PA,EP)

Insertions in other masses 11: E in S 8 (26.2.4,9,18; 26.4.4; 26.5.4,11; 26.8.10; 26.10.6) E in P 1 (26.9.4) P between S and E 2 (26.5.13,14)

Displacements within masses 12: S 8 (26.2.3,6,14,16; 26.4.7; 26.5.7; 26.10.2,4) P 2 (26.2.27; 26.3.9) E 3 (26.2.25; 26.5.16)

Texts introducing titles 17: S 2 (26.1.1; 26.2.1) S 11 P 1 E 3 (26.7.1-15)

Codal title texts 7: E 2 (26.4.11; 26.10.12) S 5 (26.1.14-18)

Text introducing mass 1: S 1 (26.3.2)

Total displacements 48/200 = 24 per cent

27.1. E 1-10, S or P 11 (Paul 1 excus. tut.)*, E 12 (Mod. 3 exc.)-18 S 19-23 (Ulp. 2 resp.), P 24 (Pap. 11 quaest.)*, S 25 (Ulp. 2 off. proc.),

S or P 26 (Paul 1 excus. tut.), <mass codal S 27 (Marcian. 5 reg.), P 28 (Pap. 5 resp.), S 29 (Marcian. 2 inst.)> P 30 (Pap. 5 resp.)-32 (Paul 7 quaest.), 33 (Paul 23 quaest.)*, 34 (Paul 7 quaest.)-38 (Paul 2 sent.), 39 (Tryph. 13 disp.)*, 40 (Paul 2 sent.), 41 (Hermogen. 2 iur. epit.), 42 (Paul 1 cogn.)*, 43 (Hermogen. 2 iur. epit.)-46.

27.2. S 1-5 P 6.

27.3. <intro. S 1 (Ulp. 36 ed.)>, S 2 (Paul 8 Sab.)-7 (Ulp. 35 ed.), P 8 (Pap. 28 quaest.)*, S 9 (Ulp. 35 ed.)-15 E 16-17 P 18 (Pap. 25 quaest.), S 19 (Ulp. 1 resp.)*, P 20 (Pap. 2 resp.)-25.

27.4. S 1 (Ulp. 36 ed.), 2 (Iul. 21 dig.)*, 3 (Ulp. 36 ed.), 4 (Iul. 21 dig.)-5 E 6.

27.5. S 1 E 2-4 (Pomp. 16 QM), <codal E 5 (Ulp. 10 ed.)>.

27.6. E 1-10 S 11-12.

27.7. S 1-5 P 6-8.

27.8. S 1-2 (Ulp. 3 disp.), 3 (Iul. 21 dig.)*, 4 (Ulp. 3 disp.), 5 (Iul. 21 dig.) E 6-9.

27.9. S 1 (Ulp. 35 ed.), S or P 2 (Paul 1 or. d. Sev.)*, 3 (Ulp. 35 ed.), S or P 4 (Paul 1 or. d. Sev.)*, 5 (Ulp. 35 ed.), 6 (Ulp. 2 omn. trib.)*, 7 (Ulp. 35 ed.)-12 (Marcian. 1 form. hyp.), S or P 13 (Paul 1 or. d. Sev.) P 14 (Paul 9 resp.).

27.10. S 1 (Ulp. 1 Sab.), 2 (Paul 1 off. proc.)*, 3 (Ulp. 31 Sab.)-9 E 10-12 (Marcell. 1 dig.), <mass codal E 13 (Gai. 3 ed. prov.)>, P 14-17.

Total texts 148 S 65 P 36 E 42 A 0 S or P 5

Initial masses S 8 (27.2-5,7-10: SP,SEP,SE,SE,SP,SE,SP,SEP) E 2 (27.1,6: ESP,ES)

Insertions in other masses 4: S in P 1 (27.3.19) S or P in E 1 (27.1.11) P in S 2 (27.1.24; 27.3.8)

Displacements within masses 9: S 6 (27.4.2; 27.8.3; 27.9.2,4,6; 27.10.2) P 3 (27.1.33,39,42)

Text introducing title 1: S 1 (27.3.1)

Codal title text 1: E 1 (27.5.5)

Codal mass texts 4: S 2 P 1 (27.1.27-29) E 1 (27.10.13)

Total displacements 19/138 = 14 per cent

28.1. <intro. E 1 (Mod. 2 pand.), S 2 (Lab. 1 post. Iav. epit., S not A), P 3 (Pap. 14 quaest. S 4 (Gai. 2 inst.), 5 (Ulp. 6 Sab.), 6 (Gai. 17 ed. prov.), E 7 (Macer 1 leg. vices.), S 8 (Gai. 17 ed. prov.), 9 (Ulp. 45 ed.), P 10 (Paul 3 sent.), S 11 (Ulp. 10 Sab.)-14 (Paul 2 reg.), E 15 (Ulp. 12 ed.), S 16 (Pomp. 1 reg.), P 17 (Paul 3 sent.)> S 18 (Ulp. 1 Sab.), E 19 (Mod. 6 pand.)*, 20 (Ulp. 1 Sab.)-25 E 26-28 P 29-31.

28.2. S 1 (Ulp. 1 Sab.), 2 (Ulp. 6 reg.)*, 3 (Ulp. 1 Sab.)-4 (Ulp. 3 Sab.), E 5 (Iavolen. 1 Cass.)*, S 6 (Ulp. 3 Sab.)-14 (Afr. 4 quaest.), 15 (Ulp. 1 Sab.)*, 16 (Afr. 4 quaest.)-17 E 18-22 P 23-28 (Tryph. 20 quaest.), <mass codal 29 (Scae. 6 quaest.)> <title codal S 30 (Gai. 17 ed. prov.), 31 (Paul 2 Sab.), 32 (Marcian. 2 reg.)>.

28.3. <intro. P 1 (Pap. 1 def.)>, S 2 (Ulp. 2 Sab.)-3 (Ulp. 3 Sab.), 4 (Ulp. 4 disp.)*, 5 (Ulp. 3 Sab.)-9 (Paul 2 Sab.), E 10 (Paul 1 Vitell.)*, S 11 (Ulp. 46 ed.)-14 E 15-16 P 17-19 A 20.

28.4. S 1-2 E 3 P 4.

28.5. S 1-4 (Ulp. 4 Sab.), 5 (Iul. 29 dig.)*, 6 (Ulp. 4 Sab.), 7 (Iul. 30 dig.)*, 8 (Iul. 2 Urs. Fer.)*, 9 (Ulp. 5 Sab.)-10 (Paul 1 Sab.), E 11 (Iavolen. 7 epist.)*, S 12 (Paul 2 Sab.)-13 (Ulp. 7 Sab.), E 14 (Iavolen. 1 Cass.)*, 15 (Ulp. 7 Sab.), 16 (Iul. 30 dig.)*, 17 (Ulp. 7 Sab.), E 18 (Paul 1 Vitell.)*, 19 (Ulp. 7 Sab.)-21 (Pomp. 1 Sab.), 22 (Iul. 30 dig.)*, 23 (Pomp. 1 Sab.), E 24 (Cels. 16 dig.)*, S 25 (Ulp. 6 reg.)*, E 26 (Cels. 16 dig.)*, S 27 (Pomp. 3 Sab.)-29 (Pomp. 5 Sab.), E 30 (Ulp. 21 ed.)*, S 31 (Gai. 17 ed. prov.)-33 (Gai. ed. urb. 2 test.), P 34 (Pap. 1 def.)*, S 35 (Ulp. 4 disp.)-38 (Iul. 30 dig.), 39 (Marcian. 2 reg.)*, 40 (Iul. 30 dig.)-41 (Iul. 30 dig.), E 42 (Pomp. 12 var. lect.)*, S 43 (Iul. 64 dig.), 44 (Paul 1 Ael. Sent.)*, 45 (Alfen. Var. 5 dig.)-57 E 58-70 (Proc. 2 epist.), P 71 (Pap. 6 resp.)*, E 72 (Paul 5 Iul.Pap.)-75 P 76-79 (Pap. 6 resp.), 80 (Pap. 1 def.)*, 81 (Pap. 6 resp.)-91 (Tryph. 21 disp.), <codal apart from Appendix P 92 (Paul 5 sent.)>, A 93.

28.6. <intro. E 1 (Mod. 2 pand.), S 2 (Ulp. 6 Sab.)> E 3 (Mod. 1 diff.)-6 (Terent. Clem. 4 Iul. Pap.), P between E and S 7 (Pap. 6 resp.)* S 8 (Ulp. 4 Sab.), 9 (Lab. 1 post. Iav. epit., S not A)*, 10 (Ulp. 4 Sab.), 11 (Paul 1 Sab.), P 12 (Pap. 3 quaest.)*, S 13 (Pomp. 1 Sab.), 14 (Pomp. 2 Sab.), P 15 (Pap. 6 resp.)*, S 16 (Pomp. 3 Sab.)-18 (Ulp. 16 Sab.), 19 (Iul. 30 dig.)*, 20 (Ulp. 16 Sab.)-22 (Gai. 15 ed. prov.), P 23 (Pap. 6 resp.)*, S 24 Ulp. (4 disp.),-28 (Iul. 62 dig.), P 29 (Scae. 15 quaest.)* S 30 (Iul. 78 dig.)-39 P 40-47 A 48.

28.7. S 1-11 (Ulp. 8 disp), P 12 (Hermogen. 3 iur. epit.)*, S 13 (Iul. 30 dig.)-14 (Marcian. 4 inst.), P 15 (Pap. 16 quaest.)*, S 16 Marcian. 4 inst.)-20 (Lab. 2 post. Iav. epit., S not A) E 21 (Cels. 16 dig.), S 22 (Gai. 18 ed. prov.)*, E 23 (Marcell. 12 dig.), P 24 (Pap. 6 resp.)*, E 25 (Mod. 9 reg.), 26 (Pomp. 2 QM)*, 27 (Mod. 8 resp.) P 28 (Pap. 13 quaest.).

28.8. E 1-3 (Ulp. 60 ed.), 4 (Ulp. 61 ed.)*, 5 (Ulp. 60 ed.)-10 A 11 (Iavolen. 4 post. Lab., not S).

Total texts 267 S 148 P 52 E 63 A 4

Initial masses S 6 (28.1-5,7: SEP,SEP,SEPA,SEP,SEPA,SEP) E 2 (28.6,8: ESPA,EA)

Insertions in other masses 21: S in E 1 (28.7.22) P in S 7 (28.5.34; 28.6.12,15,23,29; 28.7.12,15) P in E 2 (28.5.71; 28.7.24) P between E and S 1 (28.6.7) E in S 10 (28.1.19; 28.2.5; 28.3.10; 28.5.11,14,18,24,26,30,42)

Displacement within masses 16: S 13 (28.2.2,15; 28.3.4; 28.5.5,7,8,16,22,25,39,44; 28.6.9,19) P 1 (28.5.80) E 2 (28.7.26; 28.8.4)

Texts introducing titles 20: S 11 P 3 E 3 (28.1.1-17) P 1 (28.3.1) E 1 S 1 (28.6.1-2)

Codal title texts 3: S 3 (28.2.30-32)

Codal mass texts 1: P 1 (28.2.29)

Codal apart from Appendix 1: E 1 (28.5.92)

Total displacements 62/259 = 24 per cent

29.1. <intro. S 1 (Ulp. 45 ed.), 2 (Gai. 15 ed. prov.), 3 (Ulp. 2 Sab.)> S 4 (Ulp. 1 Sab.)-7 (Ulp. 9 Sab.), E 8 (Marcell. 10 dig.)*, S 9 (Ulp. 9 Sab.)-11 (Ulp. 45 ed.), P 12 (Pap. 6 resp.)*, S 13 (Ulp. 45 ed.), P 14 (Maeci. 4 fid.)*, S 15 (Ulp. 45 ed.)-17 (Gai. 15 ed. prov.), P 18 (Tryph. 18 disp.)*, S 19 (Ulp. 4 disp.)-22 (Marcian. 4 inst.), E 23 (Tertull. 1 castr. pec.)*, S 24 (Flor. 10 inst.)-26 (Macer 2 mil.), P 27 (Pap. 6 resp.)*, <mass codal S 28 (Ulp. 36 Sab.)> E 29 (Marcell. 10 dig.), P 30 (Paul 7 quaest.)*, E 31 (Marcell. 13 dig.),-33 P 34-41 (Tryph. 18 disp.), <codal S 42 (Ulp. 41 ed.), P 43 (Pap. 6 resp.), S 44 (Ulp. 41 ed.)>.

29.2. <intro. S 1 (Paul 2 Sab.), 2 (Ulp. 4 Sab.), 3 (Ulp. 6 Sab.), 4 (Ulp. 3 Sab.)> S 5 (Ulp. 1 Sab.)-11 (Pomp. 3 Sab.), E 12 (Ulp. 11 ed.)*, S 13 (Ulp. 7 Sab.)-15 (Ulp. 7 Sab.), E 16 (Ulp. 24 ed.)*, S 17 (Ulp. 7 Sab.)-18 (Paul 2 Sab.), E 19 (Paul 59 ed.)*, E 20 (Ulp. 61 ed.)*, S 21 (Ulp. 7 Sab.)-32 (Ulp. 8 Sab.), E 33 (Paul 12 Plaut.)*, S 34 (Ulp. 8 Sab.)-40 (Ulp. 4 disp.), 41 (Iul. 26 dig.)*, 42 (Ulp. 4 disp.)-47 (Afr. 4 quaest.), 48 P (Paul 1 manual.)*, S 49 (Afr. 4 quaest.), E 50 (Mod. 1 heur.)*, S 51 (Afr. 4 quaest.), 52 (Marcian. 4 inst.), E 53 (Gai. 14 Iul. Pap.)*, S 54 (Flor. 8 inst.), 55 (Marcian. 2 reg.), E 56 (Paul 57 ed.)*, 57 (Gai. 23 ed. prov.)*, S 58 (Paul 2 reg.)-60 (Iavolen. 1 post. Lab.), 61 (Macer 1 off. praes.)*, 62 Iavolen. 1 post. Lab.), 63 (Pomp. 1 reg.)*, 64 (Iavolen. 2 post. Lab.), <mass codal 65 S (Paul 2 Sab.), E 66 (Ulp. 61 ed.), S 67 (Ulp. 1 reg.)>, <mass intro. E 68 (Paul 5 Iul.Pap.)> E 69 (Ulp. 60 ed.)-83 P 84-97 A 98-99.

29.3. S 1-4 (Ulp. 50 ed.), E 5 (Paul 8 Plaut.)*, S 6 (Ulp. 50 ed.)-8 E 9-12.

29.4. <intro. S 1 (Ulp. 50 ed.)>, S 2 (Ulp. 7 Sab.), 3 (Pomp. 3 Sab.), 4 (Ulp. 50 ed.), E 5 Marcell. 12 dig.)*, S 6 (Ulp. 50 ed.), E 7 (Marcell. 12 dig.)*, 8 (Ulp. 50 ed.)-10 (Ulp. 50 ed.) E 11 (Iavolen. 7 epist.)*, S 12 (Ulp. 50 ed.)-22 (Iul. 31 dig.), <mass codal 23 (Ulp. 46 ed.)> E 24-25 P 26-30.

29.5. S 1(Ulp. 50 ed.), E 2 (Callist. 5 cogn.)*, S 3 (Ulp. 50 ed.), P 4 (Pap. 6 resp.)*, 5 (Ulp. 50 ed.), 6 (Paul 46 ed.), 7 (Paul 1 SC Silan.)*, 8 (Paul 56 ed.),-10 (Paul 1 SC Silan.), P 11 (Tryph. 2 disp.)*, S 12 (Paul 1 SC Silan.)-15 E 16-19 P 20-23 <codal S 24 (Ulp. 50 ed.), 25 (Gai. 1 ed. prov.), A 26 Scae. 34 dig.), E 27 (Callist. 1 iur. fisc.)>.

29.6. S 1-2.

29.7. S 1-4 (Iul. 63 dig.), P 5 (Pap. 7 resp.)*, S 6 (Marcian. 7 inst.)-7 (Marcian. 2 reg.) 8 E between S and P 9 (Marcell. 9 dig.)*, P 10-11 (Pap. 19 quaest.), 12 (Pap. 20 quaest.)*, 13 (Pap. 19 quaest.)-14 (Scae. 8 quaest.), S 15 (Afr. 2 quaest.)*, P 16 (Paul 21 quaest.)-17 E 18-20.

Total texts 234 S 131 P 48 E 51 A 3 E or A 1

Initial masses S 7 (29.1-7: SEP,SEPA,SE,SEP,SEPA,S,SPE)

Insertions in other masses 27: S in P 1 (29.7.15) P in S 8 (29.1.12,14,18,27; 29.2.48; 29.5.4,11; 29.7.5) P in E 1 (29.1.30) E in S 16 (29.1.8,23; 29.2.12,16,19,20,33,50,53,56,57; 29.3.5; 29.4.5,7,11; 29.5.2) E between S and P 1 (29.7.9)

Displacement within masses 5: S 4 (29.2.41,61,63; 29.5.7) P 1 (29.7.12)

Texts introducing titles 8: S 8 (29.1.1-3; 29.2.1-4; 29.4.1)

Codal title texts 7: S 2 P 1 (29.1.42-44) S 2 E 1 A 1 (29.5.24-27)

Text introducing mass 1: E 1 (29.2.68)

Codal mass texts 5: S 1 (29.1.28); S 2 E 1 (29.2.65-67) S 1 (29.4.23)

Total displacements 53/227 = 22 per cent

30. <intro. E (Ulp. 67 ed.), P 2 (Ulp. 1 fid.)> S 3 (Ulp. 4 Sab.)-5 (Paul 1 Sab.), 6 (Iul. 33 dig.)*, 7 (Paul 2 Sab.)-10 (Paul 2 Sab.), P 11 (Pap. 9 quaest.)*, S 12 (Pomp. 3 Sab.)-17 (Ulp. 15 Sab.), 18 (Iul. 31 dig.)*, 19 (Ulp. 15 Sab.)-26 (Pomp. 5 Sab.), E 27 (Paul 9 Plaut.)*, S 28 (Ulp. 19 Sab.), E 29 (Paul 6 Iul.Pap.)*, 30 (Ulp. 19 Sab.)-32 (Ulp. 20 Sab.), 33 (Paul 3 reg.)*, 34 (Ulp. 21 Sab.)-39 (Ulp. 21 Sab.), P 40 (Ulp. 2 fid.)*, S 41 (Ulp. 21 Sab.), P 42 (Ulp. 2 fid.)*, S 43 (Ulp. 21 Sab.)-45 (Pomp. 6 Sab.), A 46 (Pomp. 9 epist.)*, S 47 (Ulp. 22 Sab.)-50 (Ulp. 24 Sab.), P 51 (Pap. 4 quaest.)*, S 52 (Paul 4 Sab.)-57 (Ulp. 33 Sab.), P 58

(Pap. 9 resp.)*, S 59 Ulp. 33 ed.), 60 (Iul. 39 dig.)*, P 61 (Pap. 9 resp.)*, S 62 (Paul 41 ed.), E 63 (Cels. 17 dig.)*, S 64 (Gai. 15 ed. prov.)-75 (Ulp. 5 disp.), 76 (Iul. 34 dig.)*, 77 (Ulp. 5 disp.)-82 (Iul. 33 dig.), E 83 (Marcell. 13 dig.)*, S 84 (Iul. 33 dig.), E 85 (Paul 11 Plaut.)*, S 86 (Iul. 34 dig.), P 87 (Pap. 18 quaest.)*, S 88 (Marcian. 6 inst.)*, 89 (Iul. 36 dig.), P 90 (Pap. 18 quaest.)*, S 91 (Iul. 36 dig.)-92 (Iul. 39 dig.), P 93 (Ulp. 1 fid.)*, S 94 (Iul. 39 dig.), P 95 (Ulp. 1 fid.)*, S 96 (Iul. 39 dig.)-105 (Iul. 1 Minic.), 106 (Alfen. Var. 2 dig.)*, 107 (Afr. 2 quaest.)-127 (Paul 1 iur. cod.), <codal S 128 (Marcian. 2 inst.)>.

Total texts 128 S 111 P 11 E 6 A 1

Initial mass S 1 (30: S)

Insertions in other masses 16: P in S 10 (30.11,40,42,51,58,61,87,90,93,95) E in S 5 (30.27,29,63,83,85) A in S 1 (30.46)

Displacements within masses 7: S 7 (30.6,18,33,60,76,88,106)

Texts introducing title 2: E 1 P 1 (30.1,2)

Codal title text 1: S 1 (30.128)

Total displacements 26/127 = 20 per cent

31. <intro. S 1 (Ulp. 9 Sab.)> E 2-4 (Paul 4 Plaut.), P 5 (Paul 7 quaest.)*, 6 (Paul 1 leg. Falc.)*, E 8 (Paul 9 Plaut.), 9 (Mod. 9 reg.)*, 10 (Iavolen. 1 Plaut.), 11 (Pomp. 7 Plaut.), 12 (Paul 2 Vitell.)*, 13 (Pomp. 7 Plaut.), 14 (Paul 4 Vitell.)-23 (Marcell. 13 dig.), P 24 (Ulp. 2 fid.)*, E 25 (Marcell. 15 dig.)-49 (Paul 5 Iul. Pap.), 50 (Marcell. 18 dig.)*, 51 (Ulp. 8 Iul. Pap.)-63 (Callist. 4 ed. mon.) P 64-67 (Pap. 19 quaest.), 68 (Paul 11 quaest.)*, 69 (Pap. 19 quaest.)-70 (Pap. 20 quaest.), 71 (Pap. 8 resp.)*, 72 (Pap. 23 quaest.)-89.

Total texts 89 S 1 P 29 E 59 A 0

Initial mass E 1 (31: EP)

Insertions in other masses 3: P in E 3 (31.5,6,24)

Displacements within masses 5: P 2 (31.68,71) E 3 (31.9,12,50)

Texts introducing title 1: S 1 (31.1)

Total displacements 9/88 = 10 per cent

32. P 1-3 (Ulp. 1 fid.), 4 (Paul 4 sent.)*, 5 (Ulp. 1 fid.)-28 A 29-42 <codal E 43 (Cels. 15 dig.)>* /// S 44 (Pomp. 2 Sab.), 45 (Ulp. 22 Sab.), E 46 (Paul 2 Vitell.)*, S 47 (Ulp. 22 Sab.)-65 (Marcian. 7 inst.), P 66 (Paul 3 sent.)*, S 67 (Marcian. 7 inst.)-69 (Marcell. 1 resp.), <mass codal 70 (Ulp. 22 Sab.), 71 (Ulp. 20 Sab.), 72 (Paul 4 Sab.), 73 (Ulp. 20 Sab.), 74 (Pomp. 6 Sab.), 75 (Ulp. 20 Sab.), 76 (Ulp. 2 ed.)>, E 77 (Iavolen. 1 Plaut.)-90 P 91-99 (Paul 1 instr. signif.) A 100 (Iavolen. 2 post. Lab., not S)-103.

Total texts 103 S 31 P 37 E 17 A 18

Initial mass P 1/2 S 1/2 (32: PA///SEPA)

Insertions in other masses 3: E in S 1 (32.46) P in S 1 (32.66) E between A and S 1 (32.43)

Displacement within mass 1: P 1 (32.4)

Codal mass texts 7: S 7 (32.70-76)

Total displacements 11/102 = 11 per cent

33.1. S 1-3 (Ulp. 24 Sab.), E 4-8 P 9-16 A 17 (Labeo 2 post. Iav. epit.)-21 <codal S 22 (Alfen. Var. 2 dig.), 23 (Marcian. 6 inst.), 24 (Marcian. 8 inst.) P 25 (Valens 2 fid.)>.

33.2. S 1 (Paul 3 Sab.), P 2 (Pap. 17 quaest.)*, S 3 (Paul 3 Sab.)-10 (Iul. 78 dig.), 11 (Iul. 1 Minic.)*, 12 (Alfen. Var. 2 dig.) E 13-16 (Mod. 9 resp.), P 17 (Scae. 3 resp.)*, E 18 (Mod. 9 resp.)-23 P 24-29 A 30 (Iavolen. 2 post. Lab., not S)-37 <codal P 38 (Scae. 3 resp.), 39 (Scae. 6 resp.), S 40 (Alfen. Var. 8 dig.), S or A 41 (Iavolen. 2 post Lab.), A 42 (Iavolen. 5 post. Lab.), 43 (Venul. 10 act.)>.

33.3. S 1 E 2-4 P 5-7.

33.4. S 1-5 (Marcian. 3 reg.), 6 (Lab. 2 post. Iav. epit., not A) P 7-12 (Scae. 3 resp.) A 13-14 <codal S 15 (Gai. 2 ed. urb. leg.), E 16 (Paul 2 Vitell.), P 17 (Scae. 3 resp.)>.

33.5. S 1-4 (Paul 3 Sab.), 5 (Afr. 5 quaest.)*, 6 (Pomp. 6 Sab.), P 7 (Paul 10 quaest.)*, S 8 (Pomp. 6 Sab.)-12 E 13-17 P 18-19 A 20-22.

33.6. S 1-4 (Paul 4 Sab.), 5 (Iul. 15 dig.), E 6 (Proc. 5 epist.), A 7 (Iavolen. 2 post. Lab.)- 8 (Pomp. 6 epist.) /// S 9 (Ulp. 23 Sab.), P 10 (Hermogen. 4 iur. epit.)*, S 11-14 E 15 (Proc. 2 epist.) A 16 (Iavolen. 3 post. Lab.).

33.7. S 1 (Paul 4 Sab.), P 2 (Pap. 7 resp.)-3 (Pap. 8 res.), A 4 (Iavolen. 2 post Lab., not Sab.)-7 /// S 8-10 (Ulp. 20 Sab.), E 11 (Iavolen. 2 Cass.)*, S 12 (Ulp. 20 Sab.)-13 (Paul 4 Sab.), E 14 (Paul 2 Vitell.)*, S 15 (Pomp. 6 Sab.)-17 (Marcian. 7 inst.) E 18 (Paul 2 Vitell.) P 19-24 A 25 (Iavolen. 2 post. Lab., not S), 26 (Iavolen. 5 post. Lab., not S)-29.

33.8. S 1 (Paul 4 Sab.), 2 (Gai. 18 ed. prov.)*, 3 (Paul 4 Sab.), 4 (Gai. 18 ed. prov.)*, 5 (Paul 4 Sab.)-12 (Iul. 37 dig.), E 13 (Cels. 19 dig.)*, S 14 (Alfen.Var. 5 dig.)- 16 (Afr. 5 quaest.), E 17 (Iavolen. 2 Cass.)*, S 18 (Marcian. 6 inst.) P 19 Pap.(7 resp.), S 20 (Marcian. 7 inst.)*, P 21 (Scae. 8 quaest.) A 22 (Lab. 2 post. Iav. epit.)-23 <codal S 24 (Ulp. 43 Sab.), E 25 (Cels. 19 dig.), P 26 (Scae. 3 resp.)>.

33.9. <intro. S 1(Ulp. 24 Sab.), 2 (Marcian. 3 reg.)> S 3 (Ulp. 22 Sab.)-6 P 7.

33.10. S 1 (Pomp. 6 Sab.), 2 (Flor. 12 inst.)*, 3 (Paul 4 Sab.), P 4 (Paul 1 instr. signif.)*, S 5 (Paul 4 Sab.)-6 E 7-8 P 9 A 10 (Iavolen. 3 post. Lab., not S), 11 (Iavolen. 10 post. Lab., not S)-12 <codal E 13 (Mod. 9 resp., 14 (Callist. 3 cogn.)>.

Total texts 206 S 85 P 47 E 36 A 37 S or A 1

Initial masses S 10 (33.1-10: SEPA,SEPA,SEP, SPA,SEPA,SEA///SEA, SA///SEPA,SPA,SP,SEPA

Insertions in other masses 10: S in P 1 (33.8.20) P in S 4 (33.2.2; 33.5.7; 33.6.10; 33.10.4) P in E 1 (33.2.17) E in S 4 (33.7.11,14; 33.8.13,17)

Displacement within masses 5: S 5 (33.2.11; 33.5.5; 33.8.2,4; 33.10.2)

Texts introducing title 2: S 2 (33.9.1-2)

Codal title texts 18: S 3 P 1 (33.1.22-25) P 2 S 1 S or A 2 (33.2.38-43) S 1 E 1 P 1 (33.4.15-17) S 1 E 1 P 1 (33.8.24-26) E 2 (33.10.13-14)

Total displacements 35/196 = 18 per cent

34.1. S 1-2 E 3-6 <mass intro. P 7 (Paul 14 resp.)> , 8 (Pap.7 resp.)-14 A 15-19 <codal P 20 (Scae. 3 resp.), 21 (Ulp. 2 fid.), 22 (Valens 1 fid.), 23 (Paul 4 Nerat.)>.

34.2. S 1-2 (Afr. 2 quaest.), E 3 (Cels. 19 dig.)*, 4 (Paul 54 ed.)*, S 5 (Afr. 2 quaest.)-6 (Marcell. 1 resp.) E 7-11 P 12 (Pap. 17 quaest.), A 13 (Scae. 15 dig.), S 14 (Pomp. 5 Sab.)*, A 15 (Scae. 15 dig.)-16 (Scae. 18 dig.), S 17 (Ulp. 21 Sab.)*, A 18 (Scae. 22 dig.) /// S 19-30, 31 (Lab. 2 post. Iav. epit., not A) E 32-34 P 35-38 A 39 (Iavolen. 2 post. Lab., not S)-40.

34.3. S 1-3 (Ulp. 23 Sab.), E 4 (Pomp. 7 Plaut.)*, S 5 (Ulp. 23 Sab.), E 6 (Iavolen. 6 epist.)*, S 7 (Ulp. 23 Sab.)-13 (Iul. 81 dig.) P between S and E 14 (Ulp. 1 fid.)* E 15-16 (Paul 9 Plaut.), S or A 17 (Iavolen. 2 post. Lab.)*, E 18 (Paul 9 Plaut.)-21 (Terent. Clem. 12 Iul. Pap.) P 22-27 A 28 <codal E 29 (Paul 6 Iul. Pap.), P 30 (Paul 10 quaest.), 31 (Scae. 3 resp.)>.

34.4. S 1-3 (Ulp. 24 Sab.), 4 (Ulp. 33 Sab.)*, 5 (Gai. 2 ed. urb.)*, E 6 (Paul 5 Iul.Pap.)*, S 7 (Ulp. 24 Sab.), 8 (Iul. 32 dig.)*, 9 (Ulp. 5 disp.), 10 (Iul. 37 dig.), 11 (Iul. 54 dig.), 12 (Ulp. 50 Sab.)*, 13 (Marcian. 6 inst.)-16 E 17-21 P 22-29 A 30 (Scae. 20 dig.)*, 31 (Scae. 14 dig.), 32 (Venul. 10 act.).

34.5. P 1-9 S 10-16(Marcian. 3 reg.), E 17 (Paul 1 Plaut.)*, S 18 (Marcian. 3 reg.), <mass codal 19 (Ulp. 25 Sab.)> E 20 (Paul 12 Plaut.), 21 (Paul 14 Plaut.), 22 (Iavolen. 5 Cass.)*, 23 (Gai. 5 Iul. Pap.)*, 24 (Marcell. 11 dig.)-27 A 28 (Iavolen. 3 post. Lab., not S)-29.

34.6. S 1-2.

34.7. <intro. E 1 (Cels. 35 Dig.)>, E 2 (Paul 9 Plaut.), P 3 S 4-5.

34.8. S 1-3 E 4 P 5.

34.9. S 1-3 E 4-10 P 11-23 (Gai. 1 tac. fid.), <codal apart from Appendix 24 (Pap. 18 quaest.), 25 (Pap. 18 resp.)> A 26.

Total texts 193 S 66 P 60 E 48 A 18 S or A 1

Initial masses S 7 (34.1,2,3,4,6,8,9: SEAP,SEPA/SEPA,SEPA,SEPA,S, SEP, SEPA) P 1 (34.5 PSEA) E 1 (34.7: EPS)

Insertions in other masses 10: S in A 2 (34.2.14,17) S or A in E 1 (34.3.17) P between S and E 1 (34.3.14) E in S 6 (34.2.3,4; 34.3.4,6; 34.4.6; 34.5.17)

Displacement within masses 7: S 5 (34.4.4,5,8,12) E 2 (34.5.22,23) A 1 (34.4.30)

Texts introducing title 1: E 1 (34.7.1)

Codal title texts 7: P 4 (34.1.20-23) E 1 P 2 (34.3.29-31)

Codal apart from Appendix 2: P 2 (34.9.24-25)

Mass intro. 1: P1 (34.1.7)

Mass codal 1: S 1 (34.5.19)

Total displacements 29/184 = 16 per cent

35.1. <intro. E 1 (Pomp. 3 QM)>, S 2 (Ulp. 5 Sab.)-40 (Iavolen. 2 post. Lab.) <mass codal S 41 (Ulp. 34 ed.), 42 (Afr. 2 quaest.)>, E 43 (Paul 8 Plaut.)-58 (Pomp. 10 var. lect.), 59 (Ulp. 13 Iul.Pap.)*, 60 (Paul 7 Iul.Pap.) 61 (Ulp. 8 Iul.Pap.)-64 (Terent. Clem. 5 Iul. Pap.), <mass codal 65 (Paul 62 ed.), 66 (Mod. 10 resp.), 67 (Iavolen. 11 epist.), 68 (Iavolen. 2 Cass.), 69 Gai. (10 Iul.Pap.)> P 70-92 (Ulp. 5 fid.), 93 (Pap. 8 resp.)*, 94 (Hermogen. 1 iur. epit.)-95 (Hermogen. 4 iur. epit.), 96 (Paul 1 Nerat.), 97 (Paul 2 Nerat.)-98 (Paul 3 Nerat. <mass codal P 99 (Pap. 18 quaest.), 100 (Pap. 7 resp.), 101 (Pap. 8 resp.), 102 (Pap. 9 resp.), 103 (Paul 14 quaest.), 104 (Paul 14 resp.), A 105 (Pomp. 5 epist.)*, S 106 (Iul. 35 dig.), P 107 (Gai. 1 cas.)>, A 108 (Scae. 19 dig.)-112 (Pomp. 12 epist.), <codal A 113 (Paul 2 imp. sent.)>.

35.2. <intro. P 1 (Paul 1 leg. Falc.), E 2 (Marcell. 22 dig.) P 3 (Paul 1 leg. Falc.), 4 (Pap. 16 resp.), 5 (Pap. 8 resp.), 6 (Venul. 13 stip.)> P 7 (Pap. 7 quaest.)-33 (Paul 3 fid.) S 34 (Iul. 42 dig.)*, 35 (Ulp. 6 disp.)*, P 36 (Paul 3 fid.)-40 E 41-50 (Cels. 14 dig.), S 51(Iul. 61 dig.)*, E 52 (Marcell. 9 dig.)-68 S 69 (Pomp. 5 Sab.)-74 (Gai. 3 leg. ed. urb), 75 (Iul. dig. 40)*, 76 (Gai. 3 leg. ed. urb)-92 <codal apart from Appendix P 93 (Pap. 20 quaest.)>, A 94-96.

35.3. E 1-7 P 8-9.

Total texts 218 S 69 P 75 E 64 A 10

Initial masses S 1 (35.1: SEPA) P 1 (35.2: PESA) E 1 (35.3: EP)
Insertions in other masses 3: S in P 2 (35.2.34,35) S in E 1 (35.2.51)
Displacements within masses 3: S 2 (35.1.59; 35.2.75) P 1 (35.1.93)
Texts introducing titles 7: E 1 (35.1.1) P 5 E 1 (35.2.1-6)
Codal title text 1: A 1 (35.1.113)
Codal apart from Appendix 1: P1 (35.2.93)
Codal mass texts 16: S 2 (35.1.41-42) E 5 (35.1.65-69) P 7 A 1 S 1 (35.1.99-107)
Total displacements 31/215 = 14 per cent

36.1. <intro. P 1 (Ulp. 3 fid.), E 2 (Cels. 21 dig.), P 3 (Ulp. 3 fid.)-4 (Ulp. 4 fid.), 5 (Maeci. 6 fid.), 6 (Ulp. 4 fid.), 7 (Maeci. 4 fid.)-11 (Ulp. 4 fid.), 12 (Pap. 20 quaest.), 13 (Ulp. 4 fid.), 14 (Hermogen. 4 iur. epit.), 15 (Ulp. 4 fid.)-17 (Ulp. 4 fid.), 18 (Ulp. 2 fid.)> S 19-24 (Iul. 39 dig.), P 25 (Pap. 15 quaest.)*, S 26 (Iul. 39 dig.), S or P 27 (Paul 1 SCC)*, 28 (Iul. 40 dig.)-32 E 33 (Cels. 20 dig.)*, S 34 (Marcian. 8 inst.)-36 E 37-41 (Paul 20 ed.), P 42 (Paul 2 fid.)*, E 43 (Paul 20 ed.)-49 <mass intro. P 50 (Paul 14 resp.)>, 51 (Pap. 3 quaest.)-54 (Pap. 19 quaest.), 55 (Pap. 20 quaest.)*, 56 (Pap. 19 quaest.)-76 (Paul 2 decr.) A 77-80 (Scae. 21 dig.), 81 (Scae. 1 quaest. pub. trac.) <codal A 82 (Scae. 5?/15 dig.), 83 (Paul 1 imp. sent.)>, Q 84? 85?

36.2. S 1-2 (Ulp. 15 Sab.), 3 (Ulp. 5 disp.)*, 4 (Ulp. 19 Sab.)-7 (Ulp. 20 Sab.), 8 (Ulp. 24 Sab.)*, 9 (Ulp. 21 Sab.)-10 (Ulp. 23 Sab.), 11 (Iul. 37 dig.)*, 12 (Ulp. 23 Sab.)-20 E 21-24 P 25-29 A 30-31.

36.3. E 1 (Ulp. 79 ed.), P 2 (Pap. 28 quaest.)*, E 3 (Ulp. 79 ed.), <mass codal 4 (Ulp. 15 ed.)>, P 5 (Pap. 28 quaest.)-7 S 8-13 <codal apart from Appendix E 14 (Ulp. 79 ed.), 15 (Paul 75 ed.), 16 (Gai. 27 ed. prov.), 17 (Paul 48 ed.)> A 18.

36.4. S 1 (Ulp. 52 ed.), E 2 (Ulp. 79 ed.)*, S 3 (Ulp. 52 ed.), P 4 (Pap. 28 quaest.)*, S 5 (Ulp. 52 ed.)-7 P 8 (Pap. 6 quaest.)-11 (Hermogen. 4 iur. epit.), <mass codal 12 (Maeci. 12 fid.)> E 13 Callist. 3 ed. mon.) A 14-15 Q 16,17.

Total texts 151 S 46 P 61 E 27 A 12 S or P 1 Q 4

Initial masses S 3 (36.1,2,4: SEPA,SEPA,SPEA) E 1 (36.3: EPSA)
Insertions in other masses 6: P in S 2 (36.1.25; 36.4.4) P in E 2 (36.1.42; 36.3.2) E in S 2 (36.1.33; 36.4.2)
Displacement within masses 5: S 3 (36.2.3,8,11) S or P in S 1 (36.1.27) P 1 (36.1.55)

Texts introducing title 18: P 17 E 1 (36.1.1-18)
Codal title texts 2: A 2 (36.1.82-83)
Codal apart from Appendix 4: E 4 (36.3.14-17)
Text introducing mass 1: P1 (36.1.50)
Codal mass texts 2: E 1 (36.3.4) P 1 (36.4.12)
Total displacements 38/143 = 21 per cent

37.1. <intro. S 1 (Ulp. 39 ed.), E 2 (Ulp. 14 ed.), S 3 Ulp. 39 ed.), E 4 (Gai. 8 Iul.Pap.), 5 (Ulp. 39 ed.), 6 (Paul 41 ed.)> S 7 (Ulp. 1 Sab.), E 8 (Paul 8 Plaut.)*, S 9 (Pomp. 2 Sab.)-13 P 14-16.

37.2. S 1.

37.3. P 1 S 2.

37.4. S 1 (Ulp. 39 ed.), P 2 (Hermogen. 3 iur. epit.)*, S 3 (Ulp. 39. ed.), 4 (Paul 41 ed.), 5 (Iul. 24 dig.)*, 6 (Paul 41 ed.)-15 (Marcian. 5 reg.), <mass codal S 16 (Pomp. 4 Sab.), 17 (Ulp. 35 Sab.)> P 18-20 E 21.

37.5. S 1 (Ulp. 40 ed.), 2 (Iul. 23 dig.)*, 3 (Ulp. 40 ed.), 4 (Iul. 23 dig.)*, 5 (Ulp. 40 ed.), S 6 (Iul. 23 dig.)*, P 7 (Tryph. 16 disp.)*, 8 (Ulp. 40 ed.)-12 (Ulp. 40 ed.), P 13 (Tryph. 2 disp.)*, S 14 (Ulp. 40 ed.)-20 P 21-24 E 25.

37.6. S 1-2 (Paul 41 ed.), 3 (Iul. 23 dig.)-4 E 5-7 P 8-11 <codal S 12 (Paul 41 ed.)>.

37.7. S 1-3 E 4 P 5-6 (Pap. 6 resp.), 7 (Paul 11 resp.)*, 8 (Pap. 11 resp.)-9.

37.8. S 1-2 E 3-4 (Mod. 6 pand.), <mass codal E 5 (Mod. 6 diff.)>, P 6-7.

37.9. S 1-2 (Paul 41 ed.), P 3 (Hermogen. 3 iur. epit.)*, S 4 (Paul 41 ed.)-8 (Paul 1 adult.), <mass codal S 9 (Ulp. 15 Sab.)>, P 10 (Paul 7 quaest.).

37.10. S 1 (Ulp. 41 ed.), 2 (Marcian. 14 inst.)*, 3 (Ulp. 41 ed.), 4 (Iul. 24 dig.)*, 5 (Ulp. 41 ed.)-9 E 10 P 11-15 <codal S 16 (Paul 41 ed.)>.

37.11. S 1-8 (Iul. 28 Dig.), <mass codal S 9 (Pomp. 2 Sab.)> E 10 P 11-12.

37.12. S 1-2 E 3-4 P 5.

37.13. S 1.

37.14. <intro. S 1 (Ulp. 9 off. proc.)>, S 2 (Ulp. 1 opin.)-6 E 7-9 (Mod. 9 reg.), 10 (Terent. Clem. 9 Iul. Pap.)*, 11 (Ulp. 11 Iul. Pap.)*, 12 (Mod. 1 resp.)-17 P 18-23 A 24.

37.15. S 1-4 E 5-9 P 10 (Tryph. 17 disp.), <codal 11 (Pap.13 resp.)>.

Total texts 172 S 96 P 42 E 33 A 1

Initial masses S 14 (37.1,2,4,5,6,7,8,9,10,11,12,13,14,15: SP,S,SPE,SPE, SEP, SEP,SEP,SP,SEP, SEP,SEP,S,SEPA,SEP) P 1 (37.3: PS).

Insertions in other masses 5: P in S 4 (37.4.2; 37.5.7,13; 37.9.3) E in S 1 (37.1.8)

Displacements within masses 9: S 6 (37.4.5; 37.5.2,4,6; 37.10.2,4) P 1 (37.7.7) E 2 (37.14.10,11)

Texts introducing titles 7: S 4 E 2 (37.1.1-6) S 1 (37.14.1)

Codal title texts 3: S 2 (37.6.12; 37.10.16) P 1 (37.15.11)

Codal mass texts 5: S 3 (37.4.16-17); E 1 (37.8.5); S 2 (37.9.9; 37.11.9)

Total displacements 29/157 = 18 per cent

38.1. <intro. S 1 (Paul 1 var. lect.), 2 (Ulp. 38 ed.), 3 (Pomp. 6 Sab.)> S 4 (Pomp. 4 Sab.)- 10 (Pomp. 5 Sab.), 11 (Iul. 22 dig.)*, 12 (Pomp. 15 Sab.), 13 (Ulp. 38 ed.), E 14 (Terent. Clem. 8 Iul.Pap.)*, S 15 (Ulp. 38 ed.), 16 (Paul 40 ed.), 17 (Paul 1 iur. patr.)*, 18 (Paul 40 ed.)-20 (Paul 40 ed.), E 21 (Iavolen. 6 Cass.)*, S 22 (Gai. 14 ed. prov.)-28 (Paul 1 iur. patr.) E 29-38 (Callist. 3 ed. mon.), <mass codal E 39 (Paul 7 Plaut.)> P 40-51.

38.2. <intro. S 1 (Ulp. 42 ed.)>, S 2 (Pomp. 4 Sab.)-10 (Ulp. 44 ed.), 11 (Iul. 26 dig.)*, 12 (Ulp. 44 ed.), 13 (Iul. 26 ed.)*, 14 (Ulp. 45 ed.), P 15 (Tryph. 17 disp.)*, 16 (Ulp. 45 ed.)-21 (Iul. 26 dig.), 22 (Marcian. 1 inst.)*, 23 (Iul. 27 dig.)-29 E 30-40 P 41-50 A 51.

38.3. S 1.

38.4. S 1 (Ulp. 14 Sab.), A 2 (Pomp. 4 SCC)*, S 3 (Ulp. 14 Sab.), A 4 (Pomp. 4 SCC)*, 5 (Ulp. 14 Sab.)-7 E 8-10 P 11 A 12-13.

38.5. S 1 (Ulp. 44 ed.), 2 (Marcian. 3 reg.)*, 3 (Ulp. 44 ed.), 4 (Ulp. 43 ed.)*, 5 (Paul 42 ed.)-6 (Iul. 26 dig.) P 7 (Scae. 5 quaest.)*, 8 (Iul. 26 dig.)-11 E 12-13.

38.6. <intro. S 1 (Ulp. 44 ed.), 2 (Iul. 27 dig.)>, S 3 (Ulp. 8 Sab.)-6 P 7-9.

38.7. <intro. S 1 (Iul. 28 dig.)> S 2 (Ulp. 46 ed.)-4 E 5 P 6.

38.8. S 1-4 (Ulp. 6 reg.), <mass codal 5 (Pomp. 4 Sab.), 6 (Ulp. 45 ed.)> E 7-8 P 9-10.

38.9. S 1 P 2.

38.10. E 1 (Gai. 8 ed. prov.), S 2 (Ulp. 46 ed.)*, E 3 (Gai. 8 ed. prov.), 4 (Mod. 12 pand.), 5 (Paul 6 Plaut.),* 6 (Ulp. 5 Iul. Pap.) S 7 <mass intro. P 8 (Pomp. 1 enchir.)>, 9 (Paul 4 sent.), P or A 10 (Paul 1 grad. adfin.).

38.11. S 1.

38.12. S 1 P 2.

38.13. S 1.

38.14. S 1.

38.15. <intro. E 1 (Mod. 6 pand.)>, S 2 (Ulp. 49 ed.) -4 E 5 (Marcell. 9 dig.).

38.16. S 1-6 (Iul. 59 dig.), E 7 (Cels. 28 dig.)*, S 8 (Iul. 59 dig.)-9 E 10-14 P 15-16.

38.17. S 1-2 E 3-4 P 5-9 A 10.

Total texts 202 S 106 P 42 E 47 A 6 P or A 1

Initial masses S 16 (38.1-9, 11-17: SEP,SEPA,S,SEPA,SE,SP,SEP,SEP, SP,S,SP,S,S,SE,SEP,SEPA) E 1 (38.10: ESPA)

Insertions in other masses 8: S in E 1 (38.10.2) P in S 2 (38.2.15; 38.5.7) E in S 3 (38.1.14,21; 38.16.7) A in S 2 (38.4.2,4)

Displacements within masses 8: S 7 (38.1.11,17; 38.2.11,13,22; 38.5.2,4) E 1 (38.10.5)

Texts introducing titles 8: S 7 (38.1.1-3; 38.2.1; 38.6.1-2; 38.7.1) E 1 (38.15.1)

Text introducing mass 1: P 1 (38.10.8)

Codal mass texts 3: E 1 (38.1.39); S 2 (38.8.5,6)

Total displacements 28/185 = 15 per cent

39.1. <intro. E 1 (Ulp. 52 ed.), S 2 (Iul. 49 dig.), E 3 (Ulp. 52 ed.)-5 (Ulp. 52 ed.), S 6 (Iul. 41 dig.), E 7(Ulp. 52 ed.)-9 (Gai. ed. urb. oper. nov. nunt.)> S 10 (Ulp. 45 Sab.)-15 E 16 (Ulp. 13 ed.), 17 (Paul 67 ed.), P 18 (Pap. 3 quaest.)*, 19 (Paul 12 quaest.)*, E 20 (Ulp. 71 ed.)-23 (Iavolen. 7 epist.).

39.2. E 1 (Ulp. 1 ed.), 2 (Gai. 28 ed. prov.)*, S 3 (Paul 47 ed.)*, E 4 (Ulp. 1 ed.)-20 (Gai. 19 ed. prov.), 21 (Paul 8 Plaut.)*, 22 (Paul 10 Plaut.)*, 23 (Ulp. 63 ed.)-32 S 33-44 P 45-46 (Paul 1 sent.), <codal S 47 (Nerat. 6 membr.), 48 (Marcian. 1 delat.)>.

39.3. E 1-6 (Ulp. 53 ed.), 7 (Paul 18 ed.)*, 8 (Ulp. 53 ed.)-11 (Paul 49 ed.), S 12 (Paul 16 Sab.)*, E 13 (Gai. pr.urb. aq. pluv. arc.), 14 (Paul 49 ed.), S 15 (Paul 16 Sab.)*, 16 (Pomp. 20 Sab.)*, E 17 (Paul 15 Plaut.)-19 (Pomp. 14 QM), S 20 (Pomp. 34 Sab.)*, E 21 (Pomp. 32 QM), 22 (Pomp. 10 var. lect.) S 23 (Paul 16 Sab.)-25 (Iul. 5 Minic.), P 26 (Scae. 4 resp.).

39.4. E 1-7 P 8-11 S 12-16.

39.5. <intro. S 1 (Iul. 17 dig.), 2 (Iul. 60 dig.), E 3 (Ulp. 76 ed.)> S 4 (Pomp. 17 Sab.)-16 (Ulp. 2 resp.) E 17-26 P 27-29 (Pap. 12 resp.), S 30 (Marcian. 1 delat.)*, 31 P (Pap. 12 resp.)-34 A 35.

39.6. <intro. S (Marcian. 9 inst.), 2 (Ulp. 32 Sab.), 3 (Paul 7 Sab.), 4 (Gai. 1 rer. cott.), 5 (Ulp. 2 inst.), 6 (Paul 7 Sab.), 7 (Ulp. 32 Sab.)> S 8 (Ulp. 7 Sab.)-28 (Marcell. 1 resp.) E 29-38 (Marcell. 1 Iul.Pap.), <mass codal 39 (Paul 17 Plaut.)>, P 40-44.

Total texts 192 S 81 P 21 E 89 A 1

Initial masses S 3 (39.1,5,6: SE,SEPA,SEP) E 3 (39.2,3,4: ESP,ESP,EPS)

Insertions in other masses 8: S in P 1 (39.5.30) S in E 5 (39.2.3; 39.3.12,15,16,20) P in E 2 (39.1.18,19)

Displacement within masses 4: E 4 (39.2.2,21,22; 39.3.7)

Texts introducing titles 19: S 2 E 7 (39.1.1-9) S 2 E 1 (39.5.1-3) S 7 (39.6.1-7)

Codal title texts 2: S 2 (39.2.47-48)

Codal mass text 1: E 1 (39.6.39)

Total displacements 34/186 = 18 per cent

40.1. S 1-4 (Ulp. 6 disp.), 5 (Marcian. 2 inst.)*, 6 (Alfen. Var. 4 dig.)-9 A between S and E 10 (2 imp. sent.)* E 11-18 P 19-25 A 26 (Iavolen. 4 post. Lab., not E).

40.2. S 1-7 E 8 (Ulp. 5 ed.)* S 9-11 (Ulp. 6 off. proc.), 12 (Ulp. 2 Ael. Sent.)*, 13 (Ulp. 6 off. proc.), 14 (Marcian. 4 reg.)*, -16 (Ulp. 2 Ael. Sent.) E 17-21 P 22-25.

40.3. S 1-2 P3.

40.4. S 1-24, 25 (Ulp. 4 reg.), 26 (Marcian. 1 reg.)- 28 (Paul 1 iur. .codicill.) A between S and E 29 (Scae. 23 dig.)* E 30-32 P 33 (Paul 12 quaest.)*, E 34-46 (45 Mod. 3 pand.) P 47-55 (Maec. 2 fid.), 56 (Paul 1 fid.), 57 (Gai. 3 manual.), <mass codal P 58 (Maec. 3 fid.)> A 59 (Scae. 23 dig.)-61.

40.5. E 1-2 (Ulp. 60 ed.), 3 (Ulp. 65 ed.)*, 4 (Ulp. 60 ed.)-16 A 17-20 P 21-35 (Maec. 15 fid.), 36-8 (Paul 3 decr.), <mass codal P 39 (Paul 13/15 resp.), 40 (15 resp.), 41 (Scae. 4 resp.), 42 (Maec. 7 fid.)>, S 43-53 (Marcian. 4 reg.), P 54 (Maec. 16 fid.)*, S 55 (Marcian. 4 reg.)- 56.

40.6. E 1.

40.7. <intro. S 1 (Paul 5 Sab.)>, 2-18 E 19-32 P 33-38 A 39 (Iavolen. 4 post. Lab., not S)-42.

40.8. E 1-3 S 4-7 P 8-9.

40.9. S 1-5, P 6 (Scae. 16 quaest.)*, S 7-17 E 18-24 P 25-29 <codal S 30 (Ulp. 4 Ael. Sent.), E 31 (Terent. Clem. 5 leg. Iul. Pap.), 32 (Terent. Clem. 8 leg. Iul.Pap.)>.

40.10. P 1-2 S 3 E 4 (Ulp. 3 leg. Iul.Pap.), 5 (Paul 9 leg. Iul.Pap.), <codal 6 (Ulp. 1 leg. Iul.Pap.)>.

40.11. <intro. S 1 (Ulp. 2 resp.)>, S 2 (Maec. 1 inst.), P 3-4 E 5.

40.12. E 1-19 (Paul 51 ed.), 20 (Ulp. 55 ed.), 21 (Mod. 1 poen.)*, 22 (Ulp. 55 ed.)-29 S 30-34 P 35-41 A 42-44.

40.13. S 1 E 2 A 3 (Pomp. 11 epist. et var. lect.) P 4-5.

40.14. E 1 S 2 A 3 P 4-5 <codal S 6>.

40.15. S 1 P 2-3 E or A 4.

40.16. E 1-4 P 5.

Total texts 330 S 118 P 80 E 113 A 19

Initial mass S 9 (40.1.2.3,4,7,9,11,13,15: SAEP, SEP, SP, SEPA, SEPA, SEP, SPE, SEP, SPEA) P 1 (40.10: PSE) E 6 (40.5,6,8,12,14,16: EAPS, E, ESP, ESPA, ESAP,EP)

Insertions in other masses 6: P in S 2 (40.5.54, 40.9.6) P in E 1 (40.4.33) E in S 1 (40.2.8), A between S and E 2 (40.1.10, 40.4.29)

Displacements within masses 5: S 4 (40.1.5; 40.2.12,14; 40.5.3) E 2 (40.12.21)

Texts introducing titles 2: S 2 (40.7.1; 40.11.1)

Codal title texts 5: S 1 (40.14.6), S 1 E 2 (40.9.30-32) E 1 (40.10.6)

Codal mass texts 5: P 5 (40.4.58; 40.5.39-42)

Total displacements 23/314 = 8 per cent

41.1. <intro. S (1 Gai. 2 rer. cott.-12 (Callist. 2 inst.), 13 (Nerat. 6 reg.), 14 (Nerat. 5 membr.), 16 (Nerat. 5 reg.), 16 (Flor. 6 inst.)> S 17 (Ulp. 1 Sab.)-24 (Paul 14 Sab.), 25 (Callist. 2 inst.),* 26 (Paul 14 Sab.)-33 (Ulp. 4 disp.), 34 (Ulp. 4 cens.),* 35 (Ulp. 7 disp.)-40 E 41-56 (Proc. 8 epist.), <mass codal E 57 (Paul 6 Plaut.), 58 (Iavolen. 11 Cass.)> P 59-63 A 64-66.

41.2. E 1 (Paul 54 ed.), 2 Ulp. (70 ed.)*, 3 (Paul 54 ed.)-5 (Paul 63 ed.), 6 (Ulp. 70 ed.), 7 (Paul 54 ed.)* E 8 (Paul 65 ed.)-9 (Gai. 25 ed. prov.), 10 (Ulp. 69 ed.)*, 11 (Paul 65 ed.)- 28 S 29-36 (Iul. 13 dig.), 37 (Marcian. 11 form. hyp.)*, 38 (Iul. 44 dig.)-43 P 44 (Pap. 23 quaest.), 45 (Pap. 2 def.)*, 46 (Pap. 23 quaest.)-50 A 51 (Iavolen. 5 post. Lab., not S)-53.

41.3. <intro. E 1 (Gai. 21 ed. prov.), 2 (Paul 54 ed.), 3 (Mod. 5 pand.), 4 (Paul 54 ed.), 5 (Gai. 21 ed. prov.)> E 6 (Ulp. 11 ed.), S 7 (Ulp. 27 Sab.)*, E 8-25 S 26-41 P 42-48 A 49.

41.4. E 1-5 S 6-7, 8 (Iul. 2 Minic.)*, 9 (Iul. 3 Urs. Fer.), 10 (Iul. 2 Minic.)-11 P 12-13 A 14.

41.5. S 1-2 E 3-4.

41.6. E 1-3 S 4 P 5-6.

41.7. E 1-3 S 4-7 P 8.

41.8. S 1 E 2 (Paul 54 ed.), P 3 (Pap. 23 quaest.)*, E 4 (Paul 54 ed.)-5 (Iavolen. 7 Cass.), S 6 (Pomp. 32 Sab.)*, E 7 (Iavolen. 7 Cass.), P 8 (Pap. 23 quaest.)-9.

41.9. S 1 E 2 A 3.
41.10. E 1-2 S 3-5.

Total texts 217 S 91 P 37 E 90 A 9

Initial mass S 4 (41.1, 41.5, 41.8, 41.9: SEPA, SE, SEP, SE) E 6 (41.2, 41.3, 41.4, 41.6, 41.7, 41.10: ESPA, ESPA, EPA, ESP, ESP, ES)
Insertions in other masses 3: S in E 2 (41.3.7; 41.8.6) P in E 1 (41.8.3)
Displacement within masses 8: S 3 (41.1.25,34; 41.2.37) P 1 (41.2.45) E 4 (41.2.2,7,10; 41.4.8)
Texts introducing titles 21: S 16 (41.1.1-16) E 5 (41.3.1-5)
Codal mass texts 2: E 2 (41.1.57-58)
Total displacements 34/207 = 16 per cent

42.1. <intro. E 1 (Mod. 7 pand.)>, E 2-15 (Ulp. 3 off. cons.) /// E 16 (Ulp. 63 ed.), 17 (Ulp. 10 ed.)*, 18 (Up. 66 ed.), 19 (Paul 6 Plaut.), 20 (Mod. 2 diff.)*, 21 (Paul 6 Plaut.), 22 Pomp. 21 QM)*, 23 (Paul 6 Plaut.), 24 (Pomp. 4 Plaut.), 25 (Paul 60 ed.)*, 26 (Ulp. 77 ed.)*, 27 (Mod. 1 resp.)-35 (Pap. Iust. 2 const.), <mass codal E 36 (Paul 17 ed.), 37 (Marcell. 3 dig.), 38 (Paul 17 ed.), 39 (Cels. 3 dig.)> P 40-52 (Tryph. 12 disp.), <mass codal P 53 (Hermogen. 1 iur. epit.), 54 (Paul 1 sent.)>, S 55-63 A 64.

42.2. E 1-4 S 5-7 (Afr. 5 quaest.), <codal 8 (Paul 4 Sab.)>.

42.3. E 1-7 S 8-9.

42.4. <intro. E 1 (Ulp. 12 ed.)> E 2 (Ulp. 5 ed.), 3 (Ulp. 59 ed.), 4 (Paul 58 ed.)*, 5 (Ulp. 59 ed.)-12 P 13-15.

42.5. E 1 (Gai. 23 ed. prov.) 2 (Paul 58 ed.)*, 3 (Gai. 23 ed prov.)- 30 S 31-35 (Marcian. 1 form. hyp.), <mass codal S 36 (Ulp. 45 Sab.)> P 37-39.

42.6. E 1 P 2-5 S 6-7.

42.7. E 1-4 S 5.

42.8. E 1 (Ulp. 66 ed.), 2 (Ulp. 73 ed.)*, 3 (Ulp. 66 ed.), 4 (Paul 68 ed.)*, 5 (Gai. 26 ed. prov.)*, 6 (Ulp. 66 ed.)-7 (Paul 62 ed.), A 8 (Venul. 6 interdict.)*, E 9-10, A 11 (Venul. 6 interdict.)*, E 12 (Marcell. 18 dig.), <mass codal E 13 (Paul 68 ed.)> S 14-15 (Iul. 49 dig.), P 16 (Pap. 5 resp.)*, S 17 (Iul. 49 dig.) P 18-22 A 23-25.

Total texts 172 S 27 P 31 E 108 A 6

Initial mass E 8 (42.1-8: EPSA,ES,ES,EP,ESP,EPS,ES,ESPA)
Insertions in other masses 3: P in S 1 (42.8.16) A in E 2 (42.8.8,11)
Displacements within masses 10: E 10 (42.1.17,20,22,25,26; 42.4.4; 42.5.2; 42.8.2,4,5)

Texts introducing titles 2: E 1 (42.1.1) S 1 (42.4.1)

Codal title text 1: S 1 (42.2.8)

Codal mass texts 8: E 5 (42.1.36-39; 42.8.13) P 2 (42.1.53-54) S 1 (42.5.36)

Total displacements 24/164 = 15 per cent

43.1. E 1-4 S 5.

43.2. <intro. E 1 (Ulp. 67 ed.)>, E 2 (Paul 20 ed.).

43.3. E 1-2.

43.4. E 1-4.

43.5. E 1-5.

43.6. E 1 P 2-3.

43.7. S 1 (Pomp. 30 Sab.), 2 (Iul. 48 ed.)*, 3 (Ulp. or Pomp. 33 Sab.).

43.8. E 1-3 P 4 S 5-7.

43.9. E 1 P 2.

43.10. P (not E) 1.

43.11. E 1-2 P 3.

43.12. E 1 S 2-3 P 4.

43.13. E 1.

43.14. E 1.

43.15. E 1.

43.16. <intro. E 1 (Ulp. 69 ed.), 2 (Paul 65 ed.), 3 (Ulp. 69 ed.)>, E 4 (Ulp. 10 ed.)-12 S 13-17 P 18-19 A 20.

43.17. E 1-4.

43.18. E 1-2.

43.19. E 1-3 (Ulp. 70 ed.), A 4 (Venul. 1 interdict.)*, E 5 (Ulp. 70. ed.)-7.

43.20. E 1 S 2-6 P 7 A 8.

43.21. E 1-3 A 4.

43.22. E 1.

43.23. E 1 A 2.

43.24. E 1 (Ulp. 71 ed.), A 2 (Venul. 2 interdict.)*, E 3 (Ulp. 71 ed.), A 4 (Venul. 2 interdict.)*, E 5-7 (Ulp. 71 ed.), A 8 (Venul. 2 interdict.)*, E 9 (Ulp. 71 ed.), A 10 (Venul. 2 interdict.)*, E 11 (Ulp. 71 ed.), A 12 (Venul. 2 interdict.)*, E 13 (Ulp. 71 ed.), S 14 (Iul. 68 dig.)*, E 15 (Ulp. 71 ed.)-1 cn8 (Cels. 25 dig.), <mass codal E 19 (Ulp. 57 ed.)> S 20-21 A 22.

43.25. E 1.

43.26. <intro. S 1 (Ulp. 1 inst.)> E 2-4 (Ulp. 71 ed.), S 5 (Pomp. 29. Sab.)*, E 6 (Ulp. 71 ed.), A 7 (Venul. 3 interdict.)*, E 8 (Ulp. 71 ed.)-13 S 14-16 (Pomp. 29 Sab.), 17 (Pomp. 23 Sab.)*, 18 (Iul. 1 dig.)-20 A 21-22.

43.27. E 1 S 2.

43.28. E 1.

43.29. E 1 (Ulp. 71 ed.), A 2 (Venul. 4 interdict.)*, E 3 (Ulp. 71 ed.), A 4 (Venul. 4 interdict.).

43.30. E 1 (Ulp. 71 ed.), P 2 (Hermogen. 6 iur. epit.)*, E 3 (Ulp. 71 ed.), S 4 A 5.

43.31. E 1.

43.32. E 1-2.

43.33. S 1 E 2.

Total texts 154 S 35 P 11 E 91 A 17

Initial mass S 2 (43.7; 43.33 S, SE) P 1 (43.10: P) E 30 (43.1-6: ES, E, E, E, E, EP; 43.8,9,11-26: EPS, E, EP, ESP, E, E, E, ESPA, E, E, E, ESPA, EA, E, EA, ESA, E; 43.27-32: ES, E, EA, ESA, E, E,ESA)

Insertions in other masses 11: S in E 2 (43.24.14; 43.26.5) P in E 1 (43.30.2) A in E 8 (43.19.4; 43.24.2,4,8,10,12; 43.26.7; 43.29.2)

Displacements within masses 2: S 2 (43.7.2; 43.26.17)

Texts introducing titles 5: 1: E 4 (43.2.1; 43.16.1-3) S 1 (43.26.1)

Codal mass text E 1 (43.24.19)

Total displacements 19/121 = 16 per cent

44.1. E 1 (Ulp. 4 ed.), 2 (Ulp. 74 ed.)*, 3 (Gai. 1 ed. prov.)-4 (Paul 20 ed.), 5 (Paul 18 ed.)*, 6 (Paul 71 ed.)-11 S 12-16 (Afr. 9 quaest.) E 17 (Paul 70 ed.)*, S 18 (Afr. 9 quaest.)- 22 A 23 P 24.

44.2. E 1-7 (Ulp. 75 ed.), S 8 (Iul. 51 dig.)*, E 9 (Ulp. 75 ed.), S 10 (Iul. 51 dig.)*, E 11-15 (Gai. 30 ed. prov.), S 16 (Iul. 51 dig.)*, E 17 (Gai. 30 ed. prov.)- 19 S 20-27 P 28-31.

44.3. E 1-4 S 5-9 P 10-13 A 14-15 <codal S 16>.

44.4. E 1-8 S 9-11 P 12-16 A 17.

44.5. E 1-2.

44.6. E 1 P 2-3.

44.7. <intro. S 1 (Gai. 2 aur.), 2 (Gai. 3 inst.), 3 Paul (2 inst.), 4-5 (Gai. 3 aur.)> S 6-25 (Ulp. 1 reg.), <mass codal 26 (Ulp. 5 cens.)> P 27-34 E 35-58 (Ruf. 8 reg.), <mass codal E 59 (Callist. 1 ed. mon.), 60 (Ulp. 17 ed.)>, A 61.

Total texts 154 S 56 P 24 E 69 A 5

Initial mass S 1 (**44.7**: SPEA) E 6 (**44.1**-6: ESAP, ESP, ESPA, ESPA, E, EP)

Insertions in other masses 4: S in E 3 (44.2.8,10,16) E in S 1 (44.1.17)

Displacements within masses 2: E 2 (44.1.2,5)

Texts introducing titles 5: S 5 (44.7.1-5)

Codal title text 1: S 1 (44.3.16)

Codal mass texts 3: S 1 (44.7.26) E 2 (44.7.59-60)

Total displacements 15/147 = 10 per cent

45.1. <intro. S 1(Ulp. 48 Sab. –5 (Pomp. 26 Sab.)> S 6 (Ulp. 1 Sab.)-14 (Pomp. 5 Sab.), 15 (Pomp. 27 Sab.)*, 16 (Pomp. 6 Sab.)-59 (Iul. 88 dig.), E 60 (Ulp. 20 ed.)*, S 61 (Iul. 2 Urs. Fer.)-66 E 67-113 (Proc. 2 epist.), S between E and P 114 (Ulp. 17 Sab.)*, P 115-121 (Pap. 1 resp.), A 122 (Scae. 28 dig.)*, P 123 (Pap. 1 def.)-141.

45.2. <intro. E 1 (Mod. 2 reg.), 2 (Iavolen. 3 Plaut.),> S 3-8 P 9-16 E 17-19.

45.3. <intro. S 1 (Iul. 52 dig.)>, S 2-7 (Ulp. 48 Sab.), P 8 (Gai. 1 cas.)*, S 9 (Ulp. 48 Sab.), 10 (Iul. 52 dig.)*, 11 (Ulp. 48 Sab.), P 12 (Paul 10 quaest.)*, S 13 (Ulp. 48 Sab.)-16 (Paul 4 reg.), <mass codal S 17 (Pomp. 9 Sab.)> P 18-22 (Nerat. 2 resp.), E 23 (Paul 9 Plaut.)*, P 24 (Nerat. 2 resp.), 25 (Venul. 12 stip.)*, 26 (Paul 1 manual.) 28 E 29-40.

Total texts 200 S 87 P 46 E 66 A 1

Initial masses S 3 (45.1-3: SEP, SPE, SPE)

Insertions in other masses 6: S between E and P 1 (45.1.114) P in S 2 (45.3.8,12) E in S 1 (45.1.60) E in P 1 (45.3.23) A in P 1 (45.1.122)

Displacements within masses 3: S 2 (45.1.15; 45.3.10) P 1(45.3.25)

Texts introducing titles 8: S 5 (45.1.1-5) E 2 (45.2.1-2) S 1 (45.3.1)

Codal mass text 1: S 1 (45.3.17)

Total displacements 18/197 = 9 per cent

46.1. S 1- 6 (Ulp. 47 Sab.), 7 (Iul. 53 dig.)*, 8 (Ulp. 43 Sab.)-11 (Iul. 12 dig.), 12 (Iul. 43 dig.)*, 13 (Iul. 14 dig.)-19 (Iul. 4 Minic.), E 20 (Iavolen. 13 epist.)*, S 21 (Afr. 7 quaest.)-24 E 25-42 (Iavolen. 10 epist), 43 (Pomp. 7 var. lect.)*, 44 (Iavolen. 11 epist.) <mass intro. A 45 (Scae. 6 dig.)>, A 46 (Iavolen. 10 post. Lab.) P 47-70 (Gai. 1 verb. obl.), 71 (Paul 4 quaest.)*, 72 (Gai. 3 verb. obl.), <codal E 73 (Paul 73 ed.)>.

46.2. <intro. S 1 (Ulp. 46 Sab.), 2 (Ulp. 48 Sab.)> S 3 (Pomp. 1 Sab.)-16 E 17-26 P 27-34.

46.3. <intro. S 1 (Ulp. 43 Sab.), 2 (Flor. 8 inst.), 3 (Ulp. 43 Sab.), E 4 (Pomp.13 QM) S 5 (Ulp. 43 Sab.), E 6 (Paul 4 Plaut.), S 7 (Ulp. 43 Sab.), 8 (Paul 10 Sab.)> S 9 (Ulp. 24 Sab.)-12 (Ulp. 30 Sab.), 13 (Iul. 54 dig.)*, 14 (Ulp. 30 Sab.)-49 (Marcian. 1 form. hyp.), <mass codal S 50 (Paul 10 Sab.)>, E 51-84 (Proc. 7 epist.), <mass codal E 85 (Callist. 1 ed. mon.), 86 (Paul 8 ed.), 87 (Cels. 27 dig.)> A 88-89 (Scae. 29 dig.), 90 (Scae. 26 dig.)*, 91 (Lab. pith. 6)-93 P 94-107 (Pomp. 2 enchir.), <codal P 108 (Paul 2 manual.)>.

46.4. <intro. E 1 (Mod. 2 reg.)>, S 2-6 (Ulp. 47 Sab.), 7 (Ulp. 50 Sab.)*, 7 (Ulp. 48 Sab.)- 19 E 20 P 21-22 A 23.

46.5. E 1-6 (Paul 14 Plaut.), <mass codal 7 (Ulp. 14 ed.)> P 8-9 S 10 A 11.

46.6. E 1-2 (Ulp. 79 ed.), S 3 (Ulp. 35 ed.)*, E 4 (Ulp. 79 ed.)-7 (Mod. 6 reg.), < mass codal 8 (Ulp. 2 ed.)>, S 9-11 P 12.

46.7. E 1-3 (Ulp. 77 ed.), S 4 (Iul. 55 dig.)*, E 5 (Ulp. 77 ed.)-8 (Paul 74 ed.), 9 (Ulp. 14 ed.)*, 10 (Mod. 4 pand.), <mass codal E 11(Paul 74 ed.)>, S 12-16 P 17-19 A 20-21.

46.8. P 1-8 (Venul. 15 stip.), E 9 (Ulp. 9 ed.)-10 (Ulp. 80 ed.), P 11 (Hermogen. 6 iur. epit.)*, E 12 (Ulp. 80 ed.), 13 (Paul 76 ed.)*, 14 (Paul 3 Plaut.)-17 S 18 –25 Q 26.

Total texts 308 S 131 P 67 E 97 A 12 Q 1

Initial masses S 3 (46.1-3: SEAP, SEP, SEAP) P 1 (46.8: PES) E 4 (46.4-7: ESPA, EPSA, ES, ESPA)

Insertions in other masses 4: S in E 2 (46.6.3;46.7.4) P in E 1 (46.8.11) E in S 1 (46.1.20)

Displacement within masses 9: S 4 (46.1.7,12; 46.3.13; 46.4.7) P 1 (46.1.71) E 3 (46.1.43; 46.7.9; 46.8.13) A 1 (46.3.90)

Texts introducing titles 11: S 10 (46.2.1-2; 46.3.1-8) E 1 (46.4.1)

Codal title texts 2: P 1 (46.3.108) E 1 (46.1.73)

Text introducing mass 1: A 1 (46.1.45)

Codal mass texts 7: E 6 (46.3.85-87; 46.5.7; 46.6.8; 46.7.11); S 1 (46.3.50)

Total displacements 34/300 = 11 per cent

47.1. S 1-3.

47.2. <intro. S 1-8 (1 Paul 39 ed., 2 Gai. 13 ed., 3 Ulp. 41 Sab., 4 Paul 9 Sab., 5 Ulp. 41 ed., 6 Paul 9 Sab., 7 Ulp. 41 ed., 8 Gai. 13 ed.)> S 9 (Pomp. 6 Sab.), 10 (Ulp. 29 Sab.), 11 (Paul 9 Sab.)*, 12 (Ulp. 29 Sab.)-65 E 66-69 (Marcell. 8 dig.), P 70 (Scae. 4 quaest.)*, E 71 (Marcell. 8 dig.) 72 (Iavolen. 15 Cass.)*, 73 (Mod. 7 resp.)-78 P 79-90 A 91 (Iavolen. 9 post. Lab., not S)-92 <codal S 93 (Ulp. 38 ed.)>.

47.3. <intro. S 1 (Ulp. 37 ed.)>, S 2 (Ulp. 42 Sab.).

47.4. S 1-3.

47.5. S 1 (Ulp. 38 ed.).

47.6. S 1 (Ulp. 3 ed.), 2 (Iul. 23 dig.)*, 3 (Ulp. 38 ed.)-4 E 5 P 6.

47.7. S 1 (Paul 9 Sab.), P 2 (Gai. 1 XII tab.)*, S 3 (Ulp. 42 Sab.), P 4 (Gai. 1 XII tab.)*, S 5-10 E 11-12.

47.8. E 1-5 P 6.

47.9. E 1-5 (Gai. 21 ed. prov.), 6 (Callistr. 1 ed. mon.)* P 7-9 S 10-12.

47.10. <intro. E 1 (Ulp. 56 ed.)-21 (Iavolen. 9 epist.)> E 22 (Ulp. 1 ed.),.23 (Paul 4 ed.), 24 (Ulp. 15 ed.), 25 (Ulp. 18 ed.), 26 (Paul 19 ed.), 27 (Paul 7 ed.) S 28- 39 (Venul. 2 pub. iud.), 40 (Macer 2 pub. iud.)*, 41 (Nerat. 5 membr.) P 42-43 (Gai. 3 reg.) A 44 (Iavolen. 9 post. Lab.) <codal P 45 (Hermogen. 5 iur. epit.)>.

47.11. <intro. P 1 (Paul 5 sent.)> S 2-10 P 11.

47.12. E 1-5 S 6-9 P 10-11.

47.13. S 1-2.

47.14. S 1-2 E 3.

47.15. E 1 S 2-6 (Paul 1 iud. pub.), <codal 7 (Ulp. 4 cens.)>.

47.16. S 1 P 2.

47.17. S 1-3.

47.18. S 1 P 2.

47.19. S 1-3 P 4-6.

47.20. P 1 S 2-3 E 4.

47.21. E 1-3.

47.22. S 1-3 P 4.

47.23. <intro. E 1 (Paul 8 ed.)>, E 2-6 S 7 (Paul 41 ed.), <codal E 8 (Ulp. 1 ed.)>.

Total texts 249 S 141 P 34 E 71 A 3

Initial masses S 16 (47.1,2,3,4,5,6,7,11,13,14,16,17,18,19,22,23: S,SEPA,S,S,S, SEP,SP,SE,S,SE,SP,S,SP,SP,SP,S) P 1 (47.20: PSE) E 6 (47.8,9,10,12, 15,21: EP, EPS,ESPA,ESP,ES,E,ES)

Insertions in other masses 3: P in S 2 (47.7.2,4) P in E 1 (47.2.70)

Displacements within masses 3: S 2 (47.2.11; 47.10.40) E 1 (47.2.72)

Texts introducing titles 32: S 9 (47.2.1-8; 47.3.1) P 1 (47.11.1) E 22 (47.10.1-21; 47.23.1)

Codal title texts 4: S 2 (47.2.93; 47.15.7) P 1(47.10.45) E 1 (47.23.8)

Total displacements 42/226 = 19 per cent

48.1. <intro. S 1 (Macer 1 pub. iud.), E 2 (Paul 15 ed. prov.)> S 3 (Ulp. 35 Sab.)-9 Marcian. 1 pub. iud.) P 10 (Pap. 2 def.)*, S 11 (Maec. 10 pub. iud.), E 12 P 13-14.

48.2. S 1-8 (Macer 2 pub.), P 9 (Paul 5 sent.)*, 10 (Hermogen. 6 iur. epit.)*, S 11 (Macer 2 pub.)-14 E 15-20 P 21-22.

48.3. <intro. S 1 (Ulp. 2 off. proc.)>, S 2 (Pap. 1 adult.)-10 E 11-14.

48.4. <intro. S 1 (Ulp. 7 off. proc.)>, S 2 (Ulp. 8 disp.)-6 E 7 P 8-10 <codal S 11 (Ulp. 8 disp.)>.

48.5. <S 1 (Ulp. 1 adult.)>, S 2 (Ulp. 8 disp.), 3 (Ulp. 2 adult.)*, 4 (Ulp. 8 disp.), 5 (Iul. 86 dig.), 6 (Pap. 1 adult.), 7 (Marcian. 10 inst.)*, 8 (Pap. 2 adult.)-9 (Ulp. 2 adult.), 10 (Ulp. 4 adult.), 11 (Pap. 2 adult.)-12 (Pap. lib.sing. adult.), 13 (Ulp. 1 adult.), 14 (Ulp. 2 adult.), 15 (Scae. 4 reg.)*, 16 (Ulp. 2 adult.), 17 (Ulp. 1 adult.), 18 (Ulp. 2 adult.), 19 (Macer 1 iud. pub.)*, 20 (Ulp. 2 adult), 21 (Pap. 1 adult.), 22 (Ulp. 1 adult.), 23 (Pap.1 adult.), 24 (Ulp.1 adult), 25 (Macer 1 pub.)*, 26 (Ulp. 2 adult.), 27 (Ulp. 3 disp.)*, 28 (Ulp. 3 adult), 29 (Marcian. 1 iud. pub.)*, 30 (Ulp. 4 adult)-34 E 35-36 P 37-44, <codal P 45 (Pap. 4 resp.)>.

48.6. S 1 (Marcian. 14 inst.), 2 (Scae. 4 reg.)*, 3 (Marcian. 14 inst.), E 4 (Ulp. 59 ed.)*, S 5 (Marcian. 14 inst.)-8 E 9-10 P 11-12.

48.7. S 1-3 E 4-8.

48.8. S 1 (Marcian. 14 inst.), 2 (Ulp. 1 adult.)*, 3 (Marcian. 14 inst.)-6 (Venul. 1 off. proc.),* 7 (Paul 1 pub. iud.), <mass codal S 8 (Ulp. 33 ed.), 9 (Ulp. 37 ed.)> E 10-16 P 17.

48.9. S 1 (Marcian. 14 inst.), 2 (Scae. 4 reg.)*, Marcian. (14 inst.), 4 (Marcian. 1 iud. pub.)*, 5 (Marcian. 14 inst.), 6 (Ulp. 8 off. proc.), <mass codal S 7 (Ulp. 29 ed.), 8 (Ulp. 8 disp.)> E 9 S or P 10.

48.10. <intro. S 1 (Marcian. 14 inst.)>, S 2 (Paul 3 Sab.)-11 P 12-23 A 24 E 25-33.

48.11. S 1-3 (Macer 1 pub.), 4 (Venul. 3 pub.)*, 5 (Macer 1 pub.), 6 (Venul. 3 pub.)*, 7 (Macer 1 iud.) E 8 P 9.

48.12. S 1-2 E 3.

48.13. S 1-2 (Paul 1 Sab.), 3 (Ulp. 1 adult.)*, 4 (Marcian. 14 inst.)-12 E 13-15 P 16.

48.14. E 1.

48.15. S 1-3 E 4-6 P 7.

48.16. <intro. P 1 (Marcian. 1 ad SC Turp.) S or P 2 (Paul 1 poen. omn. leg.), P 3 (Paul 1 sent.)> P 4 (Pap. 15 resp.)-6 S 7 (Ulp. 8 disp.), 8 (Pap. 2 adult.), 9 (Macer 2 pub.)*, 10 (Pap. 2 adult.)- 15 (Macer 2 pub.), 16 (Paul 1 lib.sing. adult.) E 17-18.

48.17. <S 1 (Marcian. 2 pub.iud.)>, S 2 (Macer 2 pub.iud.), 3 (Marcian. (2 pub.iud.)*, 4 (Macer 2 pub.iud.) E 5.

48.18. <S 1 (Ulp. 8 off.proc.)>, S 2 (Ulp. 39 ed.)-11 E 12-16 P 17-21 (Paul 3 decr.), <codal P 22 (Paul 1 sent.)>.

48.19. <intro. S 1 (Ulp. 8 disp), 2(Ulp. 48 ed.)> S 3 (Ulp. 14 Sab.)-6 (Ulp. 9 off. proc.), E 7 (Callist. 6 cogn.)*, S 8 (Ulp. 9 off. proc.)-16 (Claud. Sat. 1 poen. pag.) <mass codal S 17 (Marcian. 1 inst.)> E 18-31, <mass codal E 32 (Ulp. 6 ed.)> P 33-40 (Paul 3 decr.), <mass codal 41 (Pap. 2 def.), 42 (Hermogen. 1 iur. epit.), 43 (Paul 1 resp.)>.

48.20. E 1 (Callist. 1 iur. fisc.), E 2 (Callist. 6 cogn.) S 3 (Ulp. 33 ed.), 4 (Pap. 2 adult.)*, 5 (Ulp. 33 ed.)-8 (Macer pub. iud.), E 9 (Callist.)*, S 10 (Macer pub. iud.)-11 (Marcian.).

48.21. S 1-3.

48.22. S 1 (Pomp. 4 Sab.), 2 (Marcian. 13 inst.)*, 3 Alfen. Var. 1 epit.-7 (Ulp. 10 off. proc.), 8 (Marcian. 2 pub.iud.)*, 9 (Ulp. 10 off. proc.), (10 Marcian. 2 pub.iud.)*, 11 (Ulp. 10 off. proc.)-16 (12 Marcian., 13 Paul, 14 Ulp., 15 Marcian., 16 Marcian.) E 17 (Pomp.), 18 (Callist.).

48.23. S 1-2 P 3-4.

48.24. S 1-2 P 3.

Total texts 349 S 197 P 68 E 81 A 1 S or P 2

Initial masses S 21 (1-13,15,17-19,21-24: SEP,SEP,SE, SEP,SEP,SEP,SE, SEP,SE,SPAE,SEP,SE,SEP, SEP,SE,SEP,SEP,S,SE,SP,SP) P 1 (48.16: PSE) E 2 (48.14,20: E,ES)

Insertions in other masses 6: P in S 3 (48.1.10; 48.2.9,10) E in S 3 (48.6.4; 48.19.7;48.20.9)

Displacements within masses 21: S 21 (48.5.3,7,15,19,25,27,29; 48.6.2; 48.8.2,7; 48.9.2,4; 48.11.4,6; 48.13.3; 48.16.9; 48.17.3; 48.20.4; 48.22.2,8,10)

Texts introducing titles 13: S 1 E 1 (48.1.1-2) S 8 (48.3.1; 48.4.1; 48.5.1; 48.10.1; 48.17.1; 48.18.1; 48.19.1-2) P 3 (48.16.1-3)

Codal title texts 6: S 1 (48.4.11) P 5 (48.5.45; 48.18.22; 48.19.41-43)

Codal mass texts 6: S 5 (48.8.8-9; 48.9.7-8; 48.19.17) E 1 (48.19.32)

Total displacements 52/325 = 18 per cent

49.1. <intro. S 1-9 (Ulp. 1 appell., 2 Macer 1 appell., 3 Ulp. 1 appell., 4 Macer 1 appell., 5 Marcian. 1 appell., 6 Ulp. 2 appell., 7 Marcian. 1 appell., 8 Ulp. 2 appell., 9 (Macer 2 appell.)> S 10 (Ulp. 8 disp)-13 E 14-21 P 22-27 A 28.

49.2. S 1-2.

49.3. S 1-2 E 3.

49.4. S 1-3.

49.5. S 1-7.

49.6. S 1.

49.7. S 1.

49.8. S 1 P 2-3.

49.9. S 1-2.

49.10. E 1 P 2.

49.11. S 1-2.

49.12. S 1.

49.13. S 1.

49.14. <intro. E 1-3 (Callist. 1 iur.fisc.), 2 (Callist. 2 iur. fisc.), 3 (Callist. 3 iur. fisc.)> E 4 (Ulp. 6 ed.)- 17 <mass intro. S 18 (Marcian. 1 delat.), P 19 (Pap. 12 resp.), 20 (Pap. 11 resp.), 21 (Paul 3 quaest.), S 22 (Marcian. 1 delat.), E 23 (Callist. 2 iur. fisc.), S 24 (Marcian. 1 delat.)>, 25 (Ulp. 19 Sab.)-34 A 35 P 36-48 (Paul 2 decret.), 49 (Paul 1 tac. fid.), <codal 50 (Paul 3 decret.)>.

49.15. E 1-2 (Marcell. 39 dig.), 3 (Pomp. 37 QM)*, 4 (Mod. 3 reg.), 5-9 P 10-12 S 13-24 (Ulp. 1 inst.), 25 (Marcian. 14 inst.)*, 26 (Flor. 6 inst.), 26 A 27 (Iavolen. 9 post. Lab., not S)-30.

49.16. E 1 (Ulp. 6 ed.), 2 (Arr. Men. 1 re. mil.)*, 3 (Mod. 4 poen.), 4 (Arr. Men. 1 re mil .)-7 S 8-14 P 15-16.

49.17. E 1-4 S 5-11 P 12-20 (Paul 1 reg. Cat.).

49.18. E 1 (Arr.Men. 3 re mil.), S 2 (Ulp. 3 opin.)-4 P 5.

Total texts 177 S 80 P 42 E 49 A 6

Initial masses S 12 (49.1-9,11-13: SEPA,S,SE,S,S,S,S,SP,S,S,S,S) E 6 (49.10, 14-18: EP,ESAP,EPSA,ESP,ESP, ESP)

Displacements within masses 3: E 3 (49.15.3,25; 49.16.2)

Texts introducing titles 12: S 9 (49.1.1-9) E 3 (49.14.1-3)

Codal title texts 1: P 1 (49.14.50)

Texts introducing mass 7: S 3 P 3 E 1 (49.14.18-24)

Total displacements 23/159 = 14 per cent

50.1. <intro. E 1 (Ulp. 2 ed.), S 2 (Ulp. 1 disp.)> S 3-10 P 11 (Pap. 2 quaest.), 12 (Pap 1 resp.)*, 13 (Pap. 2 quaest.)-15 (Pap. 1 resp.), 16 (Hermogen. 1 iur. epit.)*, 17 (Pap. 1 resp.)-24 (Scae. 2 dig. not A) E 25-38.

50.2. <intro. S 1 (Ulp. 2 opin.)>, S 2 (Ulp. 1 disp.)-4 P 5-9 E 10-13 <codal P 14 (Paul 1 quaest.)>.

50.3. <intro. S 1 Ulp. 3 off. proc.)>, S 2 (Ulp. 6 opin.).

50.4. <intro. P 1 (Hermogen. 1 epit.)>, S 2-7 E 8-14 P 15-17 (Hermogen. 1 iur. epit.), Q 18 (Arcad. Char. 1 mun. civ.).

50.5. S 1-5 P 6-12 E 13-14.

50.6. S 1-4 E 5-7.

50.7. S 1-7 P 8-12, 13 (Scae. 1 dig. not A), <mass codal 14 (Pap. 1 resp.)>, E 15-18.

50.8. S 1-3 P 4-7 E 8-13.

50.9. S 1-4 E 5 P 6 (Scae. 1 dig. not A).

50.10. S 1-3 (Ulp. 3 opin.), E 4 (Mod. 11 pand.)*, S 5 (Ulp. 1 off. cur. reip.) E 6-7.

50.11. E 1-2.

50.12. <intro. S 1 (Ulp. 1 off. cur. reip.)>, S 2 (Ulp. 1 disp.)-7 E 8-13 A 14 <codal S 15 (Ulp. 1 off. cur reip.)>.

50.13. S 1-3 E 4-5 <codal S 6 (Gai. 3 rer. cott.)>.

50.14. S 1-3.

50.15. S 1 (Ulp. 1 cens.), 2 (Ulp. 28 Sab.)*, 3 (Ulp. 2 cens.)-4 P 5 E 6-7 (Gai. 6 Iul. Pap.), <codal S or P 8 (Paul 2 cens.)>.

50.16. E 1-28 (Paul 21ed.), 29 (Ulp. 66 ed.)*, 30 (Gai. 7 ed. prov.)-88, S 89 (Pomp. 6 Sab.)*, 90 (Ulp. 29 Sab.)*, P 91 (Paul 2 fid.)*, 92 (Paul 7 quaest.)*, E 93-148 (Gai. 8 Iul.Pap.), 149 (Gai. 10 Iul. Pap.)*, 150 (Gai. 9 Iul. Pap.)-157 (Gallus 1 verb. signif.), <mass codal 158 (Celsus 25 dig.)> S 159-217 P 218-228 (Paul 1 cogn.), 229 (Paul 1 tac. fid.), 230 (Paul 1 SC Orf.), 231 (Paul 1 SC Tertull.), 232 (Gai. 1 verb. obl.)-239 A 240-241 (QM 1 ορων), 242 (Iavolen. 2 post. Lab., not S), 243 (Scae. 18 dig.)-246.

50.17. <intro. E 1 (Paul 16 Plaut.)>, S 2-71 A 72 (Iavolen. 3 post. Lab., not S)-73 P 74-86 (Paul 7 quaest.), 87 (Paul 13 quaest.)*, 88 (Scae. 5 quaest.), 101 E 102-210 (Ruf. 2 reg.), <codal 211 (Paul 69 ed.)>.

Total texts 628 S 198 P 96 E 322 A 10 S or P 1 Q 1

Initial masses S 15 (50.1-10, 50.12-15,17: SPE,SPE,S,SEP,SPE,SE,SPE, SPE,SEP,SE, SEA,SP,S,SPE,SAPE) E 2 (50.11,16: E,ESPA)

Insertions in other masses 5: S in E 2 (50.16.89,90) P in E 2 (50.16.91,92) E in S 1 (50.10.4)

Displacements within masses 6: S 1 (50.15.2) P 3 (50.1.12,16; 50.17.87) E 2 (50.16.29,149)

Texts introducing titles 7: E 1 S 1 (50.1.1-2) S 3 (50.2.1; 50.3.1; 50.12.1) P 1 (50.4.1) E 1 (50.17.1)

Codal title texts 5: S 2 (50.12.15; 50.13.6) S or P 1 (50.15.8) P 1 (50.2.14) E 1 (50.17.211)

Codal mass texts 2: P 1 (50.7.14) E 1 (50.16.158)

Total displacements 25/611 = 4 per cent

Bibliography

Alberico Gentili, *L'uso della forza nel diritto internazionale* (Giuffrè, Milan 2006)

E. **Albertario**, *Introduzine storica allo studio del diritto romano giustinianeo* (Guiffrè, Milan 1935)

V. **Arangio Ruiz**, Precedenti scolastici del Digesto, *Conferenze der il XIV centenario delle Pandette* (Univ. Cattolica del Sacro Cuore, Milan 1931) 287–319

V. **Arangio Ruiz**, 'Di alcuni fonti postclassiche del Digesto', *Memorie dell'Accademia di Scienze morali e politiche di Napoli* 54 (1931) 10f = *Rariora* (Edizioni di Storia e Letteratura, Rome 1946) 171–96

Ars boni et aequi. Festschrift W. Waldstein (Martin Schermaier, Zoltán Végh 1993)

P. **Birks**, 'Roman Law in Twentieth-Century Britain' in *Jurists Uprooted. German-Speaking Emigré Lawyers in Twentieth-Century Britain* (J. Beatson and R. Zimmermann (eds)) (Oxford University Press, Oxford 2004)

F. **Bluhme**, 'Die Ordnung der Fragmente in den Pandektentiteln' *ZGR* 4 (1820) 257–420 = *Labeo* 6 (1960) 50–96, 235–77, 368–404

H. **Buhl**, *Salvius Julianus* (Kessinger, Heidelberg 1886)

A. **Cameron**, review of Honoré, 'Tribonian' *Journal of Roman Studies* 69 (1979) 200–1

A. **Cenderelli**, *Digesto e Predigesti, Reflessioni ed ipotesi di ricerca* (Giuffrè, Milan 1983)

P. **Collinet**, *La genèse du Digeste, du Code et des Institutes de Justinien* (Sirey, Paris 1953)

Corpus Iuris Civilis (stereotype edition 3 vols, T. Mommsen, P. Krüger, R. Schoell, G. Kroll (eds)) (Weidmann, Zurich 1872 with many reprints)

Daube Noster (A. Watson (ed.) (Scottish Academic Press, Edinburgh 1974)

Gy. **Diósdi**, Das Gespenst der Pre-digesten, *Labeo* 17 (1971) 187–92

A. **Ehrenzweig**, 'Die Compilation der Digesten Justinians' *Zeitschrift für Privat und Öffenliches Recht* 28 (1901) 313–19

G. L. **Falchi**, 'Sul possibile coordinamento tra le masse bluhmiane e le partes del Digesto' *Studia et documenta historiae et iuris* 49 (1983) 51–90

G. L. **Falchi**, 'Gli spostamenti fuori massa dei frammenti del Digesto' *Sodalitas* 6 (1984) 2691–715

G. L. **Falchi**, 'Osservazioni sulle "L Decisiones" di Giustiniano' *Studi Biscardi* 5 (1984) 121–50

G. L. **Falchi**, 'Digesto e masse Bluhmiane' *Labeo* 35 (1989) 98–103

G. **Falcone**, 'Il metodo di compilazione delle Institutiones di Giustiniano' *Annali Palermo* 45 (1998) 223–426

C. **Ferrini**, 'I libri di Paolo ad Neratium' [1894] *Opere* 2 (Hoepli, Milan 1929) 229–34

Fides, humanitas, ius. Studii in onore di Luigi Labruna (Editoriale scientifica, Naples 2007)

P. de **Francisci**, 'Alcune osservazioni sul metodo dei compilatori delle Pandette' *Rendiconti del Instituto Lombardo di scienze e lettere* 2.44 (1911) 185f

P. **Furlong**, 'Justinian and Mathematics: An Analysis of the Digest's Compilation Plan' (revised U. Melbourne thesis): http://users.ox.ac.uk/~alls0079

R. **Greiner**, *Opera Neratii. Drei Textgeschichten* (Müller, Karlsruhe 1973)

A. **Guarino**, 'La méthode de la compilation' *Revue internationale des droits de l'antiquité* 4 (1957) 269–88

A. **Guarino**, 'La compilazione delle Digesta Iustiniani' *Atti della accademia di scienze morali e politichi di Napoli* 79 (1968) 527–62 = *Studi Scherillo* 2.717f

Handbuch der Lateinischen Literatur der Antike vol. 4 (R. Herzog and P. L. Schmidt (eds)) (C. H. Beck, Munich 1997); vol. 5 (R. Herzog (ed.)) (C. H. Beck, Munich 1989)

F. **Hofmann**, 'Die Compilation der Digesten Justinians' *Kritische studien von Dr. Franz Hofmann* (Manz, Vienna 1900)

A. M.(= T.) **Honoré** and A. **Rodger**, 'How the Digest Commissioners Worked' *Savigny Zeitschrift rom. abt.* 87 (1970) 246–314

T. **Honoré**, 'Work in Progress' *Law Quarterly Review* 88 (1972) 30–56

T. **Honoré**, 'Following the Trail' *Law Quarterly Review* 88 (1972) 530–42

T. **Honoré**, 'The Editing of the Digest Titles' *Savigny Zeischrift rom. abt.* 90 (1973) 262–304

T. **Honoré**, 'Labeo's *posteriora* and the Digest Commission' in *Daube Noster* (A. Watson (ed.)) (1974) 161–81

T. **Honoré**, 'The Background to Justinian's Codification' *Tulane Law Review* 48 (1974) 859–93

T. **Honoré**, 'A study of Neratius and a Reflection on Method' *Tijdschrift voor Rechtsgeschiednis* 43 (1975) 223–40

T. **Honoré**, *Tribonian* (Duckworth, London 1978)

T. **Honoré** and J. **Menner**, *Concordance to the Digest Jurists* (Clarendon Press, Oxford Microform Publications, Oxford 1980)

T. **Honoré**, 'Some suggestions for the Study of Interpolations' *Tijdschrift voor Rechtsgeschiedenis* 49 (1981) 225–49

T. **Honoré**, 'Techniques of Interpolation: D. 33.4.15–17' *Soldalitas* VI (1984) 2723–38

T. **Honoré**, *Ulpian. Pioneer of Human Rights* (2nd edn Oxford University Press, Oxford 2002)

T. **Honoré**, 'How Tribonian organised the Compilation of Justinian's Digest' *Savigny Zeitschrift rom. abt.* 121 (2004) 1–43

T. **Honoré**, 'Late Arrivals: The Appendix in Justinian's Digest Reconsidered' *Mapping the Law: Essays in Memory of Peter Birks* (A. Burrows and Lord Rodger of Earlsferry (eds)) (Oxford University Press, Oxford 2006) 497–512

T. **Honoré**, 'Justinian's Digest: The Distribution of Authors and Works to the Committees' *Roman Legal Tradition* 3:1 (M. Hoeflich and E. Mezger (eds)) (2006) 1–47

T. **Honoré**, 'Some Texts of Ulpian attributed to Paul' *Fides, humanitas, ius. Studii in onore di Luigi Labruna* (2007–8) 2529–42

G. **Hugo**, 'Der von Bluhme entdeckten Reihen sind vier' *Civilistisches Magazin* 6.4 (1837) 512–23

W. **Kaiser**, 'Digestenentstehung und Digestenüberlieferung' *Savigny Zeitschrift rom. abt.* 108 (1991) 330–50

W. **Kalb**, *Roms Juristen nach ihrer Sprache dargestellt* (Teubner, Leipzig 1890)

H. **Krüger**, *Die Herstellung der Digesten Justinians und der Gang der Exzerption* (Herstellung-Theissing, Münster 1922)

H. **Krüger**, *Studi Bonfante* (Studi-Treues, Milan 1930) 2.301–337

G. **Lanata**, *Legislazione e Natura nelle Novelle Giustinianee* (Edizioni Scientifiche Italiane, Naples 1984)

O. **Lenel**, *Palingenesia Iuris Civilis* (Tauchnitz, Leipzig 1889)

O. **Lenel**, *Das Edictum Perpetuum* (3rd edn Tauchnitz, Leipzig 1927)

D. **Liebs**, 'Variae Lectiones (Zwei Juristenschriften)' *Studi Volterra* 5 (1971) 51–88

D. **Liebs**, *Die Klagenkonkurrenz im römischen Recht* (Vandenhoeck & Ruprecht, Göttingen 1972)

D. **Liebs**, 'Recht und Rechtsliteratur' in *Handbuch der Lateinischen Literatur der Antike* (*HLL*) 5 (C. H. Beck, Munich 1989) 55–73

D. **Liebs**, 'Jurisprudenz' in *Handbuch der Lateinischen Literatur der Antike* (*HLL*) 4 (C. H. Beck, Munich 1997) 83–217

D. **Liebs**, 'Mein Ulpian' in *Altera Ratio. Klassische Phililogie zwichen Subjectivität und Wissenschaft. Festschrift für Werner Suerbaum zum 70 Geburtstag* (M. Schauer & G. Thome (eds)) (Franz Steiner, Stuttgart 2003) 74–81

D. **Liebs**, *Römische Jurisprudenz in Africa mit Studien zu den pseudopaulinishen Sentenzen* (2nd edn Duncker & Humblot, Berlin 2005)

D. **Mantovani**, *Digesto e masse Bluhmiane* (Giuffrè, Milan 1987)

D. **Mantovani**, 'Le masse Bluhmiane sone tre' *Seminarios Complutenses de Derecho Romano* 4 (1993) 87–119

F. **Millar**, 'A New Approach to the Roman Jurists' *Journal of Roman Studies* 76 (1986) 272–80

T. **Mommsen**, *Digesta Iustiniani Augusti* (2 vols, Weidmann, Berlin 1870 with reprints)

T. **Mommsen**, 'Hofmann versus Bluhme' *Savigny Zeitschrift* 22 (1901) 1–11

H. L. W. **Nelson and M. David**, *Überlieferung, Aufbau und Stil von Gai Institutiones* (Brill, Leiden 1981)

D. **Nörr**, *Römisches Recht: Geschichte und Geschchten. Der Fall Arecusa et alii: Dig. 19.1.43 sq.* (Bayerische Akademie der Wissenschaften/C. H. Beck, Munich 2005)

Opere di Contardo Ferrini (Hoepli, Milan 1929)

D. **Osler**, 'The Compilation of Justinian's Digest' *Savigny Zeitschrift rom. abt.* 102 (1985) 129–84

D. **Osler**, 'Following Bluhme: a note on Dario Mantovani, "Digesto e masse Bluhmiane"' *IVRA* 38 (1988) 147–58

P. **Pescani**, 'Il piano del Digesto e la sua attuazione' *Bulletino del instituto di diritto romano* 77 (1974) 237–405

H. **Peters**, *Die oströmischen Digstenkommentare und die Entstehung der Digesten* (Sitzungsberichte der Sächsichen Akademie der Wissenschaften, Phil-hist. Klasse 65, 1913) = Labeo 16 (1970) 183–214, 335–78

F. **Pringsheim**, 'Die Entstehungszeit des Digstenplanes und die Rechtschulen' *Atti del congresso internazionale di diritto romano* (1934) 449f

D. **Pugsley**, 'Some reflections on the compilation of Justinian's Digest' *Irish Jurist* 19 (1984) 350–9

A. **Rodger**, 'Behind the Scenes of Roman Law' *Oxford Journal of Legal Studies* 3 (1982) 382–404

G. **Rotondi**, *Scritti Giuridici* (Ulrico Hoepli, Milan 1922)

F. **Schulz**, *History of Roman Legal Science* (Oxford University Press 1946)

Sodalitas. Scritti in onore di Antonio Guarino (Jovene, Naples 1984)

L. **Solidoro**, 'Triboniano e la legislazione Giustineanea' *Labeo* 28 (1982) 74–81

A. **Soubie**, *Recherches sur les orignies des rubriques du Digeste* (Saint-Joseph, Tarbes 1960)

Studi in onore di Arnaldo Biscardi (Istituto Editoriale Universitario Cisalpino, Milan 1984)

Studi in onore di Pietro Bonfante (Giuffrè, Milan, 1929–1930)

Studi in onore di Gaetano Scherillo (Istituto Editoriale Universitario Cisalpino, Milan 1972)

Studi in onore di Edoardo Volterra (Giuffrè, Milan 1971)

R. **Syme**, 'Fiction about Roman Jurists' *Savigny Zeitschrift rom. abt.* 97 (1980) 78–104

C. **Tomulescu**, 'On the Activity of Justinian's Compilers' *Index* 2 (1971) 139–44

M. **Varvaro**, 'Contributo allo studio delle Quinquginta Decisiones' *Annali Palermo* 46 (2000) 361–539

M. **Varvaro**, 'Lo stile di Triboniano e la compilazione delle Institutiones di Giustiniano' *Studia et documenta historiae et iuris* 68 (2002) 319–98

O. Verrey, *Leges geminatae à deux auteurs et la compilation du Digeste* (Presses Centrales, Lausanne 1973)

Vocabularium Iurisprudentiae Romanae (De Gruyter, Berlin 1903–1985) = VIR

W. **Waldstein**, 'Tribonianus' *Savigny Zeitschrift rom. abt.* 97 (1980) 232–55

T. **Wallinga**, *Tanta Δεδωκεν. Two introductory constitutions to Justinian's Digest* (Forsten, Groningen 1989)

A. **Watson**, review of Honoré, 'Tribonian' *Law Quarterly Review* 94 (1978) 459

F. **Wieacker**, *Textstufen klassicher Juristen* (Vandenhoeck & Ruprecht, Göttingen 1960)

F. **Wiecaker**, *Vom Römischen Recht* (2nd edn Koehler, Stuttgart 1961)

F. **Wieacker**, 'Zur Technik der Kompilatoren' *Savigny Zeitschrift rom. abt.* 89 (1972) 293–323

F. **Wieacker**, 'Zur Herstellung der Digesten' *Ars boni et aequi. Festschrift W. Waldstein* (1993) 417–42

Index of Texts

References are to chapters and footnotes in each chapter. Texts cited in the main narrative are assigned to the nearest preceding footnote.

Index

References are to page number and the abbreviation n indicates a footnote, eg 74n

The manufacturer's authorised representative in the EU for product safety is Oxford University Press España S.A. of el Parque Empresarial San Fernando de Henares, Avenida de Castilla, 2 – 28830 Madrid (www.oup.es/en or product.safety@oup.com). OUP España S.A. also acts as importer into Spain of products made by the manufacturer.

www.ingramcontent.com/pod-product-compliance
Lightning Source LLC
LaVergne TN
LVHW101442200926
848483LV00001B/22
* 9 7 8 0 1 9 9 5 9 3 3 0 9 *